INSURRECTION

Kevin Danaher and Jason Mark

INSURRECTION

Citizen Challenges to
Corporate Power

Routledge
New York   London

Published in 2003 by
Routledge
29 West 35th Street
New York, NY 10001
www.routledge-ny.com

Published in Great Britain by
Routledge
11 New Fetter Lane
London EC4P 4EE
www.routledge.co.uk

Routledge is an imprint of the Taylor and Francis Group.
Printed in the United States of America on acid-free paper.
10 9 8 7 6 5 4 3 2 1

Library of Congress Cataloging-in-Publication Data
Danaher, Kevin, 1950-
  Insurrection: citizen challenges to corporate power / Kevin Danaher
and Jason Dove Mark.
      p. cm.
Includes bibliographical references and index.
  ISBN 0-415-94677-8 (cloth : alk. paper)
  1. Protest movements. 2. Anti-globalization movement. 3. Big
business. 4. Business ethics. 5. Corporate profits. 6.
Corporations—Taxation. I. Mark, Jason Dove. II. Title.
  HN17.5.D26 2003
  303.48'4—dc21
                                    2003009711

From Kevin for Medea.
From Jason for Mom and Dad.

Contents

Acknowledgments

OUR FIRST THANKS go to our wonderful colleagues at Global Exchange, who always give us strength in our struggles and often covered for us while we were writing this book. Special gratitude goes to Global Exchange Executive Director Kirsten Moller, whose encouragement never flagged.

We would like to thank John Gibler, Eric Simon and Claire Smith for their excellent research assistance. Medea Benjamin, Kirsten Moller and Michael O'Heaney were very helpful reading early chapter drafts and providing feedback.

Eric Nelson and Angela Chnapko at Routledge were a joy to work with.

We want to thank Peter Barnes and the folks at the Common Counsel Foundation for offering a month at the Mesa Refuge, where two chapters were written. We also appreciate the John D. and Catherine T. MacArthur Foundation, which provided financial support for the research and writing of this book. Many thanks to Arianna Huffington for contributing the Foreword.

Finally, big hugs to our partners Medea (Kevin) and Shannon (Jason) for their critical feedback, encouragement, and, of course, romance.

Foreword
by Arianna Huffington

AS THE POWERFUL STORIES in this book show, the dawn of the 21st century has brought a renewed fervor for social activism, as well as proof that groups of committed individuals—even small ones—can make a huge difference in the world.

And thank goodness for that, for we are living in a time of Lilliputian public figures and downsized political leadership. As a quick glance at the nightly news will make abundantly clear, our leaders seem to be suffering from either single-minded fanaticism or a severe case of congenital spinelessness.

It's as though a curse has been placed on modern politicians so that the moment they throw their hat in the ring, they are drained of all boldness, creativity, and the ability to inspire.

Today's political landscape is littered with artificial leaders who can't even get dressed in the morning without consulting the latest numbers. God forbid they should put on boxers if 65 percent of the public "strongly agrees" they should wear briefs.

Far from being out of touch, our leaders are much too aware of every passing whim. Politicians have become pathological people-pleasers, addicted to the short-term buzz of a bump in the polls and indifferent to the long-term effect.

The irony is that this craven, ham-handed attempt to pander to the public has resulted in a nation whose people feel condescended to rather than heard—and in a set of leaders who have proven themselves utterly unable to lead.

Because of this sorry state of affairs, it has become increasingly clear that we can no longer delegate our need for leadership to elected officials alone. Now, more than ever, we must learn to mine the greatest and most unexploited leadership resource available to us: ourselves. We need to find the next generation of leaders by looking in the mirror.

Each one of us can—and must—take up the gauntlet to solve the problems and right the wrongs of our times. You don't have to lead vast nations or command huge armies to make a difference. In fact, it can be an asset not to fit the traditional paradigm of leadership.

Because leadership is, after all, about breaking those old paradigms—about seeing where society is stuck and providing ways to get it unstuck. And, if society is stuck at the very heart of the old leadership paradigm—Washington, DC—then getting it unstuck is the responsibility of those outside that center of power.

Of course, this is not an unprecedented phenomenon in American history. After all, in the 1960s, it wasn't elected officials who led the drive for civil rights or who were in the vanguard of the fight to end the war in Vietnam.

Perhaps the greatest example of the power of conscience and truth to affect profound change came from the civil rights movement, when political leaders were forced to follow a movement of outraged and committed citizens demanding reform.

In March 1965, when Rev. Martin Luther King, Jr. met with Lyndon Johnson to press for a voting rights bill, LBJ wavered, telling King that the votes needed weren't there. King left the meeting convinced that the votes would never be found in Washington until he turned up the heat in the rest of the country. Two days later, the "Bloody Sunday" confrontation in Selma, Alabama, captured the conscience of the nation. Five months later, the Voting Rights Act became the law of the land.

Unlike our most highly regarded presidents, Lincoln, Teddy Roosevelt, and FDR, whose source of power came from their position, King's leadership grew out of his moral authority and ability to inspire. He was the ultimate internal leader.

External leadership is when you effectively carry out the responsibilities of your position. Internal leadership comes from an inner force that compels you to make the world a better place. "There comes a time," King said in 1968, "when one must take the position that is neither safe nor politic nor popular, but he must do it because conscience tells him it is right." Unlike so many of our leaders today, King was steered by an internal compass, not the latest poll results.

Though it is true that the battle between the public interest and the special interests can be a demoralizing one, recent examples abound that give lie to the cynical notion that nothing any of us says or does can make a difference anymore.

Take the public outrage, protest, and criticism that led to the resignation of Henry Kissinger from the 9/11 investigation commission, and transformed Trent Lott from smug majority leader into bloody political chum floating in a tank of hungry sharks.

Let's start with Kissinger. Almost from the moment his appointment was announced, the president's bewildering choice of Henry the K to head the 9/11 commission stuck in the craw of most sentient Americans—with the exception of those who subscribe to the notion that it takes a thief to catch a thief. Why select the most incorrigible obfuscator of the 20th century to get to the bottom of the horrors of September 11? All across the country, people shook their heads—and their fists—and wondered: what could the White House have been thinking?

The most charitable answer was: not very much. The White House had been so cavalier about its choice—and so smug about its own popularity—that it hadn't even bothered to do the customary vetting of Kissinger's tangled web of conflicted interests.

Thankfully, the American people—led by a chorus of media pundits—were far more diligent and demanded the obvious: that Kissinger come clean about his super secret client list or step down. He chose the latter, preferring to give up on his promise to "go where the facts lead us" rather than give up his wildly lucrative consulting gig.

And it's a good thing the people were on Kissinger's case, because the "loyal opposition" certainly wasn't. No one in the Democratic leadership had the guts to call for his ouster—or even demand the release of his radioactive client list.

If the Democrats dropped the ball on Kissinger, it was the mainstream media that were asleep at the wheel on the Lott story. No fewer than a dozen reporters were present when Lott made his memorable speech at Strom Thurmond's birthday bash, waxing nostalgic about Jim Crow. But only one, ABC News producer Ed O'Keefe, thought it newsworthy. His bosses didn't share his enthusiasm however, and, after running the story on a 4:30 am broadcast, didn't use it on either "Good Morning America" or "World News Tonight." The rest of the major media outlets also initially reacted with a collective shrug.

Thank God for that great populist tool, the Internet. It was in cyberspace that scores of bloggers continued hammering away at the story, and eventually succeeded in moving it out of the shadows into the political spotlight.

These cyber-pundits—the vast majority of whom are unpaid amateurs—didn't just rail against the repulsiveness of Lott's comments and the lameness of his subsequent kinda-sorta apologies. They also were instrumental in helping connect the dots of the erstwhile Majority Leader's long history of racist stances. The blizzard of damning information they uncovered left little doubt that Lott's comments had not been, as he first claimed, merely "a poor choice of words." Politicians talk a lot about their words being "taken out of context." Well, Lott got in trouble because his words were actually put in context.

The one upside to the fact that we no longer have any real leaders, only ersatz ones slavishly addicted to following public opinion, is that, at the end of the day, public outrage really matters.

The power of the people, as this book compellingly documents, is still the foundation of democracy—and its only salvation.

INTRODUCTION
The Insurrection Against Corporate Power

A NEW REBELLIOUSNESS HAUNTS the world. With each day, more and more people are challenging the institutions that exert control over our lives. Among ordinary citizens, skepticism and even hostility to the status quo are on the rise. People are questioning the legitimacy of the money values that guide modern society. They worry that unaccountable powers are out of control. And they are taking action to combat a system that is undermining the life values they hold dear.

Unlike most people's movements of the late 20th century, this budding revolt is not primarily targeted at governments. Instead, the new rebels have set their sights on that force which during the last generation has nearly supplanted the nation-state as the possessor of true power: the transnational corporation. An insurrection against corporate rule is underway.

In the last decade a broad-based citizens' movement has challenged the post-Cold War ascendancy of corporate power and the "free market" ideology that has been used to justify the corporate takeover of governance. With a passion that has taken much of the establishment by surprise, this nascent social movement is defying the prevailing trend of deregulation, privatization, and *laissez-faire* economics. Environmental activists, human rights groups, trade unionists, and countless other citizens of conscience are demanding that corporations be held accountable to the public. Disparate forces have united to make the claim that corporations should serve the needs of the public rather than the public serving the needs of corporations.

During the last 15 years, a consensus of the comfortable has arisen which tells the public that we are at the end of history as far as corporations are concerned. Journalists, academics, and politicians have told us that the ascent of corporate power and the diminishment of government are inevitable, that resistance is futile. But a great many people are resisting those all-too-neat assurances.

The rising tide of anti-corporate discontent can be witnessed in the myriad citizens' campaigns targeting big business abuses. Environmentalists have struggled to stop companies from profiting off the destruction of old-growth forests. Human rights groups have sought to sever corporate links with abusive regimes. Public health advocates have made tobacco companies pay for misleading the public about the effects of their products. And local community groups have fought the efforts of so-called "big box" retailers such as Wal-Mart to locate in their areas. By demanding reforms in corporate behavior, citizens are asserting that corporations owe responsibilities to society.

The movement for corporate accountability is stimulating crucial debates about the role of big business in a democracy. It is declaring that corporations, as institutions that exert enormous influence over society, must be under the control of the public. In raising these issues, the corporate accountability movement is asking some of the most important questions of the new century: Who is writing the rules of the global economy? How are the rules being written? And in whose interests?

Such questions pose a clear challenge to the belief that corporations are benign forces, creators of bounty. Citizen activists are saying that, to the contrary, the transnational, limited liability corporation does more harm than good. That point of view overturns conventional definitions of progress. The corporate accountability movement is asking: What is the price of prosperity? By doing so, activists are defying the notion that leaving big business to do whatever it pleases will promote the public good.

In challenging big business behavior, the corporate accountability movement is forcing people to ask whether corporations' power has eclipsed the sovereignty of the citizens. Every attempt to rein in corporate behavior contains the question: Who is in charge, private interests or the public? Protests against corporate abuses prompt doubts about whether corporate power has rendered democracy meaningless.

For anti-corporate partisans, those initial doubts have already been answered: Corporations rule. Corporations' campaign cash elects our politicians. Their lobbyists write our laws. Their lures of private privilege corrupt our public servants. Their monopoly on the means of communication allows them to dominate public debate. In such an atmosphere, the people's voices are ignored, their decisions made void. The reach and power of unaccountable corporations pose a clear and present danger to the health of democracy.

The anti-corporate insurrection is driven by a desire to limit or revoke the powers of the modern corporation. It is a revolt against corporate rule. It is a rebellion that seeks to reclaim democracy. And it is a movement that hopes to re-establish the principle that sovereignty—ultimate political authority—rests with we, the people, not with corporations.

THE CRISIS OF CORPORATE RULE

What does it mean to say that corporations rule? How is it that today in the United States of America giant corporations are the most powerful political force in the country? And what does this mean for democracy?

Corporations are able to rule because of their immense power, and their power comes, in turn, from their incredible size. The 1980s and 1990s saw a wave of corporate mergers that dramatically increased the size of the corporations. Between 1998 and 2000 alone, the U.S. economy witnessed $4 trillion in mergers—more than in the preceding 30 years combined.[1] This merger mania cemented the concentration of economic power in the hands of a relatively small number of businesses. The Fortune 500, for example, control one-quarter off all the assets of the 3.8 million corporations in the United States.[2] The largest 1,000 companies oversee about 70 percent of the entire American economy.[3]

These behemoths also dominate the global economy. Today's corporations are globe-spanning entities of unprecedented scale. Of the world's 100 largest economies, 51 are corporations, not nation-states, as measured by corporate revenues versus Gross Domestic Product.*[4] Just 500 transnational corporations control some 70 percent of world trade, while a mere 1 percent of transnationals oversee half of all direct foreign investment.[5] The world's biggest banks and brokerage firms wield awesome power as they oversee the *daily* transfer of some $1 trillion in financial assets.

This concentration of economic power means that just a small number of giant businesses possess enormous influence over the everyday aspects of people's lives. A few oil companies put the gas in our cars, while a clique of auto companies builds the cars that we drive. Our entertainment—films, movies, books, music—is delivered by a handful of conglomerates such as Disney, Sony, Bertelsmann, and AOL/TimeWarner. The morning newspaper is often produced by a corporation—Gannett, Knight Ridder, or the Washington Post Company—as is the nightly news, which in the case of NBC is courtesy of industrial giant General Electric. A tiny collection of huge food corporations—Nestlé, Kraft (owned by tobacco giant Philip Morris), and Archer Daniels

---

* Some people have said this comparison is inaccurate because GDP measures "value-added" and therefore is much larger than corporate revenues. That is a generous description of how GDP actually works. GDP is a very crude gauge of economic activity since it counts as a positive number *all* goods and services bought and sold. For example, the Exxon oil spill in Alaska increased GDP because the clean-up costs were huge. Prison expansion—building new cellblocks and hiring new guards—also increases GDP since it spurs economic activity. Exactly what kind of value is being added by such activity? The comparison between GDP and revenues remains apt.

Midland—sells us the food that we eat. Companies like Wal-Mart and Gap Inc. provide the clothes we wear. Corporations touch each minute of our waking lives.

To be sure, consumer choice and a measure of competition give people some say in the cars available or the clothing styles on hand. But the $450 billion advertising industry ensures that the choices are kept within a permissible range and that success is defined by how much you own.

As unsettling as corporate control of our daily routines may be, it is still less pernicious than corporations' massive influence over our political system. Corporate control over the auto industry may be tolerable; corporate control over democracy is not. The weight of corporate wealth has corrupted our democracy, and it is this corruption that is the most obvious sign of corporate rule.

Corporations and government have become so intertwined that it is often difficult to see where one begins and the other ends. At times it seems as if our government is a wholly owned subsidiary of Corporate America.

At least three features of our political system reveal how corporations have come to rule, that is, how they control public powers while evading public accountability. The first is the flood of campaign contributions to politicians. Political bribery and backroom arm-twisting lead, in turn, to unwarranted subsidies for companies, so-called corporate welfare. Finally, the "revolving door" system, in which government officials become corporate executives and vice versa, has erased the distinction between the regulators and the regulated.

Corruption is a perversion of democracy. It occurs when public officials are no longer responsive to the will of the citizens. The buying and selling of politicians, the special treatment given to already profitable enterprises, and the blurring of public and private roles and responsibilities have corrupted our political system. The natural relationship between ordinary people and our elected representatives has been short-circuited by corporate power.

POLITICAL BRIBERY

During the 2000 election season, candidates for federal office and the two major political parties raised at least $2 billion, according to figures compiled by the Center for Responsive Politics and Common Cause.[6] Most of this campaign cash came from giant corporations and their executives. While other organizations such as labor unions and environmental groups also make political donations, their contributions are dwarfed by corporate giving. In the 2000 election cycle, for example, corporations outspent labor unions 13 dollars to 1. The finance, real estate, and insurance industries alone made more than $300 million in contributions during the 2000 election.

Massive cash infusions like these are often defended as free speech. Campaign contributions are described as purchasing "access" or "influence," not actually buying laws themselves. In fact, what we are seeing is bribery. Corporations are literally bribing our elected officials and buying our laws.

If "bribery" seems too strong a word, look at Title 18, Section 11, Subsection 201 of the U.S. Federal Criminal Code. The statute, entitled "Bribery of Public Officials," mandates up to 15 years in prison as well as large fines for:

> Whoever directly or indirectly, corruptly gives, offers or promises anything of value to any public official . . . with intent to influence any official act . . . or, being a public official, directly or indirectly, corruptly demands, seeks, receives, accepts, or agrees to receive or accept anything of value personally or for any other person or entity, in return for being influenced in the performance of any official act . . . .

Ask yourself this: Do the companies that give millions of dollars a year to politicians *not* intend to "influence any official act"? If this law were enforced, nearly every Member of Congress and thousands of corporate executives would be in jail.

The buying of laws is so appalling that establishment politicians have denounced it. Former Democratic Majority Leader, Senator George Mitchell (D-ME), told the *Boston Globe* in 1994 that, "This system stinks. This system is money." Senator John McCain (R-AZ) complains:

> Bribery is the way the system works. . . . The whole system is rotten. Money not only determines who is elected, it determines who runs for office. . . . All of us have been corrupted by the process. . . . We are the defenders of an elaborate influence-peddling scheme in which both parties conspire to stay in office by selling the country to the highest bidder.[7]

A quick glance at some of the most heated political issues of recent years reveals how bribery allows corporations to run the government.

Between 1989 and 2001, Enron contributed nearly $6 million to federal parties and candidates, most of it to Republicans. Enron's political action committee and the company's employees contributed $114,000 to George W. Bush during the 2000 campaign, while Enron CEO Kenneth Lay raised at least another $100,000 for the campaign. What did Enron receive for this largesse? After Bush got in the White House,

Kenneth Lay and/or representatives from Enron met at least six times with members of a government task force writing the country's energy policies. The task force eventually called for breaking up control of electricity transmission networks, a longtime Enron goal. Enron also got exemptions from federal regulations, allowing it to undertake questionable activities that contributed to the company's eventual bankruptcy.

During the last decade, the "Big Three" automakers—General Motors, Ford, and Daimler-Chrysler—have given at least $10 million in campaign contributions. At the same time, public officials have refused to ratify the Kyoto Protocol on Global Warming or increase fuel efficiency standards for automobiles. U.S. Senators who voted against raising fuel standards have received, on average, twice as much campaign cash from the car corporations as Senators who voted in favor of raising fuel efficiency.

U.S. trade policy has been manipulated. When, in March 2000, the House of Representatives was considering whether to give China permanent normal trade relations, the 200-plus companies that make up the Business Roundtable poured $4.2 million into politicians' coffers in one month alone. The 237 representatives who voted to approve closer trade relations with China received an average of $44,000 from the Business Roundtable during the 2000 election season. Representatives who voted "no" received about half that from the lobbying group.

Corporate bribery has even helped lead the United States into foreign wars. Weapons manufacturers and oil companies heavily influenced the decision to send billions of U.S. taxpayer dollars to Colombia, which is in the midst of a bloody civil war. Just 11 days before the Clinton administration laid out its proposal for the so-called "Plan Colombia," United Technologies—maker of the Blackhawk helicopter, dozens of which have been sent to Colombia—sent a $75,000 check to the Democratic Party. Bell Helicopters, another arms manufacturer, gave $1 million to officials between 1996 and 2000.

According to public opinion surveys, most Americans believe the United States should take steps to halt global warming, and a majority of citizens felt that China should not have been given new trade status until the country met human rights and labor standards.[8] But the will of the people was buried by the avalanche of corporate cash.

In a country run on bribery, politics is more a competition for dollars than a contest of ideas. Bribery has ensured that corporations call the shots and make the rules. Capital has taken over the Capitol.

CORPORATE WELFARE

Political bribery has made politicians the clients of corporations, and it has turned government into the patron of corporations. Big business lavishes money on public officials so that public money will later be lavished on big business. It is an incestuous relationship in which the biggest campaign contributors are also the largest recipients of government handouts. This abuse of power is known as corporate welfare.

Corporate welfare can be defined as any government program that benefits narrow business interests at the expense of broader taxpayers' interests. The federal government alone spends more than $125 billion a year on corporate welfare: that's nearly two weeks of paychecks from every working person in the United States.[9] The federal government is Corporate America's biggest sugar daddy, and we the people pay the costs.

Corporate welfare violates the central principle of democracy: Government is supposed to serve the interests of the general public. Whenever corporations manipulate the public purse strings for their own private benefit, ordinary citizens suffer. And that manipulation raises questions of who the government really serves. Is government run by and for the people, or by and for big business?

Corporations fleece the public through so many unfair perks and privileges that a full list is impossible here. But at least two kinds of kickbacks—subsidies and tax breaks—illustrate how corporations are skinning the citizens.

Corporate welfare is most brazen when the government gives direct cash subsidies to already profitable companies. A little-known bureaucracy called the Export-Import Bank is the king of such corporate giveaways. The Ex-Im Bank, as it is called, receives about $1 billion a year to promote the sale of U.S. goods abroad. But instead of stimulating job growth, the bank has fostered massive layoffs in the United States by helping U.S. companies move their factories overseas.

Nearly 80 percent of Ex-Im subsidies go to Fortune 500 corporations, and just 10 companies account for half of the bank's deals. The primary recipients are household names—AT&T, Boeing, General Motors, General Electric, and IBM—all profitable enterprises. During the downsizing of the 1980s and 1990s, these corporations received billions from the Ex-Im Bank while shedding hundreds of thousands of jobs. GE, for example, received $2.5 billion from the bank even as it slashed 269,000 jobs between 1975 and 1995. The Ex-Im gave at least $500 million to GM while the auto corporation laid off 245,000 people. The list of boondoggles goes on. U.S. taxpayers are literally paying to send their jobs overseas.[10]

Tax avoidance is another common corporate swindle. Corporations' bribery has led to government officials offering profitable companies a

steady stream of tax breaks. The arrangement is perverse: Even as corporations ask for handouts, they refuse to pay their fair share of taxes.

Since the end of World War II, corporate lobbying has steadily lowered the corporate share of the nation's tax burden. During the 1950s,
corporate income tax payments amounted to 4.5 percent of GDP. By the
late 1970s, corporate income taxes were 2.4 percent of GDP. Today,
corporate taxes are 1.3 percent of U.S. GDP.[11]

Some of the largest—and most politically influential—corporations
often pay no taxes at all. In 1999, Microsoft reported $12.3 billion in
profits, yet the company paid no taxes. And in the two years before that,
Microsoft's tax rate on $21.9 billion in profits was just 1.8 percent.
Worldcom paid no taxes at all in between 1999 and 2002, despite reporting $15.2 billion in profits. And in 1997, IBM received an out-
right tax *rebate* while claiming profits of $3.1 billion for that year.[12]

The corporate tax cheats and subsidy con artists are ripping off the
public. And as long as lawmakers are more concerned with helping their
fat-cat supporters than with protecting the public, the government remains an accomplice to this scam.

THE REVOLVING DOOR

Even as corporations tap the public for handouts, they say they should
not be subject to public oversight. During the last 25 years, Corporate
America has sought to expand its power and limit citizen control over
its activities by pushing an agenda of privatization and deregulation. By
trying to take over such vital services as health care, education, and
energy, corporations have sought to put public resources under private
control. At the same time, corporations have aggressively lobbied to
slash government regulation of their activities. The over-arching goal is
to increase corporate power while reducing corporate accountability.

The so-called "revolving door" phenomenon shows one way how
the corporate philosophy of power without accountability works in practice. In Washington today there is scarcely a difference between the
regulators and the regulated. Corporate executives take jobs in government posts, where they are put in charge of overseeing their buddies.
Meanwhile, many government officials leave office and quickly leap to
the executive suites or lobbying firms, where they use their government
connections to tap their former colleagues on behalf of their new corporate bosses. This is the very definition of crony capitalism.

The revolving door has been recognized as a problem for decades,
and it's a political sickness infecting Democrats and Republicans alike.
For example, during President Clinton's watch, Citibank and the Trav-
elers Group insurance company merged even though the combination

of banks and insurance companies was a violation of the law. The new company, Citigroup, quickly used its incredible power to revoke the law, a key Depression-era guard against abuse. It was a brazen example of how corporations rule. It also showed how the revolving door works. Four days after the law was overturned to suit Citigroup's interests, Treasury Secretary Robert Rubin resigned his post to join the financial conglomerate.

The present Bush administration has taken the revolving door to new lows. Bush's Justice Department—the government arm charged with punishing corporate criminals—is a revolving door merry-to-round. Attorney General John Ashcroft had to recuse himself from the Enron and Arthur Andersen investigations because during his failed 2000 Senate race he took $57,499 from Enron and $12,500 from Arthur Andersen.[13]

Corporate connections also shadow Deputy Attorney General Larry Thompson, who was put in charge of President Bush's "corporate crime task force." Before working for the government, Thompson was an attorney at the high-powered law firm King & Spaulding, which has represented Enron, ExxonMobil, and ChevronTexaco, among other large corporations. From 1997 to 2001, Thomspon also sat on the board of Providian Financial Corp. In 2000, Providian paid $400 million to settle allegations that it had used misleading marketing practices, charged excessive fees, and violated other consumer-protection laws.

The rot goes all the way to the top. Halliburton, the oil services company that Vice President Dick Cheney headed for five years, is under investigation for the same sort of accounting fraud that Worldcom was guilty of. And President Bush has been accused of the same kind of insider trading that landed Martha Stewart in hot water. With cops like these, who needs criminals?

Where there is no accountability, corruption thrives; and when the regulators and the regulated are virtually the same people, accountability is impossible. There is no check on corporate malfeasance, no balance to corporations' increasing power. And without a system of checks and balances, abuse of power is inevitable.

CORPORATE BLOWBACK

Clearly, corporate rule is a problem of dramatic proportions. In recent years many books have chronicled this crisis. Charles Derber's *Corporation Nation*, *When Corporations Rule the World* by David Korten, *No Logo* by Naomi Klein, and Joshua Karliner's *Corporate Planet*, among many others, have exposed the threat unchecked corporate power poses to a democratic society.

But this book does not dwell on the details of corporate rule. Rather, we show how in the last decade citizens across the United States have addressed the consequences of this problem. We reveal the contours of the popular challenge to corporate power.

The opposition to corporate power that arose in the United States during the 1990s caught many people by surprise. The last decade of the century, after all, was widely thought of as an era of prosperity. The stock market's value grew by leaps and bounds. U.S. corporations had shed the malaise of the 1970s and '80s and were surging ahead with innovation. Unemployment was at historic lows. When citizens picketed in front of corporate headquarters or marched in Seattle, journalists wondered: Why this backlash amid the boom?

The backlash was due to the fact that the boom bypassed millions of people. Much of the decade's gains had gone to the already rich. By 2000, the typical CEO was making 500 times the average worker; thirty years earlier, the average CEO made about 40 times as much as a typical worker. In the boom year of 1997, the average stock options package of the CEOs at the 200 largest corporations was $31 million.[14]

Even amid the hype about day traders and the "millionaire next door," many people were all too aware of the fact that a small group of corporate executives was reaping the majority of the riches. As the Nasdaq spiraled upward, two-thirds of Americans cited "corporate greed" as one of the biggest difficulties facing families. Respondents to one poll described CEO compensation as "obscene" and "sickening."[15]

Nor were Americans oblivious to the fact that the CEOs' millions were often earned as a reward for ruthlessly slashing jobs. While the country's largest corporations cut millions of jobs in an effort to reduce costs, the paychecks of executives skyrocketed. AT&T's CEO, for example, earned $16 million in a year when his company dumped 40,000 workers.[16] Most people were not buying the rationale that job losses were necessary to remain competitive. In an unequivocal challenge to the corporate line, 70 percent of respondents in one poll said layoffs were motivated by "greed."[17] To many people it seemed that CEOs were merely mercenaries contracted by Wall Street and paid per head of dismissed worker. When asked by a reporter what he thought of corporate behavior, a resident of Peoria, Illinois, was blunt: "It's all about arrogance and greed."[18]

The widespread discontent with corporations is spurred by a feeling that they have dropped whatever measure of social responsibility they once held. Many people, especially older Americans, feel that the implicit social contract between corporations and workers has been shredded. Significantly, higher-paid workers are often those most resentful of corporations, for it has been their expectations that have been downsized furthest.[19]

At one point in American history, corporations grudgingly acknowledged that they had a responsiblity to their workers and consumers. No longer. Corporations' single goal today is to increase the value of their stock price. That change in perspective was exemplified in 1997 when the influential Business Roundtable changed its position statement to read: "The paramount duty of management and board is to the shareholder."[20]

Most people, however, don't think that way. There is a large gap in values between Wall Street and Main Street. According to a survey that *BusinessWeek* commissioned in 2000, just five percent of Americans think corporations' only purpose should be to make the most profit possible; 95 percent agree that corporations should "sacrifice some of their profit for the sake of making things better for their workers and communities."[21]

The divergent worldviews helps explain people's suspicion of Wall Street. Even at the very height of the stock market ascent during the seemingly rosy days of 1999, no more than one in three Americans had an approving view of Wall Street. Since then, the percentage of citizens who approve of Wall Street has dropped back to its usual levels of less than one in five.[22] In one study taken in 2000, only 11 percent of respondents viewed corporations as "making the world a better place."[23]

As these sentiments reveal, what corporations have gained in power they have lost in legitimacy. In many ways, corporations became the victims of their own success. This is because their success came at the expense of millions of ordinary Americans. Massive layoffs, wage stagnation (coupled with excessive CEO pay), and corporations relocating production overseas are at the root of the popular backlash. Corporations fomented a blowback against themselves.

While corporations' callous behavior has spawned disgust, their sheer size has bred fear. For stockbrokers and corporate board members, the merger mania of the recent decades was a windfall. But the corporate titans born of the business weddings left many people unsettled. The new conglomerates such as Citigroup and AOL/TimeWarner seemed too big to be of any good. If even the most gigantic corporations such as Bell Atlantic and Mobil Oil could be swept away by the Wall Street twister, then the family with the corner store was little more than dust in the wind. If entire countries could be bankrupted by the whims of the financial markets, what did that mean for the average Joe or Jane?

This sense of unease was uncovered when *BusinessWeek* asked people if they thought "business has gained too much power over too many aspects of American life." During the course of two polls, 77 percent of respondents said that, yes, corporations have too much power.[24]

Clearly, Americans are anxious about the role of corporations. Even before the boom turned to bust, a sense of insecurity pervaded the country. The specter of heartless forces beyond society's control spread alarm. Outlandish CEO pay packages created resentment, while waves of layoffs fed feelings of vulnerability. And as the move of jobs overseas ignited distrust, the frequent arrogance of corporate executives lit disdain. Corporations may have been profitable during the last decade, but that doesn't mean they were popular.

Defying many people's expectations, citizens in the United States have not responded to this state of affairs with complacency. In recent years millions of people across the country saw through the patina of prosperity, shrugged off apathy, and took action to hold corporations accountable for their actions. During the most unlikely of times, a social movement against corporate power arose.

NAMING THE ENEMY

The 1990s witnessed the convergence of a wide range of citizens. Increasingly, the efforts of citizen organizations are targeted on a single villain: big business. Students, labor unions, environmentalists, and human rights defenders are coming to agree that corporations represent the greatest threat to the public interest. When it comes to naming the enemy, more and more people are citing corporate power.*

The Student Environmental Action Coalition, a nationwide network of campus environmental groups, calls "corporate crime" one of the largest problems today and has dedicated itself to "dismantling corporate rule."[25] The National Lawyers Guild, a progressive bar association, is committed to "taking on the runaway power of U.S. and multinational corporations."[26] The Alliance for Democracy, an organization founded in 1996 with the express purpose of challenging corporate power, says its mission is to "free all people from corporate domination . . . [and] establish true democracy."[27]

Larger, more mainstream organizations have shifted their energies toward tackling corporate abuses. Groups that had once focused nearly all of their efforts on changing government policies have dedicated themselves to directly challenging corporations. Amnesty International, the world's best known human rights group, has expanded its mission to include economic and cultural rights as well as political and civil ones,

---

* In a poll taken just two years after the anti-government-inspired sweep of Congress by the GOP in 1994, 46 percent of people said corporations are a bigger problem than "government waste and inefficiency."

and the organization is putting new emphasis on monitoring corporations' impact on human rights. "We must increase public pressure on corporations to be accountable [for] promoting human rights," says Folabi Olagbaju, an Amnesty International activist.[28]

The Sierra Club, one of the largest environmental groups, has been echoing that call for years. The organization has pressured what it calls "giant, corporate-owned factory farms" to stop dumping animal waste into rivers and streams. And the group has been a key member of the coalition to transform the World Trade Organization, which it says "is a government of, by and for the corporations" that is shifting "enormous power . . . from ordinary citizens to the corporations."[29]

The focus on corporate behavior has contemporary precedents. In the late 1980s, Americans seeking to help end the apartheid system in South Africa took their struggle directly to the corporations who were profiting from the racist system. Activists had first appealed to the U.S. government to break from the whites-only regime. But when those efforts resulted in only cosmetic policy changes, antiapartheid groups set their sites on the companies who were doing business in South Africa and—through a combination of shareholder actions and selective purchasing ordinances—forced hundreds of companies to halt or reduce their involvement in South Africa, helping to bring down the regime.

A decade earlier, groups such as INFACT organized a worldwide boycott of Nestlé products after it was revealed that the company was using unscrupulous practices to market its infant formula in developing countries. Nestlé salespeople in poor countries dressed as nurses and gave out free formula samples that lasted just long enough for women's breast milk to dry up. Many poor women diluted the formula with water to "stretch" the amount of formula, leading to millions of infant deaths due to malnutrition. After years of exposés, protests, and other shaming tactics, activists eventually forced Nestlé and other infant formula makers to sign a code of conduct establishing acceptable business practices.

It was not until the 1990s, however, that the number of corporate campaigns mushroomed into what could be called a movement. As economic globalization redrew the balance of power between governments and corporations, social activists concentrated their energies directly on the corporations instead of appealing for government action. Grassroots groups channeled the popular discontent with corporate behavior into campaigns against specific abuses, and the widespread concern about corporate power made itself felt via the many struggles for corporate accountability.

This political backlash took many different forms. Environmentalists compelled some of the country's largest food companies to sell dolphin-safe tuna, and shamed major retailers from offering products made with old-growth wood. Public health advocates and state officials revealed the depth of the tobacco industry's decades-long deception and forced cigarette makers to pay massive fines. In a reprise of the anti-apartheid struggle, campus-based human rights activists demanded that corporations cease doing business with the repressive regime in Burma. Labor unions and human rights groups called on clothing retailers to take responsibility for the people making their clothes. And all of these disparate forces united to challenge corporations' domination of international trade and finance agreements—the rule-making process of the new global economy.

The corporate accountability movement is strikingly diverse. Many different kinds of people, with a broad range of concerns, are battling corporate rule. Author Naomi Klein says the corporate accountability forces represent a "movement of movements." Indeed, a close look at the sweep of corporate campaigns reveals a kind of bouquet: The whole is greater than the sum of its parts. The movement's diversity is the best proof of its strength and the popular resonance of its claims.

Yet no matter what the specific grievance—environmental destruction, worker abuse, or human rights violations—corporate accountability campaigners make a uniform demand: Corporations must be answerable to more than their shareholders. Each corporate accountability struggle represents a challenge to the notion that companies are merely private enterprises instead of public actors that owe obligations to society at large. Every effort against corporate rule is a blow against impunity and a call for a truly democratic society.

THE TIP OF THE ICEBERG

The arrangement of this book reflects the structure of the corporate accountability "movement of movements." Each chapter is a different story about an important corporate campaign. They are, essentially, stand-alone narratives—separate threads—which come together in the final chapter chronicling the battles over international commercial agreements such as the WTO. But while we present a broad overview of this still-blossoming social movement, it would be a mistake to think that it is a complete picture. This is to the movement's credit: Corporate accountability forces are too broad to be captured in a single book. In Jarol Manheim's *The Death of a Thousand Cuts*, he counts 29 anti-corporate campaigns that took place between 1989 and 1999, and another 158 labor union-initiated corporate campaigns from 1974 to 2000. It's likely the figures are much higher; there have been an almost countless number of corporate accountability initiatives.[30]

Our investigation looks solely at U.S.-based corporate campaigns that involved people nationwide. That focus omits two important anti-corporate strands: campaigns based in other countries, and smaller-scale campaigns that occurred in the United States. The corporate campaigns chronicled here are just the tip of the iceberg.

Citizens in other countries have been equally active when it comes to challenging corporate power. Many of the most impassioned anti-corporate struggles have taken place in the developing world, where corporate abuses are often the worst. When it comes to the harms done by transnational corporations and the public's response to those harms, communities in the world's poor countries are on the cutting edge.

In Mexico, poor farmers have fought the clear-cutting of forests by U.S. timber company Boise-Cascade. Ecuadoran Indigenous groups have sought to prevent oil pipeline construction through their rainforests. Farmers in India have resisted Monsanto Corporation's efforts to introduce genetically modified (GM) crops, while more than 100 communities across that country fought Enron's efforts to gain control of local resource deposits. And in Nigeria, communities in the Niger Delta have struggled, at mortal risk, to ensure that oil companies operating there clean up their oil spills and return some of their profits to the impoverished villages near the modern, corporate facilities. In July 2002, more than 1,000 women took over a Chevron oil facility in the Delta, halting production for a week. "We are no longer slaves," said one of the women who seized the plant. "Even slaves realize their condition and fight for their freedom."[31]

Activists in Europe and Canada have also spearheaded many anti-corporate campaigns. Canadian citizens, along with many Australians and Europeans, have played important roles in the anti-sweatshop campaigns against Nike and the Gap. British groups have launched initiatives to expose De Beers diamond company's complicity with human rights abuses in Africa. European campaigners helped lead the international effort to hold Shell Oil accountable for rights abuses in Nigeria. The list goes on and on.

The focus on U.S. campaigns, then, is not motivated by any notion of American exceptionalism. If anything, Americans have been behind the curve in fighting corporate rule. Yet the emphasis on U.S. initiatives does entail a recognition that the stakes here in the United States are as high as anywhere: Because more of the large transnational corporations are based in the United States than in any other country, what happens in regard to corporate power in this country has a profound impact on anti-corporate struggles around the world.

Among the many corporate accountability campaigns in the United

States, we concentrate on those that have been national in scope. That is, campaigns that enlisted support from communities across the country and involved a wide range of people. Such national efforts prove the depth and breadth of the corporate accountability movement, while showing both its strengths and its limitations.

This is not to make light of the important contributions local initiatives have made to the larger corporate accountability struggle. Local campaigns to demand toxic cleanups, to stop the construction of polluting industries, or to halt proposed Wal-Marts are essential pieces of the bigger movement. Local campaigns are often derided as "NIMBYism" ("not in my back yard"), as if they are less genuine or less sophisticated because they are geographically parochial. Even a quick glance at local campaigns should dispel that idea.

Take, for example, the successful campaigns to stop Wal-Mart and other so-called "big box" retailers from moving into certain areas.* Those usually ad-hoc efforts raise vital questions about the role of transnational corporations in a community and how local resources should be employed. And they get to the heart of citizens' concerns about who is making the decisions. As a Missouri man who fought a Kmart in his community put it: "This is a multibillion-dollar corporation trying to shove a big box down our throats."[32]

Environmental justice campaigns also reveal the corporate accountability spirit of local campaigns. In cities and towns around the country, working class or people-of-color communities have challenged polluting industries, either demanding cleanup of toxins or fighting the building of dirty industries in the first place. Many of these campaigns begin from a racial justice perspective, pointing out that oil refineries and chemical plants are rarely located in white, middle-class neighborhoods. In the course of the campaigns, community activists often develop an anti-corporate analysis as they encounter unresponsiveness from company officials. Nothing breeds resentment like arrogance.

It's not that "NIMBYism" is insufficient—it's that there is not enough of it. After all, if every community in the United States were determined to stop the toxic waste incinerators and the Wal-Marts, they would have no place to go, and we would undoubtedly have a much different economy.

The other significant omission in the stories presented here is the faith-centered campaigns for corporate accountability. Faith organizations, often led by evangelical Christian denominations, have put pres-

---

* How successful? According to Wal-Mart executives, anti-Wal-Mart community coalitions manage to block two out of every three proposed locations.

sure on the major entertainment corporations to stop producing films and music albums deemed morally offensive. Many churches have taken steps to ensure that their investment portfolios do not include companies with any involvement in providing abortions. To be sure, your typical Southern Baptist minister and your average radical environmentalist have little in common. But they are both demanding, in their own ways, that corporations be held to a benchmark beyond the bottom line. They are each saying that moral values—however defined—should come before shareholder value.

THE CONTESTED TERRAIN OF THE GLOBAL ECONOMY

The controversy of the new global economy is the common thread linking the corporate accountability stories told here.* Each of these campaigns was in some way a response to economic globalization or, in the case of the tobacco industry saga, undermined by the forces of the global economy. It is the shared concern with globalization that makes these campaigns truly cutting edge. In challenging the assumptions underlying globalization, these struggles have tackled one of the newest facets of corporate rule—corporations' domination over the shaping of the global economy.

As the reach of corporations lengthens, big businesses begin to overshadow the governments that are, in theory, supposed to act as a check on corporate authority. The rise of an integrated global economy spurred the development of ever-larger and more mobile companies, speeding the concentration of corporate power. At the same time, corporations sought to deepen that power by shaping the rules of the global economy to suit their interests. By responding to these dynamics, the corporate accountability campaigns centered on globalization have challenged corporate power on its newest front.

The global economy is contested terrain. During the 1990s, a political drama began to unfold over the question of what values will guide the global economy. Citizen groups said that the interests of workers, communities, and the environment should be at the center of globalization. Corporations insisted that globalization was primarily about eas-

---

* Even within this somewhat narrow scope, we are unable to explore all of the U.S.-based campaigns challenging corporate power. Notable omissions include: the Rainforest Action Network's innovative campaigns against Mitsubishi, Home Depot, and Boise-Cascade; AmazonWatch's efforts against Occidental Petroleum and ChevronTexaco; Project Underground's targeting of mining giant Freeport-McMoRan; Greenpeace's Monsanto campaign; and the varied initiatives against Starbucks Coffee. Once again, the number of important campaigns is too great to list fully.

ing the flow of goods and services, and that, left to its own devices, the market would eventually confer benefits such as democracy and human rights. Whether the controversy was about sweatshop abuses, protecting dolphins, or the rules of the WTO, questions about the future of globalization were at the core of the debate.

The preoccupation of corporate accountability groups with the global economy has led many observers to the mistaken conclusion that the activists are "anti-globalization." Although many years in the making, the corporate accountability movement did not pop into the public consciousness until the Seattle anti-WTO protests in November 1999. During those demonstrations, and subsequent marches against the International Monetary Fund and the World Bank, reporters started to routinely refer to the activists in the streets as "anti-globalization protesters." Yet the vast majority of those opposed to the WTO or seeking to eliminate sweatshops are not against globalization; they are against *corporate* globalization.

Of the 50,000 people who demonstrated in Seattle, most were not opposed to the creation of new relationships among different nations— it was that they didn't want those relationships to be dominated by corporate interests. For corporate accountability forces, globalization isn't the enemy. Giant corporations are the enemy, and globalization is the newest field of battle.

THE REBIRTH OF A MOVEMENT

The spectacular street protests in Seattle against the WTO created misunderstanding not just about the aims of the anti-corporate movement, but also confusion about its origins. Many commentators called Seattle the birth of a movement. But 50,000 impassioned activists do not come from nowhere. It is more accurate to say that Seattle marked the coming-out party for a movement long in gestation. The WTO protests represented a convergence of forces—environmentalists, human rights defenders, trade unionists—who for years had been challenging corporate globalization in their own ways. The Seattle protests brought to the fore passions that for years had been at the edges of American political debate.

Yet even if Seattle was the birth of something new, it would be more precise to say that the protests were the *rebirth* of an American anti-corporate movement, for protests against corporations have been common throughout U.S. history. As we show in Chapter 1, for nearly 200 years, anti-corporate feelings have formed a kind of backbeat to the rhythm of American politics. The corporation has been a regular villain of American politics, a frequent bogeyman. One of the most deep-seated, and enduring, of American political values is a fear of centralized power. And few institutions wield as much power as the limited liability corporation.

The anti-corporate activists chronicled in this book are part of a long tradition of defying big business. Whether called "the money power," "Wall Street," "monopolies," "trusts," "combinations," or "Corporate America," the language of anti-corporate dissent and the rhetoric of reform are strikingly similar throughout the past century-and-a-half. Opponents of corporate power fear a loss of independence to concentrations of money so large that they exceed the reach of public accountability. They question what corporate influence means for community values. And, above all, anti-corporate crusaders worry about what corporate power means for democracy. They are alarmed by accumulations of wealth that seem incompatible with the ideals of a self-governing citizenry in which sovereignty is supposed to rest with the people.

"Wall Street owns the country," a Populist orator, Mary Ellen Lease, told a Topeka, Kansas, crowd in 1890. "It is no longer a government of the people, by the people, and for the people, but a government of Wall Street, by Wall Street, and for Wall Street."[33]

From the streets of Seattle to the frequent pickets outside corporate headquarters, one finds the very same complaint today.

CHALLENGING THE DIVINE RIGHT OF CORPORATIONS

Once upon a time, people believed in the divine right of kings. It was generally accepted that the son or daughter of the king and queen would become the next ruler. Conventional wisdom said that government was meant to be bequeathed.

But eventually those notions were overturned and a new common sense arose. A few "radicals" started opposing the idea of hereditary rule, that "most insolent of tyrannies," as Tom Paine described it. Opposition to monarchy spread. Eventually it became obvious that the people should select who governs them—that basic dignity rests in the ability to exercise control over one's own future rather than to have it dictated by a monarch.

The history of democracy—as well as much of the American experience—is the history of these principles gradually being spread to more and more of the population. At first "We, the People" applied only to white, landowning males. Through generations of struggle, the definition of "people" was steadily expanded to include the poor, blacks, and women. As the scope of democratic participation spread, principles of universal political rights sunk roots into the civic culture. Today in most of the world the idea of hereditary rule is just short of laughable.

Intertwined with the spread of democratic culture was the gradual separation of church and state. The founders of the American republic believed that, to guard against tyranny, it was essential that no one segment of the population should govern the beliefs of the nation. This idea also eventually became common sense, and today most of the world's governments are secular.

These nearly universal philosophies of democracy and freedom, however, have yet to be fully extended to the economic realm. When a tiny circle of individuals controls a country's political system, it is called plutocracy, labeled a junta, and declared a danger to freedom. When religion invades every nook of public life, it is called theocracy, and considered a threat to free conscience. Yet when a handful of giant corporations dominate our food, our media, our healthcare—even our government—it is often described as the very essence of liberty. Consumer choice has become the new definition of freedom.

The partisans of the corporate accountability movement are rebelling against this tyranny of the bottom line. They are fighting the idea that profits should trump all other values, and that economic power should be concentrated in a few hands. In doing so, anti-corporate forces are engaged in an endeavor they believe is every bit as important as the struggles of centuries past. They, too, are trying to create a new definition of common sense. They are saying that just as unelected monarchs should not rule, neither should unelected corporations. And just as no single religion should be given a monopoly over government, neither should the government be given over to monopolies. The corporate accountability movement is, at its heart, a pro-democracy movement, one that is committed to expanding the principles of democratic decision-making from the political sphere to the economic one.

Every call for accountability is a demand for democracy. In striving to hold corporations accountable for their actions, citizens seek to fulfill the idea that in a democracy no institution is above the law. At the same time, each campaign targeting corporate abuse raises crucial issues about the role of big business in a democracy. Every exposé of corporate power raises warnings that political liberty is endangered when economic control rests with an elite minority. Every corporate protest underscores the fact that without economic democracy, political democracy is crippled.

For all of its energy and accomplishments, the corporate accountability movement is still in its infant stages. Corporate rule is far from being dismantled. Yet the struggle itself is a victory. For in battling corporate abuses, millions of people have transformed themselves from passive citizens into active ones. The experience of challenging the status quo creates courage, emboldening citizens to do more. In fighting corporate power, citizens across the country have started to grasp the true meaning of democracy, which comes from the Greek roots *demos*, meaning people, and *kratos*, meaning rule: People rule.

1

CORPORATE POWER vs. PEOPLE POWER
A History of U.S. Corporate Accountability Struggles

THE UNITED STATES WAS SETTLED by corporations. For Europe's rulers the New World was a land glittering with possibilities. Yet colonialism was a risky and expensive enterprise. The construction of large ocean-going vessels and the maintenance of trade routes required a considerable amount of capital. And even once the money was raised, the investment was chancy. The limited liability corporation was an ideal mechanism for overcoming these obstacles. Colonialism spawned the first transnational corporations.

The British crown was hesitant to undertake the endeavor of colonizing non-Christian lands. Direct annexation of foreign lands was bound to be costly since it required vast sums to pay for armies. The British government preferred to colonize by proxy, to let merchants and others do the hard work.

On December 31, 1600, the British monarch, Queen Elizabeth I, granted a charter to the East India Company for the purpose of trading in spices and teas. The queen granted the 218 London merchants who would own shares in the company "legal freedom from liability."[1] This meant that if an investor put in £100 he would be held responsible for only that amount of money; if the entire enterprise went down the tubes with £1,000 in debt, the individual investor would lose only his initial investment. This arrangement—the basis of the limited liability corporation—was essential for raising large pools of money, since it protected the investors in the event of a failure.

The arrangement was also designed to benefit the British crown. The charter agreement was clear in saying that the corporation served at the pleasure of the crown. The company owed its very existence to the state. It was supposed to act in the public interest—or at least in the interest of the monarchy—which in the case of the East India Company meant challenging Holland's virtual monopoly on the lucrative spice trade. The deal benefited many constituencies. The merchants and adventurers eager to explore uncharted territories were able to bring in partners to help finance their expeditions. The partners got security for the investments. And the crown got to see its flag spread via commerce. The losers, of course, were the Indigenous people in the lands being colonized.

The British crown's attention soon turned to North America. Eager to counter the Spanish gains in the Caribbean and South America, the crown chartered corporations to explore and settle North America. The Virginia Company was chartered in 1606 and soon established the ill-fated settlement called Jamestown. In 1629 the crown granted a charter to the Massachusetts Bay Company. The Plymouth pilgrims were, officially at least, a trading corporation. The *Mayflower* was owned by the East India Company.

Despite corporations' pivotal role in the creation of the first British settlements in America, by the middle of the 17th century large companies did not play a big part in the lives of most colonists. In the small, local economies that characterized the British colonies there was no need for the grand, heavily capitalized companies that first pioneered colonization. A typical New England or Pennsylvania farmer had little contact with corporations. Most people's only relation with corporations was secondhand, via the urban merchants who imported manufactured goods from Europe.

But that relationship, however meager, eventually began to chafe, and by the latter part of the 1700s, many colonists were complaining about their dependence on Britain. Frequent targets of complaint were "monopolies," trading companies that had been given exclusive rights to some market or goods. These monopolies aroused anger because, by narrowing the market, they raised the price of imported manufactured items and commodities such as tea. The monopolies were also antithetical to the evolving republican spirit that valued a distribution of power as a check against tyranny.

The most dramatic example of this resistance to monopoly took place in Boston in December 1773. The Boston Tea Party is often thought of as the opening act of the American Revolution, and the reverberations of the tea protest did inflame the cycle of resistance and repression that grew into war. But for the protagonists of that event, the dumping of the tea into Boston Harbor was as much a strike against a corporation as it was a rebellion to the crown. When it came to naming the enemy, the rebels in Boston cited company and king alike. The Boston Tea Party was a protest against the arrogant power and corrupting influence of the largest corporation at the time, the British East India Company.

As related by Thom Hartmann in his book *Unequal Protection*, the British Parliament's passage of the Tea Act of 1773 was, in large part, intended to prop up the fortunes of the East India Company. The company was burdened my a massive surplus of tea; some 17 million pounds of the leaf sat in English warehouses. At the same time, the company was losing market share in the colonies to American smugglers. Many Members of Parliament, as well as the king, held shares in the corporation, and were eager to see the company's fortunes (and their dividends) improve. The Tea Tax not only raised the tax paid by colonial tea drinkers, but also delivered key benefits to the company. The East India Company was exempted from taxes on tea exported to the colonies, provided a tax refund on millions of pounds of unsold leaf, and given full and unlimited access to the American tea trade. With its tax exemptions in hand, the company sharply lowered the price of its tea to drive smaller importers out of business.[2]

The Tea Tax infuriated the colonists, who were outraged at having to pay a tax they had not consented to: "no taxation without representation," went the cry. Colonists were angered by the assault on local merchants, and insulted by the obvious way the East India Company had used its influence to corrupt Members of Parliament.

A 1773 article in *The Alarm*, a colonial pamphlet, reveals the anticorporate bent of resistance to the Tea Tax:

> Are we in like Manner to be given up to the Disposal of the East India Company, who have now the Assurance, to stop forth in Aid of the Minister, to execute his plan, of enslaving America? . . . They [the company] have levied War, excited Rebellions, dethroned lawful Princes, and sacrificed Millions for the Sake of Gain. The Revenues of Mighty Kingdoms have centered in their Coffers. And these not being sufficient to glut their Avarice, they have, by the most unparalleled Barbarities, Extortions, and Monopolies, stripped the miserable inhabitants of their Property, and reduced whole Provinces to Indigence and Ruin.[3]

Resistance to the Tea Tax and antipathy toward the East India Company spread through the colonies. A boycott of the company's tea was launched. In Philadelphia and New York the corporation's ships were unable to load their tea cargo. Anti-corporate pamphleteering intensified. Another edition of *The Alarm* lashed out at the East India Company's manipulation of the Parliament for its own narrow ends:

> It hath now been proved to you, That the East India Company, obtained the monopoly of that [tea] trade by bribery and corruption. That the power thus obtained they have prostituted to extortion, and the most cruel and horrible purposes, the Sun ever beheld.[4]

What came next is well known. On the night of December 16, scores of New England patriots, disguised as Native Americans, boarded the

East India Company's ships in Boston Harbor and threw overboard 342 chests of tea—90,000 pounds of the stuff—enough to make 20 million cups of tea. The protest cost the corporation nearly £1,000: in today's terms, $1 million worth of corporate property.

For many of the rebels at the Boston Tea Party, the attack on the East India Company served as a proxy strike against the crown. Yet much of the protesters' anger was directed at the company itself. In the colonists' eyes, the Tea Tax represented an abuse of power, an abuse by the corporation, whose wealth had given it the ability to pass a law that didn't serve the public interest. The East India Company's power had corrupted the government, and that was tyranny.

The Boston Tea Party was the first American protest against the inordinate power and excessive influence of a transnational corporation.

"ARTIFICIAL ARISTOCRACIES"

The Boston Tea Party notwithstanding, explicitly anti-corporate protests were rare in pre-Revolutionary America. Thomas Jefferson warned against the accumulation of wealth and the creation of "artificial aristocracies." And among many Americans it was common sense that economic inequalities posed a danger to political equality. These vaguely class-based critiques, however, never extended to corporations. Anti-corporate activities were scarce, for the simple reason that corporations themselves were few and far between.

In the early years of the republic there was not much of a national economy, but rather a collection of local economies. Corporations were uncommon because they were unnecessary. By 1800 only some 300 corporations had been granted charters in the United States.[5]

But in the first decades of the 19th century the country's economic landscape began to change. In 1818 there were some 250 banks in the United States; by 1840 there were an estimated 800 of them.[6] New transportation arteries—turnpikes and canals and, soon, steamships and the first railroads—were transforming local economies into regional ones.

Most of the turnpike construction was done by corporations, which received "special charters" to do the work. In order to create a corporation, investors had to appeal to the state legislatures, which would vote on whether to provide a charter. The arrangements were reciprocal. The state got its roads built and the builders received permission to charge a toll on the roads to recover their investment. The corporations were expected to serve the public interest: The roads were supposed to be maintained by the company, and the poorest people were exempted from having to pay the tolls. In 1800, more than two-thirds of the country's corporations were in the transportation business, and by 1810 there were

180 turnpike corporations in New England alone.[7]

While new transportation systems were linking together the country's economies, the nation's wealthy classes were transforming themselves from merchants to manufacturers. The War of 1812 had interrupted much of the trade with Europe, giving local manufacturing the chance to flourish. Textile manufacturing was the booming industry of the day. The country's first industrialists built large textile mills that needed unprecedented amounts of capital. When Francis Cabot Lowell chartered his first mill in 1813, it was initially capitalized at $400,000, about ten times the size of a typical mill of the day. To achieve economies of scale, Lowell founded an entire town—named after himself—dedicated solely to cloth production. The company's assets grew twenty-fold from 1814 to 1823. The number of workers spiraled. In 1830 the town of Lowell had 6,000 residents; six years later it had three times that many.[8]

The construction of turnpikes and canals dramatically increased the scope of U.S. economies. At the same time, the growth of manufacturing expanded the scale of the economies. The expansion of scale and scope—the creation of regional economies—gave corporations greater influence over the lives of ordinary people. Corporations, though privately controlled, began to have greater impact on the public at large.

The mill towns of New England exemplify corporations' new presence in people's lives. Young women left their farming communities—often many days' travel away—to work in the textile mills. Living in dormitories near the factories, nearly every facet of their lives was determined by the company: the time they woke up, what they ate, the amount of free time they enjoyed, when they went to bed.

In the local economy, market relationships had been personal. In the regional economy, relationships became impersonal. Without a doubt, personal relationships between workers and masters—as they were then called—were often exploitative. But with the proliferation of corporations, the exploitation took on a different character, since workers were no longer bargaining with a person, but with an institution, the company. The destinies of individuals and communities were increasingly dictated by combinations of capital that seemed frighteningly powerful.

For some members of the new manufacturing class, the corporation's collective character allowed a divorcing of private scruples from economic decisions. "Corporations will do what individuals would not dare do," wrote Peter Brooks, one of the wealthiest men in Boston. "Where dishonesty is the work of *all* the Members, every *one* can say with Macbeth in the murder of Banquo, 'thou canst not say *I* did it.'"[9]

For many Americans, however, the changes wrought by the growing corporate economy were unsettling. The human detachment fostered by economic expansion differed sharply from the close-knit farming communities most people had grown up in. And the engine of economic change, the corporation, seemed impersonal and disembodied. A consensus was growing that the corporation was slipping beyond the reach of public accountability. "Corporations have neither bodies to be kicked, nor souls to be damned," went a popular saying of the day.[10]

The sweeping transformation of the economy was creating a backlash. The economic revolution spawned a rebellion against itself. The 1830s and 1840s saw growing social unrest. In the larger cities of New York, Philadelphia, and Baltimore workers' associations were forming. By 1835, there were 50 different unions in Philadelphia alone. Strikes were increasingly common. Workers staged work stoppages to demand higher wages and, successfully, a 10-hour day. In 1834 the women workers in Lowell's textiles mills struck to protest a wage reduction. In 1835, 20 mills went on strike simultaneously. In 1836 alone there were 140 strikes in the eastern United States.[11]

The abolition, in most states, of property ownership requirements for voting further enlivened popular challenges to the changing economy. The establishment of universal* male suffrage breathed fresh air into the political arena and spawned populist parties such as the Workingmen's Party and the Equal Rights Party. The new voters were eager to put into practice the ideals set forth in the country's founding documents. But to many it seemed the promise of democracy was being blocked by the accumulation of wealth in too few hands. Legislatures were giving "special privileges" to companies and their owners. "Monopolies" were growing in number and size. The "Money Power" was corrupting public officials. The concentration of wealth and the rising power of corporations threatened the country's nascent democracy.

The most famous example of early 19th century opposition to corporate power is President Andrew Jackson's fight against the Bank of the United States. Although Jackson is often portrayed as a hero of the common people, it's a dubious title. A ruthless Indian killer, Jackson was a land speculator, merchant, and slave holder during a time when many working people considered speculators and merchants to be parasites on the country's farmers and laborers. Economic inequalities worsened during Jackson's administration and that of his successor, Martin Van Buren.[12] But politics is about perception, and Jackson was undeniably popular during his time, especially among the poor and "middling"

---

* "Universal" applied only to white males. Women were considered inconsequential, and blacks, when considered at all, were generally referred to in the most insulting and racist terms.

classes. That popularity rested in large part on his vehement attacks against the Bank of the United States and other corporations.

The Bank of the United States was the brainchild of Alexander Hamilton, the aristocratic first Treasury Secretary of the United States. Hamilton thought that ensuring social stability and insulating the government from "the rabble" would require giving the wealthier classes a direct stake in the young state. The Bank was designed to accomplish this. It was an odd institution, a contradictory mix of private functions and public investment. The Bank was privately controlled, yet it was the official repository of public funds. One-fifth of its $35 million in capital came from government deposits. It could use its capital however it liked and its profits went to its private investors. At the same time, the Bank paid no taxes, and the government deposits did not earn any interest. In return for these privileges the Bank paid the government $500,000 a year, transferred public funds without charge, and allowed the government to appoint one-fifth of its directors.

Today we might call this arrangement "corporate welfare." For the Bank's supporters, that was precisely the point: to guarantee the rich a role in managing the government's money.

But for most citizens, the Bank of the United States represented everything they disliked about corporations. "Dangerous and pernicious to the Government and the people," as one anti-Bank Senator said.[13] It was, first of all, a monopoly. Its charter said that Congress could not create any other institution like it. This status gave the Bank immense power: It held de facto control over the country's money supply and the credit markets. Despite its clearly public functions, the Bank was unaccountable to the people. Its directors felt they owed no responsibility to the citizenry.

Nicholas Biddle, president of the Bank, claimed that: "No officer in the Government, from the President downwards, has the least right, the least authority, the least pretence, for interference in the concerns of the bank."[14]

For most people, the idea that the Bank was independent of the will of the public was frightening. The Bank's unique control over the country's financial markets gave it power rivaling that of the federal government. Andrew Jackson's Attorney General, Roger B. Taney,* wrote to Congress:

---

* Taney's populism extended only to white males. As Chief Justice of the Supreme Court, Taney would later author the Dred Scott opinion, which said that black slaves were not people, but property.

It is a fixed principle of our political institutions to guard against the unnecessary accumulation of power over property and persons in any hands. And no hands are less worth to be trusted with it than those of a moneyed corporation.[15]

This sentiment represented the prevailing wisdom in the Jackson administration and of the country at large. In 1833 the president's personal secretary wrote: "Independent of its [the Bank's] misdeeds, the mere power—the bare existence of a power—is a thing irreconcilable with the nature and spirit of our institutions."[16]

The charter of the Bank of the United States was set to expire in 1836. Once created, corporations were not assured of immortality. Corporate charters regularly put a time limit on the company's operations, anywhere from 3 to 20 years. After that time the investors had to apply again to the legislature to have their charters reapproved. Corporate charters also limited the tasks a corporation could perform. The charters set out a specific function—turnpike construction, canal building, or banking—and enforced this limitation by prohibiting corporations from owning other corporations. Some sort of public service was also required. These restrictions on corporations' lifespan and operations were a way to keep the power of corporations in check. Corporations' accumulation of wealth was viewed with suspicion, and only permitted if companies were kept on a short leash.

The country's merchants and industrialists were anxious to keep the Bank alive. The Bank's loose credit policies and floating of paper money suited their interests. In the summer of 1832, conservative legislators, led by Senator Daniel Webster, passed legislation to extend the Bank's charter. But Jackson, his cabinet, and a number of progressive legislators opposed the Bank. Echoing the public sentiment of the time, Jackson and his supporters said the Bank's arrogant behavior violated the idea of popular rule.

"This powerful corporation and those who defend it," said Attorney General Taney, "seem to regard it as an independent sovereignty, and to have forgotten that it owes any duties to the People, or is bound by any laws but its own will."[17]

Jackson vetoed the bill approving the Bank's rechartering. Then, to drive the point home, he instructed the Treasury Secretary to withdraw the government's deposits from the Bank. The country's industrialists, bankers, and merchants were beside themselves with anger. Jackson was accused of "Caesarism" and derided as a "detestable, ignorant, reckless . . . tyrant."[18] But the great mass of voters—the wage-earners and the farmers—applauded Jackson's opposition to the Bank, and overwhelmingly reelected him. The Bank would eventually close its doors for good.

The fight over the Bank of the United States is just the most dramatic anti-corporate battle of the Jacksonian era. Citizen efforts to rein in corporate power were common across the country. In the first half of the 19th century, corporations were popular targets of grassroots activism.

In 1825, Pennsylvania legislators adopted powers to "revoke, alter, or annul the charter" of any corporation at any time. Delaware voters passed a constitutional amendment in 1831 limiting all corporate charters to 20 years, and Louisiana and Michigan adopted similar amendments. In 1832, the year Jackson vetoed the Bank of the United States' charter, ten Pennsylvania banks were dechartered.[19] Kentucky's legislature replaced the Bank of Kentucky with a state-controlled loan office, and Tennessee soon followed suit.[20] In 1835, the Bank of Maryland was the target of a riot in Baltimore. Similar bank riots occurred in Ohio.[21] By 1844, 19 states had amended their constitutions to make corporate charters subject to alteration or revocation by legislatures.[22]

Citizens in the early 19th century felt that the existence of monopolies violated the democratic philosophy that power should be divided and hemmed in by checks and balances. "Equal rights for all, special privileges for none," went the Jeffersonian saying. It seemed to many that monopolistic corporations benefited from such "special privileges."

In an effort to do away with those privileges, some anti-corporate activists focused their efforts on abolishing the so-called "special chartering" laws. When a legislature granted a charter to a corporation, it usually gave the company a monopoly based on either function or geography. This was one of the reciprocal benefits granted the investors: They could be sure they wouldn't face competition. In theory, the charters were beneficial in that they tied corporations to an elected body and held them accountable. In practice, however, the special chartering system often bred corruption. The wealthy and the well-connected were usually the ones to get charters, leaving other entrepreneurs out in the cold. Wealthier petitioners hired lobbyists to press their case before the legislatures. Bribes were common. The *Workingman's Advocate*, a popular newspaper, complained: "The laws for private incorporation are all partial . . . favoring one class of society to the expense of the other."[23]

Some reformers put their energy into creating "general laws of incorporation." The idea was to take the chartering process out of the hands of the legislatures and create a system whereby anyone could create a corporation by filling out the necessary paperwork. As long as you agreed to meet certain requirements—and abide by the common restrictions on the company's life span, functions, and prohibition against owning other companies—you could charter a corporation. This was supposed to elimi-nate the dreaded monopolies that had flourished under the special char-ter system. It would make the incorporating process more democratic. The question of general incorporation versus special incorporation was promoted by radicals in the legislatures, agitated over in crowded halls, debated at political conventions. The first general incorporation law was passed in 1837 in Connecticut. Other states followed.

At first, corporate owners fought the general incorporation laws. With the abolition of the special chartering system, the already established business lost its monopoly advantage. But eventually industrialists rec-ognized that the general incorporation laws were in their interest be-cause they made incorporating so much easier. Corporate owners began pressing for general incorporation laws, using the language of reform-ers to help their cause.

The steady introduction of general incorporation laws reveals an irony in the history of anti-corporate movements in the United States. A re-form initially intended to strike at the accumulated power of monopo-lies resulted in making it easier to form corporations, and in legitimiz-ing their existence. According to historian Arthur Schlesinger, "The general laws sprinkled holy water on corporations, cleansing them of the legal status of monopoly and sending them forth as benevolent agen-cies of free competition."[24] The number of corporations exploded in the 1840s and 1850s. By the 1860s there were thousands of corporations, and the post-Civil War era would come to be known as "The Age of Incorporation."

WRITING A CORPORATE BILL OF RIGHTS

Railroads structured the United States as we know it today: They were essential to forming a national economy. Where turnpikes and canals had knitted local economies into regional economies, the steady spread of railroads united the regional economies into a national one. They helped bring together a country that—as the Civil War violently dem-onstrated—had been deeply riven by geography. The railroad also helped create, and was created by, that central feature of American life, the corporation.

Twenty-one thousand miles of railroad track were laid in the United States during the 1850s. Twenty years later, 70,000 miles of railroad tracks were in operation. By 1900, 193,000 miles of rail criss-crossed the country. This could not have happened without the corporation.

Railroad building and maintenance was far more capital intensive than turnpike construction, textile manufacturing, and even banking. In the 1850s only a handful of textile mills were capitalized at more than

$1 million, and most textile plants boasted less than $250,000 in assets. During that same time, the major East-West "trunk lines"—so called because they formed the spine of the emerging rail system—cost from $17 million to $35 million to build. Even the smaller lines that went through less-populated areas required as much as $5 million to construct. With the spread of the railroad, the number of corporations exploded, and their accumulated capital grew ever larger.[25]

Even as corporations built the railroad, the railroads shaped the modern corporation. The speed and reach of the railroad introduced business owners to new challenges of complexity. To move goods and people safely and reliably, to maintain miles of track and fleets of locomotives, required a new kind of organization. A managerial class arose to oversee the vast business enterprises. Accountants, engineers, technicians, surveyors, administrators, and executives kept the trains running on time and profitably. The corporation became an institution unto itself, every bit as elaborate and hierarchical as the governments of the day.[26]

The expansion of the railroads rippled through the economy, helping to spawn other giant industries. To lay the tracks and build the carriages, iron and steel were needed, and great metal factories were formed. Coal was needed to keep the engines running. Mines proliferated, transforming entire regions. From 1860 to 1884 the amount of coal mined rose from 14 million tons per year to 100 million tons. The increase in railroad speed shortened distances, allowing for the nationalization of formerly local businesses such as meat packing, which grew into a nationwide industry with the invention of manufactured ice in 1885. Retailers took advantage of the speed and dependability of rail transport to create the first catalogue businesses that catered to communities across the country. The railroad propelled one of the greatest marches of economic growth in history.[27] The corporation was the vehicle for that growth.

The late 19th century is often referred to as the Era of the Robber Barons: a name that proves the lasting potency of anti-corporate rhetoric. The Robber Barons were men such as Andrew Carnegie, J.P. Morgan, William Vanderbilt, and John D. Rockefeller who, through the might of their corporations, dominated the business world, the political landscape, and the daily lives of tens of millions of people. In the second half of the 19th century, the breakneck growth of the economy led to a proliferation of corporations and an accumulation of wealth unlike any before. The power of the corporation—which before had been constrained by laws and legislatures—broke free from accountability to the public.

The vast increase in corporate power was due in large part to the sheer growth of corporations' size. Corporate operations now stretched across state lines. Capital investment became more and more transregional, as banks in New York funded railroads in the Midwest. Companies came to dwarf the legislatures that were supposed to guard against business abuses. In Massachusetts, for example, the Boston & Maine railroad had revenues of $40 million a year and employed 18,000 people; the Commonwealth of Massachusetts had $7 million in revenues and employed 6,000 people.[28] The increase in economies of scale made the corporations the most powerful force in the country.

Even as corporations grew in size and number, the legal bonds that had once constricted their behavior were loosened. Changes in state laws and a wave of corporate-friendly court rulings facilitated the rise of corporate power in the latter half of the 19th century. Such changes were spurred by corporations themselves, which, it often seemed, were actually running the federal and state governments. In 1876, for example, railroad lobbyists played a key role in deciding the deadlocked presidential election, which was thrown into the hands of the House of Representatives when no candidate had a majority of electoral votes. The House selected Rutherford B. Hayes, a former rail executive.[29] Corporate corruption of government became widespread. Railroad companies and land speculators manipulated the Homestead Act and strong-armed members of Congress into giving away some 100 million acres of public lands adjacent to rail lines. Construction of the Transcontinental Railroad was greased with $200,000 in cash bribes.[30]

A Senator candidly told a group of his business patrons at the turn of the last century:

> You send us to Congress, [where] we pass laws under which you make money. And out of your profits you further contribute to our campaign funds to send us back again to pass more laws that enable you to make more money.[31]

Critics dubbed the U.S. Senate the "millionaire's club," referring to both its makeup and its clear bias toward monied interests. In a memorable jab at the corrupt and money-driven spirit of the time, Mark Twain sarcastically said the country had entered a "Gilded Age."

During the Gilded Age, state and federal courts played a significant role in bolstering corporate power by overhauling companies' legal relations to government. As early as 1819, on the cusp of the Jacksonian anti-corporate backlash, the Supreme Court had ruled that corporations were not necessarily creations of the state, but could be considered an organic relationship among individuals. In a decision over the fate of Dartmouth College (*Board of Trustees of Dartmouth College v. Wood-*

ward), the justices ruled that a corporation should also be defined as a contractual agreement among different parties—not solely thought of as an artificial invention of the state—and that therefore the corporation enjoyed protection under the Constitution's language guaranteeing the inviolability of contracts. The court struck down New Hampshire's attempt to revoke the college's charter. After that, state legislatures were careful to write detailed charter revocation rules into corporate chartering laws so that the power to withdraw a charter was clearly set forth in the original contract. Still, the case set an important precedent and opened the way for corporate owners to make the case that their enterprises existed independently of any state permission.[32]

In the decades before and after the Civil War, one court judgment after another weakened the ability of governments and citizens to hold corporations accountable for their actions. Judges gave corporations the power of "eminent domain"—the ability to take private property from others with minimal compensation. Corporate-friendly judges struck down legislatures' attempts to establish wage and hour laws and statutes governing railroad rates and grain elevator charges. When it came to disputes between labor organizers and big business, courts almost always took the side of the corporations. In 1895, the Supreme Court even ruled that the Sherman Anti Trust Act—passed in 1890 to curtail the power of corporations—could be used against interstate railroad strikes, which were called a restraint of trade.[33]

The biggest boost to corporate power came in 1886. The Supreme Court unanimously ruled that corporations were entitled to protection under the Fourteenth Amendment, which guarantees all people—regardless of skin color— equal protection under the law and right to due process. In the case *Santa Clara County v. Southern Pacific Railroad*, the justices said the amendment also applied to businesses and "forbid a State to deny to any person within its jurisdiction the equal protection of the laws, [including] these corporations." The ruling sent the message that corporations didn't exist only with the permission of the people, but that corporations themselves enjoyed the very same protections as people. In that year alone, the Supreme Court tossed out 230 state laws designed to regulate corporate behavior. The idea of public control of the corporation was being turned on its head.[34]

Often corrupted by big business bribes, state legislatures did their part to grant corporations new rights and privileges by rewriting the chartering laws set up during the Jacksonian period. Company executives were eager to strike down limits on corporate size, and in 1889 they convinced the New Jersey legislature to allow corporations to own one another. Companies flocked to New Jersey after its incorporation rules were changed, greatly enriching the state's coffers. Other states, seeing how New Jersey had reaped a bounty of new investment, sped to change their incorporation laws.

A 19th century "race-to-the-bottom" occurred during which states competed to attract businesses by lowering their demands on corporations. Companies played states off one another by asking for ever looser restrictions. In the midst of a "bidding war" between New Jersey and New York, the New Jersey legislature passed an incorporation law that permitted unlimited corporate size and market share, legalized new kinds of mergers and acquisitions, reduced shareholder power in favor of company directors, and removed all time limits on the lifespan of corporate charters. Not to be outdone, Delaware* passed the most permissive incorporation law yet. Delaware's new law said business owners "may also contain [in the charter] any provision which the incorporators may choose to insert." Whereas the early charter systems had reserved for the state all powers not explicitly given to the corporation, Delaware's new process allowed corporations to define their own powers. No one but the companies themselves could set the rules for corporate behavior. The legal framework supporting the idea that corporations should be subordinate to the will of the people was being dismantled.[35]

The wealthy classes—business owners, judges, corporate lawyers—sought to justify the changes in the law with theories of "*laissez-faire*" and "Social Darwinism." The idea of *laissez-faire* stipulated that the general good would be best served when government refrained from "interfering" with business. Seeking legitimacy in the Jeffersonian idea that "the government is best which governs least," proponents of *laissez-faire* economics argued that the state and federal government should not "meddle" in the affairs of business. If government would stay out of the way, corporations' actions would benefit society at large. The *laissez-faire* mentality meshed with corporate owners' belief that their endeavors were private efforts, not public acts, and that no one had the right to tell them how to run their businesses.

"Social Darwinism" converted the evolution theory of biologist Charles Darwin into a quasi-scientific political philosophy. Just as evolution favored the "survival of the fittest" in natural selection, the Social Darwinists said, so too did human society exhibit similar evolutionary dynamics: The rich achieved their wealth because they were the

---

* Delaware's General Incorporation Law of 1899 touted itself as "the most favorable of existing general incorporation laws . . . far beyond New Jersey." This explains why, even today, a host of major U.S. corporations are formally—if not physically—based in filing cabinets in the Delaware state capital.

most able, the fittest; the poor were impoverished because they were the least able. Attempting to rein in corporate power or redistribute the wealth of corporate owners was simply unnatural. In an America riven by widening economic inequalities and increasingly dominated by a handful of mighty corporations, Social Darwinism provided a moral justification for the status quo. George F. Baer, the owner of the Phila-delphia and Reading Railroad, summed up the beliefs behind social Dar-winism when he said:

> The rights and interests of the laboring men will be protected and cared for—not by labor agitators, but by the Christian men who God in his infinite wisdom has given control of the property interests of this coun-try.[36]

THE POPULIST REBELLION

Yet the corporate make-over of U.S. society was not without contro-versy. To the majority of American families—workers and farmers— Social Darwinism looked less like the survival of the fittest than the conquest of the corrupt and the well-connected. Even as corporate ti-tans demolished the corporate accountability accomplishments of the Jacksonian period, millions of citizens resisted their efforts. For many Americans, the vast strength of corporations, their utter disregard for workers and communities, and their flagrant corruption of public offi-cials were abhorrent. Corporate power threatened democracy, and many were determined to fight it.

The 1870s, '80s, and '90s were much like the 1830s and '40s in that the rapid changes wrought by corporate expansion created widespread anxiety and anger. While corporate expansion enriched a small minor-ity, many people lived in the depths of poverty, wracked by disease and malnutrition. The vast social and economic inequalities made a mock-ery of the ideals of political equality. At the same time, the obvious political influence of corporations and their wealthy owners called into question the bedrock principles of democracy, the belief that sovereignty lies with the people. Economic upheaval often breeds social rebellion. If the Gilded Age was a halcyon time for big business, it was also a crucible of radical citizen activism.

In the last decades of the 19th century workers across the United States were organizing for better working conditions, shorter hours, and recognition of a union's right to exist. The steady migration of people from the countryside to the cities spawned in many people a sense of vulnerability. Wage labor was a visceral shock for those accustomed to feeding themselves from their own land. Working for a wage set up a dependent relationship with the boss, a relationship antithetical to the republican ideal of independence. The anxieties of dependence and vulnerability—combined with arrogant behavior on the part of many corporate owners—spurred people to organize protests. Workers felt that the corporations they worked for needed to be accountable to the people who made the companies profitable. As one workers' organization, the Knights of Labor, explained it, unions were needed to "counterbalance the power of aggregated and incorporated wealth."[37] Every worker protest was an effort to bring corporations under public control.

Strikes were common, and frequently bloody. In 1877, a railroad workers' strike in Baltimore quickly spread to other cities, paralyzing the country. In St. Louis hundreds of protesters marched behind a banner that read, "No Monopoly—Workingmen's Rights." A song written by strikers showed the workers' anti-corporate sentiments: "There's an army of strikers/Determined you'll see/Who will fight the corporations/Till the country is free." Federal and state troops violently crushed the strike, leaving some 100 people dead in towns across the nation.[38]

In 1884, women workers in New York City struck successfully for higher wages and shorter hours. Two years later, the nascent American Federation of Labor (AFL) called for a nationwide strike to demand an eight-hour day. Some 350,000 workers around the country took part in the strike. An estimated 1,400 strikes took place in 1886—about three times as many as the year before—involving half a million workers. Police and army troops often used force to halt workers' actions. Dozens of workers were killed.[39]

In 1892, workers at the Carnegie Steel plant in Homestead, Pennsylvania, struck for four months, but eventually were crushed by armed repression and the use of strikebreakers. Two years later, railroad workers at the Pullman Company in Chicago went on strike to protest low wages and dangerous working conditions. The strike soon spread to other cities, grinding the economy to a halt. President Grover Cleveland called in federal troops to force the employees back to work. An estimated 34 people were killed during the strike, which the *Locomotive Fireman's Magazine* blamed on "the greed of the corporation."[40]

Writers were also challenging the corporate status quo. In 1879 Henry George, a self-educated working man, published *Progress and Poverty*, which criticized the "monopolization of the land," called for a tax on giant landholdings, and sold millions of copies. Edward Bellamy's *Looking Backward* became equally popular with its tale of a Rip Van Winkle character who wakes up in the year 2000 to discover a socialist utopia in the United States. The book sold millions of copies and led to the creation of a network of Christian Socialist clubs across the country.

Farmers were also rebelling. During the 1870s and 1880s farmers—who still made up a majority of the population—suffered from a sharp decrease in their standard of living. Advances in farm technology led to overproduction, dramatically reducing the prices farmers received for their crops. In 1870 a bushel of corn fetched 45 cents; by 1889 a bushel of corn earned a farmer just 10 cents. At the same time, many farmers had gone deeply into debt to pay for the new steel farm machinery that increased crop yields. To make matters worse, farmers also saw the costs of transporting their harvests increase as the railroads consolidated. High shipping rates, tight credit, and growing debts had pushed many farmers to the brink of ruin. More and more farmers began to view corporations—the banks and the railroads—as the source of their woes.

In 1877 a group of disgruntled farmers met in Lampasas County, Texas, to form the Farmers Alliance. The farmers pledged to cooperate to raise commodity prices and to work together to challenge the might of the banks and the railroads. The Alliance quickly grew across the impoverished West and South, and by 1886 the Alliance boasted 100,000 members. That year farmers gathered again, this time in Cleburne, Texas, to articulate a political program. Decrying the "shameful abuses" that farmers and workers were "suffering at the hands of arrogant capitalists and powerful corporations," the Alliance called for heavy regulation of the railroads, laws against dealing in commodities futures, prohibitions on speculators buying land, and a loosening of the money supply to help the indebted. The goal, as one Alliance chapter put it, was to "overthrow all monopolies."[41]

The Farmers Alliance was the first step toward what would eventually become the Populist Movement. In the early 1890s, the deep and broad discontent that had been simmering for 20 years would boil to the surface of American politics, rattling the status quo. The Populist insurgency was the climax of an agrarian rebellion long in the making, a rebellion against the authority and influence of giant corporations.

The Populist Movement was, in part, a class movement. Populists saw a clear division between "producers"—farmers and workers, people who actually created something—and "consumers." Populism was also a regional movement. Its greatest strength was among the western and southern farmers who feared and hated the "money power" of the northeastern banks and railroads. It was also often a nativist, anti-Semitic, and racist movement. Distrust of Jews and foreigners ran through the movement, and only in some states were blacks allowed to participate.

But judged by its own rhetoric, the Populist Movement was first and foremost an anti-corporate crusade. When Populists named the enemy, they named big business. "Corporate feudality has taken the place of chattel slavery and vaunts its power in every state," a typical Populist pamphlet complained.[42] As one Populist activist said, the Populist revolt was an effort "against the encroachments of monopolies and in opposition to the growing corruption of wealth and power."[43]

By 1890 most of the U.S. rail system had been concentrated in the hands of six giant trusts. The corporations' iron-fisted grip on rail costs and credit flows compromised the independence of ordinary farmers, an independence that was key to real liberty. For farmers in the West and the South it was outrageous that bankers and corporate executives in New York and Philadelphia exercised such influence over their lives. Populist activists complained about the "colonial economy" and the power of "unseen, faraway forces." Such complaints centered questions about control: who had it, and who didn't.

In raising those questions, the Populists were challenging the very legitimacy of the corporation. Since private enterprise impacted the public interest, corporations should be controlled by the citizenry. It was an issue of sovereignty: Should the public be subordinate to the corporation, or should the corporation be subordinate to the people? The Populists sought not only to ease the effects of corporate behavior; they wanted radical change that would curb corporate power. A Nebraska farmers' journal declared:

> The corporation has absorbed the community. The community now must absorb the corporation. . . . Does not the problem of humanity demand that there shall be a better system? There MUST be a better system.[44]

The Populists did not just complain about the corporate status quo. They also worked to establish a "better system" to replace the corporate order. Farmers Alliance chapters set up cooperatives across the South and West to put into practice the idea of "democratic capitalism." The co-ops brought farmers together to buy goods in bulk so they could get lower prices. They also coordinated the collective sale of commodities such as cotton so that individual farmers, working together, could demand higher prices for their harvest. Co-op stores and warehouses were established. The co-ops sponsored picnics and parades and town hall meetings. The Farmers Alliance viewed the revitalization of community networks and community action as an antidote to corporate control. They figured that economic cooperation and anti-monopolism were two sides of the same coin. The co-ops and farmers exchanges represented the backbone of the Populist Movement, and its most important recruiting mechanism.

It was a successful strategy. By 1887 membership had doubled to 200,000. By 1889 the number of members doubled again, to 400,000. "From New York to the Golden Gate," the Farmers Alliance president told a Fourth of July rally in 1890, "the farmers have risen up and have inaugurated a movement such as the world has never seen."[45]

That movement became a powerful political force. In the elections of 1888 and 1890, Alliance-backed candidates scored a string of victories in the South and West, grabbing dozens of state legislature seats and even sending some of their members to Congress. But regional factionalism retarded the movement's efforts to develop a unique electoral identity. In the South, Alliance partisans were Democrats, while in the West they voted Republican.

By 1892 it had become clear to most Alliance members that they needed to form their own political party. Many of the early Alliance candidates abandoned Alliance policies once in office. And it was increasingly obvious that when it came to issues of corporate power the Democratic Party and the Republican Party were hardly different. Although elected president in 1884 on an anti-corporate platform, Democrat Grover Cleveland assured industrialists and bankers: "No harm shall come to any business interest as the result of administrative policy so long as I am president.[46] Republicans within the Alliance accused Cleveland of fostering "centralized corporate despotism," while Alliance Democrats scorned Republicans as servants of "monopolists, gamblers, gigantic corporations, bondholders, [and] bankers."[47] Another party was needed if the power of big business was to be curtailed.

In February 1892, the People's Party was officially formed. The party's platform called for a loose money supply in the form of greenbacks and silver currency, creation of an income tax, use of secret ballots in elections, various plans for protecting striking workers, and an end to monopolistic ownership of land. Most radical were demands for public ownership of the railroad, telephone, and telegraph systems. The vast corporate fortunes had to be brought under public control. "We believe that the powers of the government—in other words, of the people— should be expanded to end . . . oppression, injustice and poverty."[48]

The People's Party—widely known as the Populists—was not the first political insurgency of the post-Civil War era. The Greenback Party, the Anti-Monopoly Party, the Prohibition Party, and the Workingmen Party had all tried to crack the two-party system. None gained more than four percent of the vote. The People's Party held genuine promise and ignited real excitement about upending the status quo by uniting these disparate forces. From their base among debt-ridden farmers, the Populists brought together the temperance groups, workers' associations, women's organizations, and the middle-class activists of the Christian Socialist clubs. Combating corporate rule was something reformers of all stripes could get behind.

James B. Weaver was nominated as the People Party's presidential candidate. Pledging to fight what he called "the war of the trusts," Weaver spoke to crowds around the country. Volunteers spread across the prairie to urge people to vote Populist.

The results of the 1892 campaign were promising. Despite being outspent by $4 million by the two major parties, Weaver took 8.5 percent of the national vote and won the electoral votes of Colorado, Kansas, Idaho, and Nevada. Hundreds of Populist state legislators swept into office across the Plains states. Colorado and Kansas elected Populist governors. The Populists' promise of creating a "cooperative commonwealth" had struck a chord with the public.

The midterm elections of 1894 were equally encouraging. Populist candidates won some 1.5 million votes, taking seven seats in the House of Representatives and six Senate seats.

But the promise was short-lived. Despite their calls for "equal protection for labor and capital" and some valiant attempts to reach out to industrial workers, the Populists were failing to connect with voters in the industrial heartland of the Midwest and East. Though designed to be universal, the Populists' anti-corporate rhetoric carried an unmistakable agrarian and Protestant accent that turned off many Catholic urban workers. In the South, Populist efforts were frustrated by racial tensions. Southern white Democrats used the Populists' outreach to blacks—however tentative and limited—to scare away white voters. And the few blacks who were allowed to vote were alienated by the Populists' failure to fully embrace blacks, so they stuck with the party of Lincoln.

By 1896 the People's Party was in disarray. The Farmers Alliance cooperatives in the South and West were coming undone, sapping the party's strength and eliminating the reason most people had joined the Populist Movement in the first place. The passion of the grassroots struggle had cooled as the movement became entangled in the maneuverings of the electoral system. The country was in an economic depression, and some Populists figured that the downturn would give their party's anti-corporate message more resonance among voters. But most of the party's members felt that their best chance of success lay in uniting with the Democrats in a fusion ticket.

After months of heated debate, the Populists decided to campaign with the Democrats, who had nominated William Jennings Bryan, a young Congressman from Nebraska. The Democrat-Populist fusion was an uneven relationship. When the Populists asked to select the Vice

Presidential nominee, the Democrats ignored them. And though Bryan passionately embraced the Populist call for a loose money supply, the Democratic platform rejected most of the Populists' demands.

Yet even the watered-down radicalism of the Bryan campaign was enough to scare the country's corporate establishment. Business leaders knew the Populist message had a widespread appeal, and they feared that with a Democrat vehicle such ideas might actually gain power. Republicans, who were solidly pro-business, warned that a Democrat-Populist victory would lead to socialism and revolution. Under the leadership of industrialist Mark Hanna, the Republicans engineered the first modern fund-raising campaign in U.S. history, taking in millions of dollars from railroads, oil companies, and banks. The corporations feared reform, and the GOP candidate, William McKinley, used the corporate contributions to vastly outspend Bryan and win handily.

Corporate leaders had spent decades determinedly consolidating their power. As the election of 1896 demonstrated, they were equally determined not to lose it. The Populists had not fulfilled their promise of creating democratic capitalism, but their impassioned assault on the status quo reignited a national debate about the power of giant corporations. That debate was not over.

BUSTING THE TRUSTS

The Populist spirit did not die with the collapse of the People's Party. Anti-corporate sentiment in America at the turn of the 20th century was too deep and too widespread to wither away with the failure of a single political party. The Populists had raised profound questions about whether the interests of corporations were really the same as the interests of the general public. Those questions had not been answered.

In the opening decades of the 20th century, anti-corporate reformers dubbed themselves "Progressives." Though less radical than the Populists, the Progressives still centered their energies on the corporation. Big business remained public enemy number one.

Unlike the Populists, Progressives did not attack the existence of the privately run corporation. Few Progressives were so bold as to call for the nationalization of major industries. They did not seek—as the Jacksonians and Populists had—to make accumulated wealth subservient to the public. Rather, Progressives sought to soften the sharp edges of corporate capitalism, to ameliorate its worst abuses. The Progressives were believers in the power of rational thought and they argued that, if managed wisely, the economy could be made less violent and less unequal. They weren't radicals; they were technocratic reformers.

Professionals, intellectuals, and middle-class do-gooders, the

Progressives were in no position to claim to be "producers." Living mostly in urban areas, the Progressives' lifestyles were very much dependent on the corporation. This meant that the Progressives had no Populist vision of the "cooperative commonwealth" to offer. Independence from the corporations was not considered possible, and there was little talk among Progressives of trying to build an alternative system. The Progressives wanted a less abusive system, one that limited corporate behavior yet did not reach to the roots of corporate power.

What the Progressives lacked in radicalism, they made up for in widespread appeal. Unlike the Populists, the Progressive program connected with the eastern middle class and industrial workers. Labor organizers with the American Federation of Labor made strong gains among workers, especially the most skilled and best paid. At the same time, a new generation of "muckraking" journalists raised public awareness about the scope of corporate crimes. Mass circulation magazines like *Collier's* and *McClure's*—designed to cater to the middle class—filled their pages with eye-opening exposés about the Robber Barons' lawless behavior. Investigations by reporters such as Ida Tarbell and Lincoln Steffens revealed how men like Standard Oil's John D. Rockefeller and the banking mogul J.P. Morgan were using their immense power to corrupt government officials and break laws. A typical muckraking article from 1905 assailed the "secret, underhand" dealings and "piggish" greed of the "oil-barons, beef monopolists, the steel-trust millionaires, the sugar magnates, the banana kings, and their like."[49]

During the Progressive Era, concerns about the concentration of wealth and power became commonplace. Revulsion against big business gripped workers, farmers, and small businessmen alike. A growing number of people were starting to heed the Populists' warning that the power of giant corporations posed a danger to democracy.

The most popular target of anti-corporate sentiment was the trusts, the sprawling business monopolies of the era. In the wake of the depression sparked by a financial crisis in 1893, the U.S. economy underwent a wave of corporate mergers. Between 1897 and 1904, 4,227 companies were consolidated into 257 giant trusts. By 1904, a few hundred trusts controlled 40 percent of U.S. manufacturing and had a capitalization of $7 billion, seven times the size of the national debt.[50] Monopolies were growing larger and taking greater control of key industries. Standard Oil controlled 70 percent of the world's kerosene market. International Harvester sold 85 percent of all U.S. farm equipment, while U.S. Sugar held 98 percent of the country's sugar market. By 1900 the banker J.P. Morgan controlled half the nation's rail track.[51] A popular novel summed up the common view of the trusts; it was called *The*

Octopus.

The men behind the trusts thought that business consolidation was in the best interests of the economy and the country. J.P. Morgan's belief was that "combination," as he called it, was better than competition. Competition led to instability, he said, while combination created stability. Keeping control of the economy in a few select hands—Morgan sat on the boards of 48 companies, Rockefeller served on 37 boards— was supposed to create a firm and reliable business environment that would be beneficial to the public.

The public, however, didn't see the situation so rosily. Discontent continued to seethe. In 1904 there were some 4,000 strikes, four times as many as in a typical year of the previous decade.[52] The membership of the AFL leapt from 440,000 to 2 million between 1897 and 1903 as its leader, Samuel Gompers, called for "smashing the trusts."[53]

More radical groups, in particular the Socialist Party led by Eugene Debs, also saw an increase in public support. The Socialist newspaper, *Appeal to Reason*, had a half million subscribers and probably twice as many readers. Activists such as Mary Harris "Mother" Jones traveled the country giving speeches, organizing strikes and demonstrations, and condemning "the Wall Street gang of commercial pirates."[54]

Even a wealthy conservative such as Theodore Roosevelt was compelled to bash the trusts and take steps to curb business abuses. In an era when, as *The New York Times* put it, the public was full of "vindictive savagery toward corporations," attacking big business was expedient.[55]

Roosevelt was only a half-hearted Progressive, but he understood that the country wanted the government to do something about the power of the trusts. Antitrust mail was pouring into the White House and reams of antitrust bills were pending in Congress. Elected as Vice President, Roosevelt entered the White House after an anarchist assassinated President McKinley in Buffalo in 1901. The killing, combined with the growing strength of radical groups, convinced Roosevelt that the country was on the verge of a revolution.

Although Roosevelt was a reluctant reformer, he genuinely felt that only by putting some limits on business could capitalism be saved from itself. "Corporate cunning has developed faster than the laws of nation and state," Roosevelt told a reporter during his first term. "Sooner or later, unless there is a readjustment, there will come a riotous, wicked, murderous day of atonement."[56]

Like all popular presidents, Roosevelt was adept at telling people what they wanted to hear, and during the Progressive Era what people wanted to hear was an assault on the power of the trusts. Roosevelt told an audience in New England:

The great corporations which we have grown to speak of rather loosely as trusts are the creatures of State, and the State not only has the right to control them, but it is duty bound to control them. . . . The immediate necessity in dealing with the trusts is to place them under the real, not the nominal, control of some sovereign to which . . . the trusts shall owe allegiance. . . . In my opinion, this sovereign must be the National Government.[57]

Roosevelt's record as President shows that he was more rhetoric than resolve. In private he expressed ambivalence about the strength of giant corporations. But because he was spurred on by genuine Progressives at the grassroots and in Congress, Roosevelt was forced to support a corporate reform agenda. During his tenure Congress established the U.S. Department of Commerce and Labor, which included a Bureau of Corporations to investigate business abuses. Railroad regulation, which formerly had been ineffective, was strengthened in 1906 with the Hepburn Act. That same year the Pure Food and Drug Act was passed after the publication of muckraker Upton Sinclair's, *The Jungle,* raised worries about false advertising and consumer safety. The country's second largest trust, the Northern Securities Railroad Company, was broken up during this time because, as the Supreme Court affirmed, the mere power of the corporation—regardless of any ill-intent—harmed the public interest. Roosevelt was dubbed the "trustbuster."*

The Progressive wave reached its crest in 1912 and 1913. During the presidential election of 1912, candidates describing themselves as Progressives—Woodrow Wilson, a Democrat, and Roosevelt, now with the Progressive Party—took a combined 68 percent of the vote. Socialist Eugene Debs garnered 6 percent of the vote on a rising tide of class resentment due to the fact that real wages for workers had been falling for nearly 20 years even as the income of the wealthiest 1 percent of the population doubled.[58] Wilson won the race.

In some ways Wilson was more conservative than Roosevelt, but he too felt the pressing popular desire to rein in the corporations. During the first year of his term the Sixteenth and Seventeenth Amendments to the Constitution became law, respectively authorizing the creation of a federal income tax and requiring the direct election of Senators, reforms first suggested more than 20 years earlier by the Populists. Wilson oversaw the passage of the Clayton Antitrust Act, the creation of the Federal

---

* In fact, Roosevelt's successor, the more conservative William Taft, initiated more antitrust suits. And it was during the Taft administration that the most hated trust, Standard Oil, was broken into 34 separate companies.

Reserve to regulate the banking system, and the establishment of the Federal Trade Commission to control the growth of monopolies.

During the Progressive Era the attitude of government leaders toward the union movement also began to improve. Roosevelt took the unprecedented step of personally mediating a strike between coal miners and the mine owners. In 1917 Wilson became the first president to address the annual convention of the AFL. To be sure, much government hostility toward the unions remained; the courts continued to file hundreds of injunctions a year against striking workers. Still, the attention from Roosevelt and Wilson gave the anti-corporate forces of the labor movement an official recognition they had never enjoyed.

The Progressive Era reforms made a real difference in the lives of ordinary Americans. Yet the Progressive program was a far cry from the Populist platform, which had sought to resurrect the belief that corporations existed only with the consent of the people. The Populists thought the corporation should be subject to the direct control of the people, and so they demanded the nationalization of the largest industries. In contrast, as author Charles Derber explains:

> The Progressives accepted not only the Gilded Age view that corporations should be private, but also the notion that regulation's purpose was both to protect the public *and* to maximize a company's efficiency and profitability.[59]

Theodore Roosevelt conceded as much when he said: "I believe in corporations. They are indispensable instruments of our modern civilization; but I believe that they should be so supervised and so regulated that they shall act for the interests of the community as a whole."[60]

The Progressives did, however, accomplish much by challenging the dominant *laissez-faire* ideology. "I owe the public nothing," J.P. Morgan had said. The Progressives made clear that such a notion was unacceptable. By asserting that government could be a tool for promoting social welfare, the Progressives had struck a major blow against the *laissez-faire* mindset.

At the start of U.S. involvement in World War I—generally considered the end of the Progressive Era—giant corporations were still effectively running the country, exercising great authority over the public while keeping their operations privately controlled. But the Progressives had made important advances in corporate accountability. The principle had been re-established, however tentatively, that government—that is, the people, what Roosevelt called "you and me"—had a right to regulate the operations of business.

PROSPERITY BUILT ON SAND

In the years following the Progressive Era anti-corporate fervor waned, and concerns about the power of corporations dropped from the forefront of political debate. During the "Roaring Twenties" people were excited about radio, not radicalism.

The ebb in anti-corporate activism was due partly to a crackdown on dissent. In the wake of the Bolshevik revolution in Russia, "red scares" swept the United States. Many socialists and anarchists were deported, robbing the anti-corporate forces of their most dedicated activists. Even the mainstream AFL suffered a decline in strength as its membership dropped by one and one-half million workers during the decade.[61]

The erosion of union membership reflected the disposition of a country that was not in the mood for protest. All one had to do was open a magazine full of advertisements to see that corporations were supplying a material cornucopia. By 1920, for the first time in the country's history, a majority of Americans lived in cities. And for many of the new urban dwellers, city living—with its telephones and radios, movies and indoor plumbing—was a kind of real-life science fiction, a world wholly apart from what their parents had known. Corporations had made the wonders of the machine age possible.

Business had become less hated largely because the businessmen of America had become smarter. Corporate leaders realized that in the long run co-opting their opponents could be more effective than trying to conquer them. At the same time, Corporate America began to embrace advertising and public relations as tools for shaping popular opinion and deflecting antipathy. During the 1920s the corporations learned to master the fine art of seduction.

Auto manufacturer Henry Ford was among those business leaders who understood that finesse was preferable to fighting. By 1920, auto manufacturing accounted for ten percent of the national income and was starting to supplant railroads as the engine of the nation's economy. In 1925 autos were the country's third largest industry, employing hundreds of thousands of workers. Any potential worker discontent, Ford believed, could be effectively blunted if the executives made it seem that the company was on the side of the employees. Ford helped pioneer the 20th century version of "welfare capitalism" or "corporate paternalism," as some called it. Ford's motor company—along with corporations such as National Cash Register, Proctor & Gamble, and US Steel—built recreational facilities for employees, offered profit-sharing and life insurance plans, and even gave workers stock bonuses. Arguing that workers should be able to buy what they built, Ford paid his employees $5 a day, about twice the prevailing wage, and instituted a five-day work week. With good wages and a car in the garage, there was little for workers to rebel over.

If workers did have complaints, they could take their grievances to the "company union." Recognizing the appeal of unionism but fearful of facing a genuinely empowered workforce, many corporations set up company unions to head off the efforts of labor organizers. While appearing to be genuine unions, the company unions were in fact tightly held by management's hands. Corporate executives had no intention of giving workers any real say in the management of the corporation.

While corporate leaders sought to distract potential discontent within their enterprises, they also cultivated support outside the factory walls. The 1920s saw the rise of the public relations industry and the maturing of the fledgling advertising business. Mass production, after all, demanded mass consumption. As advertising grew more adept at spurring sales, it also became a sophisticated tool for molding public opinion. A few public relations pioneers saw that corporations could use ads, not just for selling a certain product, but for selling the corporation itself.

AT&T was one of the first companies to employ advertising as a political tool. The company used its ads to attack regulatory policies: "the less working conditions are made inflexible by legislative proscription, the better," one ad declared. Ads were used to depict a company dedicated to helping ordinary people: "In the Public Service," an AT&T ad headline proclaimed above a picture of a telephone connecting a family's home to the White House. The phone company promoted the notion that growing stock ownership had created a kind of democratic capitalism. "Bell System is a democracy in business," an ad said, "owned by the people it serves."[62]

By the end of the 1920s, the U.S. economy had racked up three decades of nearly steady growth. Much of the country was infused with an air of confidence. Opinion polls ranked Henry Ford just behind Jesus and Napoleon in the public's estimation of history's greatest men.

Yet the prosperity was built on sand. The apparent affluence of the cities stood in contrast to the poverty of the countryside, where years of falling crop prices after World War I led to a flood of farm foreclosures. Even within the better-off cities, millions of people lived in squalid ghettos. Seventy-one percent of families earned less than $2,500 a year, putting them below the poverty line. During the 1920s unemployment never fell below ten percent. Even those with good-paying jobs feared becoming destitute. Social researchers of the time found millions of families existing in a "world in which neither present nor future appears to hold . . . much prospect." Most of the technological gadgets of the age—the phones and the cars—had been bought on credit. As for the much-ballyhooed growth of stock ownership, only two-and-a-half percent of the population owned any shares.[63]

The economy was a house of cards. The structure collapsed, of course, in the spectacular financial crash of the Great Depression. And with that collapse the brief complacency about the role of business in society came to an end. The Great Depression inflamed public suspicion of big business, reigniting anti-corporate sentiment. The renewal of anti-corporate politics would usher in a profound alteration in the balance of power between corporations and society.

FROM CAPTAINS OF INDUSTRY
TO CORPORALS OF DISASTER

The Great Depression was a body blow to the economy. First, the stock market crash of October 1929 evaporated the champagne optimism of the country's upper classes as stocks lost three-fourths of their value in just three weeks. Then, in 1930, a banking crisis spread the panic to the country at large. Six hundred banks closed in November and December alone, more than in the entire previous year. Bankruptcies skyrocketed. In 1930 some 26,000 companies went out of business, sending the country's Gross National Product plummeting by 12 percent.

The country's manufacturing sector—which had been cutting production as early as 1928 due to an oversupply in inventories—screeched to a halt. Millions of people lost their jobs as production slowed. General Motors alone cut 100,000 positions, 40 percent of its workforce. General Electric laid off half its workforce while Ford cut two-thirds of all positions. Many who were lucky enough to keep their jobs were reduced to working part time and for lower wages. US Steel reduced wages by 10 percent, and soon the rest of the major industrial employers followed suit. By early 1932, 20 percent of workers—13 million people—were out of a job. In the major cities, soup kitchens were set up to feed the unemployed masses. In New York City, some 20,000 children suffered from malnutrition.[64]

The situation in the American countryside was far worse. Farmers had spent the 1920s struggling to feed their families as crop prices remained low. The onset of the Depression made matters impossible as crop prices plummeted 40 percent. With prices at rock bottom, many farmers didn't even bother to harvest their crops. Fruit fell from the trees and rotted on the ground for lack of buyers. Unable to pay their debts, some 20,000 families were losing their farms every month. The wave of farm foreclosures, in turn, exacerbated the banking crisis: Nearly 2,300 banks closed their doors in 1932. Millions of homeless farmers—some alone, some with their entire families—took to the highways and railroads looking for any kind of work.[65]

The country had become an economic wasteland. The estimated one-third of the population—40 million people—who had been severely poor before the Depression were now absolutely destitute. The working class was losing what little it had gained in the last generation. The Depression's impact laid bare the fact that the country's prosperity had been very narrow. As historian David Kennedy explains: "The Depression was not just a passing crisis but an episode that revealed deeply rooted structural inequalities in American society." The Depression uncovered "the human wreckage of a century of pell-mell, buccaneering, no-holds-barred, free-market . . . capitalism."[66]

Beset by misery, citizens began looking for explanations for the crisis. For many, Corporate America was an obvious villain. The corporations that had seemed like an engine of prosperity now looked more like a powder keg of catastrophe. A reformer captured the mood when he thundered at a group of corporate executives, "You may have been Captains of Industry once, but you are Corporals of Disaster now."[67]

The Depression resurrected many of the questions and demands of earlier anti-corporate movements. If *laissez-faire* principles really worked so well, many asked, then why did the economy crash? If calamities like the Depression were the result of corporations being given free rein, why give it to them? For millions of people, it was obvious that the system was out of control. The corporations seemed to be operating under imperatives with no connection to the lives of ordinary people. Families were going hungry even as crops were left to rot because harvesting the food and shipping it to the cities was not profitable.

The common opinion that the corporations were out of control and that the lack of control had sparked the Depression was eloquently expressed in John Steinbeck's bestselling novel *The Grapes of Wrath*:

> The bank is something else than men. It happens that every man in a bank hates what the bank does, and yet the bank does it. The bank is something more than men, I tell you. It's the monster. Men made it, but they can't control it.[68]

That monster had ruined the country, and yet, to the painful frustration of millions, the government seemed to be doing nothing to bring the crisis to a close. Republican President Herbert Hoover refused to offer federal aid to those out of work. Treasury Secretary Andrew Mellon said that the Depression represented the economy's natural way of purging itself. Hoover believed that the unemployed deserved assistance, but he didn't think the federal government should be providing that assistance. Hoover's tin ear was his political undoing. The vast majority of people wanted action: government initiatives to help the indigent and government programs to overhaul the economy. Appealing to those desires, Democrat Franklin Delano Roosevelt swept into the White House in 1932.

THE PRESIDENT WANTS YOU TO JOIN THE UNION

Every crisis presents an opportunity for reform. Crises create openings through which—if people are bold enough and creative enough—great changes can occur. The Depression, as terrible as it was, offered just such an opportunity. The economy's collapse ignited in people a desire for change. The prevailing wisdom held that the Depression was caused by greedy corporations that—desperate to keep profits climbing—had overproduced, creating a glut of goods that brought the market down on itself. Roosevelt and the reformers who surrounded him felt the desire for change, and they promised the American people a "New Deal."

The people who filled Roosevelt's administration came from the progressive tradition. They feared the power of "big business fascists" who wanted to "enslave America," as a member of Roosevelt's cabinet put it. Like the Progressives before them, the New Dealers didn't challenge the legitimacy of corporations; rather, they sought to use the power of the state to check corporate behavior and stabilize the economy. Where the corporation's *laissez-faire* ideas had delivered anarchy, the New Deal would provide dependability. The New Dealers viewed the upheaval of the Depression as a chance to put in place many of the proposed reforms of the Progressive Era that had never been accomplished. "This is our hour," one of FDR's advisors told his staff halfway through Roosevelt's first term. "We've got to get everything we want—a works program, social security, wages and hours, everything—now or never."[69]

During Roosevelt's first year, a slew of government policies were enacted. Federal work programs employed millions of people building roads, parks, and nature trails. An unemployment relief service was established. Roosevelt signed the Glass-Steagall Act, which increased federal supervision over Wall Street and prohibited banks, brokerage firms, and insurance companies from owning each other. The National Industrial Recovery Act set up a federal minimum wage and maximum hour guidelines, while also guaranteeing workers the right to organize unions. The government's reach into the management of business was lengthened through the National Recovery Administration,* which gave the federal government the power to direct production and prices in key

---

* The NRA was ruled unconstitutional by the Supreme Court in 1935.

industries. The federal government ventured into direct participation in the economy via the Tennessee Valley Authority, a public corporation charged with building dams and creating an electricity grid in the South.

Despite the whirlwind of changes in government policies, the Depression showed no signs of ending. The number of unemployed workers had dipped slightly, but millions of people remained without work and mired in poverty. At the end of 1933, the country's economy was half the size it had been four years earlier.

As the Depression continued to fester, discontent deepened, turned angrier and more heated. Radicalism was on the rise everywhere. In the Plains states, farmers demanded an end to farm foreclosures and attacked "the money-lords of Wall Street." In California, a dock workers' strike in San Francisco led to a general strike that shut down the city. Upton Sinclair, the socialist muckraker, ran for governor of the Golden State as a Democrat on a platform calling for confiscating idle factories and farms and turning them over to worker co-ops. In the South, Louisiana Senator Huey Long launched the Share Our Wealth Society, promised to "make every man a king," and accused Roosevelt of being in bed with "the money power." And across the country, some 30 million people set aside time every week to listen to Father Charles Coughlin, "the Radio Priest," who from his studios outside Detroit hurled rhetorical attacks against "the enemy of financial slavery" and "the ancient heresy of the concentration of wealth in the hands of a few." [70]

Roosevelt and those around him realized that the pace of reform needed to quicken. "If something is not done and starvation is going to continue," a labor leader warned the Senate, "the doors of revolt in this country are going to be thrown open."[71]

During his first inauguration, Roosevelt promised to throw the "money changers" from the temple of democracy. Yet FDR had no intention of dismantling capitalism or bringing corporations under direct public control. He wanted to preserve the system, protect it from its own excesses. To do that, Roosevelt needed to respond to the clamor for change.

New laws were passed to help the poor and regulate business. The Emergency Relief Act dramatically expanded government work programs. New taxes were levied on corporate earnings and intercorporate dividends, a clear attack on holding companies. The largest utility companies were broken up. Congress passed the Wagner Act,* which set up

---

* Though a boon to white male workers, the Wagner Act did little for women and blacks. The legislation exempted agricultural workers and domestics: two sectors staffed largely by African-Americans and women. The Wagner Act's racism was characteristic of New Deal programs. To enlist the support of southern Democrats, the White House often agreed not to give blacks the same protections offered to whites.

the National Labor Relations Board to oversee industrial disputes and protect workers' rights. In the most far-reaching reform, the Social Security Act of 1935 established a system to provide unemployment insurance to workers, old age pensions to the elderly, and aid to dependent children. The New Dealers understood that to ensure social stability, they needed to give people some measure of social security.

At the same time, Roosevelt sharpened his rhetorical assaults against corporations and accumulated wealth. To some conservative observers, it seemed FDR was going out of his way to antagonize the wealthy classes. If so, it was because those inside the White House understood that bashing big business—"economic tyranny," as FDR called it—was simply smart politics. Amid the economy's rubble, corporations were a popular punching bag.

During a rousing campaign speech at Madison Square Garden, Roosevelt attacked the "business and financial monopoly, speculation, reckless banking, class antagonism, war profiteering" and "organized money." "I should like to have it said of my first Administration that in it the forces of selfishness and lust of power met their match. I should like to have it said of my second Administration that in it these forces met their master."[72] The crowd went wild.

In many ways, Roosevelt's rhetorical stab at accumulated wealth substituted insult for real injury. His reforms were far from radical, and the White House regularly watered down proposals from the more liberal Congress. Nevertheless, the tone of Roosevelt's rhetoric and the reach of his programs unnerved the country's financial elite. Feeling besieged, the business community lashed out at FDR. He was derided as a "traitor to his class," a communist, a socialist. One corporate executive took to calling the President "Stalin Delano Roosevelt."

Business interests also found cause for dismay in the wave of labor activism sweeping the country. The flip side of popular dislike for big business was an improvement in public opinion toward unionism: If the bosses were the villains, the workers became the natural heroes. Equally important, the government's posture toward labor unions had dramatically shifted. The Norris-La Guardia Act of 1932 limited the ability of the federal courts to issue injunctions against striking workers, robbing corporate executives of one of their most dependable weapons against labor activists. The Wagner Act, passed three years later, set into law the workers' right to organize. FDR was quoted as saying that if he worked in a factory, the first thing he would do would be to join a union. Union activists now had the formal recognition they had always sought.

The labor movement was, along with the rest of the country, becoming more radical. Since its creation during the Gilded Age, the AFL had been a sort of working class country club. The Federation concentrated its efforts on organizing the highest paid workers while neglecting the less skilled workers and blacks. The AFL disdained industrial union-ism—organizing workers by industry—and instead embraced craft unionism in which workers were organized by position. That strategy had long handicapped the Federation's growth and fed resentment within the labor movement.

In 1935, eight unions, frustrated by the AFL's failure to become more active and militant in the midst of the Depression crisis, split off from the Federation and formed the Congress of Industrial Organizations (CIO). CIO activists immediately launched aggressive organizing cam-paigns across the country. CIO head John Lewis traveled the country urging workers to form unions. In speeches Lewis attacked "the money trust," "the robber barons of industry," and the "economic royalists." CIO organizers used patriotic themes. "Fordism is Fascism and Union-ism is Americanism," went one slogan. "The President Wants You to Join the Union," claimed a widespread union recruiting poster.[73]

The CIO's most dramatic victory came in December 1936 when work-ers at the General Motors plant in Flint, Michigan, staged one of the first "sit-down" strikes in an effort to demand recognition from GM. They occupied one of the key buildings at the plant, strangling the factory's production. Workers soon took over other buildings. Police attacked the workers and a judge ordered the strikers to evacuate the plant, but the workers held their places. The governor of Michigan, a pro-labor Democrat, refused to use the National Guard to break the strike; Roosevelt urged GM executives to meet the union's demands. The work-ers' strength, combined with benign neutrality on the part of the gov-ernment, forced management to fold. GM said it would recognize the union, bringing the strike to a close after 44 days.

The auto workers' victory sparked a surge of strikes across the coun-try. More than 400 sit-down strikes took place in 1937 as workers pressed for demands as basic as union recognition and improved working con-ditions. Some business leaders, fearful of the effectiveness of the sit-down strike, decided to meet union demands without a struggle. In March 1937, US Steel—one of the most brutal union-busting firms—said it would recognize the steelworkers' union, grant a pay-hike, agree to an eight-hour day and a 40-hour week, and pay workers time-and-a-half for overtime.

The CIO activists weren't trying to overthrow the system, they sim-ply wanted a say in how the corporations they worked for were man-aged. John Lewis called it "industrial democracy." As Lewis explained it, industrial democracy centered on the question "of whether the working population of this country shall have a voice in determining their destiny or whether they shall serve as indentured servants for a financial and economic dictatorship."[74] Industrial democracy held that corporations had to be accountable to the people. It was a philosophy that resonated with most Americans. During the 1930s, organized labor grew rapidly as eight million people joined unions. At the start of World War II, one out of four nonagricultural workers was a union member.

By the late 1930s, as military tensions in Europe and Asia were heating up, New Deal reforms were winding down. The New Deal programs had been politically prudent and, for the most part, piecemeal. Yet taken together they had within just a few years transformed the nation, especially when it came to relations between corporations and the rest of society. One of the New Deal's greatest accomplishments came in giving teeth to the Progressive Era principle that corporations should be accountable to the public.

For the first time in the country's history, corporate executives now had to contend with a genuinely powerful labor movement that had the ability to shut down industry. Three generations of labor activists had struggled for their rights to freedom of association and the ability to form unions. As soon as workers secured that right, and the government agreed to be a neutral arbiter, the potential of organized labor was able to manifest itself. US Steel conceded to steelworker demands, not because it feared the political power of the government, but because it feared the economic power of the unions.[75]

The growth of the federal government via the New Deal added another counterbalance to corporate power. Before the Depression, the federal government had been an anemic creature. At the beginning of the economy's collapse President Hoover said the government could not do much because it was too small. FDR overcame objections such as Hoover's by expanding the size of government. Roosevelt and his New Dealers legitimized government as an agent of social change. With the establishment of the Social Security Administration, the federal government for the first time became a real presence in people's lives. It was a presence most people appreciated.

The growth of the federal bureaucracy also made the government a significant presence in the operations of business. Wage and hour regulations, new taxes on corporate earnings, and the establishment of labor dispute panels inserted the government directly into the inner workings of the corporation. With the creation of the Securities and Exchange Commission, government regulators insinuated themselves into the very heart of corporate capitalism, Wall Street. The government now had the ability to exert significant influence over the behavior of big business.

By the start of World War II, the notion that corporations worked best when regulated least was buried. Inordinate corporate power now faced strong adversaries. The growth of the federal government and the new force of organized labor meant that corporations were no longer unquestionably the most powerful force in the country.

FROM COMPLACENCY TO CONSUMER ALERTS

In 1952 the influential political economist John Kenneth Galbraith published the book, *American Capitalism* in which he examined the relationship between the 20th century corporation and the rest of society. Galbraith took it as a given that corporations wielded enormous clout: "The American is controlled, livelihood and soul, by the large corporation," he wrote. The most effective antidote to such power, Galbraith believed, existed in the combination of union muscle, government regulation, consumer vigilance, and genuine competition in the marketplace. Together, these forces formed what Galbraith called "countervailing power." Such a countervailing power was the best way to check the influence and authority of the giant corporations.[76]

Establishing this kind of countervailing power marked one of the central accomplishments of the New Deal. The government's new regulatory authority and the unshackling of organized labor meant that corporations now had to contend with truly powerful rivals. The New Deal did not extinguish corporate power but it did set up institutions to counterbalance corporate power.

After World War II, the American economy was highly concentrated, an essentially oligopolistic system centered on a handful of industrial giants. For New Deal liberals this was of no real concern so long as the system guaranteed stability and security rather than the economic anarchy that characterized the Depression. Oligopolies were acceptable since they would keep the system sound. There was little to fear from giant corporations if countervailing power kept them in their place.

As the Cold War riled international relations, within the U.S. relations among business, labor, and government became more cordial as corporations came to accept government regulations and union contracts as regular, if unfortunate, costs of doing business. Those costs were easier to swallow because the largest companies faced only a handful of domestic competitors. And for American businesses in the post-war era there was no foreign competition since Europe and Asia were trying to recover from ruin. The chairman of Standard Oil of New Jersey summed up business leaders' outlook when he said in a 1951 speech: "The job of management is to maintain an equitable and working balance among the claims of various directly interested groups . . . stockholders, employees, customers, and the public at large."[77]

The 1950s and 1960s were mostly quiet in terms of anti-corporate activism. Consistently rising incomes tamed dislike of big business: Between 1947 and 1973 workers saw their real wages increase by an average of three percent a year, with the biggest gains going to the poorest one-fifth of families. The reality of countervailing power fostered complacency about corporations. Plus, the red-baiting of McCarthyism chilled social activism. The liberals and radicals who did continue to push for change put much of their energy into struggling for the abolition of the South's Jim Crow system.

As always, however, there were rumblings of dissent about corporate influence. Social critics complained about the era's uniformity. The strict hierarchies of a staid, oligopolistic economy seemed to have bred an equally staid, regimented, and conformist culture. The man in the gray flannel suit—the perfect corporate bureaucrat—was a symbol of the age. A few public figures warned about the consequences of the increasing interconnectedness between business and government. During World War II, the country's corporations had been enlisted in the service of the government to help win the war. Some people were starting to wonder if the government was not now working in the service of the corporations, especially the influential armaments industry. President Dwight Eisenhower, commander of U.S. forces in Europe during World War II, most famously expressed this concern when he cautioned against the unwarranted influence of the "military-industrial complex."

Still others, meanwhile, warned that the institutions of countervailing power weren't as effective at checking corporate authority as some claimed. According to those voices, the corporate establishment remained too powerful, the unions and the government had been co-opted by that power, and big business was still a threat to democracy. This opinion was clearly articulated in the Port Huron Statement of 1962, the founding document of Students for a Democratic Society and a virtual Magna Carta of the so-called New Left.

> It is not possible to believe that true democracy can exist where a minority utterly controls enormous wealth and democracy. . . . We can no longer rely on competition of the many to assure that business enterprise is responsive to social needs. . . . Nor can we trust the corporate bureaucracy to be socially responsible or to develop a 'corporate conscience' that is democratic. . . . We must consider changes in the rules of society by challenging the unchallenged politics of American corporations.[78]

But the anti-corporate movement budding on college campuses became preoccupied with the Vietnam War. A critique of corporate power colored the edges of anti-war rhetoric, with assaults on the military-industrial complex being common. Yet the peace movement was never primarily an anti-corporate effort.

Not all activists were consumed by opposing the war. A few kept their sites on the behavior of big business. In the rebellious years of the late 1960s and early 1970s, suspicion of the powers-that-be became widespread, almost intuitive. Distrust of the country's institutions fell on government and corporations alike. Amid the rebellious spirit of that turbulent time, a new corporate accountability energy arose.

Two popular books sparked fresh challenges to corporate prerogatives. In his book, *Unsafe at Any Speed*, Ralph Nader, a young Harvard-trained attorney, showed how General Motors was disregarding safety features that it knew would save lives in auto accidents. Nader's indictment of GM was unforgiving: The company was deliberately endangering consumers in order to make a buck. The shock of that message made Nader a national figure. Biologist Rachel Carson stirred up a similar storm with her book, *Silent Spring*, which revealed how the use of toxic pesticides was destroying the environment.

The books, combined with their authors' courage in the face of harsh industry intimidation, spurred the growth of the consumer rights and environmental movements. A host of public interest organizations were formed: the Environmental Defense Fund, the Consumer Federation of America, Common Cause, the Center for Auto Safety, the Natural Resources Defense Council, and Public Citizen. The nation's largest existing environmental group, the Sierra Club, which had been politically irrelevant for decades, was reinvigorated under the leadership of David Brower. Within a few years, a wide range of citizen action groups had sprung up to serve as watchdogs over corporate behavior.

Together, the nascent consumer and environmental movements deepened the corporate critiques they had inherited from Progressive and New Deal reformers. The new corporate accountability activists put fresh attention on how corporations' day-to-day activities impacted the public. Consumer groups showed that corporations regularly cut corners, neglected available best-practices, and resisted socially beneficial innovations in order to keep costs low. Environmentalists exposed the way in which companies routinely dumped their toxic wastes into the water and the air to save disposal charges. A flood of media exposés and carefully documented reports revealed a corporate system whose profits depended on shifting the costs of negative externalities—economist language for costly consequences—onto the public. Corporations' profitability, the activists explained, rested on socializing costs and privatizing profits. The solution, the new generation of crusaders felt, was to ensure that the public, via the government, could hold corporations accountable for their actions.

In response to citizen pressure, Congress in the late 1960s and early 1970s passed a slew of reform measures. The Environmental Protection Agency (EPA) was created to clean up polluted environments and regulate corporations' disposal of toxins. The Occupational Safety and Health Administration (OSHA) was set up to monitor on-the-job injuries and workplace hazards, while the Equal Opportunity Employment Commission was established to prevent racial or gender discrimination in the office and the factory. The Consumer Product Safety Commission and the National Highway Transportation Safety Administration were created to minimize consumer abuses. In the wake of the Watergate scandal, new restrictions were placed on donations to politicians to limit the political influence of corporations and wealthy individuals.

Yet new regulations and government agencies did not get to the heart of the question, posed by Ralph Nader in a 1967 speech, about whether corporations' "concentration of economic and political power . . . transcends the tolerance of a democratic society."[79] Nevertheless the spread of so-called "process regulations"—government rules over the way products were made—marked a significant advance in holding corporations accountable. Government's reach into the day-to-day operations of business had been dramatically lengthened.

By the mid-1970s, corporations were subject to the strictest public oversight they had endured since the Jacksonian period more than 140 years earlier. A new generation of reformers had proved that, despite all its power, big business could still be made to bend to the public will.

GREED IS GOOD?

Even as consumer and environmental activists were achieving real gains in the early 1970s, a big business backlash was brewing. Conservative thinkers were preparing an assault on the principle that corporations owed obligations to society at large. That intellectual attack on corporate accountability ideals would eventually influence decision-makers at the highest levels of government. Many of the New Deal and Naderite accomplishments would be rolled back, or placed under almost constant siege. Since 1980 the United States has experienced a kind of corporate counter-reformation that has dramatically increased the power of big business and again raised the specter of corporate rule.

The corporate counter-reformation began—not in executive boardrooms—but in the halls of academia. Economists at the University of

Chicago, led by the influential Milton Friedman, started arguing against the notion of corporate responsibility. "What does it mean to say that the corporate executive has a 'social responsibility' in his capacity as businessman?" Friedman wrote in 1970. "Insofar as [the executive's] actions in accord with his 'social responsibility' reduce returns to his stockholders, he is spending their money. . . . [People] can do good— but only at their expense." For Friedman, there was no such thing as *res publica*—a public interest apart from individual self-interest. A corporation's sole responsibility lay in increasing its profits and its share price. Greed was a public virtue, and big business worked best when it was freed from any notions of accountability to the general public.[80]

Critics derided Friedman's ideas as "free-market fundamentalism" or "corporate libertarianism." But among pro-business conservatives, the theories of the so-called Chicago School quickly became influential. Regardless of whether one disdained or celebrated Friedman's ideas, it was clear that *laissez-faire* ideology was staging a comeback.

The ideas of the Chicago School were catapulted from theory into practice with the election of Ronald Reagan in 1980. During the two Reagan administrations, and later under President George H.W. Bush, conservatives scaled back government efforts to check corporate behavior. For Reaganite conservatives, government was society's worst enemy, a threat to true liberty. In many ways, conservative criticisms of the federal government echoed liberal critiques of big business: big government was too powerful, inefficient, and unresponsive to the needs of ordinary people. Following these beliefs, pro-business conservatives set about—in a piecemeal and covert fashion that often escaped the public's notice—to dismantle government oversight of corporations.

The Reaganites' most obvious move on behalf of Corporate America came via deregulation. Some steps toward deregulation had started under the Democratic administration of President Jimmy Carter, who initiated deregulation of the airline industry. But once Reagan was in office the drive toward deregulation of the economy accelerated greatly. The savings and loan industry was deregulated, as were other key sectors of banking and finance. Reagan signed an Executive Order requiring all government agencies to undertake impact studies weighing the costs to business of any proposed regulations.

The Reagan White House appointed pro-business individuals to key posts at regulatory agencies. While the regulatory system was kept in place, enforcement of public interest laws became virtually meaningless. The director of the EPA, for example, conceded that he didn't even believe in environmental regulations for business. Critics complained that a revolving door system existed at many government agencies in which the people who were supposed to be overseeing business behavior were often former executives themselves. The government's ability to act as a check on corporate power had been gutted.

Meanwhile, the Reagan administration also targeted the labor movement. For several decades the country's trade unions had been suffering a decline in membership from their 1950s peak, when about one out of three workers belonged to a union. The drop-off in members was due to an exodus of manufacturing companies overseas and also to labor's own complacency and failure to organize new workers. During the Reagan years, organized labor's fortunes dropped further as the government became openly hostile to trade unions.

In 1981, Reagan sent a shot across labor's bow when he fired thousands of striking air traffic controllers: government workers who were, in part, protesting the deregulation of the airline industry. Reagan's breaking of the air traffic controllers' strike sent a clear message to the nation that the White House was no friend of labor. Reagan then appointed business sympathizers to important positions on the National Labor Relations Board (NLRB) and within the Department of Labor. Officials at the NLRB threw roadblocks in the way of union organizing drives and hamstrung strike attempts. Union membership spiraled downward.

With government oversight of big business largely neutered and the strength of organized labor on the decline, the two central pillars of countervailing power were coming undone. Corporations stepped into the breach. The largest companies slashed millions of jobs. Some of the layoffs were a genuine response to new global competition as U.S. companies moved production abroad. But many firings were opportunistic, with corporations taking advantage of weakened unions.

The country's financial elite also became more aggressive. Banking houses and investment funds started putting pressure on firms they felt were not doing enough to boost profits. So-called corporate raiders staged hostile takeovers of companies whose directors they thought were not acting as ruthlessly as they could to cut costs and jobs. Milton Friedman's belief that corporate executives' only responsibility was to increase stock value was becoming the conventional wisdom in business board rooms. The prevailing mindset of the corporate establishment was captured by Gordon Gecko, the only half-fictional protagonist of Oliver Stone's movie *Wall Street*, who proclaimed with utter sincerity: "Greed is good."

Yet even as companies cut their workforces, they were growing larger. The 1980s witnessed a "merger mania" as companies swallowed other companies. A third of companies listed on the Fortune 500 in 1980 had lost their independence by 1990.[81] This frenzy of amalgamation was spurred by companies' desire to succeed in the new global economy.

The end of the Cold War had ushered in, with lightening speed, an era of economic globalization. Globalization, while posing a challenge to corporate managers, also offered corporations vast opportunities to increase their profits. The erosion of countervailing power had increased corporate power relative to government and labor. Economic globalization was now expanding corporate power in absolute terms.

Increases in the scale and scope of economies always lead to corresponding growth in corporate power. The railroad transformed the United States from a collection of regional economies to a truly national economy, and that transformation expanded the size of the railroad corporations. Likewise, the creation of new communication and transportation technologies and the lowering of international economic barriers with the end of the Cold War integrated the world's national economies into a global economy. And this global economy, encouraged by corporations themselves, is now expanding the power of the corporation. Many corporations have become transnational enterprises, with their operations and influence spreading across the planet.

Just as the railroads once dwarfed state governments, so do corporations today eclipse many national governments. Of the world's 100 largest economies, 50 are transnational corporations, not nation-states.[82] The combined sales of the world's ten largest companies is as large as the aggregate GDP of the world's 100 smallest countries. General Motors' sales revenues are equal to the combined GDP of nine African and Asian countries wherein lives 10 percent of the world's population.[83] The sheer size and global reach of transnational corporations gives them awesome power. Just as U.S. corporations once played states against each other in a bid to reduce charter requirements, so too can transnational corporations today play entire nations against each other as companies demand looser environmental and labor regulations. Even a relatively affluent country such as Ireland must be careful to curry corporate favor; one-half of that country's jobs and two-thirds of its total economic output are dependent on foreign firms.[84] Entire countries find themselves at the mercy of the new global financial markets. And those markets are often horribly capricious, as the Mexican economic crisis of 1995 and the East Asian financial crisis of 1997-98 demonstrated. In those episodes, the sudden departure of foreign investors led to massive recessions that threw tens of millions of people into poverty.

During the 1990s, as the pace of economic globalization sped up, the wave of U.S. corporate mergers accelerated. The merger mania of the 1990s made that of the 1980s look tame by comparison as corporations became larger and more powerful. The U.S. banking industry underwent an intense concentration as Chase Manhattan and Chemical Bank merged, NationsBank bought out Bank of America, and Citicorp merged with the insurance firm Traveler's Group. The information and entertainment industry experienced similar concentration. Disney took over the ABC television network. TimeWarner took over Turner Broadcasting, only to be bought out by America Online. Phone companies merged with such speed that it was difficult to keep track of who owned whom. Each year between 1994 and 1999 broke the preceding merger record.

At the same time, the growth of the Internet and related services sent stock market prices skyrocketing. A kind of financial euphoria seized many people as business prognosticators offered a vision of a "new economy" in which the business cycle of boom and bust would be transcended. In this atmosphere of glib wealth, some commentators couldn't help but notice the similarities with the Gilded Age of a century earlier.

The comparison seemed apt. The excitement of the railroad had become the promise of the Internet. The frontier was now cyberspace, with Bill Gates playing the part of John D. Rockefeller and Microsoft acting as Standard Oil. Social Darwinism was a bit old-fashioned, but free-market fundamentalism was as hip as could be. Even the political atmosphere was similar. Corporations again seemed to be running the government, and campaign finance scandals were once more in the headlines. Bill Clinton seemed like a 20th century version of Democrat Grover Cleveland, the strike breaker and friend of big business. Clinton oversaw the deregulation of the telecommunications industry and the repeal of New Deal laws that prohibited banks and insurance companies from owning each other. As if carrying a torch for Corporate America, Clinton proclaimed that "the Era of Big Government is over."

But the Gilded Age, remember, was as much a time of popular insurrection as it was corporate ascendancy. Concentration of power rarely comes without conflict, and the 1990s was no exception. Even in the midst of the boom, a citizen backlash was forming. The 1990s saw the rise of a vibrant, diverse, and energetic movement dedicated to challenging business as usual. People around the country organized grassroots campaigns to tackle company abuses and demand that corporations be held accountable. In the process, activists laid the foundation of a social movement with the potential to be even more influential than any of the earlier American anti-corporate movements.

The rest of this book presents some of their stories.

2

"WOULD YOU WANT *YOUR* SISTER TO WORK THERE?"
The Conflict Over Sweatshops

WHEN CHARLES KERNAGHAN PREPARED to appear before a congressional committee in the spring of 1996 to testify on abuses in overseas factories making clothes for U.S. retailers, he didn't expect much publicity. Kernaghan, a longtime labor rights activist and director of the New York City-based National Labor Committee (NLC), had done exposés on factory abuses before, and most of them had failed to gain widespread attention. In recent months the issue of sweatshops had begun to receive more notice, as proven by Kernaghan's just-completed campaign to force the Gap to accept independent monitoring of a factory in El Salvador. But aside from some garment industry trade unionists and a scattering of veteran social justice activists, most people in the United States didn't even know sweatshops existed.

Only one reporter, from the *Los Angeles Times*, listened as Kernaghan told members of Congress how workers in Honduras, some as young as 13 years old, had been forced to work 12-hour shifts, up to 75 hours a week, earning only 31 cents an hour making apparel for Wal-Mart's Kathie Lee Gifford clothing line. The next day the article was tucked back in the newspaper's business section.

The story could have ended there, just another bit of information about exploitation in a far-off country. But two days later, on May 1, Gifford went on her popular national television show, *Live with Regis and Kathie Lee*, and emotionally denounced Kernaghan.

"And I truly resent this man impugning my integrity!," Gifford told her national audience, wiping away tears.

> You can say I'm ugly. You can say I'm not talented. But when you say I don't care about children and that I will exploit them for some sort of monetary gain—for once, mister, you better answer your phone because my attorney is calling you today. How dare you![1]

Celebrities are not supposed to cry on national television, and they aren't supposed to threaten to sue people. Gifford's outburst made national news, and so did sweatshops, which for decades had been beyond the American consciousness. Gifford's tears helped spark a new social movement to abolish sweatshop abuses and protect workers' rights.

Today, the campaign to end worker abuses in the United States and abroad is one of the largest, most energetic, and most sophisticated social movements in the country. Unions, religious groups, women's groups, and people of color organizations have all participated in the anti-sweatshop struggle. Labor rights have also grabbed the attention of students, putting anti-sweatshop organizing at the center of the largest surge in campus activism in a generation. In recent years, the intensity of the anti-sweatshop activists has distinguished them as one of the most vigorous strands of the larger anti-corporate globalization movement.

Before the Gifford revelation and other exposés like it, most people only read about sweatshops in history books. Today people read about sweatshops in their daily newspapers. In a few years, anti-sweatshop activists put labor rights on the public agenda, fundamentally changing popular attitudes about how corporations treat their workers. U.S.-based retail corporations once said they held no responsibility for the workers making their clothes if those workers were employed by subcontractors, as most of them are. Corporations such as Nike and Disney said they couldn't be held accountable for what happened to workers in China and Central America. Today, many corporations grudgingly recognize that they have an obligation to the people who make their goods.

By forcing that admission from some of the largest corporations in the United States, the anti-sweatshop movement dramatically altered the debate about the new global economy. Sweatshops became a metaphor of the global economy's lawlessness. Doubts about who benefits from globalization increase with each sweatshop revelation.

The anti-sweatshop movement succeeded in altering the public debate and changing popular attitudes through a combination of old-fashioned strategies and 21st century tactics. Labor rights activists have employed the proven tools of muckraking and exposés to make their issue known. They've built coalitions among different constituencies to push their demands. Student anti-sweatshop groups have updated the sit-ins and building occupations of the 1960s. And more than any other corporate accountability struggle, the activists behind the sweatshop campaigns made attacks on corporations' brand names a centerpiece of their efforts. In targeting the corporations' images, the anti-sweatshop movement showed that branding is a tool that can be used by social activists just as effectively as it is used by the corporations themselves.

Nikki Fortunato Bas, director of the organization, SweatshopWatch, says the anti-sweatshop movement has had a powerful impact on public consciousness.

Everyone can visualize what a sweatshop is—that's a success, that people
are identifying big corporations as responsible for sweatshops is a huge
leap forward. The terms of the debate have changed. People are more
willing to say that those who control the profits should be accountable. .
. . I can't remember a time when so many people were motivated by
issues of economic justice.[2]

Yet despite these achievements, sweatshops persist. The corporations
may have admitted a responsibility to the workers who make their products, but there remains a gap between that rhetorical recognition and
actually taking action to solve the problem. The U.S. retail industry has
changed its tune, but for the most part it hasn't changed its behavior.

"There has been tremendous accomplishment in consciousness raising on the issue of sweatshops since the mid-'90's," says Jeff Ballinger,
a veteran labor rights activist who has documented abuses in Nike subcontractor factories since 1988. "In terms of victories, however, I think
we have come up nearly empty-handed in terms of demonstrable gains
for workers."

The lack of clear-cut victories for workers reveals the immense difficulties of compelling corporations to change their behavior in a
borderless economy. Focusing as it has on the inequities of globalization, the anti-sweatshop campaigns have had to grapple with the complexities of restraining corporations in the environment of the global
economy like few other social movements. The disconnect between corporations' promises and their actual reforms is challenging the movement to rethink its strategy.

As it struggles to define real corporate accountability, the anti-sweatshop movement is learning how to fight corporations in a globalized
economy. The struggle is part of the victory.

DO YOU KNOW WHERE YOUR
UNDERWEAR IS MADE?

Despite great technological advances, no one has yet figured out a way
to replace the sewing machine. The softness of the garments used to
make our clothes, along with the complicated patterns involved, means
that apparel production doesn't easily lend itself to mechanization. For
more than 150 years, the sewing machine has been, and today remains,
the best way to mass produce clothing. In the 21st century we continue
to make clothing much as we did in the 19th century.

This means that clothing manufacturing is necessarily a labor-inten-
sive industry. A worker, usually a woman, sits or stands at a sewing
machine and pieces together portions of cloth.[3] Every blouse, every pair

of jeans, every t-shirt, and every pair of shoes has to be tailored by a person. Everything we wear is made by someone.

Garment manufacturing is also a low-capital enterprise. You don't need much equipment to make a pair of shorts. At its most basic, a garment shop can consist of little more than some pressing machines, and rows and rows of sewing machines. A shoe factory or a state-of-the-art apparel shop may include a bit more machinery, but, in general, setting up a garment shop requires far less capital than building, say, a cola bottling plant or an auto factory.

The low-tech nature of clothing manufacturing makes garment production an attractive enterprise for poor countries looking to industrialize. For a country with few natural resources, but plenty of impoverished people willing to work for almost nothing, a garment industry can seem like a treasure. Those kinds of countries have very little to offer global corporations besides low-wage labor, and so garment factories are what they get.

The key characteristic of the new global economy is the increased mobility and flexibility given to big capital. Corporations now have more freedom than ever to locate in whatever countries offer the lowest wages and the loosest regulations. The intensely competitive retail industry has taken advantage of this new dynamic.

If sweatshops have become a metaphor for globalization's excesses, it is because garment factories are the shock troops of corporate globalization. Visit a country that has recently opened itself up to foreign investment and you will find a host of garment factories, even if there are very few other transnational enterprises present. Cambodia and the Indian Ocean island nation of Mauritius are typical examples: poor countries that have attracted scores of garment manufacturers but little else.

These disparate forces meet in an unfortunate mix. A footloose industry searches the world for the cheapest wages. Governments that are desperate for any kind of investment auction off their workers at shockingly low wages. Government regulators, eager to keep foreign investors happy, look the other way when environmental destruction and human rights abuses occur. It is this combination of profit-seeking and frantic pursuit of foreign investment that creates the race to the bottom underlying the resurgence of sweatshops.

YOU'LL KNOW ONE IF YOU SEE ONE

There are different ways to define a sweatshop. According to the U.S. Department of Labor, a sweatshop is any factory that violates more than one of the country's fundamental labor laws, which include paying a minimum wage and keeping a time card, paying overtime, and paying on time.[4] The Union of Needletrades Industrial and Textile Employees (UNITE), the U.S. garment workers union, says any shop that does not respect workers' right to organize an independent union is a sweatshop. The labor rights and corporate accountability groups that have led the anti-sweatshop campaigns would add to those definitions any factory that does not pay its workers a living wage, that is, a wage that can support the basic needs of a small family.

To keep labor costs low, apparel shop owners usually pay workers a "piece rate." Instead of getting paid by the hour like most workers, piece-rate workers get paid for the number of items they complete in a shift. If workers hope to earn a decent income, they have to work hard and long. Basically, they have to sweat.

Around the world, garment workers spend much more than 40 hours per week at their sewing machines making the clothes and shoes that eventually make their way to retailers' shelves. Verbal, physical, and sexual abuse are common. Workplace injuries occur regularly. The wages are low, usually below poverty levels. And when workers try to organize to defend their interests and assert their dignity, their efforts are repressed. In country after country, the stories are hauntingly the same.

Workers at a plant in El Salvador, for example, say they are frequently required to work mandatory overtime as they sew jerseys for the National Basketball Association. That means they often put in 11-hour shifts, six days a week. If the workers refuse to work overtime, they lose a day's pay.[5] In Indonesia, workers making Nike shoes have told labor rights groups that their biggest complaint is being compelled to work excessive overtime hours. Some weeks workers must put in more than 70 hours. Cambodian workers say they are sometimes forced to work from 6:15 a.m. to 10 p.m., and occasionally are not allowed to take Sundays off.[6] Workers in Mexico making jeans say that sometimes they are forced to work all-night shifts, and are prevented from leaving the factory by armed security guards.

The pace of work in apparel factories depends on the orders coming from the retail companies in the United States, which means that the work schedule, though always demanding, sometimes reaches a fever pitch. In China, workers making shoes call the months of May and June— the period when the shoes must be produced so they will be on U.S. shelves in time for the holidays—the "Black Season." At that time, workers are expected to work 16-hour shifts, seven days a week. Chinese laborers have been known to die after marathon shifts, and have coined a name for such incidents: *guolaosi*, meaning "overwork death."[7]

A Mexican worker, Alvaro Saavedra Anzures, told labor rights investigators:

I spend all day on my feet, working with hot vapor that usually burns my skin, and by the end of the day my arms and shoulders are in pain. We have to meet the quota of 1,000 pieces per day. That translates to more than a piece every minute. The quota is so high that we cannot even go to the bathroom or drink water or anything for the whole day.[8]

In this grueling atmosphere of desperate cost-cutting and arbitrary production quotas, work is accorded little value and workers are afforded little dignity. "They don't respect us as human beings," a Nicaraguan worker told factory monitors.[9]

Verbal abuse is common, and workers regularly report being bullied by shop managers. Those suspected of not working fast enough are usually the target of shouting and yelling by managers. Physical abuse is also not unusual. Workers at a factory in Mexico making collegiate apparel for Reebok and Nike have said managers regularly hit them.[10]

Sexual abuse is endemic. Most garment workers are women, the vast majority of them in their teens or twenties. Factory owners say they mostly hire young women workers because their fingers are more nimble and they work faster. The reality is more complicated. Shop owners look for young women because they are easier to intimidate and less likely to organize unions. It's partly true. Many workers in poor countries are girls who have left their homes for the first time to earn money for their families. Homesickness and isolation are common complaints, and the alienation they feel inhibits them from standing up to abusive managers. It also makes them more vulnerable to sexual harassment.

In the *maquiladoras* along the U.S.-Mexico border, factory managers who want to weed out pregnant workers to avoid paying maternity benefits force women workers to prove they are menstruating, a demeaning procedure that is against Mexican law.[11] Mandatory pregnancy tests are also common in El Salvador, and women who test positive are fired, also in violation of that country's laws.[12] A survey of Nike workers in Indonesia revealed that almost one of every ten workers questioned had received unwanted sexual advances, and several workers had been forced to have sex with managers.[13]

Workplace injuries and exposure to toxic chemicals pose a daily risk to apparel workers. To prevent workers from stealing items they are producing, factories sometimes lock the doors and windows, creating a fire hazard. In many factories, workers are not given masks for their noses and mouths, exposing them to dangerous fumes and tiny cloth fibers that lodge in the lungs.

"The windows were small and there was hardly any ventilation," a

Chinese worker who became paralyzed after prolonged glue exposure told a reporter. "As soon as the machines were on, we had to turn the fans off. It smelled horrible."[14]

In response to negative publicity and demands from labor rights groups, some retailers have begun pressuring their subcontractor factories to address the most egregious health and safety violations. Today, many visitors to garment factories remark on how clean and orderly the shops look. But the bright image of the well-ordered shop floor contrasts sharply with conditions outside the factories. The shantytowns and squalid dormitories of the free trade zones reveal that a sweatshop is defined as much by what surrounds the factory as by the factory itself. The manufacturer may have invested in its factory, but it has not invested in its workers. That disconnect is the core of the sweatshop problem: low wages. Workers' biggest complaint is that, despite working long, hard hours, they do not earn enough to live in dignity.

In their drive to post profits that will please investors on Wall Street, the U.S. retail industry has become ruthlessly competitive. As sales have stagnated and corporations spend ever-increasing amounts on marketing, the companies have tried to cut their costs on the production end.[15] The retailers put pressure on their subcontracting manufacturers to keep prices down, and the manufacturers in turn squeeze the workers, forcing them to work harder for less.

A comparison of workers' wages and retail prices of the products they produce is instructive. A worker in El Salvador earns about 24 cents for each NBA jersey she makes, which then sells for $140 in the United States.[16] Workers in Mexico producing jeans for the Gap earn about 28 cents an hour.[17] In poorer countries, the wages are even lower. In China, for example, some workers making clothing for Disney receive as little as 16 cents per hour.[18]

When presented with these facts, the corporations respond that you simply cannot compare wages in the United States—where the minimum wage is $5.15 an hour—with wages in countries such as China. And, the corporations claim, their manufacturers are already paying the local minimum wage. On the first point, labor rights activists agree: You can't compare U.S. wages with those in other countries. At issue, labor rights activists say, is not whether overseas workers should be paid at U.S. rates, but that they should be paid a living wage in the local context, enough to be able to support a family or save for the future. Minimum wages in most countries are nowhere near what would be considered a living wage. That's because developing countries, in their efforts to attract investment, deliberately keep their wages low. In addition, many companies do not even pay the local minimum wage.

Labor rights groups have calculated that a living wage in China would be about 87 cents an hour, or more than four times what the worker making 16 cents now gets. The 60 cents an hour the Salvadoran NBA seamstresses earn is only about a third of the cost of living, and even the Salvadoran government says that 60 cents per hour leaves a worker in "abject poverty."[19] Likewise, the women making Gap jeans say they would have to earn about three times what they do to support their families.[20] When Nike workers at seven of the company's subcontractor plants in Central and South America were asked about earnings, two-thirds said they didn't make enough to put away savings or support others.[21]

"I spend each penny very carefully," a Chinese worker told labor rights activists. "In fact, I seldom buy meat."[22]

At issue, say workers and their advocates, is not whether the companies set up shop in poorer countries, but *how* they do it. "We're not against foreign investment in Nicaragua," a worker there told rights groups. "But we are against exploitation."[23]

Unfortunately for workers, the current system is a trap. The apparel manufacturers fear that if they raise their workers' wages, and therefore their prices to the U.S. retailers, the retailers will go someplace with even cheaper workers. The threat is real. Because the garment industry is so mobile, and because the purchasing by the retailers is so flexible, any country that raises its wages or enforces its workers' rights runs the risk of pricing itself out of the market. Wages stay low because retail corporations demand the cheapest price possible.

No country illustrates this logic better than the United States. While many people see sweatshops as a problem for poor countries, the United States is suffering a sweatshop epidemic as well.

Every year, U.S. consumers spend more than $180 billion on apparel. In 1980, the United States produced more than two-thirds of its own clothing. But so many retailers have shifted their production overseas that today the United States imports more than two-thirds of its apparel.

The pricing pressure put on the few manufacturers still in the United States is extreme. After all, how can a U.S. worker, even earning only the minimum wage, compete on cost terms with a Chinese worker? That pressure has led garment shops to cut as many corners as they can. Overtime pay, time cards, health benefits, and unionization rights are largely a thing of the past. According to the U.S. Department of Labor, more than 60 percent of all garment factories in Los Angeles, the U.S. city with the largest garment industry, are sweatshops.[24]

If workers in the United States try to fight for better standards, managers threaten to move the factory to another country. That's exactly what happened when the garment workers union UNITE tried to organize Guess? factories in Los Angeles in 1996 and 1997. Within a year Guess? moved 40 percent of its Los Angeles production to Mexico.

Clearly, the race to the bottom is real. Regardless of which country they live in, garment workers endure long hours, hard work in demeaning environments, and low wages.

If the conditions and wages in sweatshops are so terrible, why do workers tolerate it? Often they don't. In countries around the world, garment workers have sought to improve their situation by trying to organize unions. Those efforts, however, are frequently crushed. Union organizers have been beaten, thrown in jail, blacklisted, and even killed. In some countries with thriving apparel industries, such as China and Vietnam, independent unions are outlawed. In others, such as Mexico and Indonesia, the government often cooperates with factory owners as they try to bust organizing drives. In a few countries with strong labor histories, such as Nicaragua and the Philippines, unions are tolerated, but not in the free trade zones where most sweatshops are located.

In suppressing the basic right to freedom of association, factory owners are profiting from repression. Each time a U.S. company with ties to such a factory fails to denounce a union-busting effort, it is complicit in the abuse.

That argument goes to the heart of the anti-sweatshop movement. Labor rights activists have demanded that corporations be held accountable for what happens to the workers who make their goods. In making that demand, the movement has questioned the assumptions behind the global economy: Who is benefiting, and at what costs?

SLAVERY IN AMERICA

For years, sweatshops went unreported. In the atmosphere of the much-heralded information age economy, sweatshops were perceived to be a fixture from an earlier era. That perception changed in 1995 and 1996 as the term sweatshop reemerged because of two startling episodes: the made-for-television Gifford controversy, and the discovery of a brutal sweatshop in Los Angeles.

The latter shock came during the summer of 1995. In August, federal agents raided a home in the Los Angeles suburb of El Monte and discovered dozens of women who were being forced to sew clothes for such big name corporations as Montgomery Ward and Macy's. The women, 72 in all, were immigrants from Thailand who had paid substantial fees to be smuggled into the United States. When they arrived, their passports were confiscated and they were told they would have to work off their debts. It was a system of indentured labor, illegal under

U.S. law.

The smugglers forced the women to sew day and night, sometimes for as long as 84 hours a week, for an average of about $1.60 an hour. Some workers were earning as little as 69 cents an hour. One woman hadn't left the El Monte home for two-and-a-half years.[25] "It's hard to say the word 'slavery' in America," a Department of Labor official commented after the raid. "But the awful thing is . . . this story is not unique."[26]

The El Monte story was front page news, the subject of talk shows and newspaper columns. The brutal conditions in El Monte were a wake-up call. It forced many people to consider, perhaps for the first time, where their clothing came from, who made it, and how. A woman told the *Los Angeles Times* three weeks after the El Monte raid:

> This whole [sweatshop case] has made me stop and think about what I'm buying. I don't normally think about things like that when I shop for clothes. If I knew this skirt was made by people sacrificed like those women, I wouldn't buy it. I'd feel too guilty.[27]

Prior to the El Monte scandal, Secretary of Labor Robert Reich had been trying to engage major U.S. retailers on the issue, calling sweatshops a "national disgrace." But absent any popular concern over working conditions in the garment industry, Reich's efforts had gained little traction. In the wake of the El Monte uproar, Reich called the retail executives to Washington to discuss ways of preventing sweatshop apparel from being sold in American stores.[28]

The large clothing retailers were not ready to cooperate. The brand name corporations didn't see sweatshops as their problem because they weren't making the products they sold. Ending workplace abuses was the responsibility of the manufacturers and the manufacturers' subcontractors. An official from the National Retail Federation, an industry umbrella group, told California lawmakers:

> Retailers are not the problem—unscrupulous garment manufacturers are the problem. Turning retail merchandisers into . . . labor inspectors is neither an appropriate nor an effective solution to this problem.[29]

That notion of unaccountability was set to evaporate in the bright glare of controversy. A wave of bad publicity would overwhelm the retail industry's argument that it wasn't responsible for sweatshop conditions. The year 1996 was to become "the year of the sweatshop."

"THEY SUCK AWAY OUR LIVES"

The second big shock that awakened Americans to the plight of sweatshop workers was the Kathie Lee Gifford story, which broke in May 1996. The Gifford controversy went beyond the El Monte scandal in that it exposed the reality of the *global* sweatshop, the origin of most of America's clothes. Second, it firmly attached a brand name image onto the portrait of the exploitative sweatshop. In the El Monte case, the role of the retailers who had sold the clothes made by indentured laborers went almost unnoticed. With Gifford, the story was as much about the celebrity as it was about sweatshops. The close connection between the star and the sweatshop helped illustrate for ordinary people the link between the retailers and the workers who make the clothes they sell.

The scandal would not have become front-page news had Gifford not erupted on national television. "Kathie Lee made the whole thing herself, she blew it," says Kernaghan. "She was very arrogant, and she thought she could bully us. It backfired."[30]

First Gifford had to tackle Kernaghan's congressional testimony that teenage girls in Honduras were regularly being forced to work 12-hour shifts to produce her clothing line. Then, just three weeks after the Honduras disclosures, Kernhaghan's National Labor Committee scored another hit against Gifford when it uncovered a New York City sweatshop just blocks from Gifford's television studio which was making clothes for the star. The shop manager had bilked the workers out of hundreds of dollars in back pay. When Gifford's sportscaster husband, Frank Gifford, went to the factory with $9,000 in cash to pay the workers himself, an entourage of reporters and cameras followed.[31]

There are two things reporters, especially reporters with the tabloids, love: celebrities and scandal. The Gifford story had both. A popular morning talk show host and the frequent cover girl for women's magazines like *Good Housekeeping*, Gifford was a big name. The scandal came from the hypocrisy of her compassionate persona versus the hard reality of the sweatshop workers making the clothes that earned Gifford $9 million a year. How could this wholesome icon be profiting from something as unsavory as sweatshops?

Similar contradictions would begin to trouble other brand names, forming the essence of the sweatshop controversy. In exposing sweatshop conditions, labor rights activists revealed the stark contrast between the sleek brand image and the shameful way in which the products were made.

Reporters and editors suddenly were desperate for other titillating sweatshop examples. What other companies were guilty?

Activists responded: Nike and Disney. Just as with Gifford, it was the disconnect between the companies' carefully cultivated public images and the reality of exploitation behind their products that drove the public's fascination. Abusive working conditions seemed out of sync with Disney's American-as-apple-pie image. The poverty wages of Nike workers didn't jibe with the company's hip posturing in its $1-billion-a-year marketing campaign.

The media ate it up. A front page story in the *Los Angeles Times* showed that workers in Haiti making Mickey Mouse t-shirts and Pocahontas pajamas were barely making enough to survive. The basic costs of living—food, transportation, housing—devoured most of the $2.40 the workers earned each day. "They suck away our lives as if they are popsicles," one worker told the *Times*.[32] Making clothes for Disney, it turned out, was no fairy tale.

Nike suffered similarly bad publicity in June of 1996. First, *Life* magazine ran a story titled, "Six Cents an Hour" describing how children in Pakistan were making soccer balls sold by Nike. The article featured a photo of an adorable yet desperate-looking little boy staring up from his work, a half-sewn soccer ball with Nike's ubiquitous "swoosh" clearly emblazoned. Then *New York Times* columnist Bob Herbert wrote two stories—"Nike's Pyramid Scheme" and "From Sweatshops to Aerobics"—blasting the company. Herbert wrote:

> [Nike founder and CEO] Phil Knight has an extraordinary racket going for him. There is absolutely no better way to get rich than to exploit both the worker and the consumer. If you can get your product made for next to nothing, and get people to buy it for exorbitant prices, you get to live at the top of the pyramid.[33]

Nike's top icon, basketball star Michael Jordan, also became a target of the media's newfound sweatshop fascination. Reporters questioned Jordan about whether he too, like Gifford, had some responsibility for resisting sweatshops. The athlete was nonplussed by the controversy, responding simply: "I don't know the situation. Why should I? I'm trying to do my job. Hopefully Nike will do the right thing."[34]

Sports writers were not impressed. "As for 'not knowing the complete situation,' why not look into it," wrote one sports columnist after Jordan's casual dismissal of the issue. "Or pay someone responsible to investigate or go there. Indonesia has golf courses."[35]

With assaults like that, the nascent anti-sweatshop movement had the public's attention. Activists immediately began gearing up public education campaigns to take their message directly to the grassroots.

"I HAVE NEVER TRIED ON THE SHOES"

The growing number of groups working on the sweatshop issue knew they had to speak directly to average consumers if they wanted to be able to pressure the retail corporations. With a political system largely shaped by corporate campaign contributions, the will of the U.S. government to regulate the behavior of transnational corporations is limited. At the same time, the globalization of capital had restrained the power of labor unions, whose leverage is restricted by borders, to hold corporations accountable. So instead of trying to end sweatshop abuses where they occur—at the point of production—the anti-sweatshop campaigners targeted the companies at the point of sale. Activists would convince citizens that they should demand a higher standard of accountability from the retail corporations. The strategy made sense. The buck, after all, starts with the consumer.

In making their case, the labor rights activists appealed to traditional notions of decency and fairness. It was simply wrong, activists said, for the workers to be paid so little and treated so poorly when the corporations they served were profitable and their executives famously rich. To drive the point home, activists juxtaposed workers' wages with the retail price of the garments and the income of top executives.

Kernaghan frequently compared the wage for a worker in Haiti making Disney nightgowns—7 cents for each piece—with the retail price ($11.97) of the garment at Wal-Mart.[36] In the first quarter of 1996 Disney posted a profit of $496 million, while Disney CEO Michael Eisner's total compensation amounted to an estimated $97,000 per hour.[37] Activists targeting Nike's labor record noted how a typical Indonesian worker earned $2.20 a day while a pair of Air Jordans retailed for $140. They pointed out that Nike's profits had tripled from 1988 to 1993, and that Nike's founder and CEO Phil Knight was one of the richest men in the world, with a net worth of about $4.5 billion.[38]

In demonstrating these figures and making their argument for workers to be treated fairly, activists were not just questioning the retail corporations' profit from sweatshop repression, they were also challenging the inequalities promoted by the global economy. By exposing the stark inequities between the suffering producers in poor countries and affluent consumers in the rich countries, the anti-sweatshop campaigners were challenging the free-market fundamentalism that sought to justify such inequalities.

No one demonstrated the harsh reality of those inequalities better than the workers themselves, and when activists sponsored U.S. visits for two foreign garment workers it brought new emotional force to the growing sweatshop controversy.

First came 15-year-old Wendy Diaz, a Honduran girl who had worked since the age of 13 sewing pants for Wal-Mart's Kathie Lee Gifford clothing line. In late May she appeared at a Capitol Hill press conference where Democratic lawmakers called on retailers to begin taking steps to eliminate sweatshops. Diaz told the assembled reporters:

> If I could talk to Kathie Lee, I would ask her to help us, to end the maltreatment, so that they would stop yelling at us and hitting us. [The supervisors] insult us and yell at us to work faster. Sometimes they throw the garment in your face, or grab and shove you.[39]

Two weeks later Diaz repeated her tale to the House Committee on International Relations, telling the lawmakers about the frequent use of underage workers. "About 100 minors like me—13, 14, 15 years old—some even 12," she said. "Many of us would like to go to night school but we can't because they constantly force us to work."[40]

Americans heard similar reports of abuse when Cicih Sukaesih, an Indonesian woman, was brought to the United States by the human rights group Global Exchange to talk about her experience working in Nike subcontractor plants and how she had been fired and blacklisted for trying to form a union. In city after city she visited, Sukaesih visited a Nike Town accompanied by a crowd of protesters with signs such as "Just Do It: Stomp on Workers Rights."

The first time she saw what a pair of Nikes sells for at a Foot Locker in Washington, DC, she was stunned by the $120 price. "That's more than two months of my salary," she said. "Why are these shoes so expensive? I have never tried on the shoes, after all my time at Nike." Global Exchange bought her a pair of Nikes and, in an emotional scene, she donned them for the first time.

Sukaesih's shock at the price of the shoes revealed, in a single expression, the injustice the activists were trying to illustrate. The inequities of the global economy, in which some people are consumers while the vast majority are merely producers, could not have been made clearer.

Pressure on the retailers was building. The Clinton administration, eager to show it was responding to the issue, was preparing for a retailers' summit. Newspaper columnists were clamoring for some kind of action. Democrats in Congress said they would push for anti-sweatshop legislation if the retailers didn't take steps to police themselves.

In less than a year, sweatshops had become a national issue.

"WE ALREADY HAVE A WORKER"

Clinton's Secretary of Labor, Robert Reich, had tried to engage major retailers on the sweatshop issue in the wake of the El Monte scandal, but his efforts had gone nowhere. The Gifford uproar, however, combined with the increased scrutiny of other major corporations, gave Reich the political opening to take a more assertive stance toward the retailers and to force them to begin discussions about ending sweatshops.

In late May, at the height of the Gifford scandal, the Department of Labor accused two major retailers (Macy's and JC Penney) of selling merchandise made in sweatshops.[41] A few days after these companies were singled out, Secretary Reich announced that 50 percent of all garment shops in the United States were sweatshops.[42] The public rebuke and the release of the up-to-date sweatshop numbers marked a sharp escalation in the federal government's rhetoric.

But most retailers still resisted reform. "We don't set policy within the factories," a Nike executive had said when questioned about labor abuses before the company got caught in the storm of bad publicity. "It is their business to run."[43]

"We're a very small part of what is transpiring in Haiti," a Disney spokesperson said. "We have nothing to do with the operation of the government, nothing to do with the standards of living of these people."[44]

Activists and a growing number of consumers felt differently. They believed the retailers had a clear responsibility to improve the standard of living of the people making their clothes.

In mid-July Reich hosted what he called a "Fashion Industry Forum" at Marymount University in Virginia. The forum was designed as a "brainstorming session" to give retailers, government officials, and labor rights groups a chance to discuss appropriate action against sweatshops. While the participants all agreed that sweatshops were abhorrent, there was no consensus on how to actually abolish them.

Labor rights activists wanted real government enforcement and independent monitoring of garment factories. But Reich was reluctant to commit new federal resources, arguing that "government can't do it all." The National Retailers Federation, meanwhile, was opposed to requiring retailers to participate in monitoring. The retailers said what was needed was an end to the "blame game."

Reich called the forum a "turning point" in the crusade to end sweatshops.[45] Labor rights activists were not impressed. To them, the forum was more a photo opportunity than a real working summit. The anti-sweatshop groups were especially upset that Cicih Sukaesih had been refused entrance to the forum because, as the event organizers said, they already had a worker there.[46] Sukaesih's treatment confirmed activists' fears that the forum was more about repairing the retailers' battered image and advancing the Clinton administration's electoral agenda than addressing the needs of sweatshop workers.

Although Reich's intentions seemed genuine, activists suspected that the administration wanted to deflect public attention away from the way sweatshop exposés were raising doubts about the free market agenda. It was an election year, after all, and part of Clinton's reelection bid rested on emphasizing the alleged benefits of the North American Free Trade Agreement (NAFTA). But the country's labor unions were opposed to NAFTA, and the president needed organized labor's support to win. Addressing the sweatshop issue gave Clinton a way to show labor that he was concerned about the issues that mattered to workers.[47]

Clinton tried to demonstrate that commitment when, just two weeks after the fashion forum, he appeared in a Rose Garden ceremony with Kathie Lee Gifford and Phil Knight to announce the creation of a White House task force to eliminate sweatshops. Clinton told reporters that more than a dozen retail companies, several non-governmental organizations, and the garment workers union UNITE would work together in a newly formed Apparel Industry Partnership (AIP). The task force's goal would be to create a "no sweat" label assuring decent working conditions. "Human rights and labor rights are not brand names," the President said. "They are the most basic products of our democracy."[48]

The retailers' federation said it wouldn't support the labeling initiative. Another important industry group, the American Apparel Manufacturers Association, also turned down the President's invitation. An association spokesperson said the labeling plan was unworkable, and that, in any case, consumers wouldn't pay attention to it.[49]

For their part, the organizations that had been working hardest to uncover labor rights abuses were caught off guard by the announcement. On the one hand, it was encouraging that major corporations such as Nike were at least willing to engage with adversaries like UNITE and the Interfaith Center on Corporate Responsibility (ICCR), a task force member and Nike critic. At the same time, most activists were suspicious of the initiative.

In announcing the task force's creation, the President and the corporate executives steered clear of specifics. As some reporters noted, the Rose Garden ceremony was "reduced mainly to a statement of good intentions."[50] The danger with the task force, many activists believed, was that rhetoric would take the place of real action. Activists feared that instead of fighting sweatshops, they would now have to direct their attention to challenging an institution they saw as bogus. The task force threatened to defuse the movement's energy and the public's attention.

"Generally, 'code' discussions have helped shift the media frame from 'workers battling abusive bosses' to 'nagging [non-governmental organizations] displeased with this or that CEO," says longtime Nike critic Jeff Ballinger. "That's a clear victory for the corporations."[51]

Of major concern for activists was the voluntary nature of the AIP.

The Clinton team wasn't demanding anything from the retail corporations. There was no suggestion of any government legislation, just a "task force." Clinton was merely requesting that the corporations police themselves. The arrangement offered no guarantee of accountability.

After the White House ceremony, several anti-sweatshop organizations wrote to Secretary Reich outlining these concerns. Noting that Nike had recently rejected the idea of independent monitoring in correspondence to a non-governmental organization, the letter warned that "Nike could use its position on the Clinton Administration's advisory committee to evade issues relating to its contractors."[52]

With the task force already a reality, expressing such reservations was all the AIP's critics could do until the partnership released its plan of action, which was scheduled to occur within six months.

As 1996 wore on, the pressure campaigns began to show new signs of progress. A growing number of people were writing the companies, phoning them, or visiting their stores to demand they pay their workers a living wage and guarantee workers' right to form independent unions. In October, leaders from 36 religious groups—Baptists, Catholics, Methodists, Episcopalians, Jews, and others—pledged that they would mobilize their communities to battle sweatshop practices. Calling sweatshops a "deep moral issue," the religious leaders committed to use the power of the pulpit to encourage their congregations to contact retailers and demand change.[53]

High school students became involved in the anti-sweatshop crusade. In Los Angeles, students got the local school board to agree not to purchase soccer balls made with child labor.[54] In Portland, Oregon, right near Nike's global headquarters in Beaverton, students and local activists united to question whether the school board should accept money from Nike. The board eventually decided to take the donation, but only after a heated debate.[55]

With the start of the holiday shopping season, labor rights groups redoubled their efforts to get people to think about the origin of their purchases and to demand that retailers be accountable to their workers. The National Labor Committee organized dozens of protests outside Disney stores. Teachers in the United States and Canada showed the NLC film, "Mickey Mouse Goes to Haiti," to their classrooms. Students eagerly responded to the call for a living wage for workers. More than 6,000 of them sent letters to Disney CEO Michael Eisner asking that he treat workers better. A 16-year-old in Kansas wrote:

> It really hurts me to know that Disney, the family I grew up with and learned from, doesn't even pay these workers enough to eat. I don't see

how you can walk down the street without having to hide your face because of guilt.[56]

Ordinary citizens were starting to see that the much-heralded consumer bargains came at a human cost. "A fresh set of questions has begun to flicker in the collective brain of Shopping America," *Los Angeles Times* columnist Peter King wrote at the height of the holiday buying season. "Where does this stuff come from? Under what conditions was it stitched, sewn, woven, assembled, molded? Who did the work, and for what pay?"[57]

A *U.S. News & World Report* poll showed that 6 in 10 Americans were concerned about the working conditions under which products are made in the United States; and 9 in 10 were concerned about working conditions in Asia and Latin America.[58] And U.S. consumers were increasingly willing to do something about those concerns. A Marymount University study found that 80 percent of interviewees would pay more for a garment if they knew it was not made in a sweatshop.[59]

The activists' appeal to basic values and to a sense of fairness was working. There was now a market for a "No Sweat" label. The challenge was to bring such a label into existence.

JUST *DON'T* DO IT

Long before the El Monte slave laborers or Kathie Lee Gifford's tears made headlines, labor rights activists were scrutinizing the conditions at overseas plants making shoes and clothing for Nike. In 1988, Jeff Ballinger, a labor lawyer, was sent to Indonesia by the AFL-CIO to investigate whether factories producing goods for American corporations were respecting workers' rights. Ballinger's investigation soon led to Nike, which indirectly employed tens of thousands of people in the archipelago nation. He learned that Nike's subcontractors routinely repressed union organizing efforts, and that many of Nike's vendors were not even paying the Indonesian minimum wage.[60]

In 1992, *Harper's* magazine published a story by Ballinger, "Nike, the New Free-Trade Heel," which demonstrated how the shoe maker was earning impressive profits by paying its workers starvation wages. The article, based on the pay stub of an Indonesian worker named Sadisah, showed that Nike's 1991 profits of $287 million were thanks largely to Sadisah's wage of 14 cents per hour.[61] Those earnings, the article explained, didn't even meet the Indonesian government's already-loose standard for "minimum physical need."[62]

For the next several years, the labor investigator mailed regular updates of conditions in Nike's subcontractor to about 30 journalists around the world. But Ballinger's critique was ahead of its time. The story never caught on—until, that is, Gifford's hypocrisy became a national sensation. Equipped with a storehouse of Nike horror stories, Ballinger was well prepared to deliver an unflattering picture of Nike's business practices to the press. Several organizations soon joined Ballinger's fight, including the nascent Campaign for Labor Rights, Global Exchange, and the Interfaith Center for Corporate Responsibility (ICCR). With these new forces, Ballinger's one-man operation, called Press for Change, grew into a public relations nightmare for Nike.

As author Naomi Klein shows in her book, *No Logo*, Nike and its founder, Phil Knight, were innovators when it came to focusing on marketing a brand image rather than simply selling a product. "There is no value in making things anymore," Knight said. "The value is added by careful research, by innovation and by marketing."[63] For Nike, the most important part of the company's investment was image-making. Since 1997, the company has spent nearly $1 billion per year on marketing: holding focus groups with consumers to test which messages work best, developing advertising campaigns, and paying for ad space.[64] From 1999 to 2000, Nike's spending on advertising alone—not including all the other elements involved with marketing as a whole—increased from $240 million to $349 million.[65] With expenditures like those, Nike had to cut costs somewhere.

Nike closed its last U.S. plants, located in Maine, in the 1980s. From there it moved its production to South Korea and Taiwan, at that time relatively low-wage countries with skilled labor forces. By the mid-1980s, the South Korean city of Pusan was known as the "sneaker capital of the world."[66] But as workers organized unions and pushed up wages in those countries—and as Korean labor unions became stronger with the fall of the country's authoritarian regime—Nike had to find cheaper labor. Soon the company had moved almost all of its shoe production to three countries: Indonesia, at that time controlled by the brutal dictator Suharto, and the authoritarian regimes of Vietnam and China. All three countries offered cheap wages, and in all three independent unions were either outlawed or routinely repressed.

Nike's single-minded search for cheap labor and docile workforces paid off impressively. From 1988 to 1993, the company's profits tripled, distinguishing the company and its founder as trendsetters.[67] The company's business model of "brands, not products" had become a frequent topic of business school seminars, and CEO Knight was a popular speaker with MBA audiences. In driving the race to the bottom, however, Nike had unwittingly set itself directly in the sights of corporate accountability activists. As Jeff Ballinger puts it:

I would describe the dramatic emergence of the sweatshop story as sort of a train wreck. Just as the big-name brands and department stores began outsourcing all of their production to contractors, the industry was moving to the most corrupt and repressive places in the world. . . . While business school case studies were heaping praise on corporations for shedding responsibility for manufacturing, the seeds were being sewn for a tremendous upheaval, once the contractors' brutal practices were exposed.[68]

The anti-sweatshop groups focused on Nike because it was an industry leader. Activists figured that if they could reform Nike's practices, the rest of the shoe brands would follow. The idea was to make positive change trickle down, just as negative change had done before. Nikki Fortunato Bas of SweatshopWatch says:

It has definitely made sense to go after the biggest companies: Nike, Wal-Mart, Gap. They're the ones that set the standards. If you get them to change, the other smaller companies will have to follow. You can create a race to the top.[69]

In order to change Nike's business practices, and thereby redefine the industry's standards for good behavior, the activists would have to accomplish two goals. First, they needed to expose the chasm between Nike's public image and the reality of its production practices. Second, they would have to turn the company's own best customers against it. To do that, the labor rights groups decided to concentrate their energy on attacking the lifeblood of Nike's success: its brand image.

To be sure, other corporate accountability campaigns had used the brand attack before. Student groups trying to compel corporations to leave Burma had forced Pepsi out of that country by undermining brand loyalty among the company's most valued customers: high school and college students. The environmentalists who sought to get the Heinz corporation to agree to dolphin-safe tuna plastered tuna cans with guerilla marketing stickers equating tuna with death. And the activists at Rainforest Action Network had created media stunts that made the car company Mitsubishi synonymous with rainforest destruction. As one Greenpeace activist has said of the development of the brand name attack, "it was like discovering gunpowder."[70]

When it came to Nike, the image assault was the center of the pressure campaign. That's because Nike stood out as a company built on image. The brand, as Knight has said, "is sacred."[71] The company's greatest strength would come to be its most vulnerable weakness.

Nike is, according to Naomi Klein, "the definitive story of the transcendent nineties superbrand."[72] Nike doesn't sell sports shoes or sweatshirts; instead it sells a symbol—the ubiquitous swoosh—that translates into a host of perceptions and emotions. Nike is different things to different people. The middle-aged white man wearing a Nike golf shirt at the country club, the teenage girl who aspires to be an athlete, the young African-American man at a basketball court—all of them have their own conceptions of what Nike means. For some people, Nike is the very idea of sport: strength under pressure, perseverance, competitiveness. For others, Nike is the essence of hip-hop street cool, the diverse, multicultural future.

This range of meanings is possible because Nike has invested billions of dollars to craft these different feelings. But the dynamic is also due to the nature of branding itself. A brand is more fluid metaphor than fixed definition, so it can accommodate a spectrum of interpretations. The brand is a cultural chameleon.[73] People are able to shape brands to their personality even as their personality conforms to the brand. What corporate accountability activists discovered was that if brands were culturally absorbent, it meant new meanings could be attached to them. Activists could redefine what the brand meant. Whereas the swoosh once meant success, it would now mean sweatshops.

The martial art Aikido teaches that one must use his opponent's force against them. Nike's swoosh, personified by the company's two biggest icons—Michael Jordan and Tiger Woods—was all about winning. But in creating a win-at-any-cost image, Nike had created a class of losers: the workers making the actual product. Success, activists argued, is a team sport. The workers deserved their fair share of Nike's prosperity.

The Aikido strategy was neatly summed up by a story in the *The New York Times Magazine* titled "Swoon of the Swoosh." As Medea Benjamin, a cofounder of Global Exchange, told the magazine's reporter: "We figured out . . . that the only way to make our campaign against Nike's labor practices work was to try to make the swoosh uncool."[74]

To make Nike uncool, the activists knew they would have to create their own images that could go toe-to-toe with the company's carefully tailored persona. That would mean keeping Nike's labor practices in the press, ensuring that an unflattering picture of the corporation emerged in the public mind. For the most part, then, the Nike campaign was a media war, a battle over perceptions.

By 1997 Nike had already received a strong dose of bad publicity. Bob Herbert's columns in *The New York Times*, along with similar columns from other writers, had given the company a black eye. The controversy over Michael Jordan's role, the *Life* magazine story about child laborers, and a CBS *48 Hours* investigation in the fall of 1996 had tarnished the company's reputation.

The pressure got hotter in March 1997 when a new organization, Vietnam Labor Watch, released a report showing that women in Vietnam making shoes for Nike had been physically abused by their Korean managers. The managers frequently hit the workers, and on one occasion managers had forced the employees to run around the factory in the hot sun until a dozen collapsed. The workers were being punished because they hadn't worn regulation shoes to the plant. Worse still, workers at the Nike factory regularly went hungry because they didn't earn enough for basic subsistence.

The report was written by a Vietnamese native, Thuyen Nguyen, who had lived in the United States since age 11. A New Jersey technology consultant, Nguyen was no radical. But when he saw the *48 Hours* report, he was determined to see for himself if conditions in the factories were really as bad as the press was saying. When Nguyen asked Nike to tour the factories, the company obliged, figuring that the businessman Nguyen, unlike the activists at Global Exchange and Press for Change, would report favorably. There was a major problem with Nike's strategy, however—the truth. As Nguyen's report concluded, the Vietnamese women were forced to work "like animals."[75]

Bob Herbert of *The New York Times* wrote:

> The idea that factory workers don't make enough to eat properly is hardly a matter of concern to Nike. Nike is important because it epitomizes the triumph of monetary values over all others, and the corresponding devaluation of those peculiar interests and values we once thought of as human.[76]

Nike hardly had a chance to recover from the Vietnam debacle when another scandal hit. In April 1997, 10,000 workers at a Nike subcontractor plant in Indonesia went on strike to protest the factory's failure to pay the country's minimum wage. Indonesia had just raised its minimum wage to $2.36 a day from $2.16, but three Nike subcontractors, together employing more than 40,000 people, had asked for exemptions. Workers at one of the plants, outraged by the move, staged a one-day work stoppage.[77]

The news seemed incredible. How could a wildly profitable company not afford a 20-cent-per-day increase? "Last year Nike raked in record profits of over $670 million," Global Exchange's Medea Benjamin told reporters. "And now the subcontractors say it would be a 'hardship' to pay their workers 20 additional cents a day."[78]

Nike tried to repair the damage, saying there had been a "misunder-standing" and that the company had ordered its subcontractors to pay the minimum wage.[79] But it was too late; the damage was done. The company's critics began to pile on in earnest. Increasingly, newspaper writers weren't just attacking Nike's labor practices; they were also jux-taposing those abuses with the corporation's massive media expendi-tures. Columnists were assaulting Nike's aggressive marketing as over-bearing. The journalist attacks redefined the anti-sweatshop campaign as a struggle against Nike's insidious mind control.[80]

"[Nike] may own every famous athlete, every pro and college team," wrote *Detroit Free Press* columnist Mitch Albom. "They may spend billions on brainwashing disguised as advertising, sticking their swoosh on every noble thing that ever happened in America and claiming it as their own. But they're not getting my mind." *San Francisco Examiner* writer Stephanie Salter, preferring to write "N--e" since "journalists use dashes when they print obscene or offensive words," made a similar criticism. "I'm picking on N--e because it is the biggest, the coolest. . . . Because you can't walk a block without seeing its logo."[81]

Perhaps the most influential criticism came not from a writer, but from Pulitzer Prize-winning cartoonist Gary Trudeau, the creator of *Doonesbury*. With 50 million readers nationwide, *Doonesbury* is a hugely popular mainstream institution. Trudeau's anti-Nike story lines in 1997, totaling several weeks all together, brought the company's sweatshop controversy to an entirely new audience. Combining biting wit with damning evidence sent to him by groups such as Global Exchange, *Doonesbury*'s treatment of Nike brought a much-needed pop culture sensibility to the anti-sweatshop campaign.

The sweatshop story had spun out of the corporation's control. Nike may have distinguished itself as one of the most sophisticated market-ers in the world, but, as the growing controversy showed, it had a tin ear for public relations. When the sweatshop scandal struck Kathie Lee Gifford, the celebrity smartly made the issue her own by offering a *mea culpa* and promising to work with the Department of Labor. Nike, on the other hand, responded with obfuscation. Unfortunately for the company's image handlers, the attempt to spin the facts backfired.

In February of 1997, Nike hired Andrew Young to conduct what it said would be an independent investigation of its factories. The first African-American mayor of Atlanta and President Carter's Ambassa-dor to the United Nations, Young boasted the liberal credentials Nike needed to repair its reputation. Young's organization, GoodWorks In-ternational, released its findings on working conditions in Nike subcon-tractor factories in June. Anti-sweatshop groups had obtained a leaked copy of the report, and they were well prepared to debunk Young's conclusions when reporters called for comment.

In his report, Young called the Nike factories he had visited "clean, organized, adequately ventilated, and well lit," and said he had found no evidence of widespread mistreatment of workers. The labor rights activists, noting that Young hadn't brought his own translator but instead relied on those provided by the manufacturer, questioned the report's independence and called the investigation "shallow." Pointing out that GoodWorks was asked by Nike not to address the wage issue, and that Young refused to reveal how much Nike paid him for his research, the company's critics derided the report as "fluff."[82]

Journalists were also skeptical. "The report all but ignores what may be the most important concern of Nike's foreign workers—wages," a *BusinessWeek* editorial said. The neoliberal *New Republic*, a staunch pro-free trade publication, called the report "a classic sham."[83]

Even as Nike's brand took a beating, activists refused to call for a boycott of the company's products. The decision not to boycott Nike may sound counterintuitive. After all, boycotts represent a powerful way to threaten a company's bottom line. But the labor rights and corporate accountability organizations coordinating the anti-Nike campaign had good reasons for resisting such a move. Logistically, activists realized, boycotts are problematic. They are hard to start, and even harder to stop. Once a boycott is called, activists must decide what is a sufficient concession by the targeted company to cancel the boycott. It's a high-risk strategy that can divide organizations over the definition of victory.

The anti-sweatshop groups' real resistance to the boycott, though, came from the workers on whose behalf they advocate. If a boycott were to actually catch on and depress Nike sales, it would limit the company's orders and threaten to throw people out of work. For that reason, the workers themselves never supported the idea of a boycott; so neither did their supporters in the United States.

The anti-sweatshop activists weren't asking people to refrain from buying Nike products; instead, they asked consumers to *threaten* Nike that they wouldn't buy its products anymore. Ideally, that threat would force the company to raise its workers' wages. To make the threat credible, the Nike foes needed to speak directly to the consumers. In the fall of 1997, the activists did exactly that, co-opting Nike's own marketing messages to communicate with some of the retailer's key consumers: youth of color, women, and university students.

Young, urban, people of color represent one of Nike's core sales targets. The enduring popularity of Nike gear among urban youth gives Nike an imprimatur of cool. As long as young people in the cities wear

Nike—and as long as their suburban peers keep emulating them—the company can maintain its status as an arbiter of style.

It should be no wonder, then, that executives at Nike flipped out when they heard that a group of black and Latino kids from the Bronx were preparing to demonstrate in front of the Nike Town in Manhattan. When Mike Gitelson, a social worker at a neighborhood center in the Bronx, told the center's kids about how the shoes they were buying for $100 to $180 were made by workers earning just $2 a day, the kids were angry. It seemed clear to them: Nike was ripping them off. The kids wrote letters to the company complaining about how they had been taken for chumps and how, as they saw it, the company owed them some money. When the company only responded with form letters, the youth became even angrier and decided to organize a protest.[84]

Nike flew a senior vice president to New York to try to talk the kids out of holding the protest. The corporate spin didn't work. On September 27, about 200 kids held a "shoe-in" in front of the Manhattan Nike Town, dumping hundreds of old Nikes at the store's front door.

"You got to use the lingo when you're talking about that," one of the protest participants, Leo Johnson, told *The New York Times*, explaining how he was able to talk about Nike's exploitative practices with his peers. "Yo, dude, you're being suckers if you pay $100 for a sneaker that costs $5 to make."[85]

A 13-year-old stared into a Fox News camera and delivered a message to the executives back in Oregon. "Nike, we made you," he said. "We can break you."[86]

Nike received a similar message just one month later. A coalition of women's rights groups coordinated by Global Exchange attacked Nike for its aggressive marketing aimed at women consumers while the overwhelming majority of Nike's factory workers were underpaid females. With 40 to 45 percent of the company's sales going to women, Nike knew it had to attract and retain that important sector.[87] Nike's advertising gurus had developed a series of hypnotic commercials appealing to women's aspirations for equality and athletic recognition. "I believe 'babe' is a four-letter word," a woman athlete in one commercial told viewers. "I believe high heels are a conspiracy against women."[88]

The message behind the commercials was admirable. But Nike's theme of women empowerment didn't mesh with the fact that tens of thousands of women working in Nike factories around the world were abused by managers and were paid such low wages that they couldn't afford to buy a pair of the shoes they produced.

On October 28, 1997, 15 women's organizations, including the Ms. Foundation, the Feminist Majority, and the National Organization for

Women, sent a letter to Nike and held a press conference denouncing the contradiction. "While the women who wear Nike shoes in the United States are encouraged to perform their personal best," the letter said, "the Indonesian, Vietnamese, and Chinese women making the shoes often suffer from inadequate wages, corporal punishment, forced overtime, and/or sexual harassment."[89]

Even as the women's groups were preparing their complaint, the backlash spread to a new quarter: college campuses. Nike has licensing agreements and endorsement deals with 200 colleges and universities across North America. In the fall of 1997 a number of students started to question whether their schools should be involved with a corporation known for its complicity in human rights abuses.

When anti-sweatshop groups called for an "international day of action" against Nike on October 18, citizens in 85 cities in 13 countries organized protests outside their local Nike Towns or other Nike sellers. Twenty protests occurred on college campuses, as students leafleted fans outside football games and other sporting events. The student protesters demanded an end to their universities' contractual relationships with Nike unless the company improved the wages and working conditions for its overseas workers. Just as with the Bronx youth, the student rebellion marked a serious threat to the corporation's image. Nike immediately dispatched representatives to meet with college administrators around the country to calm the controversy.[90]

The criticism kept coming. In a letter to Phil Knight, 75 members of Congress chastised Nike for playing a pivotal role in the industrial exodus from U.S. urban centers. "Apparently, Nike believes that workers in the United States are good enough to purchase your shoes, but are no longer worthy enough to produce them," the representatives wrote.[91]

If the public relations staff at Nike thought things couldn't get any worse, they were wrong. In early November, *The New York Times* ran a front page article, "Nike Shoe Plant in Vietnam Is Called Unsafe for Workers," which revealed that 77 percent of workers in one factory suffered from respiratory problems due to the toxic glues they used in making the company's running shoes. Based on a leaked internal study prepared for Nike by the accounting firm Ernst & Young, the story said that the workers' exposure to carcinogens exceeded the local legal standards by 177 times in some parts of the plant. This was one of the same factories that Andrew Young had called adequately ventilated. Whatever credibility Nike may have once enjoyed was now in shreds.[92]

Beset by the media, facing rebellion from some of its best customers, and suffering from falling stock prices, the company was at its nadir. Nike—the athletic corporation *extraordinaire*, the company whose entire ethos was all about winning—was on the ropes.

THE WHITE HOUSE TO THE RESCUE?

Nike, of course, didn't take its critics' abuse lying down. At the center of Nike's effort to salvage its reputation was the company's involvement in President Clinton's White House task force on sweatshops.

When Clinton, joined by Phil Knight and Kathie Lee Gifford, created the Apparel Industry Partnership in the summer of 1996, the President announced that within six months the partnership would develop a corporate code of conduct to eliminate sweatshop abuses. Six months later, the negotiations were stalled and there was still no code.

The White House task force consisted of 10 major U.S. retail corporations, a collection of human rights and corporate accountability nongovernmental organizations (NGOs), and the garment workers union UNITE. The NGOs and UNITE wanted the corporations to agree that any factory paying below a living wage should be considered a sweatshop. They also thought that factories requiring employees to work more than 48 hours a week should be called sweatshops. But the retailers wouldn't budge. They felt that a "prevailing wage"—that is, the wage set by the market—or a minimum wage, whichever was higher, should be enough for workers. And they said workers should be able to work up to 60 hours per week. On those points the retailers weren't prepared to compromise, and as the negotiations stretched into February 1997, the talks seemed headed for collapse.[93]

But negotiators kept talking, and in April 1997 the task force announced the standards companies would have to meet to gain the coveted "No Sweat" label. The corporations had won on the major points. A prevailing wage, or minimum wage, would set the standard for compensation, and workers would be permitted to spend up to 60 hours a week at their factories, sometimes even longer in "extraordinary circumstances." The final resolution revealed an imbalance of power. Because the standards were meant to be voluntary—no laws would compel the corporations to reform—the retailers had more weight at the bargaining table. The union and its allies made most of the concessions.

The NGOs that had shunned the negotiations—among them Global Exchange, Press for Change, and the Campaign for Labor Rights—were ready to critique the deal as soon as it was announced. As they had feared when the task force was first announced, the activists were now spending their time challenging this blue ribbon panel instead of fighting actual sweatshops. But they had little choice. The groups that had worked so hard to expose sweatshop abuses needed to make clear that without a living wage even the most well-kept factory was still exploitative.

The day the deal was announced, anti-sweatshop groups blasted the accord. They noted that there was no definition of what "extraordinary circumstance" meant for overtime pay. They pointed out that, although the companies had agreed to freedom of association for workers, the companies would still do business in places like China and would not be expected to put pressure on national governments to allow independent unions. They criticized as weak the rules regarding independent monitoring. Most of all, they attacked the new code's wage standards, highlighting the fact the "No Sweat" code would not even require factories to pay overtime rates. Elaine Bernard, a Harvard University academic who had worked closely with labor rights groups, said the new code would simply create a "kinder, gentler sweatshop."[94]

Even some outside observers felt that the code could have gone farther. Editorialists at the *San Francisco Examiner* and *The New York Times* complained that the code lacked precise commitments. "The code is so littered with loopholes," the *Times* said, "its impact will probably be limited unless public and press attention remains fixed on the problems of sweatshop workers."[95]

But the code did contain a silver lining. By making commitments, however weak, to oversee conditions in their subcontractor factories, the major retailers had conceded that they did, in fact, have a responsibility to the workers making their goods. The concession marked an important step for the corporate accountability movement. A precedent now existed for holding all transnational corporations, not just apparel companies, accountable for their foreign operations.

With the "No Sweat" standards in place, the task force turned its attention to creating a monitoring system. The retailers' commitments, although unsatisfactory to many labor rights groups, would mean nothing unless they could be enforced. The abuses in factories making shoes for Nike—a company that had developed its own internal code in 1992—had already demonstrated that.

Developing a monitoring mechanism would eventually take twice as much time as creating the standards. That's because monitoring touched on the crucial issue of transparency. How much of their operations would the corporations allow the public to see?

As a new round of negotiations began, the representatives from business, labor, and the public interest community faced several key questions. Who should do the monitoring? And should the monitoring reports be made public?

UNITE and the NGOs wanted human rights organizations and religious groups from the factory countries to do the plant inspections. "In no way should employers be the only ones monitoring what they're doing," UNITE's president said when the standards were announced. "We're saying monitoring shouldn't be left totally in the hands of the companies. You can't have the foxes watching the chickens."[96]

The retailers wanted their accounting firms to do the monitoring, even though the union and the NGOs said they did not consider such firms truly independent. The labor and human rights groups wanted the monitors to inform consumers when they discovered violations. The corporations said violations shouldn't be disclosed. The talks again drifted into stalemate for months.

Finally, in November of 1998, 20 months after the original announcement of the "No Sweat" standards, the Apparel Industry Partnership announced that it had devised a monitoring mechanism that would be implemented by a new institution, the Fair Labor Association (FLA). But it was a stillborn birth. UNITE and the venerable Interfaith Center for Corporate Responsibility (ICCR) said they would not participate because the monitoring system didn't provide adequate transparency.

Under the system created by the FLA, many of the monitors would be from for-profit accounting firms such as Ernst & Young, though they would be encouraged to consult with local human rights and faith-based NGOs. Monitors would not disclose factory violations to the public; instead, monitoring reports would go directly to the retailers, which would then have the opportunity to remedy the situation. In the first three years after a company agreed to the code, 30 percent of a retailers' suppliers would be inspected. In each subsequent year, an additional 10 percent of a corporation's subcontractors would be monitored.[97]

UNITE and the ICCR felt the arrangement failed the basic tests for public accountability, openness, and independence. "The monitoring is badly flawed," a UNITE official said. "We don't think it's very independent monitoring and the companies pick their monitors and the factories to be monitored so there won't be surprise inspections."[98]

The union's biggest criticism, though, was that the standards did not include a living wage. The union had come to agree with the vast majority of anti-sweatshop activists that a garment factory that did not pay its workers a living wage was a sweatshop—period. "How can you talk about eliminating sweatshops without making a commitment to pay a living wage?" a union representative asked.[99]

The retailers defended the plan, saying that if the requirements were stricter they would have little chance of convincing the rest of the industry to join the voluntary system. Some of the companies originally involved in the task force had already left because they felt the standards were too burdensome.

The failure of the retailers and the anti-sweatshop groups to even come close to an agreement on wages reveals a fundamental divide between the two sides. Anti-sweatshop activists and corporate executives tend to talk past each other. Whereas business leaders say the market alone should determine wages, the workers' advocates think that corporations should go beyond the market arithmetic and be accountable to standards of social justice. As the disagreement shows, the sweatshop controversy is very much a competition between different value systems. Activists say values of justice should inform wage levels. The retailers, anchored firmly to money values, disagree. Reaching consensus is difficult because the two sides aren't speaking the same language.

The wide differences in opinion were made clear in the responses to the FLA's creation. President Clinton called the accord a "historic step." Global Exchange—fearing that the agreement could do more harm than good if consumers falsely believed that the FLA system could eliminate sweatshops—called it a "step backward."[100]

With the departure of UNITE, ICCR, and several companies from the White House task force, the Fair Labor Association faced a crisis of legitimacy. Several of the FLA's members feared that without union participation, consumers would feel little reassurance that apparel produced under the agreement's guidelines was not made in sweatshops.

At the same time, a similar uncertainty afflicted the anti-sweatshop movement as a whole. The groups who had done so much to educate America about sweatshops were at an impasse, uncertain where to go next and what to do. After two heady years of sweatshop exposés, the media's attention was beginning to wane. And the reform package of the Clinton administration—voluntary regulation by the retailers themselves—offered no guarantee of accountability or meaningful change.

Fortunately for labor activists, a new force was about to reinvigorate the anti-sweatshop movement. Within a few months, sweatshops would again become a burning issue on colleges and universities across the United States. The new student energy would spark the largest campus movement since the anti-apartheid protests of the 1980s, while at the same time giving new life to the older labor rights campaigns.

STUDENTS TAKE THE LEAD

In the winter of 1999, anti-sweatshop activism exploded on campuses around the United States, altering campus politics in America and, at the same time, engaging thousands of young people in the struggle against corporate globalization.

The anti-sweatshop issue gained popularity on college campuses by showing that the political is personal. Already, the larger anti-sweatshop movement had illustrated for people the connection between the clothes we wear and the identities of people on the other side of the globe. In creating a national student movement for workers' rights, campus activists relied on making the same connection. The campus labor groups focused on the clothing bearing their schools' names. They made the political personal and the global local.

Collegiate apparel is a lucrative business. Although they account for only a sliver of the entire U.S. apparel industry, sales of Michigan Wolverines caps, Georgetown Hoya t-shirts, UCLA Bruins sweatshirts, and thousands of similar college name brand clothing items constitute a $2.5 billion annual business.[101] In raising questions about where those campus symbols came from, who made them, and under what conditions, student activists challenged their peers to look closely at the promises and perils of the global economy.

The idea for investigating the collegiate apparel industry arose in the summer of 1997, when students interning at UNITE began thinking about how they could bring the anti-sweatshop movement to their campuses. The UNITE interns began researching their colleges' clothing, and they soon learned that their schools earned royalties, often in the millions of dollars, by selling companies ("licensees") the right to manufacture clothing with the university's logo. The licensees would then contract out the garment production to dozens of factories in the United States and overseas. The system was conducive to perpetuating sweatshops because the licensees regularly moved production orders from one factory to another, according to where the cheapest bids were.[102]

The students decided that universities needed strict codes of conduct which the licensees would have to agree to in order to get the university contracts. The students agreed that several key elements should be contained in the codes: paying workers a living wage, guaranteeing workers' right to organize independent unions, prohibiting physical and sexual abuse, and disclosing factory locations. The final demand, disclosure, represented a new twist from the existing demands of the anti-sweatshop movement. Recognizing that sweatshops flourished because of the secrecy of the subcontracting system, the students felt that public disclosure of factory locations was essential for creating transparency in the industry. Without transparency, there could be no accountability, no real opportunity for independent monitoring.

The nascent student movement had jumped directly into the most complicated question bedeviling labor rights groups: How to actually go about abolishing sweatshop abuses? That question would dominate students' efforts. With a sophisticated mix of passion, pragmatism, and idealism, the student movement tackled issues that had confounded veteran activists.

In the fall of 1997, students at several universities began meeting with their schools' administrators to discuss apparel codes of conduct. Progress was painfully slow at all the campuses except for Duke University in North Carolina. The Duke students had several advantages over their peers. First, the campus already had a sizable anti-sweatshop campaign, a reaction to the university's endorsement relationship with Nike. Second, the students were aided by a university licensing director who shared the students' concerns about sweatshops, and a fairly sympathetic administration that from the start included students in the code of conduct discussion. That didn't mean the negotiations went smoothly. The licensing corporations aggressively guarded their own interests. But by March 1998, a code was adopted that included workers' right to freedom of association, public disclosure of factory locations, and independent monitoring. To the Duke students' disappointment, the code did not include a living wage requirement. Still, it was far more than any other college activists had achieved.

In July 1998, in an effort to build an institution through which the students could push their demands with greater coordination and force, 60 representatives from 30 campuses formed a national umbrella organization, United Students Against Sweatshops (USAS). That same summer, students from Harvard, Georgetown, Brown, and the University of Illinois participated in a fact-finding trip to investigate the origins of college baseball caps, a fashion staple among undergraduates. The students learned that the mostly teenage girls in the Dominican Republic making baseball caps for American universities were earning about $40 for a 56-hour work week. Their investigation showed that when a student pays $20 for a cap sold in the student union, the university receives about $1.50, and the worker who made the cap gets eight cents.[103] The fact-finding trip gave students their first chance to see how the workers really live, inspiring new commitment.

Instilled with a fresh sense of purpose, equipped with the hard facts connecting campus gear to worker exploitation, and now bolstered by a national network of like-minded activists, students returned to their campuses in the fall of 1998 prepared to push their administrators for meaningful corporate codes of conduct.

OPPOSING SWEATSHOPS ISN'T RADICAL

The energized and organized campus anti-sweatshop groups began their code of conduct campaigns by educating fellow students about the university's connection with sweatshops. Activists leafleted in front of student unions and sporting events. They held rallies and gathered signatures on petitions. Diverse student constituencies joined the call for university codes of conduct. Campus feminists criticized the routine sexual harassment of women workers in garment factories. Organizations representing Latino and Asian students were drawn to the issue through concerns about the racism of the global production chain. The sweatshop issue was forging new student coalitions, bringing together groups that hadn't collaborated before.

To secure their classmates' support for their demands, campus anti-sweatshop activists employed many of the same arguments that had proven effective for the larger labor rights movement. Instead of talking in the jargon of economics, the student activists appealed to a basic sense of fairness.

One of the key organizers of the anti-sweatshop campaign at the University of Wisconsin at Madison, Thomas Wheately, says:

> There was the moral message: talking about the actual working conditions and living situations of the workers. Then there was the university pride message; Bucky the Badger being dragged through the mud. We even made up stickers with Bucky behind bars.[104]

The dual arguments gave students a language they could use to reach a larger cross-section of students. In relying on common values to make their point, students were able to overcome political prejudices. A Michigan organizer, Rachel Paster, explained it this way:

> One reason we've been so successful is that opposition to sweatshops isn't radical. Although I'm sure lots of us are all for overthrowing the corporate power structure, the human rights issues are what make a lot of people get involved and put their energies into rallies, sit-ins, etc. We have support not just from students on the far left, but from those students in the middle who don't consider themselves radical.[105]

Despite a growing number of students demanding labor codes of conduct, administrators at most schools were stonewalling. Surprised at the sudden student interest in the formerly arcane issue of collegiate licensing, many administrators convened working groups and task forces to sort out the controversy. At some schools—to the shock of the campus activists—students weren't included in the code discussions at all. Across the country, progress on the issue was slow or nonexistent. As students headed home for their winter vacations at the end of 1998, Duke remained the only university in the United States with a code of conduct for its licensees.

CORPORATE CAMOUFLAGE?

As the student pressure for strict licensee codes of conduct mounted in fall of 1998, officials at an organization called the Collegiate Licensing Corporation (CLC) began to worry that strict codes would complicate business. The CLC represented 170 colleges and universities, and its sole job was to mediate and coordinate contracts between schools and the licensing corporations, big companies such as Champion, Russell, Nike, and Reebok, and smaller ones like Jostens and Nutmeg Mills.[106] The licensing corporation announced that it would develop a uniform code for all of its member schools. Throughout the fall, students repeatedly asked for input into the creation of the code, but were rebuffed.

The students were outraged when they came back from the winter vacation to find a CLC code that did not meet any of their demands. Afraid that their administrators would en masse adopt the CLC proposal—and frustrated by the endless meetings with university officials that seemed to be going nowhere—students headed in a more militant direction. Reaching back to the proven student protest tactics of the 1960s, the anti-sweatshop activists began to stage sit-ins and occupy buildings to push their demands. The needs of garment workers around the world were now the biggest issue in campus politics.

In February, students at Duke and Georgetown University staged sit-ins in the offices of their university presidents demanding that the schools not adopt the CLC code. Within days, both schools agreed to full public disclosure. The new spirit of militancy spread from there. In Madison, Wisconsin, dozens of students occupied the chancellor's office even though administrators at Madison had already agreed to public disclosure after students and professors organized a series of forums and town hall meetings. Now students wanted a clause on protecting women's rights and a living wage guarantee. The occupation of the chancellor's office was entering its fifth day when school officials agreed to the women's rights protection and to conduct a living wage study.[107]

Other protests and sit-ins followed. Students at the University of Michigan and the University of Arizona occupied school offices, each winning public disclosure. At Yale, students staged a "knit-in" to highlight worker abuse. At the University of California-Berkeley activists organized a "sweatshop fashion show" in which amateur models paraded the university logo as an announcer described the conditions in which the clothes were made.[108] And when University of California students from several campuses held a demonstration in front of the university president's office, they were joined by two Members of Congress. The campaign was gaining momentum.

The wave of protests grabbed the country's attention. Complaints about the younger generation's apathy were misplaced, it seemed. News reporters agreed: The anti-sweatshop movement had caused the biggest surge of campus protests since the anti-apartheid movement.[109]

But the new wave of political protest was different from earlier agitation. First, it was technologically sophisticated. Students were coordinating their actions with e-mail networks and nationwide conference calls; at sit-ins, cell phones and media contact lists were common. Second, the students' demands revealed a deep streak of pragmatism. Even if the student activists were implicitly questioning the inequities of the global economy as a whole, their central demands—disclosure of factory locations and better pay—were eminently reasonable.

"We're not asking for a revolution," Tico Almeida, a senior who led a Duke sit-in told a reporter. "We're just asking for improvement of working conditions. It doesn't seem a lot to ask."[110]

The protests and sit-ins achieved some important gains. The CLC code was effectively dead, and students had secured real commitments from university officials, especially in the area of public disclosure. But then the ground suddenly shifted beneath the students' feet.

NEW SUPPORT FOR THE FLA

In mid-March university administrators, looking for a way to enforce their new codes and apparently believing they could gain some political cover by the move, began affiliating with the Fair Labor Association. Unwittingly, the students' activism had strengthened the hand of the stumbling FLA. Former Wisconsin student leader Wheately says:

> When all the universities started signing onto the FLA we saw that as the administrators trying to take cover. It was a smart move for the FLA, which at the time was suffering from a crisis of legitimacy. They could now say, 'Look, America's leading educational institutions are involved.'[111]

If the university administrators thought they would impress the students by joining the FLA, they were wrong. It only made matters worse. The student activists were now outraged that the universities had betrayed them by joining the FLA behind their backs. Just like the labor rights groups before them, the students complained that the FLA's voluntary regulation wouldn't protect workers.

"Corporations are the ones we're trying to monitor, and they have too much control over the process," a Brown University student said in April 1999, after 56 schools had joined the FLA.[112]

As the turbulent school year came to a close, students shifted to pressuring administrators not to join the FLA. But it was too late: By the end of the semester, more than 100 schools had affiliated with the FLA. Students now had the summer respite to decide whether to try to reform the FLA from the inside or try to create a parallel institution.

In early July 2000, students from dozens of colleges and universities gathered in Washington, DC, for the United Students Against Sweatshops' first annual conference. The most important item on the agenda was the FLA: whether to "mend it or end it." Some students argued that they would not be able to get their universities to leave the association and so they might as well work to improve it. Student participation in the FLA would strengthen the position of those NGOs still involved in the FLA who were hoping to reform the institution. The other side said that if they participated in the FLA they would end up giving legitimacy to a retailer-dominated system, and in the process limit the chances for developing another monitoring system. After days of debate, the anti-association stance prevailed, and on the last day of the conference hundreds of students staged a protest against the FLA at the offices of the Department of Labor.[113]

CREATING A NEW SYSTEM

Students now faced the daunting task of creating a worker protection system from scratch, a process which had taken the White House task force more than two years to complete. Through the end of summer and into the beginning of the fall, the students, with the assistance of UNITE and several anti-sweatshop groups, worked to create an alternative to the FLA. The new system, which would be called the Worker Rights Consortium (WRC), would require public disclosure of factories and encourage schools to adopt a living wage provision. Unlike the FLA, however, the WRC would not be a monitoring system. Instead, it would create a structure for workers to voice their complaints and grievances without fear of reprisals. Then, international NGOs, local human rights groups, and labor unions and others would have the chance to assist the workers in improving their situation.

The shift in strategy revealed a new consensus emerging within the labor rights movement that too much emphasis had been put on codes of conduct. Factory monitoring, a growing number of people agreed, was only a stopgap measure and could never fully eliminate sweatshop abuses. As the FLA impasse showed, corporations weren't willing to open themselves up to public view, nor could they be trusted to police themselves. And even if the retailers did agree to independent and unannounced inspections, the resources didn't exist to monitor every garment plant in the world. Corporations such as Gap and Wal-Mart had their production spread out in thousands of factories in dozens of countries. Monitoring them all would be a logistical nightmare.

The key to ending sweatshop abuses, the labor activists agreed, was worker empowerment, ensuring that workers had the ability to stand up for themselves. Essentially, that meant giving workers the chance to form independent unions. In the long run, the labor rights groups and students believed, unionization was the best hope for raising wages and guarding against abuses. At their best, codes of conduct would open up the space for union organizing by letting both workers and corporations know that someone was watching.

"If you're really interested in stopping sweatshops and empowering workers, codes of conduct can't be a substitute for collective bargaining," says Charlie Eaton, who helped spearhead anti-sweatshop activities at New York University just after the WRC was created. "But codes can be a means to an end."[114]

In late October 1999, the students unveiled the finished plan for the Worker Rights Consortium and invited universities and colleges to join. The new group would create a system for workers to make confidential complaints about factory conditions to respected labor rights groups, thereby establishing the workers themselves as frontline monitors. The WRC would maintain a database of factory names and locations producing collegiate apparel, and conduct training for workers at plants to instruct them of their rights. The group's governing board would consist of university administrators, students, and labor rights groups. Licensing corporations and retailers would not be included in the decision-making: essentially, no voluntary self-policing allowed.[115]

Just a week before the WRC was unveiled, Nike had announced that it would disclose the names and locations of 41 of its subcontracting plants in 11 countries making t-shirts, sweatshirts, and other apparel carrying school names. The move marked an important victory for the student movement, and it gave fresh momentum to their call for universities to join the WRC. If Nike was willing to open up its factories, the students said, then there was little reason universities and their licensees couldn't agree to the WRC's disclosure requirement. "What Nike did is important," a student activist said at the time of Nike's announcement. "It blows open the whole notion that other companies are putting forward that they can't make such disclosures."[116]

In embracing the unglamorous task of dealing with enforcement systems, the student movement displayed an admirable sophistication. But the focus on the complexities of possible solutions to the sweatshop problem had complicated campus organizing. The whirlwind of acronyms now involved in any discussion of worker abuses posed an obstacle to bringing new students into the anti-sweatshop struggle.

"After the WRC became the center of things, the debate did become a bit muddled," says Wheately. "There would be these banners up saying, 'WRC not FLA,' and people would walk by saying, 'What's wrong with Florida?'"[117]

The campus activists were able to overcome this dilemma and maintain their energy and momentum by staying focused on the central issues: sweatshops and worker abuse. At the same time, they worked to convince students that this was a winnable campaign.

"We went out there and we said, 'There is something *you* can do to fight sweatshops,'" says Eaton. "For a lot of people, corporate globalization is really scary, but they feel it's too big to tackle. We said, 'If you want to challenge corporate globalization but don't know how, here's a way, by changing the behavior in your community.'"[118]

The strategy worked. Around the United States, student activity intensified, and universities responded to activist pressure and joined the Worker Rights Consortium. By April 2000, more than 30 colleges and universities had affiliated with the WRC. April 7 was the date set for the consortium's founding conference and the deadline for schools to join the group. With the deadline approaching, a new wave of protests and sit-ins swept across campuses as students increased the pressure on their administrators to affiliate with the WRC.

In Madison, Wisconsin, dozens of students occupied the administration building for 89 hours until the administration called in the police. Fifty-four protesters were arrested.[119] At the University of Iowa, 100 students confronted the university president in her office and demanded the school join the WRC. At Penn State, the University of Oregon, and University of Kentucky, students erected tent cities outside the administration building; 12 students were arrested at Kentucky, and police arrested 11 at Oregon. Similar sit-ins and occupations also occurred at Tulane University in New Orleans and the University of Minnesota.[120] At Purdue University, five students engaged in a 10-day hunger strike.

The students' message was being heard. "It's a real sign of commitment to his cause," a parent of a Purdue hunger striker told the press. "I've never read the tags before. I look at the tags now."[121] And the protests were accomplishing their goal. By the time of the WRC's founding conference, 44 schools had agreed to join the consortium.

THE NIKE BACKLASH

Across the United States, students were celebrating their victories when a powerful backlash occurred. Nike, apparently in response to Brown University's decision to affiliate with the WRC, said it was ending an agreement to provide equipment and uniforms to the school's men's and women's hockey teams. Nike executives called Brown's decision to join the WRC "arbitrary."[122] A few weeks later, the company announced it was terminating contract negotiations with the University of Michigan, another WRC school, over a 6-year, $3.5 million licensing agreement.[123] Students said the company was retaliating against the schools because of their involvement in the WRC. They were right. On April 24, Nike founder Phil Knight announced he was canceling a $30 million gift to his alma mater, the University of Oregon, because of that school's just-announced affiliation with the WRC.

Nike had once again demonstrated its tin ear for public relations. The termination of the licensing contracts and, especially, the cancellation of the donation to the University of Oregon led to headlines around the United States. The WRC and the FLA were getting more attention than they ever had before, and that new attention worked to the students' advantage. To many people, it looked as if Nike and Knight were trying to intimidate and bully the universities and the student activists. Knight had again come across as the evil capitalist from Central Casting. Knight said in a statement explaining why he cancelled his donation:

> I was shocked . . . to find out that the University of Oregon had joined the Workers Rights Consortium. With this move, the University inserted itself into the new global economy where I make my living. And inserted itself on the wrong side, fumbling a teachable moment.[124]

Clearly, Knight was not getting the message. Nike's central complaint with the WRC was that no corporate representatives were on its board. Nike and Knight apparently didn't understand that was precisely the idea. The retailers were being asked to surrender some of their power to other stakeholders. The very point of citizen and student anti-sweatshop activism during the past four years had been to insert more voices into the rule-making of the global economy. In keeping retailers out of the WRC, the movement was questioning the assumption that only a handful of corporations and their executives should be deciding how the global economy is run.

Eventually, the University of Oregon backed down and agreed not to join the WRC. The other schools held firm, however, and when it came to Michigan, it was Nike that had to surrender. The company needed the school—and the visibility that came with the university's high-powered athletic program—more than the school needed Nike. Despite the pressure by Nike, colleges and universities continued to join the WRC. At last count, 112 schools belonged to the consortium.

THE BIG TEST

The Worker Rights Consortium faced its first major test in January of 2001, less than a year after its inception. Just after New Year's, workers at a Korean-owned plant called Kuk Dong in Atlixco, Mexico, went on strike. The workers, who were making collegiate-licensed gear for Reebok and Nike, called the work stoppage to protest the factory's inedible cafeteria food and the firing of five fellow employees who had stood up to complain about the food. Two days into the strike, local police in full riot gear entered the Kuk Dong grounds and attacked the approximately 300 workers occupying the factory; four people were sent to the hospital, and two pregnant women suffered miscarriages.

The strike at Kuk Dong and the police attack attracted widespread media coverage. The WRC quickly responded, sending a fact-finding delegation to the plant. After conducting a week of confidential interviews with workers, the WRC investigators concluded that there was "substantial, credible evidence" of serious labor rights violations at the factory. Some workers were being paid less than Mexico's minimum wage. A number of workers were under legal age. And workers' attempts to form an independent union, not connected to the state's governing party or the plant owners, had been repressed by the factory management.[125]

The WRC called on Reebok and Nike to urge their subcontractor to rehire the terminated workers, address the wage and age violations, and allow for a free and fair union election. At the same time, WRC demanded that the retailers not "cut and run" from Kuk Dong. In the past, brand name corporations, including Nike, had tried to distance themselves from factory horror stories by simply severing their relationship with the controversial plant, a quick fix that did nobody, especially the workers, any good.[126] The students told the retailers that if they were genuinely interested in improving the lives of the Kuk Dong workers, they should keep contracting with the factory and work to reform it.

To press their demands, the students organized protests and rallies around the United States. Students at WRC-affiliated schools also met with their administrators to encourage them to contact Nike and Reebok directly and urge the retailers to fix the situation. The pressure worked. Reebok pressed the Kuk Dong management to allow the workers to hold a free union election. After hiring a respected monitoring group called Verité to inspect the plant, Nike called for the fired workers to be reinstated, brought in international labor experts to talk to the workers about their rights, and created a remediation plan for the plant. Both companies promised they would keep sending orders to the factory.

In the long run, the WRC involvement proved key. By putting international attention on the factory, the WRC helped give workers the space to stand up for themselves. In September 2001, after an 18-month organizing campaign, the factory workers signed a collective bargaining agreement with the plant management. The union, SITEMEX, is one of the first independent unions in Mexico's maquiladora sector.

LESSONS LEARNED

The Kuk Dong experience demonstrated that a monitoring system geared toward workers can succeed. It also showed that, when facing strong citizen pressure, transnational corporations such as Nike and Reebok will, however grudgingly, take steps to improve factory conditions and guarantee workers' rights. A *Washington Post* editorial hailed the WRC's Kuk Dong campaign as a success and a model. The win gave students confidence that they were on the right track.[127]

"You have to get a foothold somewhere, and build an ethical base in an unethical industry," says NYU student Eaton. "And that's what the WRC can do. It can sound the firm alarm."

The WRC's Kuk Dong success is one example of the small, but significant, achievements gained by the anti-sweatshop movement. At the very least, the sweatshop controversy and continuing factory exposés have forced the companies to be more vigilant internally. At the beginning of the 1990s, for-profit accounting firms did virtually no factory inspections; in 2000, the accounting firm PriceWaterhouseCoopers, an industry leader in the field, inspected 6,000 plants worldwide.[128] Since their results are not made public and the auditors are closely tied to the people they are investigating, such inspections are hardly models of accountability. And they often miss abuses, as shown by the worker revolt at Kuk Dong, a plant inspected by PriceWaterhouseCoopers. Still, the increase in internal monitoring has eliminated some of the most egregious abuses, such as blocked fire exits and workplace safety violations. Forcing some corporations to disclose their factory locations has also been a victory since anti-sweatshop groups now have a way of connecting directly with workers.

The movement's most important success so far has been getting the retail corporations to concede they have an obligation to the workers in subcontractor factories. The value of that success should not be underestimated. When the revelations about Kathie Lee Gifford's sweatshop involvement first landed in the spotlight, the celebrity tearily asked her television viewers, "I'm supposed to be personally responsible for everything that happens around the world?"[129] No, you're not responsible for *everything* that happens in the world, the labor rights groups told Gifford, but you should be accountable to the workers who make the clothes that earn you millions of dollars every year.

The new prevailing attitude on retailer accountability is illustrated by two new "joint liability" laws in California and New York, the garment centers of the United States. Under the new laws, retailers can be held liable for labor laws their subcontractors violate, and can be forced to pay workers' wages themselves in cases where employees have been cheated. The existence of these laws reveals a shift in the political debate over the definition of corporate accountability.[130]

These achievements don't mean, however, that the anti-sweatshop movement has been entirely victorious. It's one thing to compel a corporation to acknowledge new obligations; it's a far more difficult task to actually force a corporation to change its behavior. Workers' rights abuses and poverty wages remain a daily injustice in the United States and in dozens of other countries around the world. The anti-sweatshop movement may have shifted the public debate about corporate globalization, but at the same time it has revealed the difficulties in setting a floor for standards that can be enforced.

The anti-sweatshop campaigners' pressure on the big, brand name retail corporations makes sense in an industry that is at once concentrated in ownership yet diffuse in production. Nike has hundreds of suppliers and a subcontractor workforce of half a million people. Wal-Mart alone buys from 20,000 suppliers.[131] Although the manufacturers are spread out all over the globe, the retailers are a relatively tight-knit group. Just 14 well-known retailers control some 70 percent of the U.S. apparel market, and it is those retailers who set prices and therefore dictate what garment workers will get paid.[132] In such an environment, focusing on the retailers gets at the heart of the accountability issue.

Yet putting pressure on the retailers is not enough. The brand attack, activists are learning, only goes so far. A clear example of this is Nike's continued intransigence when it comes to improving workers' wages.

In May of 1998, after suffering two years of negative publicity that had scorched the company's image, Nike CEO Phil Knight delivered a speech before the National Press Club in Washington, DC, in which he offered a sort of *mea culpa*. Noting that the sweatshop controversy had made his company's name "synonymous with slave wages, forced overtime and arbitrary abuse," Knight promised that his company would soon undertake a series of reforms. Nike would adopt new policies regarding health and safety, child labor, independent monitoring, and workers' education. The speech won the company rave reviews from pundits. *The New York Times* editorial page said the announced reforms "set a standard other companies should match." *Washington Post* columnist E.J. Dionne called Knight's performance a "breakthrough for American and international human rights campaigners."[133]

But a May 2001 report by Global Exchange showed that three years after the speech, Nike workers continue to work for subsistence wages, are regularly forced to work overtime hours, and suffer repression and intimidation if they try to organize unions or speak to labor rights investigators or reporters. Nike, the report concludes, has treated sweatshop abuses as more of a public relations inconvenience than as a serious social justice and human rights issue.[134]

Nike's resistance to fundamental change, and its critics' inability to force it to change, point to some of the limitations of the brand-based attack. Citizens groups were able to embarrass Nike and redefine its responsibility to its foreign workers by tarnishing the swoosh. But if the brand can be changed to mean something its creators never intended, it can also be changed back. Malleability goes both ways; brands can recover. If a company invests enough money in repairing its brand, it will be able to create whatever meanings it likes and, in the long run at least, wipe out whatever negative associations may once have existed. The sweatshop controversy was a public relations and imaging problem for Nike. And so Nike responded with a public relations solution, tinkering around the edges just enough to distract the public's attention.

There is another weakness with brand attack, this one strategic instead of tactical. It affects only certain companies. While a number of major retailers have been burned by sweatshop revelations, a great portion of the apparel industry has flown under activists' radar and come away unscathed by the labor rights controversies. The merchandising outfits and discount stores have not been the target of public scrutiny. That means the factories producing the generic shoes and no-name shirts may be even worse than the factories producing goods for the brand name giants. A cruel irony of the anti-sweatshop campaigns is that the Nike sneaker may be made in better conditions than the generic shoe sitting next to it on the shelf.

The dilemma is illustrated by the industry's response to the Fair Labor Association. While most labor rights activists see the FLA as not going far enough, most of the retail industry has refused to participate because they say its rules go too far. Indeed, only a handful of companies—mostly brand name retailers who have been hit with sweatshop publicity—belong to the FLA.[135]

The FLA's limitations reveal the fundamental weakness of voluntary initiatives. The FLA includes no enforceable government mandate. And because there is no law that compels retailers to eliminate sweatshop abuses abroad, most companies—whose natural instinct is to increase profits no matter what the social cost—have no incentive to join the group.

In an era of free market fundamentalism, in which the state is dominated by corporate interests, corporate accountability forces have little opportunity to pass laws that will force changes in corporate behavior. This leaves activists with few options but to ask corporations to voluntarily change their way of doing business. Voluntary efforts represent a kind of first line of defense for groups seeking to reform corporations. But because the onus for change hangs on the whims of corporate directors, voluntary efforts offer no guarantee of real change.

The necessity for mandatory rules to govern corporate behavior points to the difference between corporate responsibility and corporate accountability. Business leaders and government officials often use the language of responsibility, while social activists prefer the term accountability. The first term connotes only voluntary action, while the second signifies mandatory action. Responsibility suggests a general course of action; accountability requires specific actions.

In order to eliminate sweatshop abuses, mandatory rules are needed. Achieving accountability will require a fundamental redrawing of the balance of power between corporations and citizens.

SHIFTING THE LOCUS OF POWER

The lack of progress in ending sweatshops is partly explained by the disconnect in values between industry and activists. Labor rights groups have argued that the retailers could easily raise workers' wages and keep consumer prices steady if only they would sacrifice some of their profits. But that is not a move any retailer is yet ready to make. The problem activists face is a systemic one.

The ongoing standoff has forced the anti-sweatshop movement to rethink its strategy and reconsider how best to go about ensuring meaningful accountability and helping workers improve their lives. "I would say we face the challenge of remaking ourselves," says Charles Kernaghan. "If we stay with the same old stories, we'll peter out."

Labor rights groups have concluded that, while it is important to pressure the retailers, the anti-sweatshop movement must focus more on empowering workers, as it did with the WRC's test case at the Kuk Dong factory. A global industry demands a global social movement.

"I think the goal, which is a huge goal, is building a truly international labor movement," says SweatshopWatch's Nikki Bas. "We're up against a lot in trying to build a global movement, but more and more people are focused on that."[136]

Some activists say the pieces are beginning to be put in place to build such a movement. Under the leadership of John Sweeney, the AFL-CIO has become more internationalist than ever before, coming to realize that in the global economy a strictly nationalist trade unionism can't cope with transnational capital. The AFL-CIO's "solidarity centers" in Mexico, Cambodia, Indonesia and many other countries around the world exemplify a new philosophy. The centers are designed to give local workers the support they need to build strong labor movements in their countries. "We're helping these unions get stronger," an AFL-CIO trainer in Cambodia has said. "We're helping them build independent and democratic unions."[137] That kind of initiative, combined with the vigilance provided by the Worker Rights Consortium, is laying the foundation for a more internationalist labor movement in the United States.

This political shift could also give anti-sweatshop groups the chance to realize another essential goal: creating model factories and developing a real "No Sweat" alternative. "One of the challenges to the anti-sweatshop movement is that we live in such a consumer society," says Bas. "Unless we provide an alternative—clean [sweat free] clothes—people don't feel they can get involved."

Bas's point of view offers an important lesson for all corporate accountability activists: Giving people alternatives to the status quo is an absolute must. At the height of the anti-Nike campaign the most frequent question campaigners received from the general public was, "If I don't buy Nike, what should I buy?" In failing to offer a quick and viable answer, activists handicapped their chances of success. The simple fact is that sweatshop abuses will never be eliminated until people are given a way to opt out of the current system. And unless people are given that alternative route, many will hestitate becoming active citizens. Providing a hope-filled vision of the future is essential to engaging people's imaginations and energy. The vocabulary of promise is preferable to dwelling on the perils of the present.

The lesson is underscored by the experience of the environmentalists who sought to stop dolphin killings in the Pacific Ocean, a struggle chronicled in the next chapter. Environmental groups succeeded in stemming the slaughter of dolphins, not only because the abuse was so gruesome, but because they provided an easy alternative: dolphin-safe tuna. The contrast between a horrific reality and a readily available alternative led millions of consumers to opt for the less-damaging alternative. If the anti-sweatshop movement had known this lesson in advance, they would have developed a two-track strategy: pressuring corporations to stop sweatshop abuses, while at the same time facilitating the production and marketing of clothing produced under certified humane conditions.

"We're not going to take the American people with us if we just keep saying, 'This is a nightmare,'" Kernaghan says. "There's not a single person in this country that doesn't want a 'No Sweat' label. . . . We need to push the FLA on its ass and get it out of the way and restart the whole discussion [about a No Sweat label] today."

Steadily, the U.S. anti-sweatshop movement is becoming less anti-retailer and more pro-worker. Activists say it's a natural evolution. The movement must continue broadening the definition of corporate accountability by going beyond just agitating at the point of consumption and attacking the brand. It must organize consumers and workers so they can support each other in building a new way to produce and market products that is not based on exploitation.

This evolving strategy is a major test. It will mean challenging not just individual corporations or a single industry, but the entire system of corporate rule. "Can we use our leverage to affect more than one factory?" ponders student activist Eaton. "I think that's where the anti-sweatshop movement is going: from holding corporations accountable for their actions to actually shifting the locus of power, and changing who is actually making the decisions."

3

FLIPPER vs. THE WTO
The Fight for Dolphin-Safe Tuna

ON APRIL 12, 1990, H.J. HEINZ CO., one of the largest U.S. food processing corporations and the owner of StarKist Seafood, surprised both its competitors and the environmental community when it announced that within three months it would sell only tuna that was "dolphin-safe." Within hours the country's two other major tuna brands, Bumble Bee Seafoods and Chicken of the Sea, pledged that they too would stop selling tuna caught in nets proven deadly to dolphins. By the end of that year, Congress would pass and President Bush would sign legislation establishing a federal dolphin-safe label for all tuna sold in the United States. Coming after two years of an intense citizens' campaign on behalf of dolphins, the companies' decisions marked a triumph for grassroots environmentalism. The tuna industry's capitulation to consumer concerns, accompanied by the federal legislation, promised to end the routine killing of 100,000 to 200,000 dolphins every year.

But within just nine months, the environmental groups' victory for dolphins would become tangled in the complicated nets of international trade policy. In January 1991, Mexico, confronting an embargo of its tuna catch, filed a complaint with a then-little known trade dispute court challenging the U.S. dolphin protection laws as a barrier to free trade. The European Community soon launched a similar complaint. By 1995, laws banning the importation of dolphin-deadly tuna into the United States would be under full assault, the victim of international trade rules. In 1997, the U.S. Congress passed new legislation that many environmentalists said would lead to new increases in dolphin killings. Today all three major U.S. tuna companies maintain their dolphin-safe pledge. The U.S. government, however, has retreated from its earlier commitment to ending tuna fishing methods that have proven deadly to dolphins.

The effort to save dolphins from brutal and deadly fishing methods is a fine example of how organized citizen pressure can improve the practices of an entire industry. At the same time, the history of the dolphin-safe campaign reveals the limitations of any national regulations in the era of globalization. With a barrage of lawsuits, creative use of the national media, determined public education strategies, and street protests, environmental groups succeeding in transforming corporate and government policy in little more than two years. The environmental community then spent more than a decade defending that success.

The struggle between U.S. environmentalists and foreign fishermen over tuna fishing methods was among the first illustrations of the tensions between promoting social and environmental concerns and advancing free trade. It sent a signal to corporate accountability groups that their gains could easily be erased by forces far beyond their control. And it led, eventually, to a new determination by progressives to challenge the institutions that write the rules for the global economy.

When the campaigners at the San Francisco-based group Earth Island Institute began their crusade to free dolphins from tuna nets, they never imagined their relatively modest aims would become wrapped up in the complicated rule-making of global governance.

Mark Palmer, a biologist at Earth Island Institute who has worked for more than a decade to protect dolphins from tuna nets, put it this way.

> The fact that trade rules and this bizarre tribunal would overturn environmental laws caught us by surprise. We never figured that there would be a reckoning where the U.S. would have to choose between free trade and protecting dolphins.[1]

AN OCEAN GENOCIDE

For reasons not completely understood by marine biologists, schools of mature yellowfin tuna in the Eastern Tropical Pacific (ETP)—an area roughly bounded by San Diego, the coast of Chile, and Hawaii—like to swim below herds of dolphins. Fishermen in the ETP have been aware of this pattern for generations, and naturally they've used it to their advantage. When a tuna boat sees a herd of dolphins, it can be reasonably sure that there's a catch nearby.

Before the 1950s, tuna fishermen in the eastern Pacific caught yellowfin tuna with the simple use of rod, line, and baitless hook lowered beneath the dolphin herds. Then the tuna fleets realized they could dramatically increase their catch by encircling the dolphin herds using a method called purse-seine netting. Tuna fishermen targeted dolphin herds, chased them down, and encircled them with purselike nets to catch the tuna beneath. The method sharply increased tuna catches. But there was a terrible consequence: The nets also captured the dolphins, drowning and mortally wounding scores of the marine mammals.

Initially dolphin populations didn't suffer too seriously from the new fishing methods because the fishing crews lacked the skill to encircle an entire dolphin herd. Then fishing technologies improved, and fishing crews got better at encircling dolphin herds, using speedboats to find the animals and seal bombs (concussion grenades used to ward off seals) to corral them into tight areas. Tuna boats began to use stronger and bigger nets, some 300 feet deep and almost a mile long, that made it harder for the dolphins to escape. Mass dolphin drownings became common. The introduction of powerful hydraulic winches to pull in the nets led to many dolphins being dragged onto ship decks or, even worse, into the winches themselves.

The purse-seine innovations dramatically increased tuna harvests: During one fifteen year period, the tuna catch grew fivefold. At the same time, dolphin deaths from tuna fishing shot up alarmingly.

Marine biologists estimate that the original combined population of spotted dolphins, spinner dolphins, and so-called common dolphins in the ETP was 8 million. By the end of the 1960s, somewhere between 250,000 and 500,000 dolphins were dying in tuna nets in the ETP every year. The number is imprecise because while it is known for certain that hundreds of thousands of dolphins died in the nets themselves, an untold number suffered mortal wounds; though many were able to escape the nets, with crushed noses or shattered fins they became easy prey for sharks.[2]

In the early 1970s, the growing number of dolphin deaths caused by tuna fishermen caught the attention of marine biologists, who alerted U.S. environmental groups to the slaughter. Even the fishermen started to become concerned about the high rates of dolphin casualties. The tuna skippers in the ETP realized that if they destroyed the dolphin herds they would lose their best method for capturing tuna.

Partially in response to the dolphin genocide underway in the eastern Pacific, in 1972 the U.S. Congress passed the Marine Mammal Protection Act (MMPA). The law—which was also intended to stop the slaughter of whales and the killing of North Atlantic seal pups—was part of a wave of conservation legislation, including the Endangered Species Act, that swept Congress that year.

The MMPA stated:

It shall be the immediate goal that the incidental kill or incidental serious injury of marine mammals permitted in the course of commercial fishing operations be reduced to insignificant levels approaching a zero mortality and serious injury rate.[3]

To reach that goal, the MMPA established a schedule and a quota system for eventually—if not immediately—decreasing the deaths. The act provided funds to research new fishing methods and dolphin-saving techniques. It also set up a system for placing observers from the National Marine Fisheries Service (NMFS) on tuna boats.

The U.S. tuna fleet's number of dolphin kills started to decline after the MMPA went into effect. Fishing boats began to employ what they called a "back down method" whereby they would lower and sink the net after encircling the dolphin herds to let the animals escape. The development of finer mesh nets reduced the risk of dolphins becoming entangled and drowning. Many boats started using rafts and even divers to physically pull the dolphins out of the purse-seine nets and into freedom. In 1975, before the MMPA rules went into effect, researchers estimated that 166,645 dolphins died in nets of U.S. tuna boats. By 1977, the official estimate was only 25,452 deaths.[4]

REGULATING A TRANSNATIONAL PROBLEM
But the MMPA didn't solve the problem of dolphin killing. Despite the decline in dolphin deaths caused by U.S. fishing boats, dolphin species in the ETP continued to suffer terrible losses.

Dolphin deaths didn't stop for two reasons. First, President Ronald Reagan, in keeping with his ideological opposition to government regulation, abandoned the MMPA's commitment to a "zero mortality rate" early in his term and permitted weak oversight of the U.S. fleets. Second, and more important, the number of U.S. fishing boats was steadily declining. A larger and larger share of the tuna harvest was being caught on foreign ships not bound by U.S. government regulations.

In 1981 the MMPA, under tuna industry pressure, was amended to allow the killing of 20,500 dolphins every year. The Reagan administration greatly reduced the funds for research into dolphin-saving techniques, regulations were loosened, and monitoring became lax. Even the limited rules kept in place by the administration were not enforced.

The MMPA called for observers to be placed on U.S.-registered tuna boats. The observers had two responsibilities: to ensure that tuna boats were using the best available technology, and to tally the number of dolphins killed on each voyage. But the Reagan administration cut the number of NMFS observers in half. A lawsuit by the San Diego-based American Tunaboat Association then succeeded in removing all observers from the boats for nearly three years. Even after the observers were restored by an appeals court, only about one-third of all tuna boats carried observers.

When observers did make it onto the boats, they faced such severe harassment from the fishing crews that their work was compromised. Tuna skippers resented having outside regulators on their boats, and ship owners complained that supplying a berth for the observers cost too much. NMFS observers reported frequent pressure from tuna boat captains to falsify dolphin kill numbers. Harassment of observers ranged from tuna skippers' expletive-filled tirades to actual physical threats. Observers said that fishing crews sometimes threw seal bombs at them to force them to retreat from their observation posts.[5] Clearly the tuna industry—which aside from suing to keep NMFS observers off their boats had also blocked rules aimed at stopping nighttime fishing—did not want to change.

The industry's aversion to reform was abetted by the Reagan administration's reluctance to hold the boats accountable to the law. The government's own auditors found enforcement of the MMPA to be lax. A 1987 review of the NMFS office in San Diego by the Commerce Department's Inspector General concluded that:

> Enforcement seems to have been lenient. Prosecution has been selective, settlements have been characterized by protracted negotiations to accommodate the tuna industry, and settlements have been for amounts much less than those originally sought. . . . In eleven recent cases of reported violations, no notices of violations were issued to the offenders. . . . We were told by NMFS staff with long-standing and intimate knowledge of tuna fishing operations that fines have been so low compared to incomes that skippers have knowingly violated the regulations and accepted the fines.[6]

Environmentalists and former NMFS observers estimated that, because of underreporting, U.S. fleets were killing twice as many dolphins as government records showed: about 50,000 dolphins a year, far exceeding the number allowed under the 1981 quotas. At least 800,000 dolphins died from U.S. tuna boat nets between 1972 and 1989, environmental groups said.[7]

But this represented only a fraction of all the dolphin deaths in the ETP. In 1972, U.S. fishing boats were causing 87 percent of all dolphin deaths in the ETP; a decade later, the U.S. fleet was causing 15 percent of all deaths. The shift came about because of changes in the makeup of the ETP tuna fleet. In the 1960s, virtually every tuna boat in the ETP sailed under the American flag. By 1986, only about 30 percent of tuna vessels were U.S.-registered because other governments began offering more lax regulations. And the dolphin kills on foreign vessels were four times higher than on U.S. boats, environmental groups and the U.S. government estimated.[8]

The gradual shift of the tuna industry to foreign boats reflected the

larger changes wrought by economic globalization. As U.S. food processing companies looked to cut their costs, they naturally sought producers in countries with lower wages. Over the years major tuna marketers shifted their purchasing to foreign boats and canneries that offered lower prices for their catches than did U.S. fishermen.

The MMPA-mandated regulations also contributed to the decline of
the U.S. tuna fleet. Tuna boat owners, seeking to evade even the weakest of poorly enforced rules, simply re-flagged their ships. From 1979
to 1989, an estimated 68 boats, or two-thirds of the U.S. fleet, reflagged
with foreign fleets.[9] Most of these boats remained under the command
of U.S. skippers, and many of them stayed under the control of their
original owner, even if the ownership nominally changed. The rules
instituted by the MMPA helped to relocate dolphin killings to ships beyond U.S. control.

In a sense, the success achieved by the environmental movement in
passing the original MMPA was self-defeating. While the regulations
were national in scope— affecting only the U.S. fishing fleet—the industry and the problems it was creating were transnational.

Feeling that the dolphin regulations had put it at a competitive disad-
vantage to other fleets, the U.S. tuna industry pushed for and received
changes to the MMPA in 1984. The tuna industry had two goals—to
weaken the U.S. regulations and to ensure that their foreign competitors
were held to the same standards. The amended legislation, pushed by
conservative Senator John Breaux (D-LA) at the behest of the American Tunaboat Association, did both of these things. First, the amended
MMPA locked in the rollback in standards. Second, and far more importantly from the point of view of the dolphins, the new rules mandated that foreign tuna fleets demonstrate that they were using dolphin-
saving procedures similar to U.S. boats or face a ban on imports of their
tuna. Foreign fleets—by 1984, one-third larger than the U.S. fleet—
were now on notice that they had to reduce their dolphin kill numbers to
rates "comparable" to the U.S. numbers or else risk losing access to the
lucrative U.S. market.

A law was now in place that had the power to force a reduction of
dolphin kills on both U.S. and foreign tuna boats. The question then
facing environmentalists was whether the law would be enforced. Unfortunately for the dolphins, it was not.

"LIKE TRYING TO DROWN A CAVALRY"
In 1985, Earth Island Institute initiated its campaign against setting nets
on dolphins. The environmental advocacy around the dolphin-tuna issue that had occurred in the early 1970s was largely driven by Greenpeace

and the Environmental Defense Fund. But with the passage of the MMPA in 1972 and the subsequent decline in dolphin kills by U.S. boats, those two organizations felt they couldn't do any more and that the congressional atmosphere was unsympathetic to further regulation. In the mid-1980s, Earth Island was left as the only major environmental group focused on dolphin killings in the eastern Pacific.

Earth Island first attempted to raise public awareness about the dolphin killings through reports and articles in its quarterly publication, *Earth Island Journal*. But the group's public education efforts weren't gaining traction beyond a dedicated core of conservationists and animal rights activists. While the numbers on paper were horrific—at least 125,000 dolphins were still dying each year in tuna nets, marine biologists estimated—Earth Island lacked a way to capture the attention of the mainstream public and the national media. The issue needed drama.

Earth Island got its chance to build that drama in the summer of 1987, when a self-described drifter named Sam LaBudde cruised into the group's offices. A dedicated environmentalist, LaBudde was shocked by the dolphin story. He later recalled:

> I was informed about environmental issues. I knew about the depletion of the ozone layer before most people did, and about the destruction of the rainforests. But I had thought whales and dolphins were sacrosanct species, above abuses. Nobody had told me they were being captured in nets, with speedboats and explosives and helicopters.[10]

LaBudde asked what he could do to help. The directors at Earth Island told him what they needed most was film footage to bolster the reams of documentation they already had on paper. LaBudde, who had once worked as an NMFS observer in the Bering Sea, said he thought he could get on one of the tuna boats working the eastern Pacific. The Earth Island activists were skeptical that he could land a position on a tuna trawler—and they were also unsure that LaBudde would even go through with his promise—but they told him that if he got onto a boat they would try to get him a camera.

In September 1987, after spending weeks cajoling ship captains in the Mexican port of Ensenada, LaBudde got a position on the Panamanian boat *Maria Luisa*. LaBudde immediately called his contacts at Earth Island, and within a day they shipped him an 8-millimeter Sony camcorder. During the next four-and-a-half months on the *Maria Luisa*—first working one of the speedboats used to corral the dolphins and then later as the ship's cook—LaBudde, despite an unfriendly crew, a hostile captain, and the constant fear of discovery, managed to get five hours of graphic footage of dolphin killings. In early 1988, LaBudde sent his tapes up to San Francisco, where they were edited into a powerful 11-minute film.[11]

The footage was exactly what Earth Island needed to make the dolphin killings real for average Americans. In one scene the film shows a dolphin caught by its beak in the net—head bent backwards, dorsal fin bent sideways, mouth half open—as it's dragged into the hydraulic power block and crushed. Another scene showed a tight bunch of a few dozen animals trapped below the surface; each time a dolphin seems about to escape, the net pushes it back down; finally the dolphins, one after another, stop struggling and die. At one point the film shows at least 1,000 dolphins captured in a net, thrashing about trying to escape. LaBudde described the carnage as "somebody trying to drown a cavalry."

Equipped with this imagery, in the spring of 1988 Earth Island started developing a strategy for eliminating dolphin deaths in tuna nets. The group came up with a three-prong plan. Earth Island would use lawsuits to compel the government to enforce the 1984 amendments to the MMPA, which were not being implemented. It would use Congress, which was about to consider the routine reauthorization of the MMPA, to tighten existing dolphin rules and create new ones. And the group would force U.S. corporations marketing tuna to understand that they, too, had a responsibility to halt the killing of dolphins.

The third strategy was the most novel and, arguably, the most important. The MMPA's failure to eliminate dolphin killings by U.S. ships and its inability to reduce the number of dolphins killed by foreign fleets made it clear that holding the tuna processors accountable for their actions would be essential in protecting dolphins. Since the problem was transnational, the environmental community would have to focus on the corporate marketers of tuna, who were also transnational.

From a market standpoint, the strategy made perfect sense. The United States is the world's largest consumer of tuna, eating more than half of the yearly catch—830,000 tons, making tuna sales a $1 billion market.[12] And the three largest marketers of canned tuna in the United States—StarKist, Bumble Bee, and Chicken of the Sea—account for 75 percent of all tuna eaten by Americans. If Earth Island could force those corporations to stop buying tuna caught in encirclement, market pressure—the closure of the world's biggest market—would compel the fishermen to change their practices. The key to pressuring the companies to change their policies would be consumer sentiment. Capturing the hearts and minds of the public would be crucial to success.

Earth Island released LaBudde's film to the television networks in March 1988. The ABC and CBS nightly news programs aired parts of footage, as did NBC's popular *Today* show. The ensuing hullabaloo convinced other major environmental groups that they, too, had to help with the effort to protect dolphins, and organizations such as Greenpeace and the U.S. Humane Society started working diligently on the issue, adding new momentum to the campaign. Far more important, the grisly footage galvanized the national consciousness. The dolphin slaughter became an instant *cause célèbre*, probably the best known and most popular of conservation efforts of that time.

Earth Island's Palmer remembers:

[LaBudde's film] was a key piece of our efforts. It shattered the tuna industry's claims that everything was alright. It convinced Members of Congress that this was a serious issue that had to be taken seriously. It made a major difference in changing the tone of the debate.

The dolphin-safe campaign, made for television, was in the end made *by* television.

DON'T KILL FLIPPER

Earth Island launched its campaign for dolphin-safe tuna on April 12, 1988. The group, along with the Marine Mammal Fund, filed a lawsuit in federal court against the Commerce Department and the NMFS for failure to enforce the provisions of the MMPA. Earth Island sent the LaBudde video to Washington, airing it during congressional hearings on the reauthorization of the MMPA. During protests outside the StarKist offices in Long Beach and the St. Louis headquarters of Chicken of the Sea, the group called on consumers to boycott tuna until the companies promised that no dolphins would be killed while catching the fish.[13]

The MMPA reauthorization was a mixed success for environmentalists. Their key demand was a four-year phaseout of tuna fishing by dolphin encirclement. But the fishing industry, saying such a ban would render them uncompetitive, defeated that request. Environmentalists did, however, succeed in getting Congress to require 100 percent NMFS observer coverage for the U.S. fleet. They won a prohibition on net setting after sundown and a ban against the use of seal bombs. And they won a requirement that by the end of 1989 foreign fleets would have to reduce their dolphin kill rate to double the U.S. number, and by 1990 to 125 percent of the U.S. number, or be subject to an embargo.

With reauthorization accomplished and the lawsuit slowly moving its way through the courts, Earth Island focused its attention on targeting grassroots consumer pressure against the tuna canning corporations. Although the boycott was against all tuna, Earth Island centered its efforts on just one of the marketers of canned tuna—StarKist, owned by

H.J. Heinz. The group believed that if could get the market leader, StarKist, to meet its demands for dolphin-safe tuna, the rest of the industry would have to follow.

In making their case for dolphin-safe tuna to consumers, Earth Island activists employed three basic arguments. They said that such a highly evolved, and increasingly rare, mammal as the dolphin shouldn't be endangered. They pointed out that the use of dolphin encirclement methods for catching tuna was unnecessary and could be abandoned. And they framed the issue as one of consumer choice.

In the battles around the shape and scope of the MMPA, environmentalists had tried to protect dolphins by reforming the supply side of the equation. When environmentalists switched their focus to the corporations selling tuna, protecting the dolphins became a market demand issue. If environmentalists could convince consumers to demand dolphin-safe tuna, the industry would have to respond. Earth Island knew that presenting dolphin protection as a "right-to-know" issue would resonate with an American public that valued choice as a central part of liberty—at least as far as liberty meant consumers' freedom to choose what they do and do not want. Equally important, from a simply tactical vantage, consumer choice was something the major tuna marketers were not prepared to argue against.

As they presented their argument for consumers' right to choose, environmentalists pointed out that setting nets on dolphins was unnecessary if all you wanted to do was eat tuna. The earlier debates over the MMPA had focused on the Eastern Tropical Pacific because that was where the dolphin slaughter was occurring. But only ten percent of the entire world tuna harvest comes from the eastern Pacific. Earth Island and its allies noted that tuna fishing could easily be done in other seas without lowering the total tuna catch. Or, they said, tuna fishermen in the eastern Pacific could simply start using techniques already perfected in other parts of the world, where tuna and dolphins don't have a symbiotic relationship.

This argument was effective in showing people that the dolphin killings were unnecessary. It also drove a wedge between the tuna marketers (StarKist, Bumble Bee, and Chicken of the Sea) who didn't care where they got their tuna from, and the U.S. tuna fishermen who fished almost exclusively in the eastern Pacific.[14] That division would prove essential for convincing the three major corporations to adopt dolphin-safe practices. During the two-year consumer boycott, the marketers opposed changes because of pressure from U.S. fishermen and concerns among their own purchasing units that tuna supplies would be hard to come by. But as it became apparent that other tuna sources were available, reformist voices within the corporations started to hold sway.

The linchpin of the consumer-choice and senseless slaughter arguments was, of course, a basic ethical appeal against animal cruelty. Environmentalists highlighted the dolphin's intelligence, its sociability, and its close similarity to humans to create a sense of empathy among the public. Even a single dolphin death, environmentalists argued, was intolerable.

Sara Meghrouni, a former Earth Island activist who started working on the dolphin campaign in the late 1980s as a grassroots organizer, put it this way:

> The fact that dolphins are mammals, and have so much romance associated with them, and that people can communicate with them was hugely important in building public sympathy. You have to convince people of the majesty of something if you want to protect it.[15]

Meghrouni says that all of Earth Island's literature and public statements were careful to remind people that dolphins, like any other mammals, nurse their young and that, just like humans, they are very social animals. Dolphins' intelligence—their communication abilities and their experience of uniquely conscious emotions like stress—was emphasized, as was each animal's uniqueness, for example the fact that every dolphin has a different colored iris.

Animal rights activists like Meghrouni were pleasantly chagrined to find that a generation of capturing and training sea mammals had made people more willing to identify with the dolphin. No one wanted to kill "Flipper."

Earth Island's campaign started to gain momentum in 1989. In January a federal court ordered the NMFS to ensure that it had observers on all U.S. tuna boats. The ruling was an important win for environmentalists because although the law already required 100 percent coverage, tuna captains had been trying to fight the rule. And the NMFS had been stalling and saying it didn't have the funds to put observers on all the boats.[16] The judge hearing the case also ruled that foreign fleets were subject to the U.S. law requiring observers on their boats, a regulation resisted by the United States Tuna Association, representing the canners. The tuna companies said that if U.S. observers were required on foreign boats, those fleets would simply refuse to sell their catch to U.S. canners.

Grassroots pressure was also mounting. Greenpeace was sending dozens of telegrams a day from consumers to the tuna companies demanding dolphin-safe tuna. Demonstrators were picketing in front of the tuna boat docks in San Diego. Earth Island's activists were busy in front of supermarkets, restaurants, and food industry conventions encouraging people to boycott tuna.

"We were trying to get people to understand the power of their dollar," remembers Meghrouni, who coordinated the tabling in front of supermarkets. "People like to know they can have what they want and still be guilt-free. It wasn't a hard sell."

Safeway announced it would no longer stock canned tuna, and the popular Hard Rock Cafe restaurants said they would also boycott tuna. Comparing dolphin killings to "the slaughter of the buffalos" and encirclement netting to "the strip-mining of the sea" was working.

The campaign started to receive assistance from two important sectors: Hollywood and school children. Teachers and elementary school children around the country responded to the dolphin issue without any formal urging from environmental groups. Requests for Earth Island's organizing packets were increasingly coming from children, and entire schools started sending dolphin-safe appeals to the tuna corporations, and also to Congress. School cafeterias joined the tuna boycott. The dolphin's familiar Flipper persona connected well with kids.

Hollywood personalities connected with the dolphins as well, and they started contributing their money and their names to the environmentalists' campaign. Jerry Moss, the powerful head of A&M Records hosted Los Angeles fundraisers to support the cause.[17] George C. Scott narrated an award-winning film for the Discovery Channel titled "Where Have All the Dolphins Gone?" The issue, with the help of star Danny Glover, even snuck into the hit film *Lethal Weapon 2*. In an early scene in the movie Glover's teenage daughter, wearing an Earth Island t-shirt, reprimands him for eating tuna.

As the dolphin campaign received more and more attention, StarKist tuna, the target of most of the consumer pressure, and H.J. Heinz, remained publicly uncooperative. Company executives repeatedly stated that the boycott was senseless. They said fishermen would simply sell their catch to other markets and continue their purse-seine fishing, keeping the dolphin in danger. But in private, executive attitudes were changing. Heinz's own consumer surveys showed that most people were sympathetic to the environmentalists' arguments and would pay more for tuna that was guaranteed to be dolphin-safe. The company officials were concerned, however, that a dolphin-safe pledge would limit their ability to purchase enough tuna to meet demand. That concern, combined with the U.S. tuna captains' resistance to change, kept Heinz from meeting environmentalists' demands.[18]

Still, the company knew it was losing on the public relations front.

On September 5, 1988, Heinz announced that it would fund new research into ways to reduce dolphin killings. Although company executives denied it, the announcement was clearly intended to defuse protests planned for the corporation's annual shareholders meeting in Pittsburg the next day. A year earlier Earth Island activists had picketed the shareholders meeting, and the upcoming protest was supposed to be even larger.

More than 50 activists protested outside the September 6 shareholders' meeting, chanting "Stop the slaughter—boycott Heinz." Two activists scaled a nearby building and unfurled a banner that read, "Heinz: Stop Killing Dolphins." The ruckus didn't reach into the meeting, where shareholders, likely pleased with a two-for-one stock split and news of growing profits for the $5.2 billion corporation, didn't raise any questions about the dolphin killings. But at a post-meeting press conference, reporters hounded Heinz chairman Anthony O'Reilly about the dolphin issue. O'Reilly agreed that the protesters had a "legitimate concern" and that "it is only natural that people would protest the killing of dolphins," but again said the boycott was ineffective and would only push fishermen to foreign markets.[19]

But the company was moving too little and too late. Political pressure was building for an end to the purse-seine fishing and a verifiable dolphin-safe tuna label. Voters in California were set to decide on a ballot measure to ban gillnet fishing in its waters. Even more threatening to the tuna companies, Members of the U.S. Congress, at the urging of environmental groups and thousands of citizens, were looking for ways to protect dolphins from tuna nets.

"CONSUMER DEMOCRACY AT ITS BEST"
In October 1989, California Representative Barbara Boxer and Delaware Senator Joseph Biden, with the backing of more than 100 colleagues, introduced into Congress the Dolphin Protection Consumer Act. The new law would create a federal label for all tuna sold in the United States. Tuna caught in purse-seine nets would carry a label reading, "The tuna in this product has been captured with technologies that are known to kill dolphins." Tuna caught using other methods would be labeled "dolphin-safe." Although the bill did not outlaw the encirclement of dolphins using purse-seine nets, it did include penalties—including fines and imprisonment—for violating the label rules. The main purpose of the legislation, according to Boxer and Biden, was to simply guarantee consumers the information they needed to choose which tuna they wanted to purchase.

The tuna canners and the fishermen vigorously opposed the bill. The tuna companies said it would be too logistically difficult to track the origin of the tuna and verify whether a particular boat had killed dolphins. The tuna fishermen complained, in a familiar refrain, that the new regulations would give foreign fleets a competitive advantage and would in effect "destroy" the U.S. fleet. Besides, the tuna fishermen said, the dolphins weren't an endangered species, and a few thousands deaths a year wouldn't deplete their numbers to unsustainable levels.[20]

Boxer, Biden, and the environmental community responded that the bill would in fact give the U.S. fleet a competitive advantage since consumer sentiment so clearly favored dolphin-safe tuna. If the foreign fleets couldn't demonstrate their tuna to be dolphin-safe, they would lose sales, and eventually they would switch to other fishing methods. The bill's sponsors also pointed out that the law contained provisions for placing observers on foreign boats. As for the logistical problems, the dolphin-safe proponents noted that Canada already had a similar system that had proved workable.

As the dolphin-safe act headed for votes in the House and Senate, executives at Heinz began to realize they were cornered. Heinz chairman O'Reilly started meeting with A&M Records chief and dolphin supporter Moss to test the depth of public anger on the issue. Those conversations helped convince O'Reilly that his company would have to make concessions. Even more important for O'Reilly, the company's own consumer surveys showed that public concern about the dolphin issue was growing. The percentage of consumers aware of the dolphin problem had jumped from 50 percent to 60 percent; the level of concern among consumers, measured on a scale of one to ten, had also increased, from six to seven. As the new numbers showed, it made good business sense to reach some sort of agreement. Still, some executives resisted meeting the activists' demands for fear that the dolphin-safe measures would lead to a price increase.[21]

In early 1990, as the directors at Heinz debated which course to take, Earth Island began preparations for declaring April 14 "National Dolphin Day." Protests were planned in front of grocery stores and StarKist and Heinz offices in 60 cities. The group was ratcheting up its efforts to brand the company "dolphin killers."

Just days before the scheduled protests, Heinz executives contacted the directors at Earth Island and said they were prepared to make a commitment to dolphin-safe tuna. On April 12, exactly two years after Earth Island first called for a boycott on all tuna, Heinz chairman O'Reilly, Earth Island head David Phillips, and Senator Biden came together at a Washington press conference to announce that the company would immediately take steps to guarantee that all of its tuna was dolphin-safe.

In front of dozens of television cameras, O'Reilly declared that his company would make dolphin protection a "crusade." He said the decision was prompted by "consumer concern," including "postcards and letters from schoolchildren." The campaign for dolphin-safe tuna represented "consumer democracy at its best," O'Reilly told reporters.[22]

Within hours, the other two major tuna canners—Bumble Bee, owned by the Thai corporation Unicord, and Chicken of the Sea, owned by Van de Camp—announced that they would also guarantee that all of their tuna was dolphin-safe.

Earth Island and the three tuna canners agreed that all the companies would immediately begin refusing any tuna caught in the Eastern Tropical Pacific without proof from official observers that no nets were set on dolphins during the entire trip. The companies also agreed to independent monitoring of their canning operations. Earth Island would be allowed to put a dozen monitors in canneries in eight countries around the world—from the Philippines to the Caribbean—who would have the authority to check the records of all tuna ships bringing in catches. Bar codes would be placed on every can of tuna to allow monitors to trace the fish back to individual boats. The companies all said they would support the legislation pending in Congress.

Congress soon passed the Dolphin Protection Act. Eighty percent of the U.S. tuna fleet immediately relocated to the western Pacific to fish for skipjack tuna which doesn't swim below dolphins. Within months of the companies' announcements, dolphin-safe tuna began appearing on store shelves nationwide.

In August, environmentalists won another victory on the dolphin's behalf. A federal court, responding to an earlier lawsuit filed by Earth Island against the Commerce Department, declared an embargo on tuna imports from Mexico, Venezuela, Panama, Ecuador, and the Polynesian nation of Vanuatu. The judge ruled that the Commerce Department had failed to enforce the 1988 provisions of the MMPA that called for tuna fishing countries to reduce their dolphin kill numbers to no more than double the U.S. rate, which in 1989 was approximately 12,000 deaths.

After decades of unlimited net setting on dolphins, the market for dolphin-deadly tuna was collapsing. The entire U.S. canned tuna industry was committed to dolphin-safe tuna, and foreign fishermen, the only ones who continued to use the purse-seine method, were facing a closed market. The activists at Earth Island figured they had won.

"We all decided it was solved," says Earth Island's Mark Palmer. "This showed us that the public can make a major difference by using different tools to pressure corporations to change their policies."

But the struggle to ensure that no dolphins were killed in tuna nets was not over. Environmental groups, having achieved their goal in just two years, would spend much of the next decade defending their gains from assault by other nations using international free trade rules. The effort to protect dolphins would lead to complicated battles in international trade courts and the U.S. Congress over how, and even whether, to keep dolphins out of tuna nets.

"THE LIMITED DOMAIN OF THE ENVIRONMENT"

When the U.S. tuna fleet began to decline in the 1980s, Mexican fishing companies were the main beneficiaries. Lower fuel, labor, and insurance costs on their boats made Mexican operations more attractive than their U.S. competitors. In 1984 the Mexican fleet first gained parity with the U.S. fleet, with each country registering 42 tuna boats. By 1986, Mexico had 10 percent more boats than the United States, making it the largest tuna fleet in the eastern Pacific. Mexico, then, had a great deal to lose from the U.S. embargo ordered in 1990. Mexican government officials estimated that the embargo would cost its tuna industry "hundreds of millions of dollars."[23]

The Mexican government began searching for a way to overturn the embargo and protect its tuna industry from U.S. laws that affected its operations. The best tool at its disposal was the dispute panel established by the General Agreement on Tariffs and Trade (GATT), an international treaty set up to promote freer trade among nations. In November 1990 Mexico requested that a GATT panel investigate whether the U.S. embargo and provisions of the MMPA constituted unreasonable restraints of trade. In January 1991, Mexico filed a formal complaint with GATT over the U.S. dolphin regulations. A month later, the U.S. embargo formally went into effect.

GATT was created right after World War II as a way to help regulate world trade. Leaders of the capitalist democracies, all-too-aware of how breakdowns in trade had helped spark the war, felt a multilateral system was needed to create trade rules that all countries would abide by. GATT was intended to lower and harmonize tariffs and import quotas while encouraging investment. As decades passed and successive GATT treaties were signed and ratified by an increasing number of nations, the GATT rules became larger in scope and started to apply to issues seemingly beyond the narrow scope of tariffs and trade. GATT's powers were bolstered by the creation of a dispute panel designed to arbitrate trade disagreements between nations. The dispute panels, however, were not given the ability to enforce their decisions; verdicts would simply constitute approval or disapproval.

The GATT dispute panel charged with reviewing the U.S. tuna embargo first met in March 1991. The panel's decision, released in August of that year, sent a chill through the environmental community.

Concerns about the impact of free trade agreements on environmental standards had been growing among activists for years. Environmentalists complained that the trade agreements favored the interests of investors and corporations over the need to protect the environment. Money values (trade and investment) were being elevated to a higher priority than life values (human rights and the environment). Activists noted that environmental provisions were entirely absent in the growing number of free trade agreements. But until the 1991 GATT ruling on the dolphin issue, those concerns had been largely philosphical. The GATT ruling provided the first real-life proof that trade rules could be used to weaken environmental regulations in the United States and abroad.

Earth Island's Mark Palmer notes:

> This showed to us the power of the free trade juggernaut. We thought, 'If they can do this to dolphins they can do this to anything.' The environmental community has been rushing to catch up and understand how insidious this could be ever since.

The three-member GATT panel, made up of former government trade bureaucrats and business people from the United States and Mexico, ruled that the U.S. embargo and the MMPA regulations violated GATT's free trade rules. The panel's decision said the embargo broke GATT restrictions on any law that attempts to regulate wildlife outside a nation's borders: The United States simply could not mandate other nations to carry observers on their ships. The GATT panel was essentially saying that the U.S. Congress could not require foreign producers to meet the same standard as domestic producers for goods sold in the United States.

In its arguments to the GATT panel, the U.S. trade negotiators tried to counter this argument, pointing out that GATT's own regulations said that nothing in the GATT "should be construed to prevent the adoption of enforcement by any contracting party of measures . . . necessary to protect human, animal, plant life or health . . . relating to the conservation of exhaustible natural resources."[24]

But the GATT arbitrators decided that the U.S. laws and the embargo had not met the standard for "necessary." To meet the qualification for "necessary," the U.S. government would need to exhaust all other alternatives before declaring an embargo. The panel ruled that the United States didn't do this, and that the MMPA regulations and standards lacked "predictability." The GATT decision did, however, uphold the dolphin-safe labeling provisions of the 1990 Dolphin Consumer Information

Act. The labels, the panel ruled, did not constitute a barrier to trade because they were not discriminatory; they simply gave consumers the choice between different production methods.

The GATT panel's central concern with the tuna embargo was that if the U.S. government's arguments were accepted, then any country could ban imports from another country "merely because the exporting country has different environmental, health and social policies from its own." This, the GATT panelists feared, would create a virtually open-ended route for any country to impose trade sanctions unilaterally, and to do so not just to enforce its own laws but to impose its standards on other countries.[25]

Environmentalists had a different fear: that the inability to use national legislation to protect international "commons" like the oceans would lead to a flood of attacks on U.S. environmental regulations. Environmental groups were shocked to realize that the ruling could be used to threaten the validity of other existing policies, including the ban against the import of ivory, laws that regulate the amount of pesticides that can be sprayed on fruits and vegetables coming into the United States, and other sections of the MMPA involving seals and whales. GATT's own lawyers confirmed these fears when they wrote that the ruling illustrated "the limited domain of the environment in trade policy."[26]

Although the GATT ruling set a dangerous precedent as far as environmentalists were concerned, the decision did not immediately affect either the MMPA or the embargo. While the GATT rules contained no mechanism for forcing the United States to comply with the decision, the Mexican government, GATT verdict in hand, could have pressured the Congress to overturn the MMPA. But it decided not to for fear that the dispute could spoil the chances of gaining congressional approval for the then-pending North American Free Trade Agreement (NAFTA). Mexican and U.S. officials worried that the dolphin case, if it went any further, would become a lightning rod for environmentalists' complaints that NAFTA would make Mexico a haven for U.S. polluters.

Mexico instead decided to take steps to reduce dolphin kills by its tuna fleet. Just weeks after the GATT ruling, Mexican President Carlos Salinas de Gortari announced that observers would be allowed on all 46 Mexican tuna boats within three months. He also said his government would fund a program to develop tuna fishing methods that would kill fewer dolphins. Earth Island dismissed the move as "cosmetic," noting that Mexican ships would still continue to encircle dolphin herds.

Still, environmentalists were content that the embargo on Mexican tuna would stay in place. They figured that the Mexican fleet, faced with a closed market in the United States and proposals in the European Parliament to create a European ban on tuna caught by encircling dolphins, would eventually change Mexican practices.

Earth Island's director, David Phillips told a reporter:

> The market for dolphin-unsafe tuna is collapsing. They can't find places to sell the tuna. The U.S. won't buy it; England, France and Germany won't buy it; Thailand won't process it. . . . Some of their last remaining markets . . . have begun to collapse.[27]

NATIONAL LAWS vs. INTERNATIONAL TRADE

In the winter of 1992, tuna fishermen from several nations, government officials, and environmentalists met in La Jolla, California, to find a way to settle the embargo dispute. A compromise was announced in March. The United States agreed to lift the ban on tuna from Venezuela and Mexico (Ecuador and Panama had since changed their fishing practices, so they were no longer affected by the embargo). In exchange for the end of the tuna ban, Mexico and Venezuela agreed to a five-year moratorium on purse-seine fishing in the eastern Pacific beginning in 1994. In the interim period, the embargoed countries would promise to steadily reduce their dolphin kill numbers to pre-1991 levels and allow observers on all their boats. Environmentalists reluctantly accepted the agreement as a way to limit the estimated 50,000 dolphins deaths that were still occurring every year in tuna nets in the eastern Pacific.[28]

That summer, Congress passed the International Dolphin Conservation Act, which fulfilled the U.S. end of the bargain. President Bush signed the bill in early October 1992. It looked as if the impasse was at an end, and, more importantly for environmentalists, that purse-seine fishing in the eastern Pacific would eventually halt. But then in November Mexican officials stunned environmentalists and U.S. government officials by announcing that they had decided to reject the La Jolla agreement. The Mexicans said the moratorium on purse-seine fishing would damage the nation's tuna industry. The embargo, they figured, was better than the net ban. The Mexican Foreign Ministry said at the time:

> Even though the new legislation raises the possibility of lifting the embargo on Mexican tuna, the consequences of the moratorium under the terms provided for in the law would be graver than the embargo currently in effect, in that it would cause a drastic reduction of the Mexican tuna fleet [and] the loss of jobs.[29]

The U.S. embargo against Mexican tuna remained in place.

Right on the heels of Mexico's reversal came another disappointment for environmentalists. A second GATT tribunal had been requested,
this time by the European Union, which was angry about an embargo
against its tuna exports to the United States.

The 1988 MMPA included among its provisions a restriction against
importing tuna from "intermediary nations," that is, countries that bought
and sold tuna from sources that were not verifiably dolphin-safe. This
rule, the so-called Pelly Amendment, required intermediary nations to
prove to the U.S. Commerce Department that they had banned tuna
from countries already banned by the U.S. government. The rule automatically went into effect in the summer of 1991, three months after the
embargo against the tuna fishing nations began. In June of that year the
U.S. Customs office first began requiring a "Tuna Certificate of Origin"
from countries such as Japan, Italy, and Spain which bought tuna from
Mexico and Venezuela and sold it to restaurants and delicatessens in the
United States. An embargo against the intermediary nations was declared by a federal judge in January 1992 in response to a lawsuit filed
by Earth Island.

Earth Island's lawsuit calling for the enforcement of the Pelly Amendment represented an implicit recognition of what tuna fishermen had
been saying for years: that U.S. boycotts would only push countries like
Mexico and Venezuela into selling their tuna catch to other nations. In
asking for the embargo against intermediary nations, environmentalists
hoped to force the Europeans to choose between selling to the U.S.
market or buying from Mexico. If the Europeans decided that their exports to the United States were more valuable, then the Mexican tuna
fleet would have little choice but to stop its purse-seine fishing. But the
Europeans figured they could continue to both buy from the Mexicans
and sell to the United States if they could show, once again, that the
U.S. law was GATT-illegal.

The second GATT panel released its ruling in May 1994. It was once
again ruled that the U.S. embargo against intermediary nations violated
GATT. But the argument of the second panel was different from that of
the first. This time the panel—directly contradicting the earlier decision— said that extraterritorial regulations like those imposed by the
MMPA were legitimate. The panel said the ban on European tuna was
illegal because it broke the GATT rules prohibiting discrimination of a
good based on production methods.[30]

For environmentalists, the new logic was even more threatening than
the old. After all, fundamental complaints about a host of production
methods—from strip-mining to clear-cutting of forests to oil drilling—
were at the heart of the environmental agenda. The ability to discrimi-

nate against certain types of production had always been essential in protecting the environment and in articulating a vision of sustainable development. If restrictions against methods of production were forbidden, it meant that a wide range of conservation laws similar to the MMPA were also at risk.

There was another crucial difference between the first ruling and the second—this time there was a chance that the decision would be enforced. On January 1, 1995, GATT was going to transform into a more powerful body, the World Trade Organization (WTO), which, unlike its predecessor, would have the power to levy sanctions to enforce its rulings. In the wake of the second GATT decision, Mexico started threatening to use the approaching WTO to call for sanctions against the United States unless it repealed the embargo.

The possibility of real trade sanctions began to shift the Washington consensus about dolphin protection. It became increasingly clear that the U.S. laws enacted just years before would have to change. The battle over the proposed changes would lead to a congressional debate that raised the question Mexican and U.S. free trade proponents sought to avoid during the NAFTA negotiations: Who is ultimately responsible for making environmental laws: national legislatures or international trade courts?

"THE DOLPHIN DEATH BILL"
In September 1995, Mexican President Ernesto Zedillo came to Washington to renegotiate the terms of the financial bailout Mexico had received when the peso collapsed less than a year earlier. While in Washington, Zedillo met at the Mexican Embassy with Clinton administration officials, representatives from the Mexican tuna fishing industry, and directors from five mainstream U.S. environmental groups to craft a way to end the embargo on Mexican tuna. During the closed-door talks, Mexico pledged new commitments to reduce, but not halt, dolphin deaths in the eastern Pacific if the U.S. government would overturn the tuna ban. The Mexicans said they would not pursue a WTO challenge against the United States if the existing dolphin-protection laws were changed.[31]

On October 5, the agreement brokered in Washington was formalized by 12 tuna fishing nations at a meeting in Panama. Under the so-called Panama Declaration, the tuna fishing countries pledged to reduce dolphin deaths toward zero, implement strategies for more sustainable tuna fishing and the protection of juvenile tuna schools, and provide incentives for fishermen who don't kill dolphins. In contrast to the La Jolla agreement of 1992, the declaration did not prohibit the encirclement of dolphins. The Panama Declaration permitted purse-seine fishing so long as onboard observers certified that no dolphins drowned during the netting. The observers would be supplied by the Inter-American Tropical Tuna Commission (IATTC), a non-governmental organization that would also enforce the other elements of the new plan.

The Panama Declaration did not represent a binding agreement. It merely called for negotiations to be established to create a binding agreement based on the pledges made in Panama. Final negotiations depended on the U.S. government first ending the tuna embargo.

On December 5, Senator Ted Stevens, an Alaskan Republican, and Senator John Breaux introduced to the U.S. Senate legislation based on the Panama Declaration. Congressman Don Young, another Republican from Alaska, sponsored the House law.

Congressional bills HR2823 (the House version) and SB1420 (the Senate bill) immediately opened a rift in the environmental community. The five organizations who had helped craft the Panama Declaration during the meeting at the Mexican Embassy in Washington—Greenpeace, the Environmental Defense Fund, the National Wildlife Federation, the Center for Marine Conservation, and the World Wildlife Fund—supported the change in the law. They argued that the embargo was no longer working since tuna boats from countries such as Mexico and Venezuela were continuing to catch fish using purse-seine methods. A better solution than the embargo's stick, the five organizations agreed, would be a carrot to reward countries that adopted better fishing methods. Greenpeace and the other organizations feared that if the embargo continued much longer, the foreign fleets would leave the monitoring program established by the La Jolla agreement, and dolphin deaths would start to climb again. The five groups, noting that the existing 1990 law affected only one fishery (the Eastern Tropical Pacific), and only one kind of fishing technique (dolphin encirclement), felt that the voluntary international enforcement mechanisms created by the new law could set a precedent for other fishery agreements around the world.

Earth Island—along with 85 other environmental groups, including the U.S. Humane Society, the Sierra Club, and Friends of the Earth—strongly disagreed. They said that allowing dolphin encirclement would make the dolphin-safe label meaningless. Calling tuna caught by dolphin encirclement "dolphin-safe" would amount to "consumer fraud," these groups argued, since many dolphins that escape from the nets die later from injuries or stress. Earth Island and its allies noted that while the Panama Declaration contained a "pledge" to reduce dolphin deaths to zero, it allowed for fishing fleets to kill up to 5,000 dolphins a year, far more than the 3,000 dolphins that observers estimated died just the year before. The bill, then, would actually permit an increase in dolphin deaths. Earth Island and others also said that the voluntary enforcement policies established in the Panama Declaration were weak and unworkable, and noted that the IATTC had never in its 10-year history levied a fine against a member nation for killing dolphins.[32]

As the legislation headed for a vote in the House, Earth Island launched a grassroots lobbying campaign against the bill, which it had labeled the "Dolphin Death Bill." The group organized congressional call-in days and ran advertisements laying out the arguments against the bill in *The New York Times* and *The Washington Times*. Student groups around the country organized demonstrations against the "death bill." And once again, Hollywood came to Earth Island's aid. James Bond star Pierce Brosnan taped a public service announcement urging citizens to call their representatives and tell them to vote against the legislation. Nearly 70 Hollywood personalities, including Tom Hanks, Sean Connery, and Sharon Stone, signed a letter to President Clinton asking him to reverse the administration's position.

Consumer groups and other citizens' organizations that had fought NAFTA joined in opposition to the legislation for broader philosophical reasons. They feared the bill would set a terrible precedent if the U.S. government changed one of its laws because of pressure from the WTO. Passage of the law would constitute a betrayal of the democratic process for the sake of global trade, these groups argued. In her testimony before a congressional committee considering HR2823, Lori Wallach, a policy analyst from Public Citizen's Global Trade Watch, outlined the concerns of the Citizens Trade Campaign, an umbrella organization made up of hundreds of groups opposed to the free trade status quo. Overturning the provisions of the earlier dolphin-protection laws because an international trade court disagreed with the U.S. regulations would represent a blow to national sovereignty, she warned. Wallach told the legislators:

> In considering these bills. This committee is not only deciding whether and how the United States will protect dolphins, but also how the U.S. Congress will relate to the orders of the WTO concerning U.S. domestic policy. . . . What is at stake here is who decides U.S. domestic policy. . . . In considering your position on the two bills offered, I urge you to consider: What law will be attacked next by the World Trade Organization? Maybe it will be something for which you have fought for decades and about which you deeply care.

This case was the first one that made GATT known to the American public. It was this real life example that brought home the threat that seemed inconceivable: an unaccountable bureaucracy in another country telling the U.S. Congress to kill a U.S. domestic law or pay sanctions to maintain it.[33]

Even the tuna industry came out against the proposed law. This was largely due to continued consumer pressure: Each time Earth Island sponsored a congressional call-in day, the group also urged its supporters to contact the tuna companies directly and demand that they maintain the existing dolphin-safe definition. The industry's opposition to changing the laws came from simple self-interest: Having already been burned by consumer outrage before, the tuna companies had no interest in risking their good name for a reform that would mean very little to them. "I believe the [dolphin-safe] definition should not be changed in the absence of consensus of scientists and public opinion," Heinz chief O'Reilly said.[34]

But in the end, the vote in the House wasn't even close. HR2823 passed in an overwhelming bipartisan vote, 320 to 108. The debate now moved to the Senate.

As the congressional battle shifted to the Senate, disagreement among environmental groups became increasingly vitriolic. Finger pointing in newspaper articles was common, and attack ads in the liberal weekly magazine, *The Nation* started to appear. Earth Island labeled the organizations supporting the bill the "Slaughterhouse Five." There were hints that directors at Greenpeace were more interested in securing positions in the Clinton administration than saving the dolphins. In response, Greenpeace suggested that Earth Island was motivated by "hundreds of thousands of dollars from StarKist, Bumble Bee and other tuna companies." Even though Earth Island does not accept corporate donations, and it does not appear that any Greenpeace directors later took jobs with the Clinton administration, each side came out of the fight looking bad.[35]

The environmental community's infighting didn't distract the two Senators who were bent on defeating the legislation—Barbara Boxer and Joseph Biden, the sponsors of the 1990 dolphin protection law. Working diligently to sway their colleagues, the senators offered alternative legislation that showed the United States could resolve the trade dispute while still guaranteeing the integrity of the dolphin-safe label. Their bill would remove the embargo on tuna fishing nations while maintaining restrictions on individual vessels that caught their tuna by dolphin encirclement.

The appeals of Boxer and Biden worked. On October 3, the legislation's sponsors withdrew the bill, recognizing that Boxer and

Biden had at least 40 senators on their side, enough to mount a filibuster. The dolphin-safe label would continue to mean that no dolphins had been encircled during the tuna catch. The embargo stayed in place.

VICTORIES ARE NEVER FINAL

Congress did eventually pass legislation that reversed earlier U.S. laws and ended the embargo. In August 1997, after another bruising political battle, Congress approved and President Clinton signed a law that halted the embargo against Mexico, Venezuela, and other countries while keeping the original definition of "dolphin-safe" to mean tuna had not been caught using purse-seine methods. Foreign fleets would be able to sell as much tuna to the United States as they liked, but they would not get to use the coveted dolphin-safe label. The law, however, gave the U.S. Secretary of Commerce the ability, after a two-year review, to redefine the label if it could be demonstrated that dolphins were not significantly harmed by being chased or caught in the nets and then released.

During the 1997 congressional fight, Earth Island again did all it could to defeat the legislation, for the second time branding legislation the "dolphin death bill." The group's efforts succeeded in gaining nearly 60 new votes in the House from the first vote. But Mexico's continuing threats to file a WTO complaint—coupled with Mexican and Venezuelan threats to abandon the Panama Declaration, a move some legislators called "environmental blackmail"—broke the Senate opposition.

The activists at Earth Island were satisfied, if not happy, with the final arrangement.

"We simply didn't have the support to beat the second bill," says Earth Island's Palmer.

> It was a compromise we would have rather not made. Still, the issue wasn't the embargo; it was the strength of the dolphin-safe guarantee. We knew people would not buy dolphin-unsafe tuna.

The environmental groups had to trust that consumers would avoid tuna without the dolphin-safe label and that those cans would sit stranded on store shelves. In the long run, foreign fleets would respond to the lost sales.

But in the spring of 1999, U.S. Commerce Secretary William Daley ordered a loosening of the dolphin-safe label definition to allow the encirclement of dolphins. For the seventh time, Earth Island took the United States to court. The group, using numbers supplied by the NMFS, showed that dolphin populations in the eastern Pacific had still not recovered from the decades of killing. For four years, the issue seesawed between government and Earth Island appeals. Then, in early 2003, the Bush administration loosened the standards and allowed tuna caught by encirclement methods to carry the dolphin-safe label.[36]

The lesson for activists in the dolphin-tuna struggle is similar to the lesson of the tobacco struggle covered in the next chapter: Perseverance and a long-term vision are essential when battling large corporations and the politicians they rent. Looking back on more than a decade of political struggles on the dolphins' behalf, Mark Palmer says he is reminded of an old saying from David Brower, the former head of the Sierra Club and founder of Friends of the Earth and Earth Island: "Conservation victories are never final. We never win. We always have to come back to fight the old battles."

4

UP IN SMOKE
Tobacco Profits vs. Public Health

ON MAY 12, 1994, STANTON GLANTZ, a researcher at the University of California, San Francisco School of Medicine and a longtime foe of the tobacco industry, received an anonymous package containing nearly 4,000 pages of what appeared to be tobacco company papers. The documents dated from the early 1950s to the early 1980s and consisted largely of internal memoranda of Brown & Williamson Tobacco, the third largest seller of cigarettes in the United States. Many of the pages were marked "confidential" or "privileged." The return address on the box was simply "Mr. Butts," the name of Gary Trudeau's allegorical Doonesbury cartoon character.[1]

Just days before, *The New York Times* had published a front-page story, "Tobacco Company Was Silent on Hazards," based on much of the same material delivered to Professor Glantz. The documents revealed that executives at Brown & Williamson, along with the chiefs of the other major tobacco corporations, had known since at least 1963 that cigarette smoking causes cancer and is addictive, facts later confirmed by the U.S. Surgeon General. The papers also provided a glimpse into how the tobacco industry had spent three decades trying to withhold those facts from smokers and government regulators and how the industry had manipulated public opinion to question the hard science about smoking's dangers. What for years had seemed obvious to anti-tobacco activists like Professor Glantz was now bolstered by hard proof: The major corporations that dominate the U.S. cigarette market had deliberately deceived the American public for decades about the nature and effects of the product they sell.

The company memos sent to Professor Glantz—which were later placed in his university's library and eventually on the Internet—would be crucial in making the case that the tobacco industry owed a major debt to the American people for the health disaster it had knowingly wrought. Those leaked documents would become as essential to the antismoking movement in the United States as the Pentagon Papers had been for opponents of the Vietnam war a generation earlier.

During the next several years, a steady drip-drop of similar revelations would destroy whatever credibility the cigarette makers once enjoyed. Private lawsuits, legal action by state attorneys general, and defections by industry whistle-blowers would succeed in prying loose tens of thousands of other pages of industry documents that showed how the corporations manipulated cigarettes to make them more addictive, targeted their marketing at children, undermined studies showing the dangers of smoking, and, in general, did everything they could to ensure that nothing would get in their way to make a profit.

The revelations of corporate deception spurred a seismic shift in public sentiment: People who once believed that smokers were to blame for their illness suddenly felt that the cigarette corporations should pay for the health costs of smoking. And that swing in popular opinion in turn energized legal and political efforts to hold the industry responsible for its perjurious past. During the 1990s, the once-untouchable tobacco industry saw its power threatened by a host of foes. In just a few years, public pressure forced a gigantic industry to admit to damning accusations and to compromise with critics once dismissed out-of-hand. In the end, the cigarette makers were compelled to agree to the largest legal settlement in U.S. history and a number of restrictions on their business practices. The industry narrowly avoided even tighter oversight, but only after spending tens of millions of dollars to defend itself.

The anti-tobacco forces represented an unlikely collection of allies. Veteran corporate accountability activists, longtime public health advocates, flashy trial lawyers, government bureaucrats, and attorneys general from both major parties came together in the 1990s to challenge a powerful industry. Ultimately, it was that combination of legal aggressiveness, grassroots energy, and government activism that chopped away at the reputation and profits of the cigarette makers. The tobacco industry's own cynicism and hubris also contributed to its woes.

Many of the individuals who played key roles in weakening the tobacco industry are not the sorts of people profiled in the other struggles detailed in this book. The Republican attorneys general, wealthy plaintiffs attorneys, and former corporate executives who helped drive the anti-tobacco struggle don't display the kind of anti-corporate consciousness found among the activists who fought against sweatshops. That makes their passion and determination all the more compelling. It shows that the basic values underlying the corporate accountability movement are not necessarily radical.

The tobacco companies committed the one crime that in the eyes of the American people makes for an unpardonable sin: They lied. The backlash against the tobacco industry offers important lessons about corporations' basic weaknesses. Any company that has ever deceived the public about its practices is vulnerable to the same kind of revolt the tobacco companies suffered.

But while the tobacco struggle reveals the depth of public suspicion about corporations, it also proves how even the most impressive achievements can fall short of larger goals. Even as the cigarette makers found their names becoming synonymous with fraud and immorality, they were able to forestall government action that would have led to lasting reforms. Deep pockets, the tobacco industry showed once again, can deflect the deepest public animosities.

The tobacco saga also reveals the limitations of national action in an era of corporate globalization. Long before activists in this country were able to mount a serious challenge to the tobacco industry's impunity, the cigarette corporations were shifting their attention to overseas markets. The anti-tobacco activists did an impressive job of shifting the public debate in the United States about tobacco use. But the transnational cigarette corporations know that shift means very little to their ability to continue making a killing in countries around the world. And, in fact, the victories achieved in the United States may even have contributed to larger, international defeats.

"Tremendous progress has been made," says Professor Glantz. "There's been a sea change. But the cigarette companies are still out there, and they're still very wealthy and powerful. ... The tobacco companies are like the Borg in 'Star Trek'—they adapt to whatever you attack them with."

TOBACCO'S DEEP ROOTS

Tobacco was first cultivated by the Indigenous peoples of America in the first century b.c., who smoked the weed on special political or religious occasions. Smoking became an international phenomenon in the 16th century after the Europeans brought the pipe back to Europe. Since then, smoking has spread to every corner of the globe. Today an estimated 1.1 billion people worldwide, or a sixth of all humanity, smoke. Cigarettes—the most popular form of ingesting tobacco—are one of the best-known and widely distributed products on the planet.[2]

The most obvious explanation for the spread and popularity of cigarettes is their addictiveness. Ninety percent of people who smoke cigarettes are addicts. By comparison, only about 10 percent of people who drink alcohol develop a compulsion to drink.

Tobacco plants contain the chemical nicotine, which, like morphine and cocaine, is a powerful drug. The odd thing about nicotine is that it acts as both a stimulant and a sedative when it reaches the brain. When the body's adrenal glands get a dose of nicotine, they release adrenaline. But when taken in large quantities, nicotine begins to block the chemical messages that the body is sending, and thus has a calming effect on the smoker.[3]

This combination of effects has made the cigarette the pacifier of the modern age. A smoke serves as both reward and consolation. It is made for the party and for quiet, lonely contemplation. For the smoker, the cigarette both fills time and slows its passage. It is the very definition of instant gratification.[4]

All of this, of course, makes for great business. The mix of addiction and intangible attraction has built one of the largest industries in history. It's easy to turn a profit when you're selling the opiate of the masses.

Tobacco's influence on the U.S. economy is huge. Every year Americans spend about $55 billion on cigarettes, more than on clothes for their children ($26.9 billion) or trips to the dentist ($45.8 billion). Tobacco is the country's sixth biggest crop and one of its most profitable: Farmers earn $4,000 an acre compared with $400 an acre for strawberries.[5] An estimated 142,000 workers are involved in the growing of tobacco, underpinning the economies of several U.S. states. Another 42,000 people earn their living from actually rolling and manufacturing cigarettes. And then there is the advertising: $5 billion a year's worth and tens of thousands of other jobs. Philip Morris alone spends $165 million annually on sponsoring museum shows, sporting events, and concerts. All together, the tobacco industry accounts for about 2 percent of all jobs in the United States. Even if the number were half that, the industry's clout would be awesome.[6]

But sales in the United States account for just a portion of U.S. cigarette corporations' business. Smoking rates in the United States have been declining since the mid-1960s. Smokers outside the United States spend approximately $300 billion a year on cigarettes. That means that worldwide smokers pay at least $350 billion annually (some estimates go as high as $400 billion) to feed their habit. Most of those sales go to just a handful of corporations.

The global tobacco industry is essentially a cartel. When people say "Big Tobacco," they are talking about four companies that control nearly the entire market: Philip Morris, RJ Reynolds, Brown & Williamson (owned by a London-based parent company, British-American Tobacco), and Lorillard. Globally, the largest transnational companies are Philip Morris and British-American Tobacco (BAT). In many nations, the largest competitor of the transnationals is a government-owned monopoly. For example, almost every smoker in China buys their cigarettes from the government's tobacco monopoly. Today, more than three-fourths of all the cigarettes in the world are made by just five companies.

The biggest commercial tobacco company in the world is Philip Morris. The corporation's popular Marlboro cigarette is the world's best-selling brand, with almost 9 percent of the world market. Along with its other brands such as Parliaments and Benson & Hedges, the company controls 50 percent of the U.S. market and almost one-fifth of worldwide sales, earning close to $50 billion a year from tobacco. The company also owns Miller Brewing and Kraft General Foods, the maker of Kool-Aid and other well-known products. But cigarettes, which account for two-thirds of company earnings, still form the heart of the business, and the company has distinguished itself among the tobacco giants by being the brashest defender against activist attacks.[7]

For decades, British-American Tobacco dominated the international cigarette trade, and it was only in 1996 that Philip Morris overtook it. With operations in more than 160 countries, BAT controls 16 percent of the international market. In 1999, it sold more than $30 billion worth of cigarettes. BAT is the parent company of the U.S. manufacturer Brown & Williamson Tobacco, which markets Kents and Lucky Strikes.

RJ Reynolds (RJR) was the largest U.S. tobacco company for much of the 20th century, relying mostly on the popularity of its Camel brands. But ever since Marlboros took off in the 1950s, RJR has struggled behind Philip Morris as the country's second largest cigarette seller. Still, the company's Camel, Winston, and Salem brands account for nearly $8 billion in yearly sales.

The other two major cigarette producers aren't companies at all, but countries: China and Japan. Although the formerly state-run Japan Tobacco has been a public company since 1994, it still is a monopoly, controlling more than 80 percent of the market in a country with the second highest per capita smoking rate in the world. In 1999, Japan Tobacco bought RJR's international division for $7.8 billion, giving it almost one-tenth of the world market and $30 billion in annual sales.

China National Tobacco is the largest of the big five in terms of customers but the smallest in terms of revenues. The government-controlled agency produces one out of every three cigarettes smoked in the world, but because tobacco prices in China are so low it brings in just $23 million a year. Still, its control of the massive Chinese market means that the agency is quite influential.[8]

All of these sales translate into massive profits for the tobacco companies. Cigarettes are an extremely lucrative business. Regardless of whether the economy is in a boom or a bust, there are always people in need of a smoke. Cigarette makers enjoy profit margins of 40 to 50 percent: twice as profitable as other consumer products business.

THE BREATH OF DEATH

While cigarette marketing is highly profitable, it is also deadly. Cigarettes are uniquely addictive, and they are also unique in that they are the only consumer product that, when used as intended, kill the user. Smoking tobacco is the most effective way for a person to get a nicotine rush. But that rush is one of the most lethal inventions in history.

Tobacco smoke contains about 4,000 different compounds, including poisons such as carbon monoxide, arsenic, cyanide, formaldehyde, and lead. When consumed regularly for years, tobacco smoke can lead to some 25 diseases. Smoking is the leading cause of lung cancer and a major source of heart disease. It is responsible for a host of other chronic lung diseases and an assortment of other cancers, and it contributes to tens of thousands of deadly strokes each year. Maternal smoking is associated with a higher risk of miscarriage, lower birth weight, and slower child development. Parental smoking contributes to sudden infant death syndrome and higher rates of child respiratory illnesses such as asthma.

On average, about 50 percent of lifetime smokers can expect to die from a tobacco-related illness. Every cigarette is said to take an average of seven minutes off a smoker's life, and a lifelong smoker will lose an average of 22 years from his or her life expectancy.[9]

Tobacco smoke even harms nonsmokers who merely happen to be around smokers. The thousands of chemicals in tobacco smoke, many of them carcinogenic, affect nonsmokers just as they do smokers, and sometimes in even worse ways. "Secondhand smoke" contributes to lung and heart diseases in nonsmokers, and people exposed to tobacco smoke as children are at greater risk of contracting lung cancer. According to the Environmental Protection Agency, secondhand smoke contributes to approximately 52,000 deaths a year.[10]

That number is just a fraction of the total deaths caused by smoking in the United States every year. Tobacco is the number one preventable cause of death: Smoking-related illnesses claim the lives of 420,000 smokers in the United States annually. This toll exceed the deaths from alcohol abuse, AIDS, traffic accidents, homicides, and suicides combined.[11]

Worldwide, smoking kills 3.5 million people annually, accounting for about 7 percent of all deaths, according to the World Health Organization. That number is expected to grow in coming decades as more and more people in the developing world take up the habit. The WHO estimates that by 2020, tobacco will cause 17.7 percent of all deaths in the developing world and 10 percent of deaths in the industrialized nations. Within a generation, smoking-related illnesses are likely to surpass infectious diseases as the leading threat to human health.

ROOTS OF OPPOSITION

For nearly as long as smoking has been popular, there have been people dedicated to pointing out tobacco's dangers and arguing against its use. Even as smoking became an aristocratic fad in 17th century England, the nation's monarch, King James I, blasted the "stinking" habit and levied a 4,000 percent tax on tobacco. In China, tobacco traffickers were decapitated. The Mogul emperor of Hindustan ordered that smokers should have their lips slit. In Russia, smokers could be sentenced to death or exile in Siberia. And in the Ottoman Empire smokers and tobacco traders faced losing their noses or ears. Over time, however, official sanctions on smoking eroded as rulers realized that their peoples' addictions could bolster national treasuries through tobacco taxes.

While many governments frowned on smoking in its earliest years, opposition in the United States was slow to take off. During colonial times, tobacco cultivation was central to the export economies of many southern slave states. But in the late 19th century, an anti-tobacco movement closely aligned with the temperance crusaders began to gain strength. As smoking rates climbed with the introduction of the mass-produced cigarette, tobacco foes started battling to prevent children from smoking. By 1890, foreshadowing initiatives a century later, 26 states had passed laws banning cigarette sales to minors.[12]

The country, however, continued to smoke, and in skyrocketing numbers. Tens of thousands of men took up the habit during World War I as the army included cigarettes in each soldier's rations. Before and after the war, mass advertising campaigns successfully urged millions more to begin buying cigarettes: Per capita smoking doubled between 1911 and 1916. One brand, RJ Reynold's Camel, gained more than 10 percent of the market in a single year largely from the cleverness of an advertising campaign equating the new cigarette with worldliness. Advertising also played an essential role in getting women to smoke. Advertisements for Lucky Strikes suggested to women that smoking would help them stay thin. Cigarette marketing aimed at women also tapped into women's aspirations for equality. The strategies worked. Between 1924 and 1931, the smoking rate among women tripled, to 14 percent.[13]

During the 1920s and 1930s, new desires for cigarettes were manufactured as the cigarette became a central prop of Hollywood films and smoking took on an aura of sophistication. During World War II, smoking's macho image was further reinforced when the U.S. Army once again supplied cigarettes to all its soldiers. By the 1950s, more than half the U.S. population smoked.

But Big Tobacco's halcyon wouldn't last for long. The industry suffered its first serious public relations defeat in 1952 when *Reader's Di-*

gest published an article, "Cancer by the Carton," which summarized the scientific research on the subject. For the first time the mainstream press was suggesting that the dangers in smoking had been withheld from the public, and the article prompted widespread worries about the links between smoking and cancer. Within just one year, from 1952 to 1953, cigarette sales fell by 8 percent.

The tobacco corporations realized they may be in trouble. Their own internal research had concluded that cigarettes have carcinogenic properties, and now health concerns were beginning to infect their consumers. On December 15, 1953, senior executives from the major tobacco companies gathered at the Plaza Hotel in Manhattan to chart a strategy for dealing with what they called the "health question." The executives and their propaganda consultants agreed to sponsor a "public relations campaign which is positive in nature and entirely 'pro-cigarettes.'" The meeting ended with an agreement by the tobacco companies to establish a group to get its message out to the public, the Tobacco Industry Research Committee, which in 1958 became the Council for Tobacco Research.[14] A political lobbying arm for the industry, the Tobacco Institute, was also formed around that time.

The December 1953 meeting in New York and the establishment of a public relations front group designed to debunk health concerns marked the beginning of Big Tobacco's counteroffensive. The industry had to contend with scientific evidence that, if accepted by the public, would certainly cut into its profits. Through a combination of skilled legal, political, and public relations tactics, the tobacco companies would try to dissemble hard science, deceive people about what they knew, and sow confusion about who was responsible for the mounting death toll.

The industry and its front groups would have their work cut out for them. During the next generation, evidence linking smoking to disease would continue to mount.

In January 1964, Surgeon General Luther L. Terry released a 387-page report demonstrating that smoking did, in fact, "contribute substantially to mortality from certain specific diseases and to the overall death rate." The report's researchers found a causal link between smoking and cancer, and said that the death rate for smokers was 70 percent higher than for nonsmokers. The report concluded: "Cigarette smoking is a health hazard of sufficient importance in the United States to warrant appropriate remedial action."[15]

The industry dismissed the findings. The Tobacco Institute said the report hardly constituted the last word in the health debate. A director of the Philip Morris board replied, "We don't accept the idea that there are harmful agents in tobacco." If these people truly believed what they were saying, then they hadn't read the industry's own internal research. In 1956, an RJR chemist had written that it was "well established" that cigarette smoke contains carcinogenic compounds. By 1957, BAT had recognized a causal relationship between cancer and smoking.[16]

But, despite the industry's best efforts, the public wasn't entirely fooled. The Surgeon General's report energized anti-tobacco forces and led to federal legislation. In 1966, the U.S. government placed a health warning on all packs of cigarettes which read, "Caution: Cigarette Smoking May Be Hazardous to Your Health." The cigarette corporations, at first enraged by what they saw as the government forcing them to disparage their own products, eventually put up only token opposition to the warnings. Ultimately, Big Tobacco's all-too-savvy attorneys noted, a warning would help insulate the companies from litigation. The warning would allow the cigarette manufacturers to argue that smokers were fully aware of the risks before they began smoking.

The industry suffered another setback in 1971, when the Federal Trade Commission banned tobacco advertising on television. At that time, an average American saw an estimated 800 cigarette commercials every year. At first, the broadcast and tobacco industries fought the proposed rules. Then the cigarette companies did an about-face. Concerned with the growing antismoking sentiments among the public and Congress, Big Tobacco volunteered to stop advertising on television, but on the condition that new cigarette warning labels wouldn't use the dreaded C-word, cancer. The industry made concessions to avoid more serious government regulation.

In any case, giving up TV advertising made good business sense. By the 1960s, the industry was spending 80 percent of its ad budget on television. The loss of TV ended up padding the companies' profits as advertising expenditures went down.[17]

During the 1970s, a grassroots anti-tobacco movement started to grow and to achieve real gains at the local and state levels through nonsmoking laws. In 1973, Arizona became the first state to pass a law restricting smoking in public places. A Scottsdale nurse, Betty Carnes, generated public support for the law by passing out thousands of "Thank You for Not Smoking" signs. In that same year, smoking was restricted on airline flights—marking the first federal restriction on smoking—at the urging of Ralph Nader's "raiders." Major corporations, starting with the aircraft manufacturer Boeing, began to ban smoking in the workplace. In 1977, the first "Great American Smoke-Out" occurred.

Slowly, Americans' health attitudes were changing, and so were their opinions about smoking. Once an acceptable habit almost any place and any time, smoking was increasingly becoming an antisocial habit.

Still, the industry's strategy of denial seemed to be working. Smoking rates continued to decline, but not as rapidly as they had in the year immediately following the Surgeon General's 1964 report. In 1981, a third of the U.S. public was still smoking.

In that same year, however, Big Tobacco saw the arrival of a new and especially passionate adversary—C. Everett Koop, Ronald Reagan's Surgeon General. For the tobacco industry, as for American business as a whole, Reagan's time in office was a golden age of hands-off *laissez-faire* policy. The administration was filled with free-market fundamentalists who believed that government regulation "interfered" with the magic of the marketplace. Agencies designed to protect consumers, such as the FTC and antitrust division of the Justice Department, saw their budgets slashed. Corporate America and the cigarette corporations were given free rein to follow their conviction that their own financial well-being was more important than any other interest, including the health of their own customers.

In this atmosphere, Dr. Koop quickly realized that there was a huge gap between what he could say and what he would actually be allowed to do, and so he converted his position into a bully pulpit and used his post like no one else had before him. He became the country's number one antismoking crusader and, largely through the use of the Surgeon General's annual report, placed the tobacco issue squarely on the national agenda. Koop displayed a masterly command of the media. With his goatee and epaulets—he donned a uniform to give himself an air of authority—he might have appeared something of an eccentric, but he grabbed the public's attention unlike any of his predecessors.

In 1982, upon the release of his first report, Koop declared smoking "the most important public health issue of our time," and said cigarettes were "the chief, single, avoidable cause of death in our society." In May 1984, during an address at the annual meeting of the American Lung Association, he challenged the country to become smoke-free by 2000. Koop called the industry a "sleazy outfit" and said it deserved scorn for flaunting "its ability to buy its way into the marketplace of ideas and pollute it with its false and deadly information."[18]

Koop also drove the science behind smoking into new areas. The Surgeon General's 1986 report focused on the effects of environmental tobacco smoke—commonly known as secondhand smoke—and concluded that "involuntary smoking is a cause of disease, including cancer, in healthy nonsmokers." In 1988 the Surgeon General went after another tobacco industry shibboleth—the claim that cigarettes are not addictive. Koop's 1988 report declared that the pharmacological properties of cigarettes "are similar to . . . drugs such as heroin and cocaine."

During the 1980s, the tobacco industry's clout in Congress and in the Reagan administration stalled any attempts at federal government regulation. Nevertheless, Big Tobacco knew the Koop reports were hurting their public image. Suddenly it was common knowledge that smoking caused cancer and contributed to other diseases.

A 1982 memo written by a Philip Morris researcher reveals the siege mentality caused by Koop's crusade.

> This company is in trouble. The cigarette industry is in trouble. If we are to survive as a viable commercial enterprise, we must act now to develop responses to smoking and health allegations from both the private and government sectors. The antismoking forces are out to bury us. . . . Let's face facts: Cigarette smoke is biologically active. Nicotine is a potent pharmacological agent. Every toxicologist, physiologist, medical doctor and most chemists know it. It's not a secret.[19]

It may not have been a secret, but, despite these internal admissions, the industry maintained its spin that smoking had not been proven to be either dangerous or addictive. In the wake of the Surgeon General's 1982 report, a representative from the Council for Tobacco Research testified before a congressional committee claining that cigarette smoking had not been scientifically established to be a cause of chronic diseases, such as cancer, cardiovascular disease, or emphysema. After Dr. Koop declared nicotine addictive, the industry replied that the Surgeon General's report "runs counter to common sense, as proved by the fact that people can and do quit smoking when they make the decision."[20]

For a quarter of a century, lies such as these had worked. The cigarette corporations, unlike any other industry, had been able to forestall government regulation, rebuff any and all legal challenges, and keep pressure for reform at bay. But that would change within just a few years of Koop's 1989 departure from his post. In the 1990s, a combination of government activism, legal creativity, and citizen action would create a massive anti-tobacco backlash. Ultimately, Big Tobacco's own once-effective machinations of deception would prove its greatest weakness. The industry's decades of victories would turn out to be pyrrhic.

UNREGULATED NICOTINE

The first serious attack on Big Tobacco's privilege came from an unlikely quarter: the federal bureaucracy. By the 1990s, the tobacco industry was the only industry of its size without any public review of the manufacture and sale of its products (the restrictions on broadcast advertising being the only real regulation). In fact, the public didn't even know the exact ingredients that went into cigarettes.

Big Tobacco had avoided government oversight through sheer political power. When Congress passed the 1916 Pure Food and Drug Act, in response to concerns over the kinds of dangerous food processing chronicled in Upton Sinclair's *The Jungle*, tobacco was excluded from the new rules. The industry argued that tobacco was neither a food nor a drug, and Members of Congress, responsive to the might of the tobacco baron Buck Duke, agreed. When government powers were expanded in 1938 under the Food, Drug, and Cosmetic Act, tobacco was again left off the list of regulated products. The 1966 law that put health warnings on cigarette packs went out of its way to prevent the Food and Drug Administration from requiring a different or additional warning.

In the 1970s and 1980s, anti-tobacco activists started urging the FDA to take steps to regulate cigarettes. It was ludicrous, the activists noted, that cigarettes—which are subject to heavier processing, more additives, and more toxins than any other product on the market—should be beyond public oversight. In response to this pressure, the FDA said that it had no jurisdiction over tobacco products because Congress had never mandated such powers. And FDA officials resisted taking even limited steps because they feared that challenging such a politically protected industry as tobacco would incur the wrath of pro-tobacco legislators and lead to agency budget cuts.

The sentiment at the FDA began to change in 1990, when President George H.W. Bush appointed 39-year-old David Kessler to head the administration. When Kessler, both a lawyer and a doctor, took over the FDA, morale was in shambles, the victim of a decade of Republican administrations' anti-regulatory policies. At first Kessler was too busy with other issues to tackle the nagging tobacco issue. But with the encouragement of some FDA veterans, Kessler decided to assemble a team of scientists and lawyers to explore whether, and how, the FDA could oversee the tobacco industry.

Kessler and his colleagues understood that the key to regulating the cigarette corporations wasn't tobacco, it was nicotine. The FDA would have to prove that cigarette makers intended to addict people. Unfortunately for the FDA officials, they didn't have that proof, though the fact that the cigarette companies had never tried to remove nicotine from tobacco bolstered their suspicions.

The FDA's tobacco control efforts were given life when Bill Clinton took over from Bush and decided to leave Kessler in his post. Kessler and his colleagues now knew they would have some political space to challenge tobacco. But the agency still needed proof of intent.

The first proof came on January 20, 1994, when two FDA officials spent several hours questioning a former RJR manager turned whistle-blower. The informant, code named "Deep Cough," told the FDA investigators that RJR had for years manipulated the nicotine level in cigarettes through the use of "reconstituted tobacco." That is, the company was taking the useless stems and scraps of the tobacco plants, adding a solvent to the by-product to extract condensed nicotine, and then spraying the concentrate onto the paper sheets used to roll cigarettes.

"We were told never to use the word 'nicotine,'" Deep Cough told the investigators. "We called it either 'impact' or 'satisfaction.' One of the company lawyers told me never to use the word 'nicotine,' because that could open us up to regulation by the FDA."[21]

On February 25, Kessler and the FDA announced plans to begin drafting rules for regulating nicotine. The announcement came in a letter to the Coalition on Smoking or Health, an anti-tobacco group. In the letter, Kessler said the Coalition's petitions were not far-reaching enough. "The focus should be on the presence of nicotine in cigarettes," Kessler wrote. "Evidence brought to our attention is accumulating that suggests that cigarette manufacturers may intend that their products contain nicotine to satisfy an addiction on the part of some of their customers."[22]

Three days after the FDA's announcement, the ABC investigative program *Day One* aired a segment featuring Deep Cough that had been in the works for months. The show accused the tobacco corporations of "spiking" cigarettes to keep their customers hooked. The Deep Cough revelations blew an irreparable whole in Big Tobacco's best and longest-standing defense—namely, that smokers themselves were responsible for any harm they had inflicted on their health. If the cigarette makers were manipulating nicotine levels, that meant they had worked to keep smokers addicted to their products, and therefore they were guilty of deliberately damaging public health.

The FDA announcement and the *Day One* accusations grabbed front page headlines around the country. Although the tobacco companies had been prepared for the *Day One* broadcast, they were completely caught off-guard by the FDA move.

Congressman Henry Waxman (D-CA) called hearings to explore the tobacco spiking charges and to consider the FDA announcement. A former smoker, Waxman was one of the most ardent congressional foes of tobacco, and for a decade he been spurring public debate about the issue and prying loose bits of industry information. On April 14, Waxman called the CEOs from the country's seven major tobacco companies to testify before the House Subcommittee on Health and the Environment.

During the six hours of hearings, Waxman and his colleagues questioned the executives about addiction, nicotine, and cancer. At one point

Congressman Ron Wyden of Oregon grabbed the microphone and asked the witnesses a point-blank question.

Wyden: "Let me ask you first, and I'd like to just go down the row, whether each of you believes that nicotine is not addictive."

William Campbell, head of Philip Morris, responded first: "I believe nicotine is not addictive, yes."

"Congressmen, cigarettes and nicotine clearly do not meet the classic definitions of addiction," said James Johnston of RJR.

Joseph Taddeo, U.S. Tobacco (a chewing tobacco manufacturer): "I don't believe nicotine or our products are addicting."

Edward Horrigan, president of Liggett: "I believe nicotine is not addictive."

Thomas Sandefur, head of Brown & Williamson: "I believe nicotine is not addictive."

Donald Johnston, American Tobacco: "And I, too, believe that nicotine is not addictive."[23]

During the next several years, as the struggle over holding Big Tobacco accountable for its actions burned hotter, that episode would be replayed thousands of times. The photo of the executives preparing to testify—in which the seven men looked more like defendants in a trial than chief executives—would be reprinted again and again. The Capitol Hill testimony marked a turning point in the tobacco war.

After years of studies showing nicotine to be addictive, the executives' responses were implausible. If the executives thought many people would believe them, then they took the American public for fools. Of course, people don't like to be lied to or taken for fools; the executives' answers before Congress would come to haunt their companies. Their testimony would lead to a Justice Department perjury investigation. And the executives' seeming indifference to public opinion would fuel the growing anti-tobacco sentiment.

"The level of dishonesty was the thing that got them nailed," Professor Glantz says. "It was the key to the litigation and the key to limiting their political power. It got people mad."

The deception was no longer working. For most of the 20th century, Big Tobacco had managed to avoid meaningful regulation by the federal government. It was also unique among large industries in deflecting all legal challenges. Even though it marketed the most dangerous legal product in the United States, the tobacco industry was able to insulate itself from the storm of product liability cases that battered other industries such as automobiles and chemicals. That was about to change. While David Kessler and his colleagues at the FDA were preparing to take on Big Tobacco, an army of attorneys was preparing to launch legal assaults the industry would not be able to defeat.

By 1994, cigarette smokers had filed more than 1,000 lawsuits against the makers of Kools, Camels, Marlboros, and Lucky Strikes. But the tobacco companies had never paid a single dollar to a plaintiff. In the one case the industry did lose, in 1990, the jury awarded zero damages. The industry accomplished this seemingly impossible feat by arguing that smokers themselves were responsible for their poor health and, in case that didn't work, simply wearing down opponents.

The first lawsuits against the tobacco corporations were filed in the 1950s, after the initial reports linking cigarettes with smoking. The industry already knew by then that their products were responsible for a variety of health problems. But the companies together agreed never to settle a case; they understood that a single concession would lead to a flood of lawsuits that would sink the industry.

Most of the cases filed by smokers or former smokers were standard product liability complaints: They accused the tobacco corporations of selling a product that was inherently faulty since, if used correctly, it led to sickness and death. The industry lawyers turned that line of reasoning on its head by arguing that smoking was a matter of personal choice. The cigarette companies, their attorneys argued, shouldn't be held liable for the voluntary decisions of individuals. After the appearance of warning labels in 1966 the industry lawyers could further argue that no less an authority that the Surgeon General said smoking was dangerous and still the plaintiff continued to smoke.[24] Time and again, juries agreed with the tobacco corporations. After all, it was common sense that smoking is bad for you. Oddly enough, smoking's very notoriety protected the industry from liability.

But most cases never saw a jury. Every time a smoker filed a lawsuit, the industry lawyers would file motions and objections to stretch out the case and fatigue the plaintiffs. Individual smokers didn't have the resources to challenge the deep-pocketed cigarette makers. An RJR attorney described the strategy in a confidential memo later made public: "To paraphrase General Patton, the way we won these cases was not by spending all of Reynolds' money, but by making the other son of a bitch spend all his."[25]

TURNING THE TABLES

In the early 1990s, two separate groups of attorneys saw ways to get around the industry's standard arguments. A collection of veteran trial lawyers would outflank Big Tobacco's personal choice argument by suing the corporations for knowingly addicting people. Meanwhile, state attorneys general would go around the companies in the other direction by arguing that nonsmokers, who never chose to smoke, were being burdened by the cost of treating their sick neighbors. Aside from novel legal arguments, the new tobacco foes had something else their predecessors lacked: the money to take on the wealthy corporations.

In March 1994, just weeks before the tobacco industry executives were to appear before Henry Waxman's congressional committee, Wendell Gauthier, a high-powered trial attorney, filed a class-action lawsuit in federal court in New Orleans against the tobacco corporations on behalf of 90 million former and current smokers. Gauthier, along with a longtime colleague, Washington, DC-based attorney John Coale, had earlier formed a coalition of lawyers called the "Castano Group," named after a former friend who had died of lung cancer.

The two lawyers were already well-known plaintiffs lawyers. Gauthier had won millions of dollars for the victims of plane crashes and hotel fires. Coale was the first American attorney on the scene after the Union Carbide disaster in Bhopal, India, during which 3,000 people died from exposure to a cyanide-based chemical; he won more than $200 million for victims and their families before a federal judge dismissed the case. The attorneys, who unabashedly described themselves as "ambulance chasers," knew that if they could secure a settlement with the tobacco companies, it would constitute one of the largest payoffs ever.

The Castano Group included 65 law firms that had each pledged $100,000 to tackle the tobacco industry. This gave Coale and Gauthier the deep pockets they needed to fight the cigarette makers. To win, the attorneys came up with a new angle: Instead of focusing on the effects of cigarettes, the Castano group would target the reason for smoking and argue that the tobacco corporations had conspired to hide tobacco's addictiveness from their customers. Smokers may have been forewarned about the health risks of smoking, the lawyers' class action suit said, but they had not been notified of the hazards of addiction. There was nothing on a pack of cigarettes that said they were addictive.[26]

The Castano lawyers had an instinct for appealing to people's distrust of overweening power. The group would take credit for popularizing the term "Big Tobacco," which quickly became an epithet. The Castano attorneys knew how to hit the companies where it hurt.

"A corporation is an entity to make money for its stockholders," Coale would say later, describing the Castano group's overarching strategy. "It's not an entity with a heart—and it's not supposed to have a heart. It is what it is. And to get a corporation's attention you take their money, or threaten to take their money. It's real simple."[27]

The Castano class action suit, the first class action ever filed against the industry, did grab Big Tobacco's attention. The cigarette makers were jolted once again in May, when the Mississippi Attorney General, Mike Moore, initiated the first state lawsuit against the industry. Now the tobacco corporations faced the potential of an even deeper set of pockets: up to 50 state governments.

Mississippi's case was based on a legal theory far more creative than the Castano class action. The tobacco companies, Attorney General Moore argued, owed the state money for the costs of treating the approximately 200,000 state Medicaid patients who suffered from smoking-related illnesses. The state, after all, had never chosen to smoke a cigarette. State taxpayers were unwilling victims who shouldn't have to pay for the tobacco companies' marketing of a dangerous product, the Mississippi lawsuit said.

On May 23, 1994, Moore filed his landmark suit against 13 tobacco companies, their wholesalers, trade associations, and industry public relations consultants. Moore told reporters: "This lawsuit is premised on a simple notion: You caused the health crisis, you pay for it. The free ride is over. It's time these billionaire tobacco companies start paying what they rightfully owe."[28] Big Tobacco couldn't expect to keep privatizing the profits while socializing the costs.

During the next several years, Moore and his associate and old friend Richard "Dickie" Scruggs would criss-cross the country urging other attorneys general to file similar suits. Scruggs, another veteran trial attorney and the brother-in-law of Senator Trent Lott (R-MS), would help drive the lawsuit, working on a fee-for-service basis because the state legislators would not agree to pay for the suit. The combination of the young, ambitious politician and the hard-nosed plaintiffs' attorney worked well, and eventually the two lawyers would get dozens of other states to join the Medicaid suits. By 1997, more than half of the states were suing Big Tobacco to recoup the costs of treating ill smokers.

FINDING THE SMOKING GUN

Mike Moore, Dick Scruggs, and the Castano lawyers had devised some clever strategies for outsmarting Big Tobacco's best court-tested arguments. The attorneys, however, still had to prove their case to make their threats to the industry credible, and, just like the FDA, proof was exactly what they lacked.

For decades, the tobacco companies had wrapped their operations in veils of secrecy as they dodged government regulation and guilty verdicts. This was done in part by maintaining that most internal company discussions were protected by attorney-client privilege. As soon as it became apparent to the industry in the 1950s that avoiding liability would have to be a major part of its business, attorneys became an integral part of almost all corporate planning. Industry lawyers vetted every research study, every high-level strategy memo, every marketing plan; almost every memorandum that came their way was stamped with "Attorney-Client privilege." Common sense suggested that the industry knew of the dangers and addictiveness of their products, but no one could prove that the industry had deceived consumers about the addictiveness of smoking or that it knew its products were deadly.

Whistle-blower revelations in the spring of 1994 supplied the first part of that proof. In March 1994, Don Barrett, a lawyer working with the Mississippi Attorney General, received an anonymous fax with a newspaper article about a man who had stolen internal documents from one of the major tobacco companies. Barrett, who had twice before unsuccessfully sued the industry, traced back the fax to Merrell Williams, the person profiled in the newspaper article. After two phone conversations during which Barrett struggled to ease Williams' fear of industry retaliation, the attorney arranged for Williams and Dick Scruggs to meet.

In 1988, Williams, a one-time drama teacher and failed entrepreneur living in Louisville, landed a job as a paralegal for Wyatt, Tarrant & Combs, Kentucky's biggest law firm. Williams and other paralegals were assigned to sorting and coding tens of thousands of pages of company memoranda and attorney correspondence from one of the firm's clients, Brown & Williamson Tobacco. Williams began reading the documents and he was shocked by what he found. It was obvious why the papers were marked confidential: The correspondence detailed, step by step, the lengths the industry had taken to hide the risks of smoking.

Williams, a smoker since the age of 19, was sickened by what he read. He began to tape originals to his body, smuggle them out of the law firm's warehouse, and photocopy them at a nearby Kinko's. During the next four years—until February 1992, when the job of sorting the documents was finally done—Williams copied some 4,000 pages of B&W documents.[29]

Williams didn't have a clear idea of what he was going to do with the documents. But Williams' mind changed in March 1993 after he had a quintuple cardiac bypass. The heart attack, he believed, was a message to use the documents to punish the tobacco companies.

Williams tried giving the documents to a tobacco foe at Northeastern University, law professor Richard Dynard, and to a reporter at the *Washington Post*, but neither person would take them; they feared the legal implications of receiving stolen documents. Williams even contacted the lawyers at Wyatt Tarrant and said he would return the papers for $2.5 million. Not surprisingly, they called that extortion and filed a lawsuit against Williams charging him with breach of contract. By the time

Williams met with Scruggs and Barrett, he was down on his luck and in serious legal trouble.

As soon as Scruggs and the rest of the Mississippi legal team began reading the documents, they realized they had the smoking gun they needed. For the first time, attorneys had industry documents that showed tobacco company executives knew cigarettes were addictive even as they publicly argued the opposite. The papers showed that B&W had abused the attorney-client privilege by deliberately routing research results through company lawyers. They also proved that the cigarette maker had lied under oath in case after case, and had refused to disclose facts that could have saved smokers' lives. A 1963 memo revealed that the cigarette makers had long known that nicotine was addictive. "Nicotine is addictive," the memo from a company lawyer said unequivocally. "We are in the business, then, of selling nicotine, an addictive drug."[30]

The documents gave Moore and his lawyers the ammunition they needed. But the Attorney General now faced the same problem as Williams had earlier—the documents had been stolen, and no court would admit them as evidence. Scruggs and the other attorneys decided they could get around this by anonymously disseminating the papers—thereby putting them in the public domain, which would allow a judge to accept them. Within days, Congressman Waxman received a set of the documents, as did the FDA and *The New York Times*. After Professor Glantz at UCSF received a set of the documents he put them on the Internet, where anyone in the world would have access to them. "When the history of this whole thing is written, there will be 'before the documents' and 'after the documents,'" says Glantz.

The anti-tobacco forces had a potent weapon in the cigarette papers. They could not, however, understand all of the material in their possession. Company researchers and executives had used code words for many subjects—including for cancer and nicotine—and much of the information was indecipherable even for trained health professionals. Luckily for the tobacco foes, another whistle-blower would soon act as their guide through the maze of the industry's conspiracy.

THE INSIDER

Jeffrey Wigand was no paid-by-the-hour paralegal; from 1989 to 1993 he had been the chief chemistry researcher at B&W and had access to the company's knowledge about tobacco and its effects. Wigand considered himself a man of science, and he decided to join B&W only because he was told he would get to work on creating a "safe" cigarette. But Wigand, a nonsmoker, quickly found himself at odds with the company culture. He often confronted executives about the science behind the company's business, and in January 1993 he was fired.

When Wigand left the company he reluctantly signed a lifelong confidentiality agreement. By 1994, he was struggling financially and had already suffered from B&W legal action against him. On April 14, Wigand watched the Waxman hearings on C-Span at his home in Louisville, and when he saw the tobacco company executives testifying under oath that they believed nicotine was not addictive he was outraged.

"I realized they were all liars," Wigand said later. "They lied with a straight face. Sandefur [the B&W CEO] was arrogant, and that really irked me. When that TV image replayed in my mind, I realized that, by my silence, I was not that far removed from the men on my screen."[31]

Wigand started talking with CBS's *60 Minutes*, and soon he was working with Kessler's FDA investigators as well. Wigand steered the FDA through the jargon of Williams' documents and brought new information to light. For example, Wigand—who out of fear of persecution went by the code name "Research"—explained to the FDA that the cigarette makers didn't have to manipulate the actual level of nicotine in a cigarette to determine how much of a dose a smoker would get. He showed them that for decades the tobacco corporations had put ammonia in the filters since ammonia made nicotine more potent. Wigand even suggested that the enduring popularity of Marlboros could be attributed to the cigarette's early use of ammonia.[32] Wigand also cooperated with Mike Moore's legal team after the attorney general promised he would fight to secure immunity for the one-time insider. Wigand told the Attorney General that B&W executives had sold products they knew to be dangerous: They had objected to removing additives, including an ingredient in rat poison, because it would affect taste.

The executives' obvious hypocrisy during the Waxman hearings angered another man closely connected to the tobacco industry: longtime smoker Grady Carter. Carter smoked Lucky Strikes, a B&W brand, for 43 years. He had never tried to quit, had never even wanted to despite constant pressure from his family, until 1991, when he was diagnosed with lung cancer and had half a lung removed.

Three years after the surgery, Carter was at home watching the nightly news when he saw the chiefs of the seven major tobacco companies raise their hands before Congress and swear nicotine wasn't addictive. "I wasn't a crusader until that very minute," Carter said later. "Then I became one. I chose to smoke, so I have to take some of the blame. But these guys lied and lied and lied and withheld evidence that might have helped me quit. I felt I wanted to get these liars."[33]

Within a year, Carter would be represented by attorney Norwood Wilner, another one of the lawyers working on the Mississippi case.

Carter and Wilner sued B&W for compensation for Carter's lung cancer. By withholding the facts about smoking, the company was liable for any life-threatening effects, the plaintiffs argued.

Carter's case was not that much different from the hundreds of other individuals who had earlier sued the cigarette makers and lost. But Carter had one big advantage his predecessors didn't enjoy: hard proof that the cigarette makers concealed evidence that smoking was dangerous and addictive. Carter's case was the first to use the B&W documents as evidence against Big Tobacco.

Perhaps more important, public sentiment was changing. A growing number of people were now saying that the cigarette corporations, not just individual smokers, were responsible for the ill effects of smoking. In 1991, just 13 percent of respondents to a poll said the cigarette companies should be held legally accountable to the families of smokers who died of smoking-related diseases; by 1996 that number had tripled.[34] The outcome of Carter's case would show that the once-invincible industry was now vulnerable.

THE TIDE BEGINS TO TURN

In the early 1950s, in the aftermath of the first exposés about the health dangers of smoking, the cigarette company executives agreed they would never settle a lawsuit brought against their products. During the next four decades, that consensus would serve as a bedrock principle for the industry and drive its strategy of disputing hard science, attacking critics, and concealing the nature and effects of its products. But finally, in 1997, the industry decided to compromise with its foes. The threat of government regulation, a turning of the legal tides, and the defection of one of the industry's smallest players would force Big Tobacco to the bargaining table.

From the spring of 1994—when the first allegations surfaced that the tobacco companies were manipulating nicotine levels in cigarettes—through the summer of 1995, Kessler and his team at the FDA had been building their case that, since nicotine was a drug, the agency should be able to regulate cigarettes. But Kessler couldn't announce plans to regulate tobacco without the support of the White House, and some people in the Clinton administration, including the President himself, had doubts about challenging the politically powerful tobacco industry. The Democrats had been trounced in the 1994 election, Newt Gingrich's counter-revolution seemed unstoppable, and Clinton was afraid of losing the 1996 election; the last thing the President wanted to do was alienate tobacco state voters.

Kessler also faced stiff resistance from conservative legislators and tobacco state representatives. As it became known that the FDA was preparing rules to regulate the industry, attacks on Kessler increased. Philip Morris, suggesting that the FDA wanted to entirely outlaw cigarettes, called Kessler a "wacko"; one southern Democrat labeled him a "headline-grabbing extremist."[35]

But Kessler had public opinion on his side. Clinton's private pollster, Dick Morris, had already done polling for the Mississippi Attorney General that showed challenging the tobacco industry was popular, especially if attacks against tobacco were aimed at protecting children. Kessler suggested to the President that making smoking a children's issue was the best way to challenge the industry. The idea would be to portray the industry as a predatory marketer bent on hooking impressionable teens on their deadly product. Clinton finally agreed.

On August 10, 1995, the President, surrounded by school children, announced the first substantive rules for the regulation of cigarettes ever proposed by the federal government. "It is time to free our teenagers from the addiction and dependency," Clinton said at the White House press conference.

> When Joe Camel tells our children smoking is cool, when billboards tell teens that smoking will lead to true romance, when Virginia Slims tells adolescents that cigarettes will make them thin and glamorous, then our children need our wisdom, our guidance, our experience.[36]

The FDA rules, which were now open to public review and comment before they would become official, established a series of restrictions on the cigarette makers. Vending machines would be banned, advertising geared toward adolescents would be prohibited, and the industry would have to pay for public education campaigns if smoking rates among teens didn't decrease. The goal was to cut teen smoking in half within seven years. The industry's ability to elude government regulation was nearing an end.

Big Tobacco suffered another serious setback seven months later, when in March 1996 the Liggett Group, the smallest of the cigarette makers, settled out of court with the class action lawyers and with five states. The company, which specialized in discount brands such as Chesterfield and generic cigarettes, agreed to pay just $26 million—$5 million over the next 10 years and as much as 7.5 percent of pretax profits for up to 25 years. In exchange, Liggett would be freed from the Medicaid lawsuits. The settlement terms may have been paltry, but the Liggett defection marked an important turn in the legal battle. The industry's decades-long united front was crumbling. At least one company realized that it made more economic sense to settle rather than fight. Soon the other tobacco corporations would come to the same conclusion.

The cigarette makers scored a minor victory in May 1996, when a federal judge dismissed the Castano group's national class action lawsuit on the grounds that the grouping of plaintiffs was too large. The Castano attorneys, however, had anticipated such a decision, and they immediately took steps to file separate class actions in the individual states. The decision had a Hydra effect: The tobacco companies soon faced 20 different class action lawsuits in state courts.

From there, Big Tobacco's fortunes kept sinking. In August, tobacco foes won two important victories. On August 9, a jury in Jacksonville, Florida, ruled in favor of Grady Carter, the Lucky Strike smoker outraged by the executives' lies, in his case against B&W. After a three-week trial and nine hours of deliberation, the jurors decided to award Carter $750,000 to reimburse him for his medical bills. Several jurors said the internal company documents had been key in reaching a decision. The verdict marked the first time any cigarette maker had been forced to pay a smoker for damages.

It was a stunning defeat, and everyone knew it—especially investors on Wall Street. Philip Morris shares dropped 12 percent in an hour, slicing $12 billion from the market value of the world's largest tobacco company. Share prices for RJR and British-American Tobacco, B&W's parent company, also fell sharply. It was becoming apparent that, unlike in the past, litigation represented a real danger to the future profitability of the industry.

A few weeks after the Carter verdict, President Clinton and David Kessler announced the publication of the final FDA rules on tobacco, formally giving legal weight to the administration's restrictions on tobacco. Since proposing the rules a year earlier, the FDA had received hundreds of thousands of public comments on the regulations, both from anti-tobacco activists and smokers. On the last day that public comments were to be accepted, the cigarette makers submitted more than 40,000 pages of their own comments. The industry hoped that by bogging the FDA down in paperwork it could delay the publication of the regulations by years. But FDA staffers had worked around the clock to process all of the opinions, and managed to prepare the final rules in just 12 months. Big Tobacco now faced immediate restrictions on the ways it could market and sell cigarettes.[37]

THE DEATH OF JOE CAMEL

Although the cigarette makers were putting on a brave face publicly, privately they were starting to worry. Mike Moore had signed up an-

other half dozen states onto his Medicaid lawsuit. The Florida verdict
was a disaster; it seemed likely that the industry would have to spend
hundreds of millions of dollars in the foreseeable future defending itself. Stock prices were falling. And if that weren't bad enough, the Justice Department had initiated five different grand jury investigations
into the companies and their executives.

In September, the CEOs of the four largest tobacco companies started
holding secret meetings at hotels in New York to decide what to do
about the increasing pressure. By December, the executives had agreed
to hire an outside counsel to begin negotiating with the state attorneys
general. The industry was preparing to settle.[38]

On March 31, 1997, Mike Moore, Dick Scruggs, the Castano Group's
John Coale, and Matthew Myers, the director of the National Center for
Tobacco-Free Kids, first met with the industry's attorneys to begin work
on a national settlement. Several items were on the table: what kind of
oversight powers the FDA would be given, how much the companies
would pay, the scope of advertising restrictions, and, most controversial, whether the industry would be given immunity from future lawsuits. For a tense and turbulent 79 days, the parties wrangled over these
issues, fortunes shifting back and forth. At different points, cigarette
companies and attorneys general walked away from the bargaining table
only to return reluctantly.

Big Tobacco had the natural advantage. The legal argument behind
the states' case was untested. The Carter verdict was just one case among
hundreds, an aberration. Plus, the industry was confident of winning its
case against the FDA; even if it lost the initial hearing, it could count on
the rules being tied up in appeals courts for years.

But during the spring the attorneys general and their allies received
some lucky breaks that kept the tobacco companies at the bargaining
table and pressured them to make one concession after another.

The first advance for the attorneys general came on March 19, when
the Liggett Group reached a new, broader agreement with 17 other states
it hadn't yet settled with. Since Liggett's initial settlement a year earlier, the number of states filing their own Medicaid complaints had grown
steadily as word had leaked out that the cigarette corporations were
ready to compromise. Attorneys general, smelling blood in the water,
knew they had much to gain by joining an effort that at first seemed
quixotic. The mounting lawsuits meant serious trouble for Liggett, which
was struggling to turn a profit. The relatively small company, already
near bankruptcy, could not afford a major payout.

In terms of compensation, the settlement was virtually worthless.
Liggett agreed to pay 25 percent of its annual pretax income for the next

25 years to the states for Medicaid reimbursements. But because Liggett had lost $14 million the year before, that promise was worth nothing. The victory for the attorneys general came in the form of an unprecedented admission: Liggett would publicly state that tobacco is addictive and causes cancer. Liggett CEO Bennett LeBow also admitted that Liggett had marketed cigarettes to children as young as 14. Most damaging to the other tobacco companies, LeBow agreed to turn over thousands of pages of company documents that would shed light on the business practices of Liggett and its competitors. The attorneys general were given fresh ammunition to make their claim that Big Tobacco had engaged in a decades-long conspiracy that cost thousands of lives.

Vice President Gore called the admission "a historic victory for the American people." Tobacco investors agreed: Philip Morris shares dropped five percent.

One month later, the cigarette makers suffered another loss when Federal Judge William Osteen ruled that the FDA could regulate tobacco products. The tobacco companies could have filed their complaint against the FDA rules in any federal court, but they chose the district court in North Carolina in an effort to get a more sympathetic hearing. When the case was handed to Judge Osteen, it appeared the strategy had paid off. Osteen grew up on his family's tobacco farm, and in the early 1970s he had lobbied on behalf of tobacco farmers for a brief time. "We don't feel we'll need to appeal," an RJR attorney said confidently after a hearing in Osteen's court.[39]

The confidence was misplaced. On April 25, Judge Osteen ruled in favor of the FDA on two of the three issues at stake. He said the FDA had the right to regulate cigarettes since Congress had never explicitly forbade it to do so, even if it had never explicitly ordered it to. Osteen also said that the FDA had every right to regulate tobacco since nicotine was, in his opinion, a drug. The judge did, however, strike down the FDA rules on restricting advertising geared toward minors. Those restrictions exceeded the administration's authority, Osteen found.

The tobacco companies immediately pledged to appeal the case. But, as everyone understood, that appeal wouldn't affect the ongoing negotiations. The industry had lost an important bargaining chip.

Once again, Wall Street investors reacted sharply. The share price of Philip Morris stock dropped another 5 percent. RJR stocks lost nearly 9 percent of their value.

The momentum was now clearly in favor of the attorneys general. In early May the tobacco companies received some good news when a Florida jury decided in favor of RJR in another case brought by an individual smoker. But by that point the states held the advantage. The number of attorneys general filing additional Medicaid suits was growing by the week. The Federal Trade Commission had just charged RJR with illegally targeting minors with its Joe Camel ads. And investors were eager for a settlement. The gathering storm of litigation clouded the industry's future and represented a substantial risk for investors. What investors wanted was stability: a clear and fixed set of government rules and a lawsuit-free atmosphere.

For the industry, immunity from future lawsuits was key. It offered the only real way for the tobacco companies to get the stable business environment they had sought for decades. But for many of the attorneys general, the idea of immunity was anathema. Most of the attorneys general agreed to it only reluctantly, and only when it looked as if cigarette companies would walk away from the deal without it.

Arguments continued through May over the amount of money the tobacco industry would pay and how it would change its business practices. With the White House pushing a compromise, the attorneys general agreed on limited liability for the cigarette makers. Details bedeviled the negotiations, and the bargaining dragged on.

Finally, on June 20, 1997, the attorneys general gathered at a Washington, DC, hotel to announce the final agreement. Billing the final compromise as a "global settlement," the lawyers for the states jubilantly laid out the terms of the settlement to a packed press conference. The cigarette companies would pay $368.5 billion over 25 years to the 40 states with Medicaid claims. Outdoor advertising, vending machines, promotions on clothing, and Internet marketing would be prohibited. The industry could no longer sponsor sports or arts events, including motor racing. Nor could the industry use human images or cartoon characters in its advertising, a provision that meant the end for Joe Camel and the Marlboro Man. And the industry would agree to FDA jurisdiction over tobacco, subject to a series of conditions. If, after all these steps were taken, teen smoking didn't fall by 30 percent within five years and 50 percent after seven years, the cigarette companies would face additional penalties.

In exchange for agreeing to these restrictions and pay-outs, the industry received what it desired most: insulation from new litigation. While lawsuits by individual smokers would still be allowed, class action lawsuits—the biggest legal threat to the industry—would be banned. And even in the individual cases, plaintiffs would not be able to claim punitive damages for past misconduct. Total damage awards would be capped at $5 billion annually.

Mike Moore was ecstatic announcing the settlement. "We are here today to announce what we think is—we know, we believe is—the most historic public health agreement in history," Moore said. "We wanted this industry to change the way it did business, and we have done that. We had to punish this industry in such a way that everybody in this country, and everybody in this world, would recognize that they had paid a higher price than any other corporation in the world. Because, frankly, this corporation has done more harm than any other corporation in history."

The 68-page settlement was, in fact, historic. The $368 billion payment represented the largest legal settlement in U.S. history. And the restriction placed on the industry's business practices marked the broadest regulations the tobacco companies had ever faced. The signed agreement, however, wasn't a done deal. The settlement needed to be approved by Congress, and that meant that a host of new voices were suddenly going to join to the discussion, which until then had largely been limited to an ad hoc coalition of lawyers and a handful of health advocates. That spelled trouble for the cigarette makers. The public and even the political establishment weren't willing to be as lenient with the industry as the attorneys general had been.

NOW COMES THE HARD PART
From the beginning of the legal negotiations the White House, which helped bring the parties to the table, had insisted that some public health groups be involved in the talks. The Clinton administration knew that if it was going to support any political settlement, it needed the backing of the public health community. That's how Matt Meyers, a longtime anti-tobacco crusader who had founded the Campaign for Tobacco-Free Kids, became a central figure during the talks. Other health groups, however, were excluded from the bargaining. That was a bad miscalculation.

Divisions between the attorneys general and the health activists had surfaced even before the final agreement was signed. On May 28, weeks before the ultimate settlement was announced, Mike Moore and Matt Myers met with 100 health advocates at a hotel in Chicago to inform them of the talks' progress and to try to convince the activists that supporting the settlement was a wise move. The activists were skeptical. Most of them had been battling the industry for years, long before Moore filed his suit in 1994, and they were suspicious of the attorneys general and the Castano lawyers. The activists, many of them wearing buttons that read "No Moore Sellout," feared that lawyers were giving the industry too much. They questioned why the talks had to be held in secret, and many argued—bolstered by Minnesota Attorney General Hubert Humphrey III, who opposed settling—that taking the cases before juries was better than an out-of-court compromise. Moore and Myers tried to convince the activists that a sure thing was better than no deal at all. After hours of discussion, Moore and Myers failed to sway the activists. The vast majority of the public health community—including activists from the American Lung Association and veterans like Glantz—opposed an accord.[40]

As soon as the June 20 settlement became public, health activists unleashed a barrage of criticism. David Kessler, who had left the FDA to teach medicine, complained that the deal undercut the ability of the federal government to oversee the industry. The attorneys general deal gave the FDA jurisdiction over the manufacture and sale of cigarettes (including the right to reduce nicotine levels starting in 2009), but with nearly impossible conditions attached. While Judge Osteen had ruled that the FDA could pass any regulation that wasn't "arbitrary or capricious," the June 20 settlement raised the bar by forcing the FDA to provide "substantial evidence of benefit" to back up its regulations.

Activists and health groups also noted that the industry payments would be tax-deductible. That meant taxpayers would pick up as much as 40 percent of the companies' tab—or about $221 billion over 25 years.[41] Also coming in for sharp criticism were the deal's penalties against the cigarette companies in case teen smoking didn't decrease. Former Surgeon General C. Everett Koop showed that even if the full $2 billion fine were levied, it would amount to only 8 cents a pack, of which 3 cents would be tax-deductible. "So the fine comes to a nickel a pack," Koop said in the days following the settlement announcement. "An unscrupulous CEO of a tobacco company could say, 'Let's market to kids all we want and raise the price by six cents a pack and make a fortune.' . . . I think we've been snookered."[42]

The industry's legal immunity got the harshest attacks. For the activists who had spent decades fighting the companies, absolving the industry of its past crimes was unthinkable. "Our chief concern has been issues of liability and whether this industry will be punished for its record of wrongdoing over the decades," an American Lung Association official said. "In terms of holding this industry accountable, it's a free ride."[43]

Indeed, the deal's immunity provisions struck at the heart of the accountability issue. By avoiding class action suits, the industry could rely on its tested strategy of outspending and fatiguing lawyers filing individual cases. And by limiting its damages, the tobacco companies knew they would be able to protect their profits. The possibility that the industry would get to continue to operate much as it had before violated the principle of accountability. There had to be some way for people to punish the cigarette makers for their behavior, and the courts offered the best way to do that. For health activists, immunity was a deal-breaker, just as for the industry the lack of immunity was one.

Because the June 20 settlement covered FDA authority and included significant changes to tort law, the agreement needed to be approved by Congress. The fight that had occurred for the last few years in the legal realm was headed for the court of public opinion. The challenge now facing the health activists was to convince Congress and the American people that the June 20 settlement was a bad deal for the public. The battle against Big Tobacco, which in recent years had been driven by a small group of lawyers, was now turning to the grassroots.

FIGHTING FOR CLEAN AIR

During the 1980s, as Dr. Koop took on Big Tobacco from his bully pulpit, a grassroots movement arose to challenge the industry at the local level. The grassroots activists, many of whom were organized through a group called Americans for Non-Smokers Rights and the local chapters of the American Lung Association, focused their energy on a key goal: passing local clean air ordinances. Like Betty Carnes, the Arizona nurse who in the 1970s successfully lobbied for the country's first restrictions on smoking in public, the grassroots activists of the '80s made smoking a quality of life issue. Nonsmokers, who constituted a majority, should not be exposed to the dangers of secondhand smoke. It was a message that resonated with the public.

The local ordinances were important in two ways: they served as a vehicle for educating people about the dangers of smoking and the duplicity of the tobacco industry, and they won. By the 1980s, the anti-tobacco activists had learned that the industry was too powerful to beat at the federal or even state level. First in 1978 and then in 1980, activists in California tried to pass statewide clean indoor air initiatives. Both lost, the victims of massive campaign spending by the tobacco industry. After those defeats, the health activists decided to take their struggle to city councils, where they knew they had more access.[44]

"If you're talking about tobacco, the basic battle you're in is about social norms and what is acceptable and not acceptable and what gives status and what takes status away," says Glantz. "You can't change norms from Washington, DC. We were trying to influence community norms at the grassroots. The higher you go up the political food chain, the more powerful the industry is and the harder it is to beat them."

The strategy worked. The tobacco companies couldn't be everywhere at once, and the local efforts built to a point where it would have been very difficult for the industry to fight them all. On the one occasion when the industry did expend substantial energy and money to fight a local ordinance—in San Francisco in 1983—the cigarette makers were branded as outside agitators seeking to interfere with local governance, and they lost. By 1986, the year Koop released his report on the effects of secondhand smoke, 192 cities and counties had passed some form of smoking restrictions; two years later, there were nearly 300 local non-smoking ordinances around the country. In 1988, the movement scored a huge victory when California voters, this time not swayed by Big Tobacco's expensive ad campaigns, passed Proposition 99. The proposition, which increased the tobacco tax by 25 cents per pack to raise $100 million annually for antismoking programs, represented the most ambitious tobacco control program in the world at the time.[45]

The local ordinances, which by 2002 numbered more than 800, were key to shifting public attitudes about tobacco. And the struggle itself was essential for building a constituency committed to fighting the industry. If many of the local health activists did not hold a corporate accountability consciousness when they began working for nonsmoking ordinances, they developed one along the way.

"A lot of our best allies were very conservative, but they thought that corporations shouldn't lie and shouldn't kill people," says Glantz. "People were motivated by a desire for clean indoor air. Then they see the tobacco corporations close up and personal and they see how evil they are and they begin to see them as evil multinational corporations."

By the early 1990s, some openly anti-corporate activists were beginning to join the fight against Big Tobacco. In 1993 the group INFACT, which in the 1970s had spearheaded the campaign against Nestlé's unethical marketing practices for baby formula in poor countries, launched a campaign calling for a boycott of Kraft and Nabisco products, owned by Philip Morris and RJR, respectively. INFACT also started investigating the cigarette makers' overseas operations. Perhaps most important, INFACT organized *smokers* against Big Tobacco.

"When the whole propaganda around smoking being a 'choice' began to erode, smokers rebelled," says Kathy Mulvey, an activist who has coordinated INFACT's tobacco campaign.

People get involved because of life and death issues, and as they get involved they start to see that a giant corporation is the root cause of the problem. That's the permanent shift of consciousness we've seen in the U.S.—the interest in holding corporations as well as individuals accountable.[46]

SADDLED WITH TOBACCO

The grassroots networks proved crucial to remodeling the June 20 settlement into legislation that reflected the demands for accountability. As the summer of 1997 wore on, lawmakers in Washington started to scrutinize the substance of the agreement, and health activists began to energize their supporters for the upcoming political battle.

The health activists targeted the Clinton White House, which had helped broker the June 20 deal but was now deciding whether to support it in full or propose changes. The American Lung Association and Public Citizen bought newspaper ads criticizing the deal. Activists urged people to call the White House. Koop and Kessler came out against the deal. With the public health community almost unanimously behind a tougher program, Clinton had little choice but to back a stricter law.

After a three-month internal debate, Clinton said he would support the settlement with some changes. Flanked by Koop, Kessler, Matt Myers, and Mike Moore, Clinton announced that he wanted to raise the price of cigarettes by $1.50 a pack if teen smoking rates didn't drop. He also proposed nondeductible, uncapped penalties on the cigarette makers if teen use didn't decline. But the President stopped short of a full endorsement of the deal, essentially throwing the political hot potato to Congress and waiting for a bill he would either veto or sign.

In January 1998, as Congress returned from its winter recess and started to consider the tobacco legislation, the cigarette makers were hit with another series of public relations setbacks. First, a biotechnology company, DNA Plant Technology Corp., pled guilty to Justice Department charges that it had illegally exported special tobacco seeds from the United States to Brazil. The admission revealed that Brown & Williamson had developed, cultivated, and then put in its cigarettes a biologically engineered strain of "super tobacco" that contained twice as much nicotine as natural tobacco. Charges about the use of high nicotine tobacco first emerged in 1994 during the FDA's initial investigations. But at that time B&W denied it had used a super crop. The guilty plea by B&W's biotech firm revealed that denial to be a lie.

Just two weeks later, Representative Waxman made public internal RJR documents he had received from a lawyer suing the industry. The memos, stretching from 1973 to 1990, illustrated how RJR had aimed its marketing at adolescents, all the while denying that it was doing so.

"They [young smokers] represent tomorrow's cigarette business," the company's vice president for marketing wrote in 1974.

As this 14-24 age group matures, they will account for a key share of the total cigarette volume for at least the next 25 years. . . . Our strategy becomes clear for our established brands: 1. Direct advertising appeal to young smokers.

A 1988 memo said that Joe Camel ads should be placed "wherever younger adult smokers hang out."[47]

The revelations sunk Big Tobacco's reputation even lower. Polls showed that a large majority of Americans—between 70 and 80 percent—mistrusted the cigarette makers and viewed them as greedy companies seeking to profit from kids.[48]

As the Senate started to consider the smoking legislation, the anti-tobacco activists put their lobbying efforts into high gear. They urged people to call and write their Senators and demand legislation that didn't include immunity for the industry. The activists appealed to citizens' suspicion of the cigarette corporations. Any deal supported by the tobacco industry itself and its investors on Wall Street—where tobacco stocks rose 15 percent on news of the June 20 settlement—was not in the public's interest, activists argued.

Many members of the Senate agreed. After weeks of debate, Senator John McCain (R-AZ) crafted a bill that was much tougher than the June 20 settlement. The bill raised the amount the industry would have to pay to $506 billion. The price of cigarettes would increase $1.10—less than what the President wanted, but twice as much as the agreement with the attorneys general called for. FDA authority over tobacco was strengthened. The annual cap on damages was raised from $5 billion to $6.5 billion. Most important, the industry lost its legal immunity. Class action lawsuits against the cigarette makers would still be permitted.

Many health activists still felt that the legislation didn't go far enough. Former Surgeon General Koop said he couldn't support the McCain bill. INFACT also opposed it. But the large health organizations, pleased that immunity was struck from the deal, supported the bill.

Now the industry had to decide whether it was going to support the new compromise. The political arithmetic was not encouraging. Polls showed the public supporting the deal, and the industry feared it could no longer count on the support of longtime allies. Even Newt Gingrich, the fiery Republican who headed the House of Representatives, opposed giving the industry any relief from lawsuits. "You guys have screwed us," Gingrich told tobacco company lobbyists as the McCain bill moved forward. "The Republican party has been saddled with tobacco."[49]

Cigarette executives decided they couldn't support the McCain bill. It didn't give them what they needed most—insulation from legal challenges—and yet it demanded what they considered to be a large number of concessions. A week after McCain's legislation moved to the Senate floor, the cigarette companies announced they would fight the deal. "Congress wants us to sign a suicide note," B&W CEO Nicholas Brookes said in announcing the industry's opposition. "We won't do that. We won't stand idly by while a legal enterprise engaged in marketing a legal product is targeted for extinction by politicians."

Within days, the industry launched a nationwide television and radio campaign to erode public support for the McCain bill. The industry's ad campaign relied on messages that had worked for the industry in fighting antismoking initiatives at the state level. The ads, 11 different ones in all, painted the smoking legislation as a major tax hike that would create a huge government bureaucracy to interfere in people's lives.

"Washington has gone haywire, proposing the same old tax and spend," one ad said. "Half a trillion dollars in new taxes . . . 17 new government bureaucracies. Cigarettes up to $5 a pack." Another ad declared: "Washington has gone cuckoo again."

The ad campaign claimed that the legislation would cause job losses among farmers and small businesses. Some ads warned that the bill would create a black market for cigarettes. "Washington is creating a serious new law enforcement problem," one spot told viewers.

During the next three months, the industry would spend at least $40 million on the nationwide campaign, three times as much as insurance companies spent on the "Harry and Louise" ads that defeated Clinton's healthcare plan in 1994.[50]

The industry also poured money into lobbying lawmakers on Capitol Hill. The cigarette makers paid an additional $10 million for lobbying. They recruited two former Senate majority leaders (one Democrat, one Republican) to argue the companies' case with former colleagues. With 200 lobbyists on their payrolls, the cigarette companies had two lobbyists for each Senator, and they quickly went to work to scuttle the bill.[51]

At the same time, the cigarette corporations flooded Washington with campaign contributions. For decades, the tobacco industry had been one of the largest campaign donors at both the state and federal levels. In 1996, the industry's giving reached a zenith. During that election year, Philip Morris was the largest corporate campaign contributor in the country, donating nearly $4 million. RJR was the seventh largest giver.[52] Between the end of the 1996 election cycle and the beginning of the fight over the McCain bill, Big Tobacco gave away another $4.3 million—$3.4 million to Republicans and $933,000 to Democrats.[53]

Debate over the legislation moved to the Senate floor at the end of May. The industry's blitzkrieg made its mark on the proceedings. Pro-tobacco senators attached "poison pill" amendments to the bill—such as raising the cap on damages to $8 billion a year—to erode the support of moderates. The bill's supporters were having a hard time defending the legislation in its entirety. The tobacco industry's public image had been sullied, but its political clout in Washington was still considerable.

As the debate dragged on, the industry's ads were beginning to have an impact. Hundreds of thousands of people were calling the toll-free number listed in the TV and radio ads, and many of those callers were taking the extra step of registering their opinions with their representatives. The ads succeeded in transforming the debate from being about child smoking to being about a tax hike. In March, polls showed that the public supported the McCain legislation by a two-to-one margin; by June, public opinion had completely reversed—people now opposed the legislation two-to-one.[54]

The shift in public sentiment gave conservative and moderate Senators the cover they needed to defeat the bill. On June 17, after four weeks of debate, the Senate voted 57 to 42 to pull the McCain legislation from the floor and shelve it indefinitely. A few Members of Congress vowed to continue fighting for comprehensive tobacco legislation, but it was clear that the issue was dead for the foreseeable future.

Once again, the tobacco industry had fought back an effort to make it pay for its past social costs and to put restrictions on its future business practices. Four years after the first proof of the industry's conspiracy of deception surfaced, the cigarette companies remained safe from any meaningful government regulation.

"This Congress is the very best that tobacco money can buy," the *Los Angeles Times* opined. "The captains of industry must surely have been pleased with their investment."[55] Wall Street certainly was. The day after the McCain bill collapsed, investors bid up the price of Philip Morris and RJR shares.

DISORDER IN THE COURT

Big Tobacco, at the expense of tens of millions of dollars, had narrowly avoided federal legislation that would have cost it billions of dollars and subjected its business practices to the oversight of the FDA. It was a clear triumph. But the industry still faced the threat of lawsuits: By June 1998 the tobacco companies were the target of more than 800 suits, many of them Medicaid reimbursement suits filed by state governments. The collapse of a congressionally approved compromise meant that the industry would have to go back to the bargaining table.

Just weeks after the McCain bill was defeated, negotiations resumed between the attorneys general and the cigarette corporations. The terms of the talks had completely changed from a year earlier. FDA powers were off the table since returning to Congress was out of the question. So was immunity, the lightning rod of earlier debates. The central question was how much the industry would have to pay.

In the months leading up to the June 20 settlement, a series of legal victories had strengthened the bargaining position of the attorneys general. Now the winds of fortune shifted the other way.

In late June an appeals judge struck down the $750,000 award given to Lucky Strike smoker Grady Carter. The court ruled that Carter's case had failed to meet a statute of limitations deadline. Three-quarters of a million dollars was a paltry sum, but the verdict delivered a psychological boost to the industry lawyers.

Then, on August 14, a federal appeals court in Richmond overturned Judge Osteen's earlier decision that the FDA had the power to regulate tobacco. In their decision, the appeals judges wrote that "Congress did not equip the FDA with tools appropriate for the regulation of tobacco." Ironically, the appeals court found that the very danger of smoking prevented the FDA from regulating the cigarettes. Because smoking had been proven to be deadly, and because the FDA was not supposed to grant approval to any drug that could endanger people's health, the administration would have no choice but to entirely ban cigarettes if it were given oversight of tobacco. But only Congress could ban cigarettes, the appeals court decided.[56]

The FDA immediately appealed the case. But the industry felt sure it would ultimately prevail. The second great threat to the industry's business practices—government regulation—appeared set to evaporate.

The ruling against the FDA gave the cigarette makers confidence that they could defeat the states' litigation. In late August, RJR and B&W pulled out of the negotiations with the attorneys general, citing frustration with talks about marketing restrictions. The companies soon came back to the table—their departure being only a tactical bluff—but the move showed that crafting a settlement satisfactory to the public would be difficult.

As the negotiations stretched into September, health activists, who were not included in the talks, were urging the attorneys general to walk away from the settlement discussions, as Massachusetts' attorney general had just done. The activists argued that despite the FDA ruling, the states still held the upper hand. Individual settlements by each state would cost the industry far more than a master settlement, activists argued. They noted that Mississippi, Texas, Florida, and Minnesota had already received $37 billion from the cigarette makers, and that the dollar payouts had increased with each new case. A $300 million award the year before for flight attendants suffering from secondhand smoke showed that the class action suits posed a real menace to the industry. And with every new case, new internal documents were coming to light, adding fresh strength to the cases against the tobacco companies.

Activists pointed to the Minnesota experience as proof that compromise with the industry was unnecessary. Minnesota Attorney General Hubert Humphrey III had from the beginning of the state suits been the industry's staunchest foe, and he had won more than any of his peers. On the verge of a jury decision, the industry settled and Humphrey received $6.6 billion from the industry and a host of restrictions to their marketing in his state. Ads on buses were to come down and so would billboard ads. Marketing on hats and t-shirts was prohibited. Humphrey even got the industry to change its practices beyond Minnesota. The tobacco companies agreed not to pay any more money to filmmakers for "product placement"; to disband the industry's "scientific" arm, the Council for Tobacco Research; and to pledge not to oppose clean indoor air laws and youth smoking laws. Humphrey also forced the industry to make public 33 million pages of internal memos.[57]

But many of the attorneys general in the talks didn't have Humphrey's zeal. And most of the attorneys general who had been involved for the past few years were feeling pressure to accomplish something. As elected officials, the attorneys general knew that if they didn't walk away with an agreement they might be punished at the polls.

On November 20, the 46 remaining states settled with the tobacco industry for $206 billion over 25 years. Under the deal, the cigarette corporations agreed to end outdoor advertising, end the use of cartoon characters in marketing, and stop the sale and distribution of merchandise with brand names on it. The industry also said it would disband its Washington front groups and pay $250 million over the next 10 years to establish a national public health foundation to combat teen smoking. The companies pledged not to market to kids, but there would be no penalties if rates of youth smoking didn't increase.

Even though it was substantially less than the earlier agreement, the $206 billion payout still represented the largest civil settlement in U.S. history. Nevertheless, the agreement was anticlimactic. Once again, the cigarette corporations had managed to get the better part of the deal.

"With the master settlement agreement, the tobacco companies are only paying for half of the harms they've caused" says INFACT's Mulvey. "What they paid is only a tiny fraction of what they could owe, and they knew that, and so that's why they wanted the deal."

A few days after the multi-state settlement was signed, Minnesota's Humphrey expressed similar sentiments in an op-ed in *The New York Times*. "The new agreement will prevent the states from achieving full justice against the tobacco manufacturers," the Attorney General wrote. "What is good news for the tobacco industry has never been good news for public health. ... The settlement, in sum, demonstrates how far we have to go."[58]

A GLOBAL SETTLEMENT?

The attorneys general first agreement with Big Tobacco was billed as a "global settlement." That description, however, was misleading. Nothing in the first attorneys general agreement, nothing in the McCain bill, and nothing in the final November 1998 master settlement addressed the U.S. cigarette companies' operations abroad. For many health activists, the omission was egregious. After all, the major cigarette producers are *transnational* corporations, more concerned with their sales outside the United States than their retail numbers here. The master settlement's failure to include international tobacco control measures means that child smokers in Manila are paying for the costs of reducing youth smoking rates in Mississippi.

Health activists' achievements against Big Tobacco in the United States—although they may have fallen short of many people's aspirations—are unquestionably impressive. But even as the cigarette makers suffered a dramatic loss of power and prestige in the United States, they were able to dramatically expand their global influence and strength. The struggle to hold Big Tobacco responsible for its actions reveals the limitations even the most effective corporate accountability campaign faces in an era of economic globalization. Today, the cigarette transnationals are making a killing off their foreign profits.

Philip Morris is the world's largest transnational tobacco corporation. In fact, the company sells more cigarettes outside the United States than it does domestically. Philip Morris's profits from overseas sales first surpassed its domestic profits in 1997. In that year, the company sold 235 billion cigarettes in the United States for a profit of $3.3 billion; it sold 711 billion cigarettes abroad, earning $4.6 billion.[59] Two-thirds of the company's cigarette sales occur overseas, and the company controls at least 15 percent of the tobacco market in 40 countries. Year after year, the company is one of the world's largest advertisers. All together, Philip Morris sells more than 17 percent of all the cigarettes smoked in the world.[60]

London-based British-American Tobacco (BAT), the parent company of Brown & Williamson, has always been a proudly international company. Although its share of the global tobacco market is slightly smaller than that of Philip Morris, the company has a longer reach than its competitor, with operations in 65 countries. In Latin America alone, it sells approximately 60 percent of all cigarettes.[61] In 1999, the company sold $30 billion worth of cigarettes around the world.

In the spring of 1999, RJR bucked industry trends and sold off its international division to Japan Tobacco. The move had nothing to do with a decline in foreign sales. In fact, in 1997, the company saw a 43 percent increase in its sales in Central Europe and 13 percent increase in the republics of the former Soviet Union. By 1998, foreign sales accounted for 41 percent of RJR's total cigarette sales, and the company had subsidiaries or licensing agreements in 56 countries.[62] The company's decision to get rid of its international arm was simply an effort to clear up debts it had incurred fighting a hostile takeover bid in the early 1990s. Before the sale to Japan Tobacco, RJR had pursued a strategy of global expansion as aggressively as its larger rivals.

The tobacco transnationals have lengthened their global reach by employing the proven crowbar tactics of primitive mercantilism and by taking advantage of new opportunities offered by economic globalization. In the 1980s, the U.S.-based transnationals manipulated U.S. trade policy to pry open markets in East Asia. After the end of the Cold War, Big Tobacco drove into the formerly socialist economies ahead of all other industries. At the same time, the cigarette makers expanded their market power in Latin America as free trade agreements changed domestic ownership laws. And in every country they have entered, the tobacco corporations have repeated the aggressive defense that worked for so long in the United States: they have fought advertising bans, health warnings and smoking restrictions; they have bullied government officials; and they have stopped at nothing to sell their deadly products without public oversight. Big Tobacco has benefited from economic globalization and free trade policies like few other industries.

"EXPORTING DEATH"

Big Tobacco clearly underestimated the U.S. public's resentment toward the industry; when the cigarette makers finally conducted polling on the public's attitudes about tobacco companies, they were shocked by the deep-seated anger the polls revealed.[63] But if the industry was blind-sided by its own hubris, it was never so blind that it didn't recognize that health attitudes were changing and that the number of smokers was declining. By the early 1980s, one out of three Americans smoked, down from 40 percent a decade before. The tobacco companies could see that their U.S. sales were sliding. Other markets had to be found. To search for and then penetrate those new markets, in 1981 Philip Morris, RJR, and B&W created the U.S. Cigarette Export Association.

The largest U.S. tobacco companies looked first to Asia, where attitudes about smoking were more positive. In Japan nearly two-thirds of men smoked, and the country had (and today still does) the second-highest per capita cigarette consumption. Cigarette warning labels meekly urge: "We should all be careful not to smoke too much." In

South Korea, about 50 percent of men smoke. For Big Tobacco, these countries represented a gold mine. But there was a major problem: State-run monopolies controlled nearly all of the Asian tobacco markets, and foreign cigarettes were banned or faced massive import taxes.

To gain entry to the Asian countries, the tobacco corporations turned to the U.S. government for help. The industry argued that the import bans and high tariffs in Asia constituted barriers to free trade. In making their case to government officials, the industry appealed to the primitive mercantilism underlying U.S. trade policy: The more U.S. goods sold abroad, the better it is for the United States (no matter what the product). The U.S. Trade Representative's (USTR) office agreed.

To pry open Asian markets, Big Tobacco and USTR officials used a Commerce Department regulation known as Section 301. Under Section 301, the USTR can invoke unilateral trade sanctions against countries that discriminate against U.S. exports. High tariffs in Japan and import restrictions in South Korea, Thailand, and Taiwan represented discrimination, the USTR felt. Trade officials and industry executives said Asian governments were using public health protection as a phony justification to protect their state monopolies. The cigarette makers had a "right" to do business in Asia, the corporations and U.S. government officials declared.

In September 1985, the U.S. government threatened Section 301 trade sanctions against Japan if it did not open up its cigarette market. Senator Jesse Helms, a powerful conservative from the tobacco state of North Carolina and chair of the Senate Agriculture Committee, bolstered the demand in a letter to the Japanese Prime Minister in the summer of 1996. It included this admonition:

> Your friends in Congress will have a better chance to stem the tide of anti-Japanese trade sentiment if and when they can cite tangible examples of your doors being opened to American products. I urge you to make a commitment to establish a timetable for allowing U.S. cigarettes a specific share of your market. May I suggest a goal of 20 percent within the next 18 months?[64]

Japan complied, lowering its taxes on foreign cigarettes and rewriting its rules on advertising. The U.S. government then made similar threats to the South Koreans and the Taiwanese. In 1996 a U.S. Embassy official in Seoul wrote to a Philip Morris executive: "I want to emphasize that the embassy and the various U.S. government agencies in Washington will keep the interests of Philip Morris and other American cigarette manufacturers in the forefront of our daily concerns."[65]

South Korea and Taiwan soon followed Japan's example and changed their tobacco policies.

One country fought back against the USTR's bullying. In the fall of 1989, Thailand challenged the U.S. demands before the dispute resolution panel of the General Agreement on Tariffs and Trade (GATT), the most important international trade body. In 1990, the GATT panel ruled that Thailand's ban on imported cigarettes violated free trade rules. The GATT panelists, however, upheld the Thai restrictions on advertising. In the other Asian countries, the U.S. government had been able to roll back advertising restrictions by arguing that they constituted de facto barriers to trade. Because the state-run tobacco companies enjoyed monopolistic market shares, the transnational cigarette makers and their USTR allies argued, the foreign corporations needed free rein to "catch up" to their competitors.[66] In every nation except Thailand, governments succumbed to that argument.

At first glance, the state-run tobacco monopolies may seem curious anachronisms. It would appear counterintuitive for a government to sell to its citizens a product it knew to be deadly and which certainly burdened the country's health care system. But most health activists didn't oppose the existence of the government tobacco monopolies. The monopolies tended to produce low-quality yet high-priced cigarettes—and that kept smoking rates in check. In some countries the cigarette monopolies even had a long history of working together with national health ministries to limit cigarette consumption. Most important, the government tobacco enterprises rarely advertised. Smoking wasn't linked with image or fashion. Without the lifestyle advertising, young people and women saw little allure in smoking.

The entry of the tobacco transnationals and the sudden appearance of cigarette advertising changed all that. Big Tobacco didn't just export cigarettes; it also exported its proven marketing savvy. Advertisements told young people that smoking was a sign of sophistication; women, who in many Asian countries had never smoked in great numbers before, were told that it was proof of liberation. Ironically, even as smoking rates declined in the United States, the tobacco transnationals used American models in ads to equate smoking with Western affluence.

As they entered the Asian countries, the tobacco transnationals went on an advertising spree, buying as much as 50 percent of the television ad time in some countries.[67] The foreign corporations sponsored rock concerts, art exhibits, and even sporting events to introduce their brands to the public. Attractive women were hired to give out free samples at discos and bars. The companies gave away hats, compact discs, t-shirts, and even motorcycles in exchange for empty packs.

"You name it and they do it," Dr. Judith Mackay, once director of the Asian Consultancy on Tobacco Control and now an official at the World Health Organization, told a reporter in the wake of the transnationals' entry into Asia.

> Wherever they can, they have overt, direct advertising—on television, on billboards, in the print media, everywhere. . . . When it comes to sponsorship, again you name it and they sponsor it. They sponsor sports and arts. Recently, in Asia, they sponsored the Camel Rally in Mongolia. They sponsored Michael Chang and Pete Sampras to play tennis in Asia. They sponsor rock concerts, karaoke bars, discos. The Hope Library in China. Training to be a psychotherapist in China. Chinese football. I could rattle off one after the other.[68]

The marketing blitz worked. In Taiwan, foreign cigarette sales went from 1 percent to 20 percent in two years. Within a year of the market opening in South Korea, U.S. companies had 6 percent of the market. In Japan, the tobacco transnationals soon controlled 22 percent of the market.[69] The advertising offensive, and the foreign companies' success, spurred the national monopolies to gear up their own marketing. Afraid of losing market share, state-run enterprises tried to beat the transnationals at their own game, creating an advertising arms race.

The entry of the cigarette transnationals, the introduction of foreign marketing campaigns, and the appearance of domestic ads caused an immediate surge in smoking rates and overall cigarette consumption. After Korea's import restrictions were lifted in 1988, smoking rates among male Korean teenagers rose from 18.4 percent to 29.8 percent in a single year; in that same period, the smoking rate among Korean female teens shot up to 8.7 percent from 1.6 percent. In Taiwan, smoking rates among high school students jumped from 22 percent to 32 percent between 1985 and 1987. And in Japan, teen smoking among males shot up from 26 to 40 percent in the years following the change in the country's tobacco regulations.[70] According to the World Health Organization, total tobacco consumption increased 15 percent between 1988 and 1990, the years immediately following the Section 301 threats.[71]

As it became apparent that the tobacco transnationals' aggressive drive into Asia and the USTR's support of the industry were prompting increased smoking, health activists started complaining that the U.S. government shouldn't be promoting the interests of the cigarette makers. The industry responded with its practiced brazenness.

"Most worldwide smokers think American tobacco is the sweetest and the tastiest," a spokesperson for the Tobacco Institute told a reporter. "It's legal here, it's legal there. What's the problem?"[72]

The problem, of course, was that the United States was, in the words of Surgeon General Koop, "exporting disease, disability, and death." A 1990 report by the U.S. General Accounting Office, a research arm of Congress, seemed to agree, noting that America's domestic health policies and its trade agenda were at "cross purposes." But U.S. policy makers didn't resolve the contradiction until 1997, when, during the height of anti-tobacco sentiment, Congress passed the Doggett Amendment. The law blocks government money from promoting the export of tobacco overseas or seeking the removal of any country's tobacco control laws, provided they affect domestic and international manufacturers alike.

By the time the Doggett Amendment was passed, however, the cigarette transnationals had figured out how to enter countries without the U.S. government wielding the sanctions crowbar. The dissolution of the Soviet Union and the fall of the Berlin Wall gave Big Tobacco a host of virgin markets. At the same time, free trade agreements were starting to change the rules of international commerce, meaning that the industry wouldn't have to resort to combative tactics to increase its reach.

The countries of Eastern Europe and the former Soviet Union are among the smokiest in the world. Of the top ten heaviest smoking nations in terms of packs per person consumed each year, five of them— Poland, Slovenia, Czech Republic, Hungary, and Slovakia—are former socialist countries. In Russia, two-thirds of men smoke. Smoking is so ingrained there that when a cigarette shortage occurred in 1990, then-President Mikhail Gorbachev arranged for Philip Morris and RJR to import more than 30 billion cigarettes to diffuse what was being called the "tobacco rebellion."[73] The cigarette airlift provided a beachhead for Big Tobacco's coming invasion of the formerly socialist nations. In the 1990s the Soviet bloc nations were for the cigarette transnationals what Asia was for them in the 1980s: new territory to be exploited.

Once again, Big Tobacco opened its offensive with an advertising and marketing charge. As in Asia, smokers in Eastern Europe had never seen tobacco advertisements. In societies unaccustomed to modern marketing techniques, the tobacco ads were especially seductive.

"All the tactics which the companies are using did not exist here before," Dr. Witold Zatonski, a Polish health activist, told a reporter as the tobacco battle raged in the United States.

> They introduced quite aggressive and sophisticated, at least for us, technical advertising. Many people were saying, 'Look. They have decorated our streets with these posters. They are very beautiful. They are putting up these beautiful pictures in public places.' Many people were

quite pleased in the beginning with this new fashion, with this new art which was developing around us.[74]

In Eastern Europe and the former Soviet Union, the tobacco corporations linked their brands to "American" themes. Winston offered a "Taste of Freedom." The Marlboro Man started appearing everywhere, offering "Total Freedom" and a "Rendezvous with America." When anti-American sentiment increased in Russia in the mid-1990s, RJR switched to marketing "Peter the Great" cigarettes for those who "believe . . . in the grandeur of Russian lands." By the mid-1990s, foreign cigarette companies accounted for 40 percent of all advertising in Russia.[75]

In the former socialist countries, the cigarette transnationals have also taken advantage of the chaos caused by the economic transition to capitalism. To keep labor and production costs low and increase their profit margins, Big Tobacco went on a buying spree in the 1990s. Between 1991 and 1997, Western tobacco corporations spent more than $3 billion buying dozens of decrepit state-owned cigarette factories.[76] In March of 1998 alone, Philip Morris, BAT, and RJR announced $480 million of new investments in Russia.[77] Aside from supplying cheap labor, the domestic production allows the transnationals to avoid import taxes. Most important, by buying up existing enterprises, the foreign tobacco corporations automatically secure valuable market share. Philip Morris has gained one-third of the Polish market through purchasing old state-run plants. In Romania, the second largest tobacco market in Eastern Europe, foreign cigarette makers also gained a third of the market this way. Seventy percent of the cigarettes consumed in Russia are produced by Big Tobacco.

As always, the industry says its expansion has not led to an increase in smoking. "We export cigarettes," a Philip Morris spokesperson said when questioned about the company's operations in the region. "We don't export smoking."[78]

Yet smoking rates throughout most of Eastern Europe and the former Soviet Union are on the rise. In Russia, cigarette consumption has increased 40 percent since 1986. Smoking among Russian children aged 10 to 14 rose from 19 percent in 1992 to 35 percent in 1993. Most of those children smoke foreign brands.[79]

Big Tobacco has also employed its strategy of simply buying up local competitors in Latin America. Before the ratification of the North American Free Trade Agreement, Mexico prohibited foreign companies from owning more than 50 percent of any enterprise. With that rule gone, the tobacco transnationals have moved into Mexico to grab the Mexican smokers' pesos, and to establish a platform for exporting cheaper cigarettes and cheaper raw tobacco leaf to the United States and Canada. In July 1997, BAT and Philip Morris paid a combined $2.1 billion to buy the first- and second-largest Mexican tobacco companies, respectively. The purchases give the two transnationals de facto control of the 15th largest cigarette market in the world.

Big Tobacco is also hoping that free trade will deliver the biggest prize of all: China. Smoking rates and per capita consumption are relatively low in China. But the sheer size of the country's population means that there are more smokers in China than there are people in the United States. One of every three smokers in the world lives in China. Whichever company makes the first inroads there stands to make a killing.

The Chinese market, however, remains largely closed. Sales of tobacco leaf, cigarette sales, and taxes on cigarettes together represent the largest source of government revenue, accounting for an estimated 12 percent of the country's budget.[80] Not surprisingly, then, the Chinese government has gone to great lengths to protect its monopoly over Chinese smokers. Despite massive advertising and a heavy black market trade, transnationals sell just 4 percent of the cigarettes smoked there.

In 1992, China, facing a Section 301 sanctions threat, signed a memorandum of understanding with the United States to lift all licensing requirements on cigarettes within two years. But the government, afraid of surrendering revenue it can't afford to lose, still hasn't complied with the agreement. That may soon change. As a condition of gaining membership in the World Trade Organization, China has agreed to phase out tobacco subsidies and lower tariffs on cigarette imports. It's expected that the government will delay implementing those promises as long as possible. Nevertheless, it's likely that China will eventually succumb to the pressures of Big Tobacco. And when that happens, if history is any guide, smoking rates and overall consumption in the world's largest country will increase amid a wave of advertising and marketing.

"If any cigarette company could capture the Chinese market," activist Judith Mackay has said, "it wouldn't matter if every smoker in North America quit tomorrow."[81]

GLOBAL RESISTANCE

According to the World Health Organization, at least 1.1 billion people older than 15 smoke. Seventy percent of those smokers live in the less-developed countries.[82] While smoking rates in the developed world are falling at a pace of about 1.1 percent a year, they are rising by 2.1 percent annually in the world's poor countries. The number of smokers is growing fastest in those countries least able to handle the health problems created by tobacco use. The trend, which already costs millions of lives every year, threatens an even greater health catastrophe. By 2020, tobacco's annual death toll will reach 10 million, with seven out of every ten deaths occurring in the developing world: a 700 percent increase from a generation before. If smoking rates continue to climb, tobacco-related deaths could in 25 years exceed the number of deaths from AIDS, tuberculosis, and childbirth complications combined.[83]

The responsibility for many of these deaths will fall squarely on the cigarette transnationals, which have pushed their way into countries around the world. But the tobacco industry's aggression hasn't gone without opposition. Worldwide, activists have fought for tobacco control measures designed to help slow the health disaster created by the industry. Confronted by persistent industry belligerence, activists are now working on a truly global solution that promises to put real restrictions on the transnationals' behavior.

For decades, many developing nations lagged behind the industrialized world in formulating and enforcing tobacco control regulations. In Asia, for example, only Hong Kong and Singapore had meaningful restrictions on tobacco by the late 1980s. But as the cigarette transnationals launched their drive into the developing world, national health officials quickly responded to the new marketing aggression. During the last decade, many countries have put in place tobacco restrictions much stronger than those in the United States and Western Europe. In South Africa a major tobacco tax increase led to a sharp drop in consumption. Warning labels on South African cigarette packs read, "Smoking Can Kill You" and include a toll-free number for addiction help. Poland has banned tobacco ads on radio and TV and requires all outdoor ads to contain a warning at least 20 percent of the size of the ad. In Thailand, a total ban on advertising has limited the transnationals to less than 5 percent of the country's cigarette market. The European Union is set to phase out all broadcast advertising, and cigarette companies will soon be prohibited from sponsoring sporting or cultural events in Canada.

Several foreign governments have even tried to copy the U.S. attorneys general Medicaid lawsuits against Big Tobacco. In the spring of 1998, Guatemala became the first nation to sue the U.S. cigarette makers when it filed a claim in U.S. federal court to recover $3.2 billion the government said it spent treating citizens suffering from tobacco-related diseases. Israel and two Canadian provinces later filed similar suits. Although a judge threw out the Guatemalan suit, attorneys in other countries are investigating ways of suing the transnationals for breaking laws against marketing to children.[84]

Of course, the cigarette makers have fiercely fought all tobacco control proposals, and on the occasions when they have lost, they have found ingenious ways to get around the enforcement of regulations. As in the United States, the industry has been a potent force in parliaments and legislatures, especially in the dozens of countries where tobacco is an important cash crop. In Ukraine, Big Tobacco successfully fought for a repeal of most of the country's restrictions on tobacco advertising. When the government of the Philippines launched a campaign to reduce child smoking, the transnationals worked to "neutralize" the effort. In Senegal, the industry succeeded in rolling back bans on advertising.[85] During the late 1980s, the industry defeated several proposed no-smoking laws in Switzerland, a country it perceives to be a bellwether for European attitudes about smoking.[86] And in China the transnationals successfully pressured directors at the state-run tobacco monopoly to stop cooperating with the country's health officials. Just as in the United States, the industry is determined to avoid any restrictions on its deadly business.

After the attorneys general announced the June 20 settlement with the tobacco companies, activists warned that a settlement in the United States without global controls would actually exacerbate public health threats in the rest of the world. Part of the activists' fears rested on the concern that national controls imposed on a transnational industry would accelerate a race to the bottom in standards. Indeed, the disparity in tobacco control regulations contributes to a danger that could undermine all rules: the threat of smuggling.

Each year about 300 billion cigarettes—or a third of all cigarettes in international commerce—are illegally smuggled. The cigarette black market costs governments at least $16 billion in lost taxes and customs revenue, money that could be used to treat sick smokers.[87] Smuggling encourages people to smoke by making cigarettes cheaper, and black market cigarettes don't have to comply with health warnings. Most important for the transnationals, smuggling creates a disincentive for governments to have high tariffs on cigarettes and it weakens local competitors. By chipping away at regulations country by country and by raising the specter of smuggling, the industry can foment doubts about the wisdom of controls in all other countries.

GLOBAL REGULATION

Efforts to establish meaningful international tobacco controls are well underway. In 1999, the member states of the World Health Organization (WHO) unanimously agreed to launch negotiations on a global tobacco treaty. Fifty nations immediately pledged financial and political support for the treaty, called the Framework Convention on Tobacco Control (FCTC). When it is adopted, the convention will become the first international health treaty to be negotiated through the WHO.

"I think the FCTC is a very positive process," says Glantz. "I'm sure the industry is doing everything they can to get rid of it. They know it means that, internationally, the genie is out of the bottle."

In the spring of 2003, WHO negotiators presented the completed treaty to countries for ratification. The FCTC addresses two key issues: smuggling and marketing. The anti-smuggling protocol involves a system for tracking cigarette exports and the creation of special labels that will allow enforcement officials to follow a pack of cigarettes from origin to destination. By clamping down on smuggling, WHO officials hope to create new incentives for governments to put in place high cigarette taxes that will eventually lower consumption. The treaty also includes tough, new restrictions on the marketing of tobacco. Terms like "light" and "ultralight" will be banned. In countries where such restrictions are constitutional, total prohibitions on cigarette advertising will be put in place. Finally, the treaty encourages countries to pass strict indoor air laws and dramatically increase tobacco taxes. The treaty will to put real limits on the way Big Tobacco conducts its business around the world.

Most countries—including nearly all developing nations, which are especially eager to clamp down on tobacco use—are expected to ratify the treaty. But the United States probably will not, nor will Germany and China.[88] While activists are disappointed that some countries will opt out of the system, they remain pleased about the precedent the treaty will set. The FCTC represents not just the first international health treaty negotiated by the WHO, but also the first binding global corporate accountability compact.

"Because we're dealing with transnational corporations, the controls have to be transnational," says INFACT's Mulvey.

OFF THE HOOK?

The struggle against Big Tobacco shows that, when it comes to battling Corporate America, activists can't hope to compete against industry on its money terms. The deep pockets of trial attorneys helped put the cigarette manufacturers on the defensive for a spell. Yet no public interest force was prepared to match the tens of millions of dollars the tobacco corporations spent to defeat the proposed McCain legislation. Evidently even the greatest swells of popular opinion can be reversed by waves of corporate cash. This proves that corporate accountability activists shouldn't try to fight fire with fire: When it comes to corporate political spending, they will always be outgunned. What's needed, then, is to get money out of the political system. In the long run, anti-corporate forces' best hopes are in disarming corporations of their ability to bribe elected officials.

The health activists' strength came from their long record of success in passing local clean air laws. By mobilizing people community by community, the anti-smoking forces were able to steadily change public attitudes about smoking while undermining the image of the cigarette makers. Seen in hindsight, health activists' biggest victories didn't come in the courts or in Congress, but in the culture wars for the public mind. In fact, it was those cultural successes—the subtle shifting of social views about smoking—that made the legal victories possible.

Those successes contain an important lesson for corporate accountability activists: Local action is often more effective than national efforts. As activists progress up the political food chain from the local, to the state, to the national and then international level, officials become generally less responsive to citizens. This explains why, as the health activists demonstrated, political change is often easier to accomplish at local levels. The scale of politics is easier to manage at the municipal or county level. Also, local politicians are often more eager allies for the simple reason that they understand that their authority is place-based, grounded in a specific geographical jurisdiction. In contrast, transnational corporations gain their economic strength from *not* being rooted in place. There is a fundamental contradiction between the economic needs of transnational capital and the political needs of local authorities.

Yet, as Big Tobacco's international reach illustrates, the lesson contains its own contradiction, and should be studied carefully. For in today's economy, even the most important local success can be undermined by the forces of the global market. Local action is essential, but it does not replace the necessity for coordinated action with global allies. The tensions between the effectiveness of local organizing and the need for global action pose a tremendous challenge for corporate accountability activists: Without the first, victory is unlikely, and without the second, lasting triumph will prove elusive. As the experience of the Free Burma activists will show in the next chapter, balancing the demands for local and global action is not easy.

The tobacco saga also proves that every political controversy has a half-life. In 1997 and 1998, tobacco represented a major political issue. At that time, challenging the cigarette makers was a wise move politically, as presidential candidate John McCain's championship of the effort demonstrated.

Today, efforts to hold the tobacco corporations accountable for their actions have faded from the public's attention. And the lack of attention means that politicians can work on the industry's behalf without facing a barrage of criticism. Big Tobacco has always worked best from the shadows.

Congressional approval of FDA regulatory power over the tobacco industry seems unlikely. The issue has been a nonstarter on Capitol Hill since the defeat of the McCain bill. Ironically, the only real supporter of FDA jurisdiction is Philip Morris, which hopes that set rules would give it the stability its Wall Street investors desire. Health activists have hesitated to support FDA legislation, afraid that any measure supported by the industry itself will prove a raw deal.

Big Tobacco has also received a boost from the Supreme Court. In March 2000, the justices upheld the earlier appeals court decision and ruled 5-4 that the FDA has no jurisdiction to regulate tobacco. The court agreed with the argument that because cigarettes are so inherently deadly, the agency would have no choice but to entirely ban them, powers it didn't have. The FDA immediately sent letters to all the states announcing the shutdown of its program to enforce laws against selling tobacco to minors, which had been a central part of its regulatory efforts.[89]

A year after the FDA decision, the Supreme Court gave the industry another boost when it struck down Massachusetts' restrictions on tobacco advertising, calling them a violation of the corporate freedom of speech. But the tobacco corporations still have not been able to get out from under the shadow of legal assaults.

In a surprising reversal of its earlier policies, in March 2003 the Bush administration's Justice Department announced that it was calling for the cigarette companies to forfeit $289 billion in profits gained from 50 years of "fraudulent" marketing tactics. Quoting from more than 38 million pages of internal cigarette company documents, the Justice Department accused the industry of running "what amounts to a criminal enterprise by manipulating nicotine levels, lying to their customers about the dangers of tobacco and directing their multibillion dollar advertising campaigns at children."[90]

Continuing the lawsuit started by the Clinton Justice Department in 1999, the new filing with the Federal District Court in Washington marked the first time the federal government put a dollar figure on the amount of "ill-gotten gains" the industry should forfeit. The Justice Department claimed that:

> ... in short, defendants' scheme to defraud permeated and influenced all facets of defendants' conduct—research, product development, advertising, marketing, legal, public relations, and communications—in a manner that has resulted in extraordinary profits for the past half-century, but has had devastating consequences for the public's health.[91]

Activists have also kept heat on the industry as they have maintained their boycott against Philip Morris' Kraft division and their efforts to pass clean indoor air laws. And the civil lawsuits against the cigarette corporations keep on coming.

In 1997 and 1998, Big Tobacco's top goal was winning immunity from legal challenges and putting a cap on liability payments to ensure a stable business environment. Such stability has proven elusive. The number of individual and class action lawsuits against the tobacco corporations continues to grow. Already, several legal challenges have delivered heavy punishment to the industry. And with every new guilty verdict against the cigarette makers, the dollar amounts grow larger.

In January 1999, a San Francisco jury awarded $51.5 million to a woman suing Philip Morris for her inoperable lung cancer. Just a few months later, an Oregon jury ordered Philip Morris to pay $81 million to the family of a man who died of lung cancer after smoking Marlboros for four decades. In the spring of 2001, jurors in Los Angeles awarded $3 billion to a lifelong Philip Morris customer and lung cancer sufferer.

While the brush fires of individual lawsuits threaten to turn into a conflagration that could cripple the industry, the biggest danger to the industry's continued profitability remains the class action lawsuits, with their possibility of gigantic damage awards.

A historic verdict against the industry in a class action trial came in 1999, when a Florida jury found that the tobacco corporations should be held responsible for addicting people to a product they knew to be deadly. A year later, after another long series of hearings to decide what the penalty should be, the six-person panel handed down the largest damage award in history: $144.8 billion.

The jurors said the industry's dishonesty and its arrogance were the main forces behind their verdict and damages decision. The industry had to be held accountable for what it had done. "For a period of 50 years, these tobacco companies denied the dangers of their product," the jury foreman said in an interview after the penalty announcement. "They belittled or denied causation of the health effects of smoking and addiction, and had the gall to challenge public health authorities."

The jurors' justification for their massive damage award is bad news, not just for the tobacco industry, but for all of Corporate America. The jurors' thinking offers a crucial lesson to the broader corporate accountability movement: Corporations or industries that mislead the public about the nature of their products are vulnerable to the same kind of assault suffered by Big Tobacco. The chemical industry (which for decades hid the effects of its products) and the auto and oil companies (which have denied the science on global warming) have good reason to be wary about future pressure campaigns. "We thought it [the damage award] was fair," the jury foreman continued.

It would bring to the forefront, for the first time in the history of this country, the issues surrounding this product and the millions of lives that have been affected by this. And it would put the companies on notice—not just the tobacco companies, all companies—concerning fraud or misrepresentation of the American public.[92]

5

CITIZEN DIPLOMACY vs.
CORPORATE PROFITS
Defending Human Rights in Burma

ON THE FIRST WEEKEND of February 1997, some 400 progressive activists from around the country gathered at American University in Washington, DC, for the first conference of the Free Burma Coalition (FBC). During the preceding year and a half, people across the United States had been working to restore democracy in the Southeast Asian country of Burma, condemned as one of the most repressive nations on Earth. By pressuring U.S.-based corporations to withdraw from Burma, the activists hoped to force the country's military rulers to implement democratic reforms. The strategy was reminiscent of the antiapartheid movement, and the FBC labeled their effort the "anti-apartheid struggle of the '90's."

The FBC had already scored some impressive victories. The year before, activists had convinced nine cities and the state of Massachusetts to approve laws restricting the purchase of goods and services from companies with operations in Burma. These so-called "selective purchasing laws" forced major corporations such as Apple Computer, Hewlett-Packard, Motorola, and Eastman Kodak to withdraw from Burma. In the summer of 1996, the U.S. Congress passed, and President Clinton signed, legislation making way for a ban on all new U.S. investment in the country. And just weeks before the American University conference, PepsiCo, which had been the central target of a wave of campus protests and boycotts, announced that it would sever all commercial relations with Burma. The conference agenda was hopeful, and the activists in Washington were confident of future success.

Unknown to many of the conference participants, a shadow hung over these victories. A month before, in January, the European Union and Japan had sent letters to U.S. trade officials complaining that the Massachusetts selective purchasing law violated World Trade Organization (WTO) regulations regarding government procurement. At the same time, the U.S. big business lobby was preparing a strategy to ensure that selective purchase laws would not interfere with corporate interests. The FBC's most potent weapon, government procurement rules targeting corporations doing business in Burma, was in jeopardy.

In June 1997, the EU asked for a WTO consultation on the Massachusetts Burma law. In April 1998 that challenge was overshadowed by a more serious threat to the activists' goals when the National Foreign Trade Council, a consortium of more than 600 U.S. transnational corporations, filed a lawsuit in federal court charging that the Massachusetts selective purchasing law was unconstitutional. The case would eventually go all the way to the U.S. Supreme Court. Unwittingly, the Free Burma Coalition's efforts to bring democracy to one brutalized country became a test case for whether local and state governments in the United States can use their purchasing power to promote social goals in a globalized economy.

The Free Burma campaign offers a bright example of grassroots democracy and corporate accountability in action. Human rights activists, determined to sever the financial support for a brutal military junta, went to university administrators, city councils, and state governments to press for economic measures against companies doing business in Burma. These efforts quickly percolated up to Washington, where lawmakers eventually approved federal sanctions against Burma.

At the same time, the campaign revealed the awesome power of the Internet and e-mail for drawing together and energizing social movements. During the first years of its existence, the Free Burma Coalition was exclusively an Internet-based operation; it had no offices or paid staff. Many of the activists at the Washington, DC, conference in early 1997 had never met before. Although they had worked closely together for more than a year, most of their communication had been via e-mail and through the FBC Website. By employing proven tactics like selective purchasing laws and new technologies like the Internet, the FBC succeeded in creating a nationwide grassroots movement that scored some real achievements.

But the Free Burma activists confronted two obstacles their antiapartheid predecessors did not have to contend with: a bolder, more organized corporate lobby hostile to their agenda, and a global economy completely unconcerned with their goals. The corporate lobby's ideological defense of free and unfettered trade eventually robbed the Free Burma forces of their most potent weapon: selective purchasing laws. And the unwillingness of other nations to duplicate the, albeit limited, U.S. sanctions against Burma allowed the military junta to stay in power.

"I was completely blindsided by the WTO challenge, and I never expected a group of corporations to fight this in federal court," says Simon Billenness, a socially responsible investment expert who coauthored the Massachusetts law and helped design the FBC's selective purchasing strategy. "I never, never expected it."[1]

The FBC did an unquestionably admirable job in achieving the objective of forcing companies to withdraw from Burma; today only one major U.S. corporation has operations there. But the coalition's central goal—freeing the Burmese from decades of autocratic rule—remains as distant today as it was at that hope-filled meeting in the winter of 1997.

A HISTORY OF OPPRESSION

Burma, a Texas-sized country of about 50 million people situated between Thailand, India, and China, has a long history of oppression. During the last two centuries the Burmese people have hardly ever enjoyed the self-determination of democracy, and for the last four decades the country has been ruled by a series of increasingly brutal military juntas.

In the 19th century and the first half of the 20th century, Burma was a colony of the British Empire. The British entered Burma in the 1820s, and by 1886 British control over the country was completed when the imperial administrators decided to make Burma a colony separate from India. The most focused efforts for independence came during World War II, as the Burmese, caught in the middle of some of the worst fighting in Asia, sided first with the Japanese and then with the British as the armies' fates changed. Led by an adept military commander named Aung San, the Burmese gained independence in 1947. In the country's first election, Aung San's political party won a landslide victory. But in April 1947, on the eve of taking power, Aung San and six of his ministers were assassinated by political rivals. A colleague of Aung San, U Nu, became leader of the newly democratic country.

For the next 15 years, the Burmese enjoyed a season of democracy. The representative government ran more or less smoothly, and the military largely stayed out of politics. Tensions between the Burman* majority and the country's many different ethnic minorities, however, strained the young country, and in 1962 military officers concerned about a breakup of the state launched a coup.

The military junta, led by a general named Ne Win, immediately suspended all civil liberties and clamped down on dissent. Armed conflicts with ethnic guerilla groups flared up along the borders. Torture, political imprisonment, and other human rights abuses became common.[2] The country's ethnic minorities suffered harsh treatment.

During the next 26 years, Ne Win's Burma Socialist Program Party (BSPP) ruled the country with a harsh grip. Student and worker demon-

---

* The word "Burmese" refers to all the people living in Burma. "Burman" applies only to the ethnic majority living in the country's central lowlands.

strations were invariably crushed by the generals. In the mid-1970s, former premier U Nu tried to launched an armed rebellion from the Thai border, but it failed to gain support. Throughout these decades, the BSPP's "Burmese Way of Socialism," characterized mainly by an extreme isolationism, steadily wrecked the economy. The country's already limited resources were poured into the military to fight the ethnic guerilla groups. Rice, the nation's main subsistence crop and once a major export, started to be in short supply.

In 1988, food shortages and general discontent with the BSPP's authoritarian rule led to rebellious anger. In March of that year, a scuffle in a tea shop in the capital Rangoon between a group of students and some police led to the killing of a student.[3] Students demanded an inquiry into the killing, and when the military rulers ignored the request nonviolent student demonstrations broke out in the capital. The student protesters were soon joined by civil servants and workers. Even the country's Buddhist monks, a pillar of Burmese society, became involved, refusing to accept rice bowl donations from soldiers as a sign of disrespect.

On August 8, hundreds of thousands of people across the country, including even some police and soldiers, turned out for massive demonstrations. (The Burmese are obsessed with numerology, and 8-8-88 was considered a significant date.) The military junta responded with force. Soldiers in Rangoon opened fire on the nonviolent protesters, killing hundreds. Despite this repression, the rebellion continued.

In early September, Ne Win responded to calls for democracy by announcing his resignation and promising elections. But a new junta was immediately formed. On September 18, the Orwellian-named State Law and Order Restoration Committee (SLORC) announced that it would halt all dissent. During the next few weeks, the renamed junta cracked down on the nascent pro-democracy movement. Independent newspapers were closed, more than a thousand opposition leaders were rounded up, and soldiers machine-gunned protesters. An estimated 10,000 people were killed during the next two years.[4]

In the midst of this chaos, a new opposition figure arose: Aung San Suu Kyi, daughter of the country's independence hero General Aung San. Born in 1945, Aung San Suu Kyi had been raised in Britain. She had married a British man, had two children there, and was largely detached from the troubles in Burma. In 1988, she returned to the country to be with her ailing mother. When the pro-democracy movement erupted, Aung San Suu Kyi took a leading role because, as the daughter of Aung San, she felt a duty to become involved with the struggle.[5]

While the SLORC tightened its grip on the country, Aung San Suu

Kyi and other opposition forces formed the National League for Democracy (NLD). SLORC, recognizing that they had a powerful adversary in Aung San Suu Kyi, placed her under house arrest in July 1989. The junta jailed scores of other senior NLD officials.

To the surprise of many, SLORC permitted elections to take place on May 27, 1990. Evidently SLORC was willing to hold open elections because the generals believed there was no way they could lose. The pro-democracy movement, led by the NLD, was shut out of the state-run media in the months leading up the election, and the party had virtually no resources compared to the SLORC-backed National Unity Party. Thousands of opposition activists, the NLD's base, had fled to Thailand, and Aung San Suu Kyi, though head of the party, was not allowed a line on the ballot. The junta was so bold it even changed the country's name to Myanmar. (To this day, the democratic opposition continues to call the country Burma.)

The results from the May 27 vote stunned the military leaders. Millions of people, an estimated 60 percent of the electorate, came out to vote. Of the 485 parliamentary seats up for grabs, the NLD won 392—more than 80 percent. Ethnic minority parties opposed to the SLORC won another 65 seats. The military's National Unity Party won just ten seats.[6] The tally was a stinging rebuke to the military rulers, revealing not just the breadth of popular opposition to the regime but also the SLORC's utter detachment from the people.

The generals refused to give up power. They nullified the results, declaring that the election had not been for parliament but instead had been conducted to form a constituent assembly that was to write new constitution. The regime again jailed hundreds of NLD activists, including this time dozens of people who had just been elected to serve in parliament. Aung San Suu Kyi was kept under house arrest. Repression across the country grew.

More than a decade after the NLD landslide, SLORC continues to rule Burma by decree.* The United Nations, human rights groups such as Amnesty International and Human Rights Watch, and the U.S. State Department agree that Burma is one of the most repressive countries on Earth. Wracked by poverty, stunted by repression, afflicted with widespread drug abuse, and facing an AIDS epidemic, the people of Burma are one of the most abused populations in the world.

The SLORC's system for keeping the Burmese population in check

---

* In 1997, the SLORC renamed itself the State Peace and Development Council in a bid to improve its image. Most Free Burma activists and the Burmese exile community continue to use the name SLORC, in a self-consciously slanderous way.

is brutally authoritarian. There is no freedom of speech or assembly. The press is tightly controlled by the military and the use of unauthorized fax machines or modems is punishable by 15 years in jail. The SLORC prohibits the formation of private civic associations, and it is illegal for more than five people to gather together publicly without a permit. Travel abroad is tightly controlled, and even within the country Burmese are expected to report to the local police if they plan on having guests sleep over at their homes.[7] Propaganda billboards warning the population not to resist the government dot the country. "Crush all internal and external domestic elements as the common enemy," says a common sign. "Even if you say you do not know the laws, you will not be forgiven," read other billboards.[8] According to the U.S. Embassy in Rangoon, there are about 1,400 political prisoners in jail.[9]

The country's ethnic minorities have suffered particularly harsh abuse. In the last ten years, SLORC has signed cease-fire agreements with 15 different ethnic insurgencies in an effort to consolidate its control. But the conflicts earlier in the decade were brutal. In the early 1990s, tens of thousands of Muslim Rohingya in western Burma were driven from their homes and into India and Bangladesh. Although most have returned, Human Rights Watch estimates that at least 20,000 Rohingya remain refugees.[10] Government attacks against the Karenni of eastern Burma in the mid-1990s were especially harsh. Dozens of villages were displaced or relocated. Torture and the execution of civilians were widespread. A few thousand armed Karenni still battle the government, and tens of thousands of refugees remain stranded in Thailand.

To maintain its tight control, SLORC has quadrupled the size of the military in the last decade to more than 400,000 soldiers. Since Burma lacks any external enemies, this force is used against the Burmese people themselves. Tens of thousands of soldiers are stationed in and around the country's major cities. The SLORC has paid for the expansion and maintenance of its army in three ways: cutting spending on social services, selling off the country's natural resources to transnational corporations, and forcing civilians to work for the military without pay.

Burma is one of the poorest countries in the world. Average annual per capita income is about $300.[11] According to the World Health Organization, only Sierra Leone's healthcare services are worse. Four out of ten children in Burma are malnourished, and the government spends just 28 cents a year per child on public schools. Spending on education has declined 70 percent since 1990.[12] The universities have been closed for most of the last decade. In comparison, just after World War II, despite suffering serious damage during the war, Burma had the best healthcare system and highest literacy rate in Southeast Asia.[13]

The SLORC routinely forces citizens to work on construction projects. Roads, airports, and railroads across the country have been built with forced labor. The military regularly compels civilians to build or repair army roads and camps or forces them to work as cooks and launderers at military bases.[14] According to Amnesty International, children as young as eight years old have been forced to work on government construction projects. Families are allowed to get out of their duties only if they pay a fee or donate food.

But reducing social spending and employing forced labor go only so far. To get the hard cash it needs to buy military hardware, the SLORC has resorted to selling off the country's vast natural resources. While the military rulers have received billions of dollars from foreign investment, the environment has suffered badly. In the early 1990s, SLORC sold logging concessions to several Thai companies, which quickly clear-cut vast tracts of teak forests. Fishing contracts, also granted to Thai corporations in the early 1990s, have led to severe overfishing by modern trawler fleets in wide areas of the Andaman Sea, off Burma's southeast coast.[15] Tin dredging on the Burmese coast has caused ocean pollution and marine life destruction.[16] And the construction of the Yadana natural gas pipeline—the country's single largest source of foreign investment—through the forests along the Thai border, has contributed to the destruction of habitats for rhinoceroses, tigers, and elephants.

The Burmese people receive almost none of the proceeds from these foreign investment projects. The money goes directly to a few hundred of the highest-ranking army officers. The vast majority of Burmese struggle to live on less than $1 a day, while the military junta and its small circle of supporters possess all the amenities of First World affluence: sport utility vehicles, satellite dishes, and big homes surrounded by well-tended lawns.[17]

Into this mix of repression and exploitation swirls another scourge—drugs. Burma is the world's second-largest producer of opium, after Afghanistan, and it is also a regional exporter of amphetamines. While Burma has always been a source of opium—the "Golden Triangle" between the frontiers of Laos, Burma, and Thailand is legendary as a source of drugs—heroin production has skyrocketed since the SLORC took control. Between 1988 and 1996, Burmese heroin production grew 400 percent.[18] Most of this heroin goes overseas, and many observers attribute a drop in the U.S. price of heroin in the mid-1990s to the increased supply from Burma. In 1996, for example, more than 60 percent of the heroin seized in New York City was produced in Burma.[19] But a portion is consumed in the country itself, and addiction rates have grown in the last decade.

The SLORC has repeatedly said that it is not involved in the drug business. This is partially true. The vast majority of the poppy cultivation occurs in the homeland of the Shan, Wa, and Kokang peoples, ethnic groups who were once at war with the SLORC and now enjoy considerable autonomy from the central government. Nevertheless, a large share of drug revenues are laundered through the conventional economy, and it is widely reported that many of the hotels in Rangoon and Mandalay have been financed with drug money. In any case, it's unquestionable that the SLORC has done little or nothing to clamp down on the drug trade; the junta simply looks the other way.

As the drug trade and its attendant addiction destroys lives in Burma and abroad, it has bred another problem for the country—HIV and AIDS. Needle-sharing among heroin users is commonplace in Burma, and 57 percent of users are HIV positive.[20] The virus has spread from heroin users to the population at large. Forty-seven percent of prostitutes are HIV positive—three times the number in Thailand and a rate comparable to the most hard-hit countries of Central Africa. The disease is also spreading in jails, where inmates donate blood for money, and in monasteries, where monks share razors to shave their heads. In the face of this growing health crisis, the SLORC has done nothing. HIV testing is rare, and condoms, once banned, are a luxury.

Amid this brutality and malignant neglect, the pro-democracy opposition continues to struggle to restore freedom to Burma. The leadership and charisma of Aung San Suu Kyi, who was awarded the Nobel Peace Prize in 1991, has allowed the movement to remain in the eye of the Burmese population and the international community. And NLD activists continue to press for change even as their numbers have been whittled by a decade of oppression. The struggle goes on.

Since 1995, human rights activists from around the world have contributed greatly to the efforts of the Burmese pro-democracy movement. By pressuring transnational corporations with business in Burma to withdraw from the country, activists, mostly in the United States, have eroded the SLORC's financial base. In their efforts to help pro-democracy forces in Burma, activists in the West educated thousands of their fellow citizens regarding the ways in which corporations profit from repression. Those efforts succeeded, in just a very short time, in striking an important blow for corporate accountability.

THE CAMPAIGN TAKES OFF

Burma seems an unlikely candidate for a grassroots solidarity movement in the United States. The country is thousands of miles away, and U.S. involvement there is limited. Partially due to Burma's decades of self-imposed isolation—and also due to the U.S. citizenry's ignorance of international affairs—the U.S. public knows little to nothing about Burma and its people. And the Burmese population in the United States is tiny, numbering only in the tens of thousands.[21] Not surprisingly, it took years before a real Free Burma campaign developed in the United States; although, when eventually created, it grew in a flash.

Following the 1990 SLORC crackdown in Burma, a brief burst of activity grabbed students in the United States. Groups of activists at a few schools tried to educate fellow students about Burma, and one university student government passed a resolution condemning Burma's government. But most of the activity was limited to a handful of campuses in Northern California, where some members of the All Burma Students Democratic Front had landed after fleeing Burma. The efforts quickly faded. By 1994, only a handful of people in the United States were focused on the plight of the Burmese—a New Jersey environmentalist, a retired schoolteacher in Chicago, the investment specialist Billenness in Boston, and a Burmese graduate student in Wisconsin.[22]

In 1995, the Free Burma effort in the United States took off. Clever organizing strategies, some technological foresight, and a significant amount of luck all played a part.

Free Burma efforts received a major boost in the summer of 1995 thanks to the unwitting help of SLORC. On July 10, the SLORC released Aung San Suu Kyi from six years of house arrest. The military junta freed Aung San Suu Kyi because her original sentence was nearing its end, and the regime felt confident that its control of the country was so tight that her release would not present a serious threat to its rule. The SLORC was largely right—five years of repression had seriously weakened the opposition, and the release of Aung San Suu Kyi alone was not enough to spark a national uprising. But the Nobel laureate's sudden freedom did succeed in grabbing the attention of the international media, catapulting Burma into public consciousness. As dozens of journalists rushed to Rangoon to interview Aung San Suu Kyi, the story became big news. Thousands of Burmese democracy supporters began congregating in front of Aung San Suu Kyi's home every weekend to hear the NLD leader speak. Feelings of hope spread among opposition leaders in Burma and their supporters abroad.

Aung San Suu Kyi's release and the accompanying flood of encouraging reports from Burma got a young Burmese exile in Madison, Wisconsin, thinking that perhaps it would be possible to reinvigorate a Free Burma campaign in the United States. Zarni (many Burmese use only one name) had come to the United States in early 1988 just before the student rebellion began in Burma. In Burma Zarni had worked as an

English teacher and a translator for tourists, and he came to the United States not for any political reasons, but merely to improve his English and earn an advanced degree. After the massacres of September 1988, Zarni decided to remain in the United States.

In 1995 Zarni had collaborated on a Hollywood film about Burma and Aung San Suu Kyi called "Beyond Rangoon." The movie did poorly at the box office, yet it helped spread the word about what was happening in the country. More importantly, it started Zarni seriously thinking about how he could increase public awareness of the situation in Burma.

An important break came in mid-October, when Zarni and two other Burmese exiles, Moe Thee Zon and Aung Na Oo, attended the national conference of the Student Environmental Action Coalition (SEAC) in Chapel Hill, North Carolina. SEAC was already a well-established activist network, with chapters on campuses across the country and close connections to some of the larger environmental groups in the United States. Zarni and his colleagues figured that if they could educate the young environmental activists about the ecological destruction committed by transnational corporations with ties to the SLORC, the environmental groups might provide a crucial base of support.

This same sort of coalition-building would prove useful in the future. The SLORC's crimes were so numerous that it was relatively easy for the Free Burma activists to enlist the support of different constituencies. Women's rights groups detested the SLORC's use of rape as a tool of war and intimidation. Workers and labor unions abhorred the forced labor in Burma. Conservatives hated the SLORC's persecution of Christian minorities and its sanction of the drug trade. The diverse organizing strategy was neatly summed up in the nascent Free Burma Coalition's motto, taken from an Ethiopian proverb, that "when spiders unite they can tie down a lion."

The appeal to the SEAC activists worked. Armed with hundreds of newly printed Free Burma posters and dozens of copies of a BBC documentary about the situation in Burma, the Madison contingent illustrated for the young environmentalists the links between the SLORC's oppression and the involvement of transnational companies in Burma: Without foreign investment, the Free Burma activists argued, the military junta would not be able to pay for its massive military and sustain its repression of the Burmese people. The BBC film and other educational primers on Burma supplied the facts about the country; the real live Burmese exiles gave a human dimension to the story. Zarni recalls:

We got there and in just 36 hours we signed up about 45 campuses. SEAC was the right place to go to do the outreach. These people were already activists.

They were already concerned about the activities of the oil corporations, and they were already concerned about social justice.

Once back in Madison, Zarni and his colleagues began preparing for an "International Day of Action to Free Burma" that they had called for October 25. Central to their organizing efforts was a new tool never before used on a major scale by social activists—the Internet.

THE SPIDERS' WORLDWIDE WEB

In September, just before the SEAC conference, Zarni formally launched the Free Burma Coalition when he and a computer programmer friend, Alex Turner, created the FBC's home page. In fact, the FBC at that time was nothing more than its Website—it had no office and no staff, and only a handful of committed volunteers aside from Zarni. At that time cyberspace was just becoming a reality. While the Internet's democratizing nature and its potential uses for social movements was already being discussed in academic circles, no one yet had actually driven an activist campaign with the new technology. The FBC billed itself as the "largest human rights campaign in cyberspace."[23]

The idea to center Free Burma communications on the Internet was a decision formed as much by economic necessity as by forward-thinking strategy.[24] Simply, the Free Burma activists had neither the time nor the money to get their message out any other way.

The website (www.freeburmacoalition.org) was housed on a University of Wisconsin server, available free to any student group. Combined with an e-mail listserve, the site proved essential for spreading the word and preparing for the late October protests. First, the site offered unmatched access to information. In spurring people to get involved with the Free Burma movement, the FBC's greatest challenge was the public's ignorance about Burma; student activists would come back from conferences on Burma and have to go find a map to locate where exactly the country was.[25] The Website gave the FBC the luxury of providing as much background information on Burma as it liked—the amount of space was endless, and the access 24 hours a day. Second, the Website allowed the FBC to supply its affiliated activists with all the materials they would need for a successful campus campaign. Sample press releases, Aung San Suu Kyi posters, and Free Burma stickers could all be downloaded directly from the FBC Website. Also, the inclusion on the site of photos of earlier protests at Madison gave heart to other activists, and created a sense of community. Finally, the growing use of e-mail on college campuses let the Burma activists communicate among each other almost instantly, at no cost and with a viral energy.

The international day of action on October 25 was a stunning success. On more than 70 campuses across the United States students staged marches, sit-ins, and pickets. "Really, the whole thing came together in just a few weeks," Zarni says.

BASHING THE BRANDS

The main target of the protests was PepsiCo, the soft drink company and owner of fast-food chains Taco Bell, Pizza Hut, and Kentucky Fried Chicken. At that time, Pepsi was a joint investor in a cola-bottling plant in Rangoon operated by a Burmese businessman who was a major SLORC supporter. The FBC charged Pepsi with taking advantage of forced labor. Because of the difficulty of converting its Burma revenue into hard currency from the volatile Burmese *kyat*, Pepsi would purchase agricultural products in Burma and then sell them in Thailand, where the company could more easily transfer its earnings into dollars, the FBC activists said. According to the FBC, many of the goods bought for resale by Pepsi were produced on farms that used forced labor.[26]

The focus on Pepsi could seem misplaced. After all, compared to the investments of major oil and gas corporations in Burma—investments which generated direct revenue for SLORC since all the oil deals went through the state-owned energy company—Pepsi's support for the military rulers was minor and circuitous. The students concentrated on Pepsi because, as a brand-driven corporation and a company with a massive presence on college and high school campuses, it was a vulnerable target. There was a kind of shock value in the targeting of Pepsi that helped gain new support for the Free Burma campaign. When students learned that a company they had intimately grown up with was involved with something intolerable, they were scandalized, and often moved to take action.[27] The campaign against Pepsi was a perfect consumer boycott: The company was being targeted by the very people it was most invested in attracting.

The Pepsi emphasis, while it demonstrates a tactical sophistication, also reveals the fundamentally anti-corporate drive of the FBC. Certainly the FBC's central goal was to support the democracy movement in Burma. Toward this end, the FBC, following the strategy of the anti-apartheid movement a decade earlier, sought to the follow the money and cut off SLORC's financial support. At the same time, however, the FBC organizers self-consciously designed their campaign to confront what they called "the corporate agenda."[28] The Free Burma activists wanted to demonstrate that it was intolerable for any corporation to do business with a government it knew to be abusive. Any involvement with an authoritarian regime—even an involvement as limited as Pepsi's in Burma—was indefensible, and citizens had a responsibility to hold corporations accountable for their actions and demand that such involvement end. The desire for profits should not trump the defense of basic human rights. A $33 billion-dollar corporation such as Pepsi could certainly afford to give up its revenues from a tiny country like Burma.

"Many people became involved because they were concerned about Burma, but then they developed an anti-corporate mentality," says Brian Schmidt, an FBC activist who designed the campaign's Boycott Pepsi stickers, 20,000 of which were eventually distributed. "They realized that it was not a unique example of corporate irresponsibility, even if Burma is a unique place. The campaign made people become anti-corporate."[29]

The FBC website underscored the corporate accountability spirit of the campaign. The primary objective of the coalition, according to the site, was "to weaken the grip of [SLORC] by cutting its substantial flow of currency provided by transnational corporations such as Total, Unocal, Texaco, and Arco, among others." Strengthening the democratic opposition within Burma was a secondary objective. The website also made explicit the campaign's claim to be the inheritor of the antiapartheid mantle. "Our mission it to build a grassroots movement inspired by and modeled after the anti-Apartheid [sic] movement in South Africa," the coalition's mission statement read.

It's easy to understand why the Free Burma forces would want to model their campaign after the South Africa struggle of the 1970s and 1980s. By claiming to be the progeny of the antiapartheid struggle, the FBC identified itself with a righteous cause. At the same time, the recent election of Nelson Mandela as President of South Africa allowed the coalition to project an aura of inevitable victory.

The comparison was not just self-aggrandizement. In fact, the connection between the Burmese struggle and the struggle of black South Africans had first been made in 1993 by Archbishop Desmond Tutu after the reverend and six other Nobel Peace Prize laureates had attempted to visit Aung San Suu Kyi but had been stopped at the Thai border. In a September 1993 essay in the *Far Eastern Economic Review*, Tutu argued that doing business with Burma would only give SLORC the political will and economic sustenance to continue its repression.[30] Targeting the corporations made sense.

The college activists attacking Pepsi largely relied on the tried and true tactics of earlier social movements. Sit-ins at Taco Bells, Pizza Huts, and KFC outlets were common. Students regularly held educational events on campus squares, urging their fellow classmates to send letters to university administrators asking that their school end any contracts with Pepsi. Activity trickled down from colleges to high schools, as university students urged even younger people to get involved in the Free Burma campaign. Anti-Pepsi pickets took place in high school cafeterias in Lawrence, Kansas, and Los Altos, California.[31]

At the same time as the student protests picked up momentum, the FBC's Internet site supplied an unlooked-for feedback effect—it became a news story in itself. National newspapers such as *USA Today* and the *Christian Science Monitor* looking for stories about the social protest possibilities of the Internet used the FBC site as pegs for articles. The attention drove greater numbers of people to the website, which in turn gave the campaign new energy, creating then still more attention. The Free Burma Coalition was made by the Internet as much as it was made for the Internet.

Two big breaks came for the Free Burma activists in the spring of 1996. In March, the Harvard University dining services denied a contract to PepsiCo after hundreds of students, urged on by Free Burma activists at Harvard, sent letters to university officials calling on the school not to do business with Pepsi. Coke instead received the contract, worth $1 million. According to the student activists at Harvard, Pepsi's refusal to disclose its operations in Burma and its insistence that it could not "take political situations into consideration" discredited the company with the dining services decision-makers as much as the student demonstrations did.[32]

Then, in the beginning of April, students at Stanford University, after gathering more than 2,000 signatures, succeeded in preventing a Taco Bell from opening in the student union. At the same time, the Free Burma activists got the student government to pass a resolution calling on their university's investment managers to support any "shareholder resolutions" calling on companies to halt their operations in Burma.

The pressure worked. On April 22, PepsiCo announced that it would sell its 40 percent share in the Rangoon bottling plant. The announcement seemed timed to mollify critics planning on attending the company's shareholder meeting just a week away, which was to include a vote on a shareholder resolution regarding Pepsi's involvement in Burma. The company's move, however, did not appease the Free Burma activists. Noting that the company would continue to maintain a franchise agreement in the country and keep selling Pepsi cola syrup to the Rangoon bottler, the FBC said it would continue to call for a boycott of the company's products. Any involvement in Burma, no matter how small, constituted support of the regime, the Free Burma forces said.

But even as the Free Burma activists continued their pressure on PepsiCo, the FBC was increasingly focusing its energies on ways to use the government—at the local, state and federal levels—to hold corporations accountable to human rights standards. The concentration on particular companies, while apparently successful, was also a major drain of energy and resources. Better to find systematic ways to attack a whole host of companies, the FBC activists figured. And so the FBC began turning its attention to so-called "selective purchasing laws."

HARNESSING THE POWER OF THE PURSE

Among progressive activists and the broader public, the South Africa antiapartheid struggle of the 1970s and 1980s is often remembered as a divestment campaign. Beginning with the state of California, dozens of state pension funds, universities, and other major investors decided to sell their shares of companies with investments in South Africa or to stop purchasing the stocks of such companies. But more central to the antiapartheid movement's success was the legislation approved by more than 100 cities and 28 states to stop doing business with companies that did business with the apartheid regime. These "selective purchasing laws" hit corporations right where they lived—on their bottom line.

Simon Billenness, a British-born investment manager at the socially responsible investment firm Trillium Asset Management in Boston, first became involved with the Free Burma movement in the summer of 1992 when, as an MBA student, he did a study called "Thinking Globally" about issues facing socially responsible investors.[33] When Billenness began talking with Free Burma activists such as Zarni, he urged the movement not to pursue a divestment strategy, but instead to focus its energies on selective purchasing laws and shareholder resolutions.

Divestment, Billenness argued, is largely a symbolic action. While divestment sends a clear message of moral outrage, it costs social activists any further leverage over a corporation while costing that corporation very little: Some other investor will surely buy up the stock, and the activists surrender their ability to exert pressure on the company. It is much more effective, Billenness told the Free Burma activists, to promote shareholder resolutions and selective purchasing laws.

Corporate charters and rules set forth by the federal Securities and Exchange Commission (SEC) allow shareholders to introduce resolutions at companies' annual investor meetings to be voted on by all proxy holders. The existence of the shareholder resolution is supposed to create a kind of corporate democracy. That is, shareholder resolutions give investors—the actual owners of corporations—a say in how their company is run. A wide range of business practices fall beyond the reach of shareholder resolutions since the SEC rules don't allow votes on specific company operations that are supposed to be within the discretion of executives and managers. Still, shareholder resolutions can be used to call for company reports on certain policies, thereby making the corporations more transparent, a crucial element of accountability.

Social activists in the United States started using shareholder resolutions during the anti-apartheid struggle. But it wasn't until the mid-1990s that activists in the corporate accountability movement began making appeals to corporate investors a routine tactic in their campaigns. So far, no progressive shareholder resolution has yet been approved by corporate investors. Most socially responsible shareholder resolutions garner around 10 percent of the vote; and while a few have received more than 30 percent of the proxies, many fail to get even 3 percent of votes, the threshold number required by the SEC to reintroduce the measure the following year. Nevertheless, shareholder resolutions are very effective at grabbing the attention of corporate executives. And they are equally effective at getting the attention of the business press, which as a matter of course covers all major shareholder meetings. Shareholder resolutions serve to increase public awareness about an issue while also forcing corporate executives onto the defensive.

Billenness advised the Burma activists that divestment should be used as a last resort, or as a way to pressure institutional investors to support progressive shareholder resolutions. But far better than either tool, according to Billenness, is the creation of government-sanctioned boycotts through the passage of selective purchasing laws.

"Selective purchasing laws hit corporations on their bottom lines, and in that respect they're much more effective than divestment, which is largely symbolic," Billenness says. "Divestment is just washing your hands of the situation. Selective purchasing laws can actually cost corporations hundreds of millions of dollars."

The student pressure on Pepsi was a primary boycott: It targeted a single corporation because of a specific abuse, namely, profiting from forced labor. Selective purchasing laws, on the other hand, represent secondary boycotts; they affect a host of companies for simply being involved with criminals. By using the power of the government's purse, the Free Burma activists would be able to hold more corporations accountable to human rights standards than they could on their own.

The very first selective purchasing laws were passed well before the explosion of campus-based activity in the fall of 1995. First in Berkeley, California, in February 1995 and then in Madison, Wisconsin, in August of that same year, small groups of Free Burma activists succeeded in getting their local city councils to pass laws restricting city contracts with companies that did business in Burma. Selective purchasing campaigns gained new strength when the campus activism took off. By the time Pepsi made the announcement of its partial withdrawal from Burma in April 1996, four other towns and cities had passed selective purchasing laws aimed at Burma: Santa Monica, Ann Arbor, San Francisco, and Oakland.

The biggest selective purchasing success came in June 1996, when the state of Massachusetts said that it, too, would restrict business with companies involved in Burma. The Massachusetts Burma law had first been introduced into the statehouse two years before, when State Representative Byron Rushing from South Boston, working with Billenness, simply dusted off the state's earlier South Africa selective purchasing law and replaced every South Africa mention with "Burma (Myanmar)."[34] The bill did not prohibit contracts with companies doing business in Burma; it simply assessed a 10 percent penalty on bids from such companies, essentially making them uncompetitive. The bill had languished due to parliamentary delays, but the sudden arrest of 250 NLD members in Burma in May, along with student activism at campuses across the Boston area, gave new momentum to the legislation. The law passed both houses of the state legislature by a simple voice vote.

Champions of the Massachusetts law worried that Republican Governor William Weld would veto the bill. A wealthy businessman and avowed free trader, Weld had expressed opposition to placing sanctions on China. Luckily for the Free Burma activists, Weld was then in the midst of a campaign for the U.S. Senate seat held by incumbent Democrat, Senator John Kerry. The year before, Kerry had supported sending counter-narcotics money to SLORC, a proposal roundly criticized by Free Burma supporters, and he had failed to support federal legislation calling for federal sanctions against the generals.[35] Suddenly Burma had become a campaign issue. If Weld supported the measure, he could make Kerry look bad in the eyes of Kerry's liberal base.

On June 25, Governor Weld, surrounded by Free Burma activists, signed the Massachusetts selective purchasing bill into law. Now, corporations with investments in Burma were facing a serious loss of business if they continued their operations in the country. The budgets of the six municipalities that already had Burma selective purchasing laws totaled just over $3 billion a year; in 1996, the state of Massachusetts had a $14.2 billion budget and spent $2 billion on outside contracts.[36]

"We expect this bill will affect millions of dollars in state business," Weld said at the signing. "It is my hope that other states and the Congress will follow our example."[37]

The governor didn't have long to wait. As the Massachusetts law was being approved in Boston, lawmakers in Washington, DC, were considering whether they, too, should take action against the SLORC.

FROM THE GRASSROOTS TO CAPITOL HILL

Burma's biggest champion in Washington was an unlikely ally, Senator Mitch McConnell, a Republican Senator from Kentucky known for his friendliness to big business. In the past, McConnell had been a vocal opponent of severing financial ties with China, another regime well-known for its systematic human rights abuses. His passion for imposing sanctions on Burma came from his desire to punish SLORC for its collaboration in the heroin trade. McConnell was also determined to oust SLORC because he feared that China's arms sales to Burma were cementing an alliance in the region inimical to U.S. strategic interests.[38] Never mind that McConnell's motivations came from a far different place than those of the openly anti-corporate FBC, the Senator's enthusiasm and determination would prove a major help to the grassroots activists, and the FBC was glad to have it.

McConnell, along with Senator Daniel Moynihan (D-NY), were proposing federal legislation that would go beyond the Massachusetts measure. They wanted Congress to impose sanctions on Burma that would bar any investments by U.S. companies, a move that would have forced corporations with existing operations to pull out of the country. McConnell had introduced a similar bill the year before, but it had gone nowhere. Now, with public interest in Burma heightened, McConnell's bill stood a strong chance of passing. Although the FBC had not focused its energies on Washington, the coalition's work had helped to shift the political debate in the capital. By making Burma a popular issue, the FBC created the political climate to make federal sanctions against the SLORC a possibility.

But the new energy on Capitol Hill did not mean that approving sanctions against Burma would be easy. McConnell and the Free Burma activists faced two formidable opponents: the Clinton White House and the oil giant Unocal.

The Clinton administration said it didn't want to see Congress place sanctions on Burma for two reasons. First, the administration said it didn't want Congress making foreign policy. This challenge came from the executive branch's desire to keep its nearly exclusive control over foreign policy making. More specifically, with regard to the Burma situation, the administration feared that without the support of other nations in Asia and Europe, unilateral sanctions would fail. Foreign policy makers needed "flexibility" to deal with the SLORC, the White House argued. Congressional sanctions would take away that flexibility.[39]

Even as White House aides worked behind the scenes to defeat the

McConnell sanctions, U.S. oil firms with interests in Burma put their lobbying might against the bill. California-based Unocal, operator of the Union 76 gas stations, led the industry opposition to the McConnell law. Already, FBC activists had targeted Unocal with protests outside Union 76 stations because of the company's large investments in Burma, and so the company was prepared to play defense. In February 1995, Unocal signed a contract with the SLORC to extract and transport natural gas from the Yadana gas field off Burma's coast. The company, along with Total of France, the Petroleum Authority of Thailand, and the SLORC-run Myanmar Oil and Gas Enterprise, planned to build a 218-mile pipeline under the Andaman Sea and then across Burma to Thailand. The $1.2 billion project was expected to earn $400 million a year when completed, including about $100 million a year each for Unocal and the SLORC.[40]

With millions of dollars already invested in the Yadana pipeline (Yadana means "treasure" in Burmese), Unocal had a clear incentive to fight McConnell's legislation, which would force the company to completely pull out of Burma. Backing Unocal were Texaco oil and Atlantic Richfield oil (Arco). Arco had invested about $50 million in two offshore oil wells. Like Unocal, both Arco and Texaco had already been targets of FBC-sponsored protests and shareholder resolutions.

The Senate battle was tough. In Senate hearings, McConnell and his allies brought in Hollywood stars, Burmese dissidents in exile, and the influential financier George Soros, who since 1994 had funded Burmese pro-democracy groups through his Open Society Institute. "It will be argued that free trade promotes free societies," Soros told the Senators. "That's a well-sounding slogan without any basis in fact. Regimes may remain repressive even as they grow rich."[41]

As the pro-sanctions forces made their case, Unocal did everything possible to make its voice heard. Company executives flew to Washington for face-to-face meetings with Senators. Lawmakers were invited to travel to Burma with Unocal officials. Unocal hired the Washington office of Edelman Public Relations to enlist the support of professors and other foreign policy experts to speak out against sanctions. And the company made use of such high-powered lobbyists as Tom Korologos, a former advisor to Senator Bob Dole's presidential campaign.[42]

The combined pressure of the White House and the oil lobby proved enough to beat McConnell's legislation. His sanctions bill was defeated in a narrow 54-45 vote.

Still, the effort by McConnell was enough to get passage of a compromise bill that, while not going as far as McConnell's legislation, at least opened up the possibility of cutting off all future U.S. investments in Burma. Sponsored by Senators William Cohen (R-ME) and Dianne Feinstein (D-CA), the compromise measure mandated the President to prohibit all future investment in Burma if the SLORC were to crack down further on the NLD or in any way threaten Aung San Suu Kyi. The Cohen-Feinstein legislation gave the Clinton administration the flexibility it wanted, and it satisfied the oil companies by guarding existing investments in Burma. By putting special pressure on its home-state Senator, Feinstein, Unocal got what it wanted most—protection for its current involvement with the SLORC. The compromise measure, attached as an amendment to a $12 billion foreign aid appropriations bill, passed the Senate 93 to 6.

In late September, President Clinton signed the foreign aid bill into law, thereby triggering the provisions of the Cohen-Feinstein amendment. Also in September, the Massachusetts law went into effect, and the results were immediate.

THE PRESSURE PAYS OFF

In early October 1996, Apple Computer became the first company to pull out of Burma because of a selective purchasing law when it announced that it would stop selling computers to Burma's government. The selective purchasing law was working exactly as it was intended to: Apple's business with Massachusetts was more valuable than its business with the SLORC.[43] A month later, Hewlett-Packard announced that it was pulling out of Burma because of the Massachusetts law. Then the wireless company Motorola, worried about losing a $40 million contract with the city of San Francisco, which also had a Burma selective purchasing law, announced it would stop doing business in Burma.

Victories for the Free Burma activists kept coming. In January 1997, PepsiCo announced that it would immediately sever all relationships with its franchiser in Burma. Though the Pepsi brass denied it, the consumer boycott against Pepsi must have had some impact on the company's decision. Throughout 1996, activists across the country kept up their campaign against PepsiCo, winning some notable victories such as Colgate University's decision not to sign a contract with Pepsi. The new federal law also played a part in Pepsi's decision. In making its withdrawal announcement, Pepsi cited "the spirit of current U.S. government foreign policy" as a reason for its move.[44] For the FBC, the Pepsi announcement clearly showed that consumers, united, could force a major corporation like Pepsi to respond to social concerns.

Other successes followed. In March an Australian town became the first government outside the United States to pass a Burma selective purchasing law. Also in March, the European Union voted to revoke all tariff privileges for Burma—a decision not as strong as the U.S. sanctions but still important symbolically. The Free Burma movement was suddenly taking on an important international dimension. Then, in May, the University of Wisconsin, responding to high-pitched student and faculty pressure, divested $250,000 in Texaco stock.

A major victory came on April 22, 1997, when Secretary of State Madeline Albright announced that within a month President Clinton would sign an Executive Order barring future U.S. investment in Burma. Since late 1996, pro-sanctions Senators and FBC activists had been strongly lobbying the White House to trigger the sanctions permitted by the Cohen-Feinstein amendment. The arrest of more than a 100 NLD members in late 1996, along with an attack on Aung San Suu Kyi's car in central Rangoon by SLORC thugs, more than met the conditions for imposing the sanctions. Pressed by a massive FBC letter-writing campaign and pressure from Capitol Hill, the White House agreed.

As the FBC activists entered the summer of 1997, they were optimistic of future successes. Clinton's Executive Order barring new investments and the impact of the selective purchasing laws meant that only a handful of major U.S. companies now remained in Burma. The Free Burma activists figured that by concentrating most of their energy on the three U.S. oil firms still in Burma—Arco, Texaco, and Unocal—they could further restrict the SLORC's revenues and take a major step in the movement for corporate accountability.

The Free Burma forces expected opposition from the oil corporations. Billenness, at least, was noticing that the oil companies were waging more sophisticated lobbying campaigns in the statehouses considering Massachusetts-style laws. But no one expected the corporate backlash to be so effective, and no one thought that a little-known but powerful international trade body called the World Trade Organization would join the fray.

During the next few years, the FBC activists would have to struggle to maintain their significant achievements. While the Free Burma movement was in the end able to keep corporations out of Burma, the ensuing fight would end up causing damage to one of the corporate accountability movement's most powerful and effective tools for social action.

THE CORPORATIONS FIGHT BACK

Billenness was right—the corporate lobby, at first caught unawares by the selective purchasing laws, became energized by the fight in Congress and started a counteroffensive against the selective purchasing strategy. "With the passage of the federal legislation, the corporations started to take the grassroots seriously," Zarni says.

Unocal and other companies did, in fact, try to fight the Massachusetts law when it was under consideration, but their single lobbyist at the Boston statehouse was, according to Billenness, rather hapless, and the Free Burma activists were able to outmaneuver the opposition.[45] Of course, in Massachusetts the FBC enjoyed some important natural advantages. For one thing, Massachusetts is a liberal state, and legislators there had a history of using their power to weigh in on international issues. More important, no major Massachusetts-based company did business in Burma when the law was passed, which meant that there was no local constituency against the legislation.

The FBC didn't enjoy similar advantages when it took its case to lawmakers in Texas, Connecticut, and California. In each of these places, corporate lobbyists, backed largely by Unocal, made the argument that punishing U.S. corporations doing business in Burma would only serve to give an advantage to Asian and European corporations with investments there. And in these states the FBC activists had to contend with powerful and wealthy local interests. Unocal is based in California, and Connecticut is host to United Technologies, which did business in Burma. The FBC lost selective purchasing drives in all three states.

The FBC was successful in 1997, however, in getting the cities of Los Angeles and New York to approve Burma selective purchasing laws. Given the size of these cities' budgets, the victories were huge; New York City has the fourth largest government budget in the country after the federal government and the states of California and New York.

As the FBC struggled against Unocal and its allies to pass selective purchasing laws around the country, the very legitimacy of the laws themselves came under attack from an unexpected direction. In June 1997 the European Union formally requested a "WTO consultation" over the Massachusetts law. Earlier in the year the EU had written a letter to the office of the U.S. Trade Representative complaining that the Massachusetts selective purchasing law violated a 1994 government procurement agreement between the EU and the United States. Because the law gave special preferences to companies that were not involved in Burma, the EU argued, it represented a barrier to fair competition. The Japanese also wrote a letter to the USTR complaining about the law. Suddenly, the FBC's efforts to restore democracy in Burma and hold corporations accountable to human rights standards were caught up in the intricacies of international trade policy.

The EU could have gone further by filing a formal complaint with the WTO. Most observers at the time agreed that the EU chose the less aggressive route because it wanted to see if it could first compel Massachusetts to voluntarily repeal the law. In fact, State Representative Byron

Rushing, the Massachusetts law's chief backer, met with EU officials to try to work out an arrangement. He said the state would change the law to affect only contracts under $500,000 for goods and service and under $6 million for construction projects if the EU would tighten its sanctions against Burma.[46] When the EU refused, Rushing said he wouldn't work to change the law, and the WTO consultation process went on.

In any case, even though the EU merely asked for a consultation instead of filing a formal complaint, the move raised some disturbing issues for corporate accountability activists. The EU was arguing that the selective purchasing law violated WTO rules that bar the use of "political" criteria in awarding government contracts.[47] That prohibition struck right at the heart of the corporate accountability agenda. After all, the FBC activists were trying to promote the idea that purchasing decisions by public institutions such as colleges and local governments *should* be informed by "political" criteria; if "political" meant opposition to human rights abuses and environmental destruction. By barring decision-making based on anything other than strict market considerations, the WTO rules could effectively block the ability of citizens to tell public institutions how the people's money should be spent.

The WTO dispute represented a clash of values and priorities. Essentially, it was a battle between the concept of popular sovereignty enshrined in the U.S. Constitution and the profit needs of transnational corporations embodied in WTO regulations. By seeking to impose a set of rules based on human rights, the Massachusetts law ran afoul of the commercial values governing international trade.[48] The WTO's decision on the Massachusetts law's possible violation of existing free trade agreements threatened to set an important precedent for how—or even whether—local governments would be able to have their purchasing decisions reflect their values in the new global economy.

Yet the WTO arbitrators never made a decision on the issue. The EU's consultation request was pushed to a back burner in late April 1998 when a business consortium called the National Foreign Trade Council (NFTC) filed a lawsuit in federal court charging that the Massachusetts law was unconstitutional.

The NFTC is a coalition of 550 U.S. manufacturing companies, financial institutions, and other large firms with large overseas interests. Among its members are found practically every blue-chip company in the United States, including corporations such as Arco, Pepsi, and Unocal that once had or continue to have operations in Burma. Founded in 1914, the council claims to be the oldest business association devoted to trade matters, and the organization's Website boasts that the group has been a "leading spokesman" of increased free trade and of the WTO.[49]

The NFTC filed its federal court challenge on behalf of a smaller and younger organization called USA Engage, a sort of NFTC spin-off. With an almost identical membership, USA Engage has a narrower agenda than the NFTC, which, much like the U.S. Chamber of Commerce, lobbies for corporate interests in general. USA Engage focuses on international trade issues and on opposing economic sanctions imposed unilaterally by the United States. Such sanctions, the group argues, don't work because, being limited to U.S. corporations, they fail to cut off a regime's financial support; at the same time, such sanctions make U.S. businesses less competitive. The ban on new U.S. companies entering Burma offered a ripe target for the group.

In the NFTC and USA Engage, the Free Burma activists faced a sophisticated and determined opponent. The NFTC-led counteroffensive revealed a business lobby prepared to aggressively defend itself against any attempts to hold corporations accountable for their actions. The challenge to the Massachusetts law and economic sanctions in general was, according to Robert Stumberg, a Georgetown University law professor who served as the FBC's legal counsel, a "state-of-the-art" campaign.[50] Using the courts, the media, and officials in Washington, the NFTC's struggle against selective purchasing laws matched in creativity and energy the FBC's efforts for corporate accountability.

The simple fact that the business community spent the money and took the effort to go after the Massachusetts selective purchasing law demonstrates that the FBC did, in fact, make some major gains for corporate accountability. After all, if the Free Burma campaign had not impacted the interests of U.S. corporations, they would not have bothered to fight it. "A broad spectrum of corporations—more than 600 companies—were willing to band together to oppose a policy that would have held only a few dozen corporations accountable," Stumberg says.

Why did the business lobby challenge the Burma selective purchasing laws even though it did not fight the South Africa laws of a decade earlier? The antiapartheid laws were adopted much more widely than the Burma laws, and U.S. business with South Africa was far larger than it ever was with the Burma. FBC activists such as Billenness and Stumberg offer several explanations for the increased aggressiveness.

Attacking the antiapartheid effort would have generated very bad publicity. With its strong backing from the African-American community and its parallels to the civil rights movement, the struggle to end apartheid was a popular and unquestionably righteous cause. In comparison, the campaign to restore democracy to Burma, though it certainly enjoyed moral authority, was not as well known and did not have a large demographic base which could identify directly with the oppressed in Burma. In striking at the Massachusetts Burma law Corporate America did not risk immediately alienating a large sector of the U.S. population. Second, in the years since the antiapartheid movement's zenith, U.S. transnational corporations had focused more on promoting free trade. The fight for the passage of the North American Free Trade Agreement honed the corporate lobby's arguments for free trade and, in general, forced the corporations to become better organized on the issue. Also, U.S. corporations had more and more investments overseas, some of which were in autocratic countries. Selective purchasing laws and secondary boycotts represented a serious obstacle to the operations of transnational enterprise. As the volume of international business grew, so did selective purchasing laws' threat to business as usual.

Perhaps the NFTC's most pressing motivation was the sudden proliferation of Burma-style laws. Inspired by the FBC successes, activists opposed to the Indonesian occupation of East Timor, the military dictatorship in Nigeria, or abuses by the Chinese government were now trying to use selective purchasing laws to cut off financial support to those regimes. Even as the NFTC prepared its lawsuit, the state of Massachusetts, again at the urging of Byron Rushing, was considering a selective purchasing law targeting companies doing business in General Suharto's Indonesia. Maryland legislators were debating whether to stop buying from companies involved with the Nigerian military dictatorship. And countless towns and cities were discussing similar moves. Like the Free Burma campaign—and unlike the antiapartheid movement—a domestic ethnic constituency didn't drive these struggles. The activists behind the campaigns to free East Timor and to bring democracy to Nigeria were motivated by a commitment to human rights and an abhorrence of corporations that profit from repression. That spelled trouble for U.S. corporations with investments overseas: If a corporate accountability movement could spring up around the relatively obscure cause of Burma, it could happen with other countries.

"When the corporations looked at similar laws targeting Nigeria and Indonesia and China, they saw the writing on the wall," Billenness says. "They knew this could get a lot worse. The lawsuit also showed that we were doing our job. When you come under serious fire, you know you're on target."

THE CASE OF BURMA GOES BEFORE THE BENCH

The NFTC and USA Engage made it very clear that their challenge to the Massachusetts law was as much about their ideological opposition to economic sanctions and their support of unfettered trade as it was about defending the interests of a few companies.[51] The legal challenge itself, billed as a "test case" by the NFTC, proved this. The lawsuit didn't allege that any corporation had been directly harmed by the law, though it did charge that the selective purchasing restriction had led to "lost opportunities" for some companies.[52] Rather, the NFTC suit challenged the Massachusetts law on broad constitutional grounds. It charged that in passing its Burma law, Massachusetts infringed on the federal government's exclusive right to make foreign policy. The suit also charged that the passage of the federal sanctions in July 1996 pre-empted the Massachusetts law, and so should make it void.

Even as the business group made its case in legal briefs, it took its argument against sanctions to the court of public opinion. In the summer of 1998, a growing number of news articles appeared questioning whether economic sanctions were effective in advancing foreign policy goals. It was a fair question. In the past, progressives had argued against sanctions against countries such as Cuba and Iraq, pointing out that economic sanctions were a blunt instrument that usually worked to hurt average citizens, especially the poorest, while entrenching local elites. It makes little sense that trade with Cuba was thought of as propping up Fidel Castro's government while trade with China was supposed to lead to a crumbling of the autocratic regime there.

The FBC activists argued that Burma was a special case. For one thing, the extremely repressive nature of the SLORC meant that unlike in, say, China or Cuba, average citizens would see very little trickle down from any foreign investment, and so putting money into the country would not help to empower the people. The Free Burma forces also noted that Burma was different from other sanctioned countries in that the call for economic restrictions came directly from the country's democratic opposition and Aung San Suu Kyi. More broadly, the FBC continued to defend the point that, as countries like Singapore and Indonesia showed, free markets don't necessarily lead to freedom.

But the FBC could not get around USA Engage's central argument that sanctions don't work unless they are multilateral. Since the Massachusetts law was first attacked, the FBC had scored important victories, most notably the withdrawal from Burma of Texaco and Arco, in September 1997 and August 1998 respectively. That left Unocal as the only U.S. company with big investments in Burma. Transnational corporations based in other countries, however, had refused to leave Burma, despite pressure from U.S. activists. Also, in the July 1997, the Association of South East Asian Nations (ASEAN), ignoring the pleas of the U.S. State Department, invited Burma to become an observing member of the confederation. The ongoing involvement of many corporations in Burma, combined with the ASEAN's refusal to isolate the country, meant that the SLORC still enjoyed a modicum of international legitimacy.

In September 1998, as the Asian financial crisis made it even more unlikely that corporations would risk pulling out of Burma, lawyers for the NFTC and the state of Massachusetts argued their case in federal court before Judge Joseph Tauro. As the NFTC attorneys—backed by the presence of EU officials in the courtroom—argued that the Massachusetts law encroached on the federal government's right to make foreign policy and was preempted by the sanctions passed by Congress, lawyers for the state vigorously defended the law.[53]

The Massachusetts attorneys noted that since the federal sanctions were approved after the Massachusetts law was passed, Congress must have been aware of the earlier law and did not intend to contradict it; if Congress had wanted to pre-empt the Massachusetts law, the state's attorneys said, they would have explicitly done so. On the central point of whether selective purchasing laws constitute foreign policy making, the state's lawyers said that the state enjoyed the same right as individual consumers to decide how to spend its money. Like any other market participant, the lawyers argued, the state, as a collection of market participants, had the right to choose not to do business with those it found morally reprehensible.

In November, Judge Tauro ruled in favor of the NFTC, writing that "state interests, no matter how noble, do not trump the federal government's exclusive foreign affairs power."[54] The judge, however, declined to rule on the NFTC's pre-emption complaint. As expected, the Massachusetts Attorney General's office immediately filed an appeal. From the moment the NFTC first challenged the law, it was anticipated that the issue—so wrapped up in questions of states rights and federalism—would eventually have to be settled by the Supreme Court.

In June 1999, the First Circuit Court of Appeals upheld the original ruling. Massachusetts appealed again, and the Supreme Court agreed to hear the case.

TAKING AWAY THE HOWITZER

The U.S. Supreme Court considered oral arguments in the Massachusetts case on March 23, 2000. What had started as an effort by a few well-meaning people to cut off financial support to a brutal military regime had now become a weighty matter of constitutional principles. In a reflection of the larger tensions created by globalization, the case pitted the interests of the business community against those of local governments. Joining the nearly 600 plaintiffs represented by the NFTC were 12 business associations who filed an *amicus* ("friend of the court") brief supporting the NFTC position. Dozens of federal officials, the EU, and 20 Members of Congress also signed briefs supporting the NFTC. The Clinton administration, after intense internal debates, also decided to support the NFTC. On the other side, eight major associations of state and local governments, 22 attorneys general, 16 city governments, 64 non-governmental organizations and 78 Members of Congress supported Massachusetts.[55] The corporations and their allies wanted to make sure that they no longer would have to deal with the inconvenience of local selective purchasing laws. The local governments hoped to retain their sovereignty to spend their money as they wished, including in ways motivated by altruism. The stakes were high indeed.

For a conservative-leaning Court committed to states' rights but also historically sympathetic to the interests of business, the case offered many complications. While the lawyers for the state tried to tap into the Court's states rights leanings, the NFTC representatives argued that a ruling in favor of Massachusetts would lead to 50 different foreign policies. The new realities of trade and globalization overshadowed both sides' arguments. Because of the increasing interconnectedness created by the growth in global trade, Massachusetts attorneys argued, local ordinances similar to the Burma selective purchasing laws were bound to increase, and it was important that the Court protect the right of state and city governments to make such laws.[56] The lawyers for the NFTC said that precisely because trade was growing it was necessary that the U.S. government speak with one voice. In questioning the attorneys for the two sides, most of the Justices seemed antagonistic to the Massachusetts' position. Only the most conservative member of the Court, Justice Antonin Scalia, appeared sympathetic to the state's argument.[57]

In the end, the Justices split the difference between the two sides. On June 19, the Justices released a unanimous 9-0 decision striking down the Massachusetts Burma law. The ruling, however, was a narrow one. The Court said that the congressional sanctions targeting Burma preempted the state and local selective purchasing laws and that the Massachusetts law therefore violated the so-called Supremacy Clause of the Constitution. But the Court stopped short of declaring all local selective purchasing laws unconstitutional. The decision focused only on the specific issue of the Burma laws.[58] While the free trade lobby succeeded in eliminating the local laws targeting corporations doing business in Burma, it failed in its larger goal of prohibiting local selective purchasing laws altogether.

For the Free Burma activists, the decision was obviously a blow. After all, the passage of selective purchasing laws had been essential for getting companies such as Apple, Motorola, and Eastman Kodak out of Burma. For the larger human rights and corporate accountability movements, the Court's ruling was a partial—though not complete—defeat. The Court of course left open, in theory, the continued use of selective purchasing laws to advance human rights and hold corporations accountable for their actions. But the Justice's decision on the issue of preemption meant that, in practice, it would be far more difficult in the future to pass selective purchasing laws.

"The corporations won," Stumberg says.

> The FBC lost. And while they didn't lose all their legal options, they lost one of their best tools. The broader human rights community also lost because if it can't apply pressure regarding Burma, they can't do it anywhere. And the states lost. They lost some of their ability to make purchasing decisions on moral values.

According to Stumberg, the Supreme Court's ruling means that future selective purchasing will only be permissible if they don't contravene existing federal foreign policies. And since there are few countries toward which Congress has not already articulated some sort of stance, the use of selective purchasing laws will be limited. Of course, Congress could easily insert language into any foreign policy bill stating that the law under consideration is not intended to pre-empt any local or state laws. But given the clout of well-financed lobby machines in Washington and the overall influence of corporate interests in the capital, approving such an exemption would be a chore for any grassroots movement. Human rights and corporate accountability groups must now be more careful than ever, Stumberg says, of making sure that sanctions passed at the federal level are not just watered-down measures designed to make it look like something is being done when in reality the sanctions let the worst offenders off the hook.

The Court case over the Massachusetts law revealed another problem for citizens groups and local lawmakers. In arguing their case that the Massachusetts Burma law represented a foray into foreign policy making, the NFTC lawyers—backed by the Clinton administration—pointed to the WTO consultation requests filed by the European Union. When the EU went to the WTO, the Massachusetts law automatically became a foreign policy issue. Under that line of reasoning, any local law that runs afoul of WTO rules could be considered an irritant to foreign policy making, and therefore be subject to constitutional review. For lawmakers intent on regulating corporations and citizens struggling for corporate accountability, the NFTC argument threatens future efforts to exert pressure from the local level.

"There's no doubt about it; secondary boycotts are effective,"

Stumberg says, using the more legal description of selective purchasing laws. "The court's decision takes away the howitzer. But just because they rolled the howitzer off the field doesn't mean you drop your rifles."

Billenness, too, says that although the Court decision represents a setback, the FBC, and the broader corporate accountability movement, will continue to struggle with whatever tools they have at their disposal. "I think the corporations won a battle but, when it comes to Burma, are losing the war," he says. "The sanctions still have an effect, the boycotts continue, and corporations are not lining up to go back into Burma. They've pulled some of our teeth, but we still have bite."

LEARNING LESSONS, KEEPING THE HEAT ON

The Free Burma Coalition's experience is a study in the law of unintended consequences: The campaign's very successes paved the way for its eventual setbacks. The FBC scored some impressive tactical victories, yet it still managed to not to win at the ultimate strategic level. The coalition's story proves that no tactic, no matter how promising, is foolproof. When activists target the consequences of corporate power—as opposed to tackling its causes—even the bigggest wins are likely fall short of lasting triumph.

But the FBC's setbacks do not mean that the Free Burma activists have given up. Like truly dedicated activists, they have used their reversals as learning opportunities while they keep up their strugggle.

Since the Supreme Court struck down the Massachusetts selective purchasing law, the FBC has continued its struggle with the best tools at its disposal. The coalition has succeeded in convincing the cities of Los Angeles, Minneapolis, and San Francisco to divest their holdings in companies that still deal with the government of Burma. Free Burma activists plan on taking their divestment demands to all the jurisdictions that passed selective purchasing laws. The FBC has also kept pressuring individual companies: shoe-maker Kenneth Cole (part of the Nike empire) and hotel chain Best Western have agreed to stop doing business in Burma.

SLORC remains in power, of course. And the military junta is still reaping considerable benefit from the one major U.S. corporation the Burma activists have not been able to drive out of Burma: the oil company Unocal. Despite years of creative activist pressure, the company refuses to pull out of Burma. Unocal's intransigence is important to note, for it demonstrates the limitations of any corporate accountability initiative that, for whatever reason, cannot leverage the powers of government to meet its objective. It shows that when grassroots activists are unable to pass laws to further their aims and are left to their own devices, those devices, no matter how sophisticated, may be insufficient to change the policies of transnational corporations.

The Free Burma forces first targeted Unocal in 1994—long before the campus-based efforts against PepsiCo took off—when they introduced a shareholders resolution at the company's annual meeting calling on Unocal executives to conduct a report of its operations in Burma. That same year, activists also introduced similar resolutions at Pepsi, Amoco, and Texaco, but those three corporations were all able to convince the SEC to strike down the resolutions as insufficiently appropriate to the companies' business. The Unocal resolution was allowed to stand. It received a surprising 15 percent of the vote, and earned the company a significant amount of unfavorable publicity about its connection to the Burmese generals.

In the years since then, Free Burma activists have gone even further in uncovering the links between the California oil corporation and the SLORC. Reports by the well-respected advocacy group EarthRights International have shown that, in the construction of the Yadana natural gas pipeline, SLORC soldiers used forced labor to build service roads. The reports have shown that SLORC soldiers forcibly displaced several villages to make way for the pipeline, in the process summarily executing, torturing, or raping resisters.[59]

But even as Unocal's name has been tarnished in the press, its image has remained unscathed—because Unocal has no real image. In the fall of 1996, in a move to remake itself as mainly an oil and gas exploration and extraction corporation, Unocal sold all its Union 76 gas stations to the Tosco corporation for $2 billion.[60] While the sale of the stations was a smart business move for Unocal, for the Free Burma forces it meant Unocal no longer had a public face to attack. Since Unocal had no retail consumer base, there was little way for the Free Burma activists to hurt the company's revenue by making it look bad.

The corporate accountability movement has shown itself to be particularly adept at the so-called "name and blame" game. That is, groups fighting against corporate policies have often relied on exposés and muckraking techniques to make a company look bad, to sully its image in the minds of consumers, and thus shame a corporation into changing its policies. As we saw earlier, the name and blame strategy was especially effective in the struggle against sweatshop abuses. And brand attacks were central to the FBC's campaign against Pepsi.

The key to branding is creating an emotional bond between consumers and a product. By getting people to identify with brands, corporations hope to create lasting connections between consumers and products. But this can backfire, as the Pepsi experience demonstrates. When students found that a product they identified with was associated with intolerable practices, their shock and outrage drove them to action.

While the power of the brand gives social activists a powerful tool for fighting corporations, offering activists the ability to use a corporation's own success against itself, it also carries limitations. The most obvious is: What to do with a corporation, for example Unocal, that has no brand? The FBC organizers learned the limitations of the brand-attack strategy all to well. After Pepsi agreed to completely pull out of Burma in January 1997, the campus energy that had been so essential to the movement started to evaporate. "When Pepsi left Burma, we lost some direction," Zarni recalls. "It was our biggest target, and after they left we lost a lot of people. We were really pressed to keep people involved after that."

Aside from having few outlets for aiming citizen anger at Unocal, the Free Burma activists also have had to struggle against the sheer size of Unocal's investment in Burma. For companies like Pepsi, Motorola, and Apple, leaving Burma represented a relatively small loss of revenue. No company likes giving up sales, but at some point a cost-benefit analysis takes place that tells corporate executives that it is wiser to change their policies than to stay with the status quo. Pepsi left because its consumer base among young people in the United States was more valuable than all of the Pepsi drinkers in Burma. Motorola left because it wanted to do business more with the city of San Francisco than it did with the SLORC; the same with Apple and the state of Massachusetts. Even the oil corporations Arco and Texaco eventually chose to leave. But whereas the Burma investments of Arco and Texaco numbered in the tens of millions of dollars, Unocal's investment there is at least $340 million—a significant 5 percent of its total business. Unocal's resistance to leaving Burma suggests that some investments are too large to walk away from.

Faced with Unocal's refusal to leave Burma, the Free Burma forces came up with a creative maneuver that would force Unocal to reconsider its involvement with the Yadana pipeline, or at least punish the company for its past involvement there. In October 1996, attorneys in Los Angeles filed a landmark lawsuit against Unocal on behalf of Burmese refugees in Thailand who claimed the SLORC military had forced them to work without pay on the Yadana pipeline. The lawyers, asking for millions of dollars in damage for their clients, based the suit on an 18th century U.S. law called the Alien Tort Claims Act that originally was designed to help U.S. citizens get compensation for pirate attacks. But the law also allows foreign citizens to sue foreign or domestic individuals for crimes committed outside the United States so long as the defendants are given notice of the lawsuit while inside the country.

In recent years, a host of similar Alien Tort Claims Act lawsuits have been filed against U.S.-based transnational corporations linked to abuses abroad. The proliferation of such suits offers corporate accountability activists an unparalleled way to use the courts to punish companies for their actions in other countries. Oil companies have become special targets of alien tort suits. Texaco has been sued for oil spills in Ecuador affecting Indigenous communities. Nigerians have sued Chevron for the killing of a protester on a Chevron oil platform in the Niger Delta. And Shell Oil has been sued for its involvement with the former military dictatorship in Nigeria. Although none of the legal challenges have been settled, the suits have nevertheless sent a signal to corporations that they may be held legally responsible for their operations in any country where they invest.

The fact-finding—or "discovery"—stage of the Unocal lawsuit took three years. Finally, in September 2000, the judge in the case, Ronald Lew, ruled that although the evidence suggested that Unocal knew that forced labor was used by SLORC forces to protect the pipeline, the plaintiffs had failed to prove that the oil company had conspired with the military or "controlled" the military's actions. "The evidence does suggest that Unocal knew forced labor was being utilized and that the joint venture benefited from the practice," the judge wrote.[61] But that evidence, the judge ruled, was insufficient to establish liability.

The Free Burma activists successfully appealed the dismissal, and the case was slated to go trial in February 2003. Since then the trial has once again been postponed. At press time, it was unclear if a trial would occur.

In this case, however, the Free Burma forces don't have to worry about going all the way to the Supreme Court. In March 2001, the High Court refused, without comment, to rule on whether a similar alien tort suit against Shell Oil is valid in U.S. courts. That means that corporate accountability activists will be able to continue using alien tort suits for the foreseeable future.

Unocal's response to the Alien Tort Claims Act suit demonstrates yet another obstacle thrown in the way of social activists by the globalization of business. In the spring of 1997, just after a federal judge refused to throw out the alien tort lawsuit against it, and as the Clinton administration took steps to impose sanctions on Burma, Unocal announced that it was opening a "twin corporate headquarters" in Malaysia. No longer would Unocal consider itself a U.S. company; now it was a "global energy" company.[62] The move hinted that Unocal was prepared to spin off a separate company if either the U.S. government imposed retroactive sanctions on Burma or if the court case went too far. The spin-off never occurred. But the episode revealed how easily it would be for a transnational corporation to simply change its base of operations if it sought to avoid regulations in a certain country. The challenge for corporate accountability activists was clear: How could local and national laws hold companies accountable for their actions if they were prepared to leave the country at the first sign of danger to their profits?

Unocal's flirtation with relocating itself outside the United States reveals one of the FBC's greatest strategic weaknesses: its inability to convince other countries to follow the U.S. lead and cut off investment in Burma. In a globalized economy, the FBC's failure to force Asian-based transnational corporations to pull out of Burma was the Achilles' heel of the movement's efforts.

With so much capital moving so quickly in so many different directions in a globalized economy, it is very difficult for activists in just one country, even a country as large as the United States, to affect business in a certain location. The FBC's efforts were undermined by transnational capital based in Thailand, Malaysia, and China that decided to keep investing in Burma. Even as the FBC met its objective of holding U.S. transnational corporations accountable to human rights standards, it could not meet its ultimate goal—real democracy in Burma—without extending that accountability to corporations based in other countries.

This points to the need for global regulations to govern the actions of transnational companies. After all, if activists want to change the behavior of corporations acting like international outlaws, then they need international rules to bring those companies within the law.

The WTO, of course, represents a kind of international rule of law. But, as the Free Burma forces painfully learned, the WTO's rules prioritize the protection of commercial interests. What is needed, then, is a new set of enforceable global rules that will also protect human rights, along with other social and environmental interests. In illustrating the need for another set of global rules, the FBC's efforts raised important questions about what values and priorities should guide the global economy. As the next chapter shows, those questions would soon explode to the surface of American politics.

6

TRADING DEMOCRACY
Rule-Making in the Global Economy

ON NOVEMBER 30, 1999, SOME 50,000 people converged on the rain-soaked streets of Seattle to protest the World Trade Organization (WTO). The organization's critics represented a wide range of public interest groups, including the bulk of the American progressive movement. Among the demonstrators' ranks were trade unionists, environmentalists, human rights activists, farmers, animal rights groups, priests and Buddhist monks, and longtime consumer advocates. Veteran activists as well as neophyte protesters marched in the streets. The demonstrators came from as many as 100 different countries. Together, this unlikely coalition of forces was about to make history.

Before the "Battle in Seattle" it is fair to say that most people in the United States, and indeed the world, had never heard of the WTO, an organization established in 1995 to write and enforce rules on international trade and investment. After the Seattle confrontation between civil society and the WTO, the organization became a household name, and not a very pretty one.

During five days of street protests, groups and individuals succeeded in dramatically altering the terms of the debate over international commercial agreements like those set up by WTO. The WTO was transformed in much of the public mind into a dangerously secretive institution that was elevating corporate interests at the expense of workers' livelihoods, environmental protection, human rights, and even democracy itself. On the first day of talks aimed at opening a new round of trade negotiations, protesters surpassed the expectations of even themselves and managed to physically shut down the WTO meeting, rattling the representatives of more than 120 governments who had traveled to Seattle. In subsequent days, the protesters would continue to dog the summit, exacerbating divisions among the negotiators inside the meeting rooms. Finally, the trade negotiators gave up on their agenda, and the meeting collapsed in failure. International civil society groups claimed victory for stopping the seemingly unstoppable WTO.

In the weeks following the dramatic showdown in Seattle, media commentators described the WTO protests as the birth of a new anti-corporate movement. But 50,000 protesters—including thousands of individuals willing to risk arrest for their beliefs—didn't come from nowhere. Rather than marking the birth of a new social movement, the Seattle demonstrations were, more accurately, the spectacular coming out party of a movement long in the making.

During the 1990s, a variety of citizens' groups organized grassroots campaigns to hold corporations accountable for their actions. Labor rights activists and trade unions demanded that large retailers be accountable to the people making their clothes. Human rights activists and students called on corporations to cease doing business with the repressive government of Burma. Environmentalists forced some of the biggest American food companies to ensure that the tuna they sold was caught without killing dolphins. In Seattle, these disparate interests came together to form a force more powerful than the sum of its parts.

"Turtles and Teamsters together at last," read one of the most frequently quoted signs from the streets of Seattle. The hand-lettered placard, held by a member of the Teamsters union, referred to the alliance between organized labor and environmentalists. The conventional wisdom had long held that the interests of trade unions and environmentalists were inimical to each other: Saving trees meant cutting jobs, or so the popular assumptions went. In Seattle those divisions were nowhere to be found. The succinct message on the placard illustrated one of the most significant features of Seattle—the strengthening of ties among unionists, greens, human rights activists, and others. By putting aside their differences and uniting in the common cause to challenge corporate power, the Seattle coalition revealed the potency and popular resonance of anti-corporate politics. The "turtles and Teamsters" unity and the collapse of the WTO talks proved that the corporate accountability movement was a force to be reckoned with.

The unlikely coalition between organized labor and environmental groups had been building for years as the two interests found they shared deep-seated concerns about the new breed of international trade and investment agreements. During the Cold War, trade policy had been the special purview of Washington technocrats and corporate lobbyists who asserted that increased commerce among nations was beneficial for everyone. Democrats and Republicans alike supported so-called free trade policies, and public involvement in the crafting of trade policy was rare. That situation changed sharply in 1993 during the debate over the North American Free Trade Agreement (NAFTA), a commercial pact between Canada, the United States, and Mexico. Suddenly, trade was front-page news again, and concerns about the impacts of trade were stirring passions among people across the United States.

The heated battle over NAFTA brought together consumer groups, labor unions, family farm organizations, and environmentalists who viewed the agreement as a vehicle for giving corporations more power at the expense of the public interest. The NAFTA dispute created bedfellows as strange as right-wing commentator and politician Pat Buchanan and left-wing consumer advocate Ralph Nader, both of whom believed the deal would undermine U.S. sovereignty.

Throughout the 1990s, confrontations would intensify as the growing "fair trade" forces* fought the General Agreement on Tariffs and Trade in 1994, presidential "fast track" trade negotiating authority in 1997, and the Multilateral Agreement on Investment in 1998. These recurring trade wars laid the foundation for the labor-environmental alliance that was so effective in Seattle.

But to call the disputes of the 1990s "trade wars" misses the point, say the leaders of the fair trade movement. Commercial agreements such as NAFTA and the WTO are about much more than trade. They represent the first steps toward a global constitution that elevates commercial values above life values (human rights and the environment), and which has been written without the consent of the world's people. These agreements threaten the very spirit of democratic decision-making.

"If this was just about trade, we'd have other fish to fry," says Lori Wallach, director of Global Trade Watch, an arm of the consumer watchdog group Public Citizen.

> The issue is the hijacking of trade to push other issues—deregulation, a sweeping corporate takeover. Within the terms of the WTO and NAFTA— these huge commercial agreements—is a huge smorgasbord of pro-corporate, antidemocratic measures.[1]

Indeed, trade alone wouldn't ignite the kind of passions seen in Seattle. The fears and anger of many of the people opposed to the WTO centered on issues of control: who they felt had it (corporations) and who lacked it (ordinary citizens).

The battle against the commercial agreements took the corporate accountability movement's analysis to an entirely new level. During the 1990s, Public Citizen, along with dozens of other organizations, be-

---

* The "fair trade" movement contains two distinct but complementary strands. One is a collection of interest groups—such as the AFL-CIO, Public Citizen, and Friends of the Earth, among dozens of others—who have sought to reform trade and investment policies. The second is those organizations that promote direct links with producers in the world's poor countries and consumers in the wealthier nations via craft stores and commodities such as coffee and chocolate. Here we are referring to the first group.

came aware that corporations were promoting NAFTA and the WTO as a way to advance a broader agenda of deregulation. Essentially, the international commercial agreements were stripping citizens, and their elected governments, of the ability to hold corporations accountable for their actions. The giant trade deals were short-circuiting the democratic process. For a growing number of people, challenging corporate power meant more than protecting dolphins or human rights, it meant protecting democracy itself. The protesters in Seattle were addressing core questions of democracy: Who has the power, and who decides?

The shared concerns about the commercial agreements' impact on democratic decision-making helped cement the fair trade alliance. While each interest group had its own priorities and its own constituency to serve, everyone agreed that pacts like NAFTA and GATT/WTO were increasing corporate power to the detriment of democracy.

"I remember a meeting in the early '90s at which we had a union and an environmental group that could hardly stand to be in the same room together," Wallach says. "But then someone said, 'I bet there's one thing we can all agree on: A democratic process that is out in the public is better than being locked in the dark.' Everybody saw these agreements as an issue of democratic decision-making."

Throughout the controversies over the international trade and investment agreements, media commentators frequently described critics as know-nothings. NAFTA and the WTO were fostering globalization, and globalization, as everyone was supposed to know, was as unstoppable as the ocean's tide.

But, as Seattle showed, the growing corporate accountability movement could make waves of its own, waves big enough to frustrate even the best-laid plans of the political establishment.

FROM CONTROVERSY TO CONSENSUS
AND BACK AGAIN

Throughout American history, trade policy has frequently been a cause of heated debate. Orthodox economic theory says that trade should benefit everyone ("a rising tide lifts all boats"). But in the real world things are rarely as neat. Some people have leaky boats or no boat at all. The truth is that trade among nations involves winners and losers. Some groups—for example, importers—find benefit in low tariff rates, while other people—industrial workers—are harmed by them. At the same time, trade is a central part of any country's relationship with other nations, and represents an important part of government policy. Combine the contest between different interest groups with the importance of trade in international relations, and it is clear why trade policies have often been a fiercely contested political issue.

In the early decades of the American Republic, and for most of the 19th century, trade was among the most divisive of political issues, second probably only to the disputes over slavery. Disagreements over how the young nation should trade with other countries divided the political parties, split farmers from industrialists, and sharpened the suspicions between North and South, East and West. The debates were so intense because, firstly, tariff rates (taxes placed on goods entering the country) were a majority share of federal government revenue and, secondly, tariffs represented a make-or-break protection for the country's nascent industrial sector. At stake in the 19th century trade debates were the size of the federal government and the future of the American economy.

The first major trade disputes in the United States occurred before there was even a country called the United States. The Boston Tea Party was a protest against British tea tariffs. On the eve of the Revolution, one of the initial acts of the First Continental Congress was a vote to stop trading with England until it changed its policies.

After the United States gained its independence, trade remained controversial. The nation's first Treasury Secretary, conservative Alexander Hamilton, pushed for high tariffs in an effort to protect the budding industries of the Northeast and allow the country to be less dependent on manufactured goods from England. Thomas Jefferson's Democrats opposed high tariffs. The small farmers who made up the party's base complained that the tariffs raised the price of manufactured goods.

These disputes carried over into the 1820s and 1830s, with the Democrats taking the anti-tariff "free trade" position and the Whig Party generally in support of higher tariffs. The debates pitted the increasingly industrialized North against small farmers in the West and the slave-holding plantation owners of the South. Under President Andrew Jackson, the Democrats decried tariffs as a sop to the wealthy classes of the East, who they said were receiving special treatment. Essentially, the Democrats were attacking the tariffs on the grounds that they were what today would be called "corporate welfare." The Whigs responded that by encouraging local manufacturing the tariffs were benefiting the country as a whole. For the most part, the tariff position prevailed, and in the decades before the Civil War, tariff rates, though relatively moderate, extended to a wide range of economic sectors.

In the second half of the 19th century, trade policy continued to fracture the country, and the debate became more intense than ever. The Republican Party, which was becoming the party of big business, was the party of protectionism, supporting the expansion of tariffs to shield American business from foreign competition. Meanwhile, farmers remained intensely resentful of the tariffs. Trade was increasingly seen as a zero-sum game: What was good for the eastern manufacturers was bound to be bad for the farmers in the West. The resentment turned to outright anger as commodity prices collapsed in the 1870s, ruining many farmers and contributing to the rise of the Populist Movement, which endorsed free trade.

The nascent American labor movement was split on the tariffs issue. Some trade unionists felt that tariffs only served to give big businesses even larger profits and gain market share that could be used against smaller enterprises, workers and consumers. Some labor activists labeled tariffs "the mother of trusts."[2] But others within the labor movement believed that by protecting industry the tariffs helped provide jobs to workers. This sort of economic nationalism was persuasive enough that protective tariffs stayed in place into the early 20th century.

During the first part of the 20th century, the U.S. government seesawed between lowering and raising tariffs. In 1913, Democratic President Woodrow Wilson cut tariffs substantially. The passage, in 1916, of the constitutional amendment permitting a federal income tax meant that, for the first time in the country's history, tariffs would no longer supply the largest portion of the government's budget. Still, the argument that tariffs were key to protecting American business continued to hold sway, and in 1921, and again in 1923, Congress increased tariffs for dozens of imported products.

The last hurrah for tariff protectionism came in 1930, when Congress passed the Smoot-Hawley Tariff (named after its authors), which raised rates for a variety of goods. In the congressional hearings over the legislation, one speaker after another hailed the benefits of high tariffs.[3] But as the Great Depression deepened, Washington's long-held belief in the benefit of high tariffs began to waver.

When Franklin Roosevelt was elected President in 1932, his administration began doing everything it could to end the Depression. Roosevelt and the Democratic Congress tried out one policy after another—government work programs, loan programs, increased government spending—to restart the economy. Part of this policy experimentation involved tinkering with trade policy. In 1934 Congress passed the Reciprocal Trade Agreements Act, which provided the President with the authority to negotiate trade deals with other countries, reversing the constitutional arrangement that gave power over trade policies to Congress. The intention of the act was to "restore the nation's standard of living" by fostering trade.[4]

World War II solidified the notion that free trade could be in America's best interest. During the war, production took off, and U.S. industry, led by the military sector, began exporting goods around the world.

This belief took hold in the postwar years as the country's largest companies boosted the idea that trade was good for everyone. After the war, many countries were in ruins, but the U.S. economy had come out of the conflict in far better shape than at the outset. The United States unquestionably had the strongest economy on earth; by one estimate, the U.S. economy accounted for 50 percent of all world production. With production continuing to grow, the United States needed new markets for its goods. And since the United States essentially controlled the global marketplace, free trade would only assist the United States in maintaining its preeminence. This position echoed the free trade agenda of Great Britain in the 19th and early 20th century, when it was the world's economic powerhouse. Free trade favors those on top.

The foreign policy establishment in Washington began to see free trade as an important Cold War tool. Cold War strategists felt that the United States could win friends by opening the U.S. market to certain countries' products, thereby gaining allies in the struggle against the Soviet Union.

The U.S. position at the top of the world economy eased tensions between corporations and labor unions. Businesses saw free trade as a way to increase sales abroad. The unions recognized that more sales equaled more jobs, and supported low tariff principles. Large corporations could afford trade unions at home if they were earning super-profits from unfree labor abroad.

A new consensus was emerging on trade issues. Protectionism was out. Free trade was in. Between 1948 and 1970, the U.S. government led the industrialized countries in six rounds of tariff reductions (i.e., cutting taxes on transnational capital). Democrats and Republicans alike supported these cuts.

As U.S. companies moved their factories out of the United States while continuing to sell here, the country lost in a double sense: It lost the jobs and local tax revenues from the runaway jobs, and it lost the tariff revenue when the products were brought back in for sale.

In the 1970s, the U.S. economy started to slip from its dominance when the oil embargo led to high inflation and President Nixon scrapped the gold standard. In 1971, the United States registered its first trade deficit since 1893. Yet support for free trade held strong. In 1974 Congress passed, by sweeping margins, a bill giving the President "fast track" trade negotiating authority. Even as the economy entered a period of stagflation—recession coupled with inflation—the United States was negotiating with other countries for a new round of tariff reductions and other free trade policies.

The first mutterings that free trade might not be in the country's best interests came in the 1980s, as the ever-growing trade deficits raised concerns that the U.S. economy was in real decline. Union support for free trade—which was strong through the 1950s, '60s, and even '70s—began to flag as organized labor realized that the trade deficit was shipping jobs out of the country. Right-wing nationalists saw the trade deficits as a symbol of weakening of U.S. power. The fact that much of the trade deficit was due to Japanese imports contributed to a nationalistic "America First" sentiment. "Buy American" campaigns spread.

In 1984, Congress responded to the growing deficits by passing a nonbinding resolution calling for an import ceiling on some products. But despite such stirrings, most of Washington was still committed to the free trade philosophy. Among the general public, unease about trade policy had not yet translated into outright opposition. The free trade consensus held.

That was about to change. An entirely new breed of trade agreements—affecting more domestic laws than any similar trade deals before them—were about to crack support for free trade. These new agreements would shift the terms of debate from free trade versus protectionism to free trade versus national sovereignty. That shift would grab the attention of the general public, in the process upending the long-standing bipartisan alliances on trade. After nearly 50 years of consensus, trade policy was once again to become a red hot political issue, igniting the passions of millions of ordinary citizens.

IT CAME FROM CANADA

In 1988, the United States and Canada signed a free trade agreement—and hardly anyone in the United States noticed. The bill approving the U.S.-Canada Free Trade Agreement (FTA) sailed through Congress. The deal hardly even made the news in the United States. But in Canada, the agreement stirred a bitter controversy and made millions of Canadians aware of the sweeping consequences of the new breed of trade deals.

Talks between the United States and Canada over the FTA began in September 1985, and for the next three years Canadian labor unions, environmentalists, and social activists mobilized to educate their fellow citizens about the dangers posed by melding the Canadian and American economies. Canadian progressives said the agreement would weaken environmental standards, loosen the country's social safety net, and lead to job losses. When it came to recognizing the potential impacts of international commercial agreements, Canadian activists were way ahead of their peers to the south.

When Canadian Prime Minister Brian Mulroney, head of the right-of-center Progressive Conservative party, first proposed a free trade agreement with the United States, most Canadians were favorable to the idea; support ran three-to-one in favor of a deal, according to one poll.[5] But as Canadian activists started organizing opposition to the agreement, support eroded. Canadian labor unions, representing nearly one-third of workers, feared that the FTA would encourage jobs to move to the United States, where the minimum wage was lower and worker benefits such as unemployment insurance were less generous. Environmentalists were afraid that merging with the larger U.S. economy would lead to a weakening of Canadian environmental regulations to make them more like U.S. laws. Many Canadians were worried that the deal would jeopardize Canada's unique cultural identity and put at risk Canada's more egalitarian social welfare system.

Many Canadian activists also warned that the agreement would deregulate big business and increase the power of corporations at the expense of ordinary people. In a pamphlet published by the newly formed Council of Canadians, Maude Barlow wrote that "Canadian institutions are now under intense pressure to operate as if they are businesses." Another critic of the FTA, Tony Clarke, cautioned that

> stateless corporations are effectively transforming nation-states to suit their interests. . . . By campaigning for . . . privatization and deregulation, business coalitions have effectively dismantled many of the powers and tools of national governments.[6]

Such critiques were building public opposition to the agreement. Resistance was so strong that the opposition Liberal Party forced an election over the free trade deal. The Conservatives won a majority of seats in the vote and Parliament soon approved the treaty. But public opinion polls showed that a majority of voters opposed it.[7]

The high stakes controversy that surrounded the FTA in Canada would eventually move south, and with it many of the same complaints about what free trade meant for workers, the environment, and the growth of corporations' power.

A North American free trade bloc was formally proposed in August of 1990, when Mexican President Carlos Salinas sent a letter to President Bush asking for talks to create a free trade zone including Mexico, the United States, and Canada. Negotiations among the three governments began in June of 1991. American non-governmental organizations, who for the most part had cared little about the U.S.-Canada FTA, began to take notice. A free trade deal with Canada—a country with a similar economy and comparable environmental and labor standards—

was one thing; but tying the U.S. economy closer to Mexico, a much poorer country that failed to enforce worker and environmental protections, was cause for real concern.

When the FTA was under consideration, Canadian groups had tried to alert American organizations that the trade deal was about more than trade: In fact, the agreement was a cloak for deregulating business. Few U.S. NGOs had heeded the warnings, but as the NAFTA talks gained steam, American activists began to listen to the Canadian critiques—and develop their own.

Some American environmentalists pointed to the improper disposal of toxics, especially along the U.S.-Mexico border, as evidence of Mexico's poor environmental record. Greenpeace warned that "free trade as defined by corporate interests" would take away the government's ability to protect the environment and put decision-making in the hands of "multinational corporations and obscure international agencies."[8] Greenpeace, along with other environmental groups, said U.S. businesses would use NAFTA to move production to Mexico so they could avoid complying with environmental regulations.

Environmentalists also feared that NAFTA could lead to a lowering of environmental standards in the U.S. In 1991—under the auspices of another trade system, the General Agreement on Tariffs and Trade (GATT)—a U.S. law intended to protect dolphins from the nets of tuna fishermen had been cited by Mexico as a violation of free trade principles (see Chapter 2). Environmental groups were afraid that businesses could use NAFTA to launch similar attacks on other environmental protections.

Those fears were shared by some consumer activists, most notably Ralph Nader's organization Public Citizen and its Global Trade Watch unit, headed by Lori Wallach, a trade lawyer. Nader had been one of the few American activists to note the importance of the U.S.-Canada FTA, and Wallach had started preparing to battle NAFTA as early as 1990. For Public Citizen, the GATT dispute over America's dolphin-protection law represented a direct assault on the democratic process. Nader and Wallach were warning other activists that NAFTA could be used to challenge hard-won regulations protecting consumers, workers, and the environment. They argued that NAFTA, by fostering deregulation of businesses, would increase the power of corporations to the detriment of the public interest.

The AFL-CIO had long supported free trade principles. But during the 1980s, manufacturing jobs started to disappear as companies moved their production facilities overseas, forcing a change in the AFL-CIO's perspective on trade policy.

The AFL-CIO feared that NAFTA would greatly accelerate the loss of manufacturing jobs. After all, if a corporation could pay a Mexican worker $3,700 a year (the average Mexican income) or a U.S. worker ten times that, the business would most likely move production south. Critics also complained that Mexican workers' wages would have little chance of rising soon since Mexican workers were routinely denied their rights to form trade unions and bargain collectively. Most workers were represented, if at all, by government-controlled unions that failed to act as real advocates for workers' interests. For the unions, NAFTA threatened "an economic and social disaster."[9]

Environmentalists, consumer activists, and trade unionists criticized NAFTA from different angles, but their attacks converged on the idea that the agreement would lead to a "race-to-the-bottom." They feared that transnational corporations would use the free trade agreement to relocate operations to Mexico, where they could avoid meaningful health and safety, workers' rights, and environmental regulations. Businesses would gravitate to the place with the weakest standards.

The disparate groups attacking NAFTA also shared a fundamental concern about the way in which the agreement was being negotiated behind closed doors. Citizen groups were entirely left out of the process, given no chance by the government negotiators to influence the trade talks. Despite frequent complaints to the office of the U.S. Trade Representative, bolstered by similar criticisms from some Members of Congress, the NAFTA negotiators refused to release any of the draft texts. Critics demanded to know why the secrecy was necessary if there was nothing to hide. For those opposed to NAFTA, the secrecy surrounding the negotiations heightened their suspicions and deepened their sense that the agreement was undemocratic. "This is not the right way to make a major policy decision in this country," a fair trade activist complained to the media during the negotiations.[10]

As the NAFTA negotiations entered their final stage in 1992, the concerns of the trade unionists, environmentalists, and consumer advocates began to attract the attention of the media and the public at large. Clearly, the agreement was going to have a powerful effect on the United States. Curiosity about NAFTA grew.

The deal started to gain popular attention as it became an issue in the presidential campaign. President George H.W. Bush was clearly in favor of the agreement. Other candidates were opposed. Former California Governor Jerry Brown, a dark horse candidate in the Democratic primaries, attacked NAFTA, echoing the complaints of environmentalists and the unions. Ross Perot, a Texas billionaire who campaigned as a "throw-the-bums-out-of-Washington" populist, was also strongly against the agreement. His campaign put NAFTA opposition at the center of its platform and drew new interest to the agreement. In the most evocative description ever attached to the deal, Perot said NAFTA would lead to a "giant sucking sound" as U.S. jobs were relocated to Mexico.

Bill Clinton, the Governor of Arkansas and the Democratic nominee for President, was undecided on the issue. Clinton was attempting to sell himself to the electorate as a "New Democrat"—that is, a more centrist, business-friendly Democrat, and supporting NAFTA, which was a priority of the American business community, fit right in with that image. Clinton had offered several pro-NAFTA statements during the primary campaign, but many of the candidate's close advisors had serious misgivings about supporting the agreement, which they knew the party's base opposed. Within the Clinton camp, opinions were split on the issue. In the end Clinton—setting a course that would steer him for the next eight years—chose a contradictory middle ground. He would support NAFTA, but only if it included "side agreements" that would help protect workers and the environment.[11]

Clinton announced his decision at an October 4 speech at North Carolina State University.

> I remain convinced that the North American Free Trade Agreement will generate growth and jobs on both sides of the border if and only if it's part of a broad-based strategy, and if and only if we address the issues still to be addressed.

It was classic Clinton, leaving NAFTA proponents and critics alike unsure what the final agreement would look like if Clinton was elected.

THE SELLING OF NAFTA

For Clinton, passing NAFTA was central to his self-image as an internationalist, a forward-thinking statesman. It was also key to his probusiness, New Democrat character. But the President had a serious problem: Several of the Democratic Party's key constituencies—among them organized labor, environmentalists, consumer groups, and small farmers—were against the agreement. By pushing NAFTA, Clinton threatened to split his own party. The President needed to find a way to pass NAFTA while preventing a schism within the Democratic Party.

Supplemental, or side, agreements to address labor and environmental issues were supposed to do the trick. But Clinton was also bound by the expectations of Corporate America, which was in favor of NAFTA but was strongly opposed to any side agreements that went too far in actually enforcing labor and environmental regulations. If the side agreements weren't binding enough, Clinton would lose the support of the AFL-CIO and some of the major environmental groups. If the side agreements were genuinely enforceable, the President would lose the support of big business. The administration had to toe a careful line.

On August 13, 1993, Mickey Kantor, Clinton's U.S. Trade Representative, released the labor and environmental side agreements that had been written with Canada and Mexico. The conservative government in Canada and Mexican President Carlos Salinas had both opposed strong side agreements, and the final result had no teeth. The environmental agreement pledged to "foster the protection and improvement of the environment," but there was no enforcement mechanism. The labor agreement called for "improving working conditions and living standards," again without providing any sanctions if that goal was not met.

NAFTA's opponents were unimpressed. The labor unions called the side agreements nothing more than a fig leaf. Public Citizen said the difference between NAFTA without side agreements and NAFTA with side agreements was "like comparing rotten fish to rotten beef."[12]

Clinton's side agreements split the environmental community. Some organizations said the agreements were better than nothing and announced they would support NAFTA. These groups included the World Wildlife Fund, the National Resources Defense Council, and the Environmental Defense Fund, among others. The Sierra Club, Greenpeace, and Friends of the Earth remained opposed.

The support of just a portion of the environmental community was not enough to give Clinton the cover he needed. The side agreements had failed to win converts among the skeptics in Congress. Representative Marcy Kaptur (D-OH) noted that while the side agreements were full of the words "investors" and "competition," they never mentioned "people" or "workers" or "farmers." Representative Dick Gephardt (D-MO), the party's leader in the House and a longtime labor ally on trade issues, was also unswayed. After reviewing the side agreements, Gephardt said he would not support NAFTA.

Clinton had failed to gain the support of key Democratic leaders and interest groups. NAFTA had been framed as an agreement for big business, so now Clinton would have to rely on big business to pass NAFTA.

The Clinton White House turned to some of the most experienced corporate lobbyists in Washington to sell the American public on NAFTA and get the deal through Congress. As chronicled by John MacArthur in his book *The Selling of "Free Trade"*, in early September of 1994, lobbyists from three dozen of the largest U.S. corporations gathered at the Washington offices of Allied Signal to plan a strategy for winning NAFTA. Lobbyists and lawyers representing some of the most influential NAFTA backers—Boeing, General Electric, Motorola, Caterpillar, and IBM, among others—were at the meeting. And so were three top Clinton aides—trade ambassador Kantor, NAFTA "czar" and future Commerce Secretary William Daley, and politico Rahm Emmanuel.[13]

The individuals assembled at the Allied Signal offices represented a kind of corporate lobbying "A-Team." They were among the most influential lobbyists in Washington, the most effective at creating (or defeating) legislation to serve their clients' interests. Most of the lobbyists in the room would soon be working with an organization called "USA*NAFTA"*: essentially a front group for the powerful Business Roundtable. During the next two months, USA*NAFTA and the White House would work closely together to make NAFTA the law of the land. The business group and Clinton aides collaborated on political tactics and media strategy, and shared polling data and messaging points with each other. When it came to NAFTA, the relationship between the White House and big business was almost seamless.

NAFTA's backers—however powerful and well organized—were facing long odds. An August Gallup Poll showed that 64 percent of Americans opposed a free trade agreement with Mexico.[14] And when William Daley did his first congressional head count to gauge how many votes he needed, he found only 19 Democrats in favor.[15]

Congressional and public resistance to NAFTA was due in large part to the work of the unions, environmentalists, and consumer groups. Opponents of the agreement had gotten a big jump on the business lobby. Throughout August, when Members of Congress were home in their districts during the summer recess, NAFTA critics had urged people to call, write, or visit their representatives. Organized labor held town hall meetings to educate people about why they should oppose NAFTA. In the weeks leading up to Labor Day, remembers one NAFTA proponent, Members of Congress "were getting the hell beat out of them."[16]

Many of the opponents' activities were coordinated through a coalition of NGOs called the Citizens Trade Campaign (CTC). Formed in 1992, the CTC included such disparate partners as Public Citizen, the United Auto Workers, the Sierra Club, the National Farmers Union, the Rainbow Coalition, and Friends of the Earth. The different members disagreed on other policy issues, but they all agreed that NAFTA was a raw deal. The CTC's efforts to defeat NAFTA laid the foundation for

---

* USA*NAFTA later became "USA*Engage." While the membership stayed the same, the group broadened its mission to promoting free trade principles in general, not just NAFTA. The group played a key role in the controversy over Burma. (See Chapter 4.)

the coalition that in late 1999 would stop the WTO in Seattle.

"When we put together the CTC in 1992, we wanted the 'you can't run-you can't hide' coalition," says Public Citizen's Lori Wallach.

Members of Congress were voting in such a way that they were screwing all of us, and then blaming the other groups. We had to all be in one room so they couldn't play us off against one another. . . . And this was not easy. Within our own constituencies, people thought we were nuts. But we realized that the scale of what we faced was so big that we had to work together.

While each of the members of the CTC articulated criticism of NAFTA that would resonate best with their constituencies, the coalition worked to developed a shared, overarching critique. According to the CTC members, NAFTA wasn't really about trade, it was about investment.

The CTC pointed out that since the United States and Canada were already parties to a free trade agreement, the real focus of NAFTA was Mexico. Multinational corporations were eager to relocate production facilities to Mexico, which had looser environmental and labor standards than the United States. Consequently, businesses moving to Mexico would get to be close to the United States while at the same time substantially cutting their costs. The corporations, however, feared Mexico's history of expropriating and nationalizing foreign-owned enterprises. And businesses were turned off by Mexican laws that required foreign companies to find Mexican partners for their operations and placed restrictions on foreign land ownership. NAFTA, then, was primarily designed to foster corporate investment in Mexico, an agenda which served both the interests of Corporate America and that of Mexican President Carlos Salinas, whose corruption-ridden government needed the investment to offset its massive foreign debt payments.

For Carla Hills, President George H.W. Bush's trade representative and the key U.S. negotiator for NAFTA, the goal was clear: "We want corporations to be able to make investments overseas without having to take a local partner, or export a given percentage of their output, to use local parts, or to meet any of a dozen other restrictions."[17]

In this agenda NAFTA's critics saw an effort by corporations to avoid any measure of accountability. Easier investment meant more opportunity to move production from one country to another, and that would give corporations greater ability to avoid regulations and even lower them by playing countries off each other. For the CTC and its allies, NAFTA was set up to give corporations more power by giving them new chances to set up business wherever they liked. Whenever NAFTA's opponents were labeled "protectionists," the CTC replied that, in fact,

NAFTA itself was protectionist—only it was intended to protect the investment of businesses, not workers or the environment.

"What we're really trying to protect here are property rights," one of the U.S. government's NAFTA negotiators has been quoted as saying.[18]

When asked by author John MacArthur to describe NAFTA, Carlos Castañeda, an NYU professor who eventually became Mexico's Foreign Minister, was more blunt: "It's totally an investment agreement. It has nothing to do with trade."[19]

But the CTC's argument that NAFTA was essentially about investment didn't make it far into the public mind. When it came to the popular debate, the NAFTA controversy hinged almost exclusively on what the deal would mean when it came to jobs. And that was largely because the media chose Ross Perot to serve as the anti-NAFTA voice.

During his failed bid for President, Perot had centered his campaign on opposition to NAFTA, seeking to tap into populist distrust of the corporate-managed, so-called "free trade." After the campaign, Perot kept up his attacks on NAFTA. The diminutive billionaire traveled the country holding anti-NAFTA rallies that drew thousands. Then, in August of 1993, Perot and an economist friend, Pat Choate, authored a book that brought together many of the arguments against NAFTA. *Save Your Job, Save Our Country: Why NAFTA Must Be Stopped Now* laid out in easy-to-read language the criticisms of the trade deal. The book sold hundreds of thousands of copies, and made best-seller lists. Its success landed Perot invitations to all the major television and radio talk shows. NAFTA's opponents had never selected Perot as their main spokesman—and, in fact, many environmentalists were displeased by some of what he had to say—but now the businessman-populist was the de facto voice of the NAFTA resistance.

The popularity of Perot's book blindsided the White House. The U.S. Trade Representative's office was so shaken that it prepared a rebuttal, "Correcting the Record," which was distributed to reporters and lawmakers. The terms of the debate had been set: For the mainstream media, NAFTA wasn't about corporate power, it was about jobs.

The White House scrambled to get out its message. The trade agreement, the White House claimed, would create 200,000 export-related jobs within the first year alone by giving American businesses new chances to sell to Mexican consumers. If the agreements didn't pass, the White House warned, a sharp drop in exports could lead to the loss of as many as 400,000 jobs. NAFTA's backers said a defeat of the agreement would rattle international financial markets and lead to a meltdown of the Mexican economy.

Meanwhile, USA*NAFTA, the business lobby, was bringing its

weight to bear. The group helped coordinate a letter signed by 238 prominent economists, including 12 Nobel laureates, stating that NAFTA was in the country's best interest. The letter gained widespread media coverage and bolstered the conventional wisdom that NAFTA would be beneficial. USA*NAFTA was also trying to drum up support for NAFTA in the country's heartland. Its grassroots efforts—labeled "astroturf" by NAFTA opponents—enlisted local business people to contact Members of Congress to support NAFTA. USA*NAFTA organized nationwide "push polls"—calls to people's homes that came off as neutral opinion polling but were really advocacy messages with a pro-NAFTA agenda. The push polls led to thousands of constituent communications being sent to congressional offices, though many of them were of dubious authenticity.[20]

President Clinton and USA*NAFTA also worked together to recruit a high-profile television spokesman—former Chrysler chair Lee Iacocca. During the 1980s, Iacocca had become the very face of American entrepreneurial spirit, and he enjoyed universal name recognition and impeccable credibility. Soon televisions spots were running across the country featuring Iacocca's NAFTA pitch. "With NAFTA, U.S. exports to Mexico are going to take off, and that means more high-paying jobs right here in the US," Iacocca told the American people.

The White House continued pushing its message that NAFTA would create hundreds of thousands of jobs. In late October, Clinton's team and USA*NAFTA organized a "NAFTA Jobs and Products Day" on the South Lawn of the White House. Caterpillar heavy machinery and Chrysler cars, among other products, sat in front of the White House as business leaders and administration officials talked about all the jobs NAFTA would create.

USA*NAFTA was spending millions of dollars on advertising and lobbying, and the President was putting all his influence behind the deal. Yet NAFTA was still struggling. House Democratic leader Gephardt was against the bill, and his lieutenant, Majority Whip David Bonior, was fiercely lobbying Democratic members to oppose NAFTA. The unions and environmental groups were turning up the heat at the grassroots. And Perot, a regular face on the television, wouldn't shut up.

The White House needed to neutralize Perot, and administration officials figured the best way of doing that would be to challenge him head on in a prime time debate. There was a big risk in facing Perot one-on-one. His down-home language was effective, and if the White House lost, it would probably mean the end of the NAFTA. But with the agreement's fate up in the air, the White House decided the gamble was worth it, and Vice President Al Gore prepared to debate Perot.

A nationally televised debate was risky, but the White House saw advantages in facing Perot, who had a reputation as an eccentric, and had shown flashes of instability. White House officials figured that if they could fluster Perot, they could win a debate. At the very least, he promised to be a far weaker debater than Ralph Nader, who had also challenged the White House to a debate and had been turned down.[21]

On November 9, less than two weeks before Congress was scheduled to vote on NAFTA, Perot and Gore appeared on CNN's "Larry King Live" for a 90-minute debate. Nearly 17 million viewers tuned in.

Sure enough, Gore quickly rattled Perot. Holding up a photograph of former Representatives Smoot and Hawley, authors of trade legislation in 1930, Gore charged that protectionism had sparked the Great Depression. He went on to challenge Perot's spending on the anti-NAFTA campaign, insinuating that Perot had something to hide.

Perot could have noted that Smoot-Hawley went into effect well into the Depression, and that its impact on the already dire economic situation remains debatable. He could have pointed out that USA*NAFTA was spending somewhere between $14 million and $18 million on its NAFTA campaign, about ten times what Perot himself had shelled out.[22] Instead, Perot became flustered and turned defensive. His arguments were rambling. He came off as just plain weird.

To anyone watching the debate, it was clear that Perot had been clobbered. The anti-NAFTA forces at the AFL-CIO and the CTC were devastated. "Perot was the worst thing that ever happened to us," a union strategist said later. "I'm watching the debate, and I just wanted to kill myself."[23]

The White House had won an important battle, destroying the credibility of the NAFTA critics' most prominent spokesperson. But the debate was by no means over. The AFL-CIO and the CTC were continuing their popular education campaigns, talking to ordinary people across the country about why NAFTA was not in the country's best interest. The deal's opponents were keeping the pressure on Members of Congress, urging them to vote "no." As the vote got closer there were still no assurances the bill would pass.

All eyes were on the House of Representatives. The Senate, generally a more conservative body, was widely expected to approve NAFTA, which meant that the grassroots citizen energy and corporate muscle was focused on the House. The lobbying was intense, with both corporate lobbyists and CTC and AFL-CIO members swarming the Capitol and trying to nail down votes. With less than a week to go before the vote, as many as 80 members remained undecided.

With the outcome in the air, and desperate to clinch the deal, the

White House decided to turn to what in Washington is know as "retail politics." That is, the President would offer Members of Congress pork barrel spending projects and other perks and favors in return for a "yes" vote on NAFTA.

In the days before the vote, the White House threw the store doors wide open. Some of the deals Clinton made with Members of Congress were connected in some way to the potential effects of NAFTA. For example, the White House gained the support of California Representative Esteban Torres by promising to establish a special development bank that would fund environmental clean-up and infrastructure projects along the border. Many other deals, however, were pure pork. Representatives from sugar-growing states were promised continued subsidies for the sugar industry. Some members from agricultural districts got a slower phase-out of certain pesticides, while others were assured that the government would continue buying crops from their districts for school lunch programs. In return for their votes, two Members requested an agreement by the Justice Department to send undocumented immigrants who were in jail in the United States back to Mexico. One Representative received the promise of a duck hunting trip with the President. In all, at least 21 vote-buying episodes were documented in a Public Citizen report titled "NAFTA's Bizarre Bazaar."[24]

In the short run, the deals paid off. On the night of November 17, the House of Representatives approved NAFTA by a surprising margin, 234-200—16 more votes than were needed. Three days later the Senate voted in favor of the deal 61-38. NAFTA would become law.

In the long run, however, the manner in which Clinton clinched the NAFTA victory would come to haunt him. The White House had won the vote, but it had failed to win the debate. Instead of focusing on convincing the American people of the alleged merits of the agreement, the White House had relied on last-minute back room deals to pass NAFTA. Rather than responding to the concerns of environmentalists, trade unionists, and small businesses, the White House had relied on the astroturf tactics of Corporate America, whose agenda—setting up new factories and investments in Mexico—was at odds with the President's goal of creating more jobs in the United States.

"Public opinion wasn't in support of [NAFTA]," a member of Mickey Kantor's staff later conceded. "We had better support than we thought, but this was not being won by hundreds of constituents."[25]

In failing to really persuade the public that NAFTA would be beneficial, Clinton had set himself up for future failures. The President had promised a great deal—jobs for ordinary people, special projects for Members of Congress—and someday those promises would come due.

Also, the White House's success came at the expense of alienating a great many rank-and-file Democrats. The environmentalists and ordinary workers who had fought so hard against NAFTA would find it hard to see why they should fight for Clinton. Nearly two-thirds of House Democrats opposed NAFTA, and Clinton's aggressive support for the deal had left many Members suspicious of the President.

Clinton got his trade deal, but only by splitting his party. The long-standing bipartisan consensus on trade was dead. With even bigger commercial agreements on the horizon, that meant bigger fights lay ahead.

A REVOLT FROM THE JUNGLE

On January 1, 1994, NAFTA went into effect with a bang, from an unexpected direction. On that day Indigenous peasants in the impoverished southern Mexican state of Chiapas launched an armed rebellion, briefly seizing roads, military outposts, and the state's second-largest town, the colonial center of San Cristóbal de las Casas, before melting back into the jungle. The rebels, who called themselves Zapatistas (after legendary revolutionary Emiliano Zapata), were revolting, they said, against 500 years of oppression. The timing of the rebellion was pointed. The rebels wanted to strike a symbolic blow against "neoliberalism," the ideology of market fundamentalism and corporate *laissez-faire* embodied in NAFTA. The Zapatistas said they wanted freedom over their lives and true democracy.

Until the Battle of Seattle in late 1999, the Zapatista rebellion would serve as the clearest example of the passions inflamed by the march of corporate globalization.

GATTZILLA EATS FLIPPER

Although unnoticed by most Americans, a shadow hung over NAFTA, the prospect of a much larger and more sweeping trade agreement. Even as the NAFTA debate raged, citizens groups, corporate lobbyists and Members of Congress had an eye on a decades-old commercial pact called the General Agreement on Tariffs and Trade (GATT). Most worrisome for fair trade forces, the newest proposed modifications to GATT were set to establish a global governing regime, the World Trade Organization, with more powers than the United Nations, yet with few of the UN's checks and balances and with far less transparency. As the NAFTA controversy cooled, another trade battle was set to begin.

The GATT system was established after World War II, when the Western capitalist countries—seeking to avoid the global economic chaos of the Great Depression—starting building a framework of rules to oversee international trade and taxation. Initially, GATT's mandate was limited to tariffs, the taxes governments place on goods coming from other countries. The central goal of successive GATT negotiations was to reduce and conform tariff rates among the major industrialized countries. The first six GATT "rounds," as the multi-year trade negotiations were called, limited themselves to this objective. In effect, GATT delivered a series of tax cuts to transnational corporations, fattening business coffers while taking money away from national governments. These tax cuts were a major contributor to the eventual fiscal crisis of the federal government because tariff income had traditionally been a significant source of revenue to the U.S. government.

In the 1970s, trade negotiators from the world's wealthiest countries expanded their discussions to include what they called "non-tariff barriers" to trade. That is, trade officials started looking at how national laws and regulations—consumer safeguards, environmental legislation, and food safety laws—were setting up "obstacles" to the unfettered flow of goods and services. In examining the impact of non-tariff barriers, trade bureaucrats began to involve themselves in evaluating whether democratically decided laws were "acceptable," whether they constituted a "reasonable" obstacle to trade among nations.

GATT negotiators first turned their attention to non-tariff barriers during the seventh round of GATT talks, the so-called Tokyo Round that occurred in the late 1970s. By this time, GATT negotiations had expanded from the initial small circle of the world's largest economies to include 99 countries. The increased number of participants slowed the talks, but by 1979 the negotiators had agreed on new rules governing countries' procurement codes (government purchasing), product standards (such as auto safety requirements), and subsidies (government payments to industries).

GATT was steadily acquiring the power to affect domestic laws, yet hardly anyone noticed. When Congress considered implementing the results of the Tokyo Round, just one union, the International Brotherhood of Electrical Workers, expressed concerns that the GATT was leading to a deregulation of businesses, and posed a threat to national sovereignty. "[If the bill becomes law] we will have subordinated the standards-making process to the international arena," the union warned.[26] Such concerns hardly had an impact on the congressional deliberations. The Trade Agreements Act of 1979 passed 395-7 in the House and 90-4 in the Senate.

In 1986, another GATT round (the Uruguay Round) was launched. By now, trade officials were focused on reducing non-tariff barriers. They also started working to establish a permanent international body that would have the power to enforce GATT rules through monetary penalties. Unbeknownst to most of the world's citizens, the foundations of the World Trade Organization were being laid.

A global trade body was not an entirely new idea. When GATT was created, its architects proposed establishing an International Trade Organization (ITO) that would regulate global commerce. Recognizing that trade could have a real impact on other areas of social policy, the ITO included rules obligating member countries to take actions to eliminate unfair labor practices. The ITO also would have allowed countries to exempt health and safety regulations from its reach. And the ITO was to have contained mechanisms, similar to UN rules, for civil society organizations to influence deliberations. President Harry Truman was in favor of the idea, but Congress never embraced the plan, and the proposal died a quiet death.

The WTO disregarded the ITO ideas. With the main intent of increasing global trade flows, the WTO was being designed to protect the interests of investors and corporations, not workers or consumers or the environment. And the WTO allowed no way for citizens to participate in decision making, or even to have access to draft documents. For the NGO community, this was cause for serious concern. The WTO threatened to limit or eliminate hard-won consumer, environmental, and workplace regulations, while at the same time giving the public no way to influence WTO policy making. The WTO would foster global trade above all other social goals.

As far back as the 1980s, some U.S. activists started worrying about the potential impacts of GATT. Mark Ritchie, founder of the Institute for Agriculture and Trade Policy, a family farm group based in Minneapolis, tried to warn fellow activists of the far-reaching effect the new trade rules could have on important regulations. GATT also caught the eye of consumer crusader Ralph Nader. According to Ritchie and Nader, transnational corporations—which were intimately involved in writing GATT's rules—were using the GATT talks as a back door to push their deregulation agenda. Trade was being used as a cloak to strike at regulations that corporations had long opposed, but felt they couldn't overturn through the regular political channels in Washington.

For example, a key concern of Ritchie's was the attempt by U.S. GATT negotiators to "harmonize" food safety standards to make it easier for massive agribusiness firms to export their products. In practice, "harmonization" meant lowering the food safety requirement. Ritchie described the first Bush administration's efforts as a plan by agribusiness giant "Cargill and their supporters . . . to go around Congress by moving the debate and ultimate decision-making to the international trade negotiations at GATT."[27] By allowing trade bureaucrats to do an end run around their own legislatures, GATT was short-circuiting the democratic process.

Critics of the GATT talks were as upset about the process of the negotiations as their substance. Ritchie, along with Public Citizen staffers and a few other groups, had been working with European NGOs to influence the GATT talks. While GATT officials and some government negotiators agreed to meet with the civil society groups, the NGOs found the GATT negotiators completely unresponsive to their concerns. To compound the distrust, GATT officials refused to release any of the negotiating drafts to the civil society groups. The secrecy deepened activists' suspicions. "There is a citizen vacuum being filled by corporate schemes," Nader wrote in 1990.[28] How was it possible that talks impacting a wide range of public policies were taking place in secret?

It was an important question, but few people were listening. Despite their best efforts, the handful of American activists sounding the alarm about the dangers posed by GATT were not being heard by the NGO community, much less the public at large.

"What we tried to argue—but people couldn't hear for the first couple of years—was that this was a corporate power grab wrapped in the happy language of trade," says Wallach. "People just thought we were crazy. But then GATTzilla ate flipper, and that was the beginning of the end of ignorance."

In 1990, environmentalists convinced Congress to pass legislation banning the importation of tuna caught in ways proven deadly to dolphins. In 1991, Mexico challenged the law via GATT's dispute panel, claiming that the U.S. dolphin-protection law was an unfair barrier to trade. In September of 1991, the trade panel ruled that the U.S. law was, in fact, GATT-illegal. According to the GATT panel, if similar laws were permitted, then any country could ban imports from another country "merely because the exporting country has different environmental, health and social policies from its own."

A subsequent GATT ruling on the tuna law raised other fears. GATT officials said the U.S. tuna law was illegal because it violated GATT rules prohibiting discrimination of goods based on "production methods." Under GATT, countries could not ban a product based on how it was produced. This logic struck right at the heart of a host of government regulations. Concerns about production methods were the basis for regulations on strip-mining, oil drilling, and logging, and the ban on goods made with child labor or forced labor. Essentially, GATT was saying that the buying and selling of products should trump all other values or priorities. And now, through the Uruguay Round, the GATT negotiators wanted to make such rules binding and enforceable through the creation of the WTO.

The warnings from Ritchie, Nader, and others about GATT were no longer academic. A U.S. environmental law was under attack because it represented an obstacle to business as usual. The GATT panel had no power to strike down the law or levy any sort of fine against the United States, but the decision sent a chill through the environmental, consumer rights, and labor communities. A host of long-standing public interest legislation seemed at risk from a little-known international body.

Arguments about how the free trade agenda was increasing corporate power at the expense of ordinary citizens had lurked at the edges of the NAFTA fight, but the question of jobs always held center stage. The debate over GATT would be different. Worries about commercial agreements' impact on democratic decision-making were set to dominate the fight over GATT. That shift would further complicate the already-messy politics of trade. GATT's threat to the national sovereignty—the ability of countries to make their own laws—was as inflammatory on the right as it was on the left. The battle over GATT would show that trade politics was splintering Republicans as much as it was fracturing the Democrats—and in the process laying the ground for a populist backlash.

CONGRESS WELCOMES GATTZILLA

In April 1994—after nearly eight years of arduous negotiations—the United States and 100 other countries closed the Uruguay Round of trade talks. Under the new agreement, a new institution, the World Trade Organization, would be formed to enforce GATT and other international commerce treaties. The WTO would have the same basic mandate as GATT—expanding global commerce—but it would enjoy vastly greater powers. Unlike GATT, the WTO would be able to levy monetary fines against any nation that violated its rules. The creation of the WTO would mark the most momentous change in global governance since the creation of the United Nations some 50 years earlier.

For the WTO to come into being, the legislatures of its member nations needed to pass a host of laws bringing their regulations into conformity with WTO rules. That meant that the U.S. Congress was about to be at center stage for another trade-related controversy.

By the time GATT talks were clinched in the spring of 1994, the Citizens Trade Campaign was well prepared to oppose the WTO's creation. The dolphin case had crystallized opposition to GATT/WTO, and given its critics plenty of ammunition for their public education campaigns. The CTC distributed thousands of pamphlets across the country featuring on the cover a monstrous "GATTzilla" squashing a dolphin in its hand while smashing the U.S. Capitol underfoot. In plain language, the pamphlet laid out the reasons why citizens should oppose GATT, referred to as "NAFTA on steroids." The central message: GATT posed a threat to democracy and the sovereignty of the American people.

The popular resonance of that message was proven during the dog days of August. CTC organizers had been working hard through the spring and summer to educate people about the dangers of GATT and to urge them to contact their representatives during the August recess. That campaigning paid off when a radio station in Kansas interviewed Ralph Nader to ask him his views about the upcoming deal. Nader laid out the criticisms against GATT and then asked listeners to call their U.S. Representatives and Senators if they were worried about the impact GATT could have. The response was overwhelming. Calls started flooding into the offices of GOP Senator Bob Dole, the Senate Minority Leader and one of the most influential people in Washington. Suddenly Dole's office was receiving up to 2,000 calls a day on the seemingly obscure issue.[29] In the country's heartland, people were worried about how the WTO was poised to impact their lives.

On August 28, Dole responded to his constituents' concerns in an op-ed published in the *Wichita Eagle*. While Dole said he was not necessarily opposed to GATT, he warned the White House and his colleagues in Congress that they were ignoring legitimate concerns about how GATT would affect American laws. He urged lawmakers to take their time in considering the legislation to implement the WTO.[30] With one of the most powerful men on Capitol Hill saying he had doubts about the commercial pact, the WTO's future seemed up in the air.

As Members of Congress returned to Washington after Labor Day, the CTC ratcheted up its campaign against GATT. CTC members took to the airwaves to make their case. In August the CTC started running anti-GATT television commercials in 12 cities across the country. In one ad, an animated version of a Trojan Horse creaks in front of the Capitol as the announcer warns that GATT is a sneak attack against U.S. consumers and workers. "This deal could cancel out U.S. laws— laws that protect our environment, ensure imported foods are safe, defend family farms and protect workers rights," the announcer says.[31] Environmental groups allied with the CTC ran full-page ads in newspapers pointing out the dangerous precedents set by the dolphin-safe tuna case. Activists put up anti-WTO posters in cities nationwide.

The NAFTA fight had created bitter divisions among the environmental community. But when it came to GATT, environmental groups were united in their opposition. The World Wildlife Federation and the Environmental Defense Fund, among other green NAFTA supporters, were badly shaken by the dolphin case, and had come to agree with the free trade critics that GATT/WTO could jeopardize environmental regulations. With the exception of the Consumers Union, every major liberal NGO was against establishing the WTO.

Many conservatives were also concerned about the WTO's impact on U.S. sovereignty. The right-wing opposition to WTO was led by Pat Buchanan, a former Nixon aide and well-known pundit who liked to think of himself as the voice of Main Street Republicans. The WTO's ability to strike at U.S. laws struck directly at the heart of Buchanan's America-First philosophy. "Not in 200 years has the United States dealt away so vast a slice of her liberty," Buchanan complained.[32] Buchanan, with help from other leading conservatives such as Phyllis Schlafly and Rush Limbaugh, launched anti-WTO radio spots across the country.

The WTO was also beginning to draw criticism from an even more unlikely corner: small businesses. For many small- and medium-sized entrepreneurs, it was clear that the WTO's benefits would fall almost exclusively to massive transnational corporations. A group called the U.S. Business and Industrial Council (USBIC) began organizing opposition to the WTO among small businesses by arguing that the deal would lead to international intervention in local economies. The USBIC started running television ads that showed the Declaration of Independence being ripped apart to reveal the letters "WTO" underneath.[33]

The USBIC tried to bring together the liberal and conservative opponents of the agreements, hosting a Capitol Hill press conference featuring both Nader and Buchanan. The press conference illustrated how trade policies were creating strange political bedfellows. Opposition to the WTO transcended conventional definitions of right and left, uniting people across the political spectrum and driving wedges into both major political parties. Resistance to the proposed commercial pact wasn't so much a matter of left versus right as it was an issue of up versus down, elites versus the populists. "People think this is being done for the multinationals at the expense of the average working man," Buchanan was quoted as saying.[34]

The populist groundswell against the WTO was complicating the White House's drive for approval. Luckily for Clinton, organized labor—which had provided much of the muscle against NAFTA—was sitting out the WTO fight. Officially, the AFL-CIO was against the WTO. But the union leadership was split on the issue. While a new generation of union leaders was strongly against the WTO, longtime union leaders were less adamant. AFL-CIO president Lane Kirkland was a member of the Council on Foreign Relations, historically a staunch free trade backer, and for decades the AFL-CIO had supported the tariff reductions overseen by GATT. Conflicted within, the AFL-CIO didn't mobilize its 13 million members the same way it had done on NAFTA.

The AFL-CIO's passivity hamstrung the WTO opposition. Without the power of organized labor, fair trade forces found it difficult to make the WTO into the kind of household name NAFTA had become, or to generate the same kind of opposition on Capitol Hill that the earlier agreement had faced. Democratic leader Dick Gephardt (D-MO), for example, said he would vote in favor of the WTO.

The Clinton administration's most important advantage, however, lay not with labor's ambivalence, but with big businesses' eager support. For Corporate America, the WTO was a much bigger and potentially more lucrative deal than NAFTA. Whereas NAFTA was centered on Mexico alone, the WTO would open new opportunities in dozens of countries around the world. Like NAFTA, GATT was more of an investment treaty than a trade agreement—what *The Washington Post* called "an insurance policy" for international investment.[35] By establishing a fixed set of rules for international business, the WTO would make it easier for corporations to move factories anywhere around the world. At the same time, the WTO's focus on eliminating non-tariff barriers to trade would loosen regulations, lowering companies' costs. One executive said GATT was "worth 10 NAFTAs combined."[36]

No wonder Corporate America put so much effort into seeing that Congress approved the creation of the WTO. In February of 1994, some 285 major American corporations had come together to form a coalition called "Alliance for GATT Now." The Alliance included Cargill, Hewlett Packard, IBM, Caterpillar, Boeing, and the country's largest pharmaceutical companies. The big business group set out to make GATT seem as American as baseball cards and hot dogs.

On September 27, President Clinton sent the WTO implementing legislation to Congress, ignoring the demands of 55 Members of Congress who had asked for more time to review the legislation. Since GATT had been negotiated using so-called "fast track" rules, Congress would have no power to modify any part of the agreement, and Congress was forced to vote up-or-down on the deal within 90 days.

The agreement, Clinton and his aides repeatedly said, represented the "biggest tax cut in history," since it would cut tariffs by an estimated $740 billion globally over ten years. The White House also claimed the WTO would create more jobs in the United States, between 300,000 and 500,000 within a few years.[37] The Clinton administration also relied on scare tactics. Officials warned that a congressional vote against the WTO would send a shock to financial markets, and White House aides pointed out that nearly the entire world was waiting for the United

States to act on the proposal. Indeed, just one-fourth of GATT countries had approved the creation of the WTO—most nations had decided not to act until the world's largest economy did so. The future of the WTO was in the hands of the U.S. Congress.

Some in Congress weren't buying the White House line. Senator Dole continued to voice deep concerns. Another prominent Republican, Senator Jesse Helms of North Carolina, asked for a delay in the vote. And Senator Ernest Hollings (D-SC) was using Senate rules to keep the WTO legislation held up in committee for 45 days. Hollings' state was dependent on textile manufacturing, and, as even the WTO's backers agreed, cuts in textile tariffs would decimate textile plants in the United States. For textile workers, GATT would do obvious harm. "The industry I work in is not going to be here in a short while," a garment worker told a reporter. "Am I afraid? Of course I'm afraid. Wouldn't you be scared?"[38]

The WTO had not grabbed the popular attention of the American people the way NAFTA had. Unlike the NAFTA battle, the WTO, which involved more than 100 countries, lacked a single bogeyman such as Mexico. For many people, the WTO was so large as to be intangible. And the sheer complexity of the agreement befuddled even veteran lawmakers. Many people in Washington conceded that most Members of Congress had not even read the 22,000 page agreement.

"There is no way that [the agreement] is broadly understood by the membership," Congresswoman Marcy Kaptur, said. "I find it incredible that they want to bring up a bill of this magnitude."[39]

The widespread ignorance on Capitol Hill of what the WTO would mean for the United States was illustrated when Ralph Nader said he would give $10,000 to the favorite charity of any Member of Congress who could correctly complete a quiz on GATT. One person, Senator Hank Brown (R-CO), took the challenge. After he finished reading the agreement, Brown, a free trader, announced he would not support GATT.

Senator Hollings' delay meant that GATT would not be voted on until after the midterm elections, during a lame duck session. Opponents were cheered by delay, believing it gave more time to educate people about the agreement.

But the Alliance for GATT Now was organizing too. Business executives were making the rounds on Capitol Hill lobbying hard for the deal. A multimillion dollar nationwide television ad campaign was underway. An astroturf group was created, "Consumers for World Trade," that lobbied Members of Congress. The organization, rather than truly representing consumers, was a front for major corporations such as Exxon, 3M, and Proctor & Gamble, among others.[40] In a rather bizarre move, corporate lobbyists sent every congressional office a set of "GATT

All Star" baseball cards featuring former Presidents and listing their involvement with the different rounds of GATT talks. The cards were intended to highlight the decades-long bipartisan support of GATT.

The political maneuverings of opponents and proponents alike were thrown into disarray when Republicans unexpectedly won huge gains during the November elections. The GOP Revolution, as it was called, upset the calculations of both sides. It had been known for weeks that the GATT vote would take place during a lame duck session. But now there were to be a great many more lame ducks—dozens of Senators and Representatives would not be returning to Washington—and no one knew how that would affect the vote.

Regardless of the lame ducks, WTO approval remained uncertain in the Senate. Because the reduction of tariffs would lead to the loss of billions of dollars in government revenue and would entail tax adjustments, Senate rules required 60 votes for passage. Senator Dole was still skeptical of the deal, and some estimated that as many as 35 votes would follow the Republican leader, making or breaking the agreement.

The big business forces put special energy on swaying Dole's vote. CEOs from the powerful Business Roundtable made personal calls to his office. Boeing held a free trade rally in Topeka, Kansas, as corporate public relations specialists leaned on the *Wichita Eagle* to take pro-WTO editorial positions.[41]

Finally, on November 23, Dole struck a deal with the White House. The GOP leader said he would support the WTO as long as a review panel was created to give Congress a way to withdraw from the WTO if it consistently ruled against U.S. laws. Dole called it a "three strikes-and-we're-out" mechanism. Privately, White House officials admitted that the United States would never pull out of the WTO once a member, and said the compromise was undertaken only to give Dole the political cover he needed to vote for the commercial agreement.[42]

Senator Dole's decision cleared the way for the rare lame duck vote. In the end, the WTO won approval relatively easily. On November 29, the House approved the measure 288 to 146. A few days later the Senate followed suit, passing the legislation 76-24 over the warnings of Senator Hollings, who called the vote "the gravest mistake the U.S. has ever made on economic policy."[43]

The WTO's creation marked a major victory for the free trade agenda and for the White House, which badly needed a legislative win after losing Democratic control of Congress. For the fair trade coalition, the creation of the WTO was a grievous setback.

Yet, as with NAFTA, the free trader's win on the WTO was a victory built on quicksand. Once again the White House and its corporate allies had relied on multimillion dollar ad campaigns and slick lobbyists to sell their agenda. "A gaudy display of corporate muscle on behalf of GATT," *New York Times* columnist Bob Herbert called it.[44] Once again, the free traders had depended on astroturf campaigning instead of real grassroots energy. And once again the White House had managed to win the legislative battle without winning the intellectual one. From the beginning of the debate, the controversy over GATT and WTO had centered on questions of democracy and sovereignty. The fair trade forces had framed the political debate in a manner that struck a deep chord among ordinary citizens. The free traders were winning in Washington, but losing on Main Street.

"NAFTA was difficult to pass. The [GATT] round is no big winner with the general public," Senator Max Baucus (D-MT), a supporter of both free trade deals, said before the WTO vote. "The academics and the multinational corporations like it, but there is beginning to be a gulf between them and the public about whether this is helping people keep their jobs and pay their mortgages."[45]

As time went by and the discussions over NAFTA and the WTO shifted from promises and rhetoric to the actual record of the free trade experience, that gulf between elites and the general public would widen even further. A populist anger was fueling the resistance to the international commercial agreements. WTO passed with bipartisan support, but the opposition was equally bipartisan: In the Senate 11 Republicans and 13 Democrats voted against GATT, while in the House 56 Republicans joined 89 Democrats in opposing the measure. That kind of broad-based opposition did not bode well for future free trade initiatives.

The fair traders had lost two important battles within the space of a year. But they could have taken some consolation from the old proverb that it is always darkest before the dawn. The CTC and its allies were poised to win a string of victories that would stun the corporate backers of international trade and investment agreements. The tide was set to turn sharply against the free trade agenda.

A FAST TRACK IN THE WRONG DIRECTION

The congressional legislation establishing the WTO was the size of several phone books: 2,000 pages of GATT rules plus some 20,000 pages just to bring U.S. laws into conformity with those rules. The NAFTA bill was similarly large. Had the agreements actually been about trade alone, they likely could have been dealt with in just hundreds of pages. But by expanding their reach into areas outside of trade, the new breed of commercial agreements had mushroomed into documents of intimidating complexity. Conventional wisdom said that in order to negotiate such complex agreements the President needed special powers to effectively engage in talks with other countries. These special powers are known as "Fast Track."

The U.S. Constitution gives Congress the power to regulate trade with other countries, while putting the President in charge of overseeing relations with "sovereign nations." This division of foreign policy responsibilities is one of the many checks and balances established by the Constitution's framers. Under Fast Track, Congress surrenders its responsibility for trade policy to the executive branch with the intention of expediting international negotiations. Fast Track prevents Congress from modifying any trade agreement negotiated by the President. The House and the Senate have to vote "yes" or "no" on the deal, and cannot make changes. This is supposed to give other countries a guarantee that the deals they negotiate with the United States won't later be changed by Congress. At the same time, Fast Track limits congressional debate on trade measures to a set period.

Although President Richard Nixon came up with the idea of Fast Track, President Gerald Ford was the first President to be given Fast Track authority by Congress. It was no coincidence that the move occurred just as GATT negotiations were beginning the foray into issues such as non-tariff barriers. As international commercial agreements started to affect domestic laws, the possibility for controversy increased, and with it trade negotiators' desire for a smoother approval process, a process insulated from the maneuverings of Congress.

Fast Track renewal was used to complete NAFTA and finish the long GATT Uruguay Round talks. Fast Track procedures also guided the Congressional battles over both commercial agreements. Debate was limited to 90 days, and Members of Congress were not permitted—as they would be with any other piece of legislation—to make amendments to the deals. Fair trade forces were determined not to let that happen again.

After NAFTA was approved, Clinton announced his intention to expand the agreement to the entire Western Hemisphere via the Free Trade Area of the Americas (FTAA). To move forward with the complex FTAA talks, the President needed Fast Track authority, but the Fast Track powers that had been given to President Bush in 1991 had lapsed. Clinton had to go to Congress and ask for Fast Track to be passed once again.

For several years the White House kept postponing Fast Track renewal. In 1995, during the first heady days of the Gingrich Revolution, the Republicans largely controlled the political momentum in Washington. In 1996 the White House decided not to push any trade-related issues, afraid of dividing Democrats in an election year. The matter didn't come up again until 1997, when Clinton pledged in his State of the Union Address that Fast Track would be a presidential priority for the year.

Yet it must have been a second-tier priority. The White House didn't introduce any Fast Track legislation during the spring or summer of that year. For the CTC and organized labor, who had long been preparing to challenge Clinton's Fast Track request, the delay was just fine. As with the WTO approval, the fair trade groups felt that they were struggling against ignorance. The public was simply unaware of Fast Track and what it meant. To complicate matters, citizens groups would be struggling not against an agreement, but a *procedure*, an arcane topic at best. The CTC strategy, then, would rest on making Fast Track a referendum on NAFTA. NAFTA was now three years old, and the initial data showed that the agreement had failed to live up to the promises of its backers. The CTC's message would be clear: "If you don't like NAFTA, you should be against Fast Track." But to make this case, the fair trade forces needed time to educate and organize.

The CTC and its allies had been preparing for Fast Track since the end of the WTO vote. The coalition had used the intervening two years to broaden and deepen its network of activists. The time also gave fair traders an opportunity to educate the public and Members of Congress about the free trade agenda. Clinton's announcement that he would move on Fast Track gave the CTC a heightened sense of urgency. Throughout the spring and summer, CTC activists nationwide stepped up pressure on Members of Congress to oppose Fast Track. And once again the fair traders used the crucial August recess to catch Senators and Representatives in their home districts and urge them to oppose Fast Track. The CTC campaign quickly showed positive results. Midsummer polls revealed that a solid majority of voters were against Fast Track, including 73 percent of "grassroots" Republicans.[46] By the time Clinton introduced Fast Track legislation in September of 1997, congressional opposition to the measure was already stiff.

The White House's delay was due in large part to the desire to craft a Fast Track that would please both citizens groups and big business. As with the NAFTA side agreements, Clinton was trapped between two diametrically opposed views, a tough position for a man well known for always wanting to please everyone. The fair trade groups wouldn't accept a Fast Track that didn't include clear provisions stating that all future agreements would including binding, enforceable protections for labor and the environment. For Corporate America such safeguards were anathema. After all, a key motive for promoting free trade was precisely to weaken environmental and labor regulations.

Ultimately, Clinton followed his usual pattern on trade matters and decided that the support of transnational corporations was more valuable than the support of traditional Democrat constituencies such as organized labor and the environmental community. Clinton's Fast Track established "workers rights and environmental protection" as negotiating objectives, but left vague how that would be done and included no real standards. The NGO community was unappeased.

Significantly, the White House's procrastination not only gave the Fast Track opposition time to prepare its campaign, but it kept the business lobby from organizing its own. Hesitant to support any Fast Track bill until it had seen the actual language of the legislation, Corporate America hadn't equipped itself for a major political fight. The fair traders were way ahead of the free traders this time.

On September 16, President Clinton formally asked Congress to give him Fast Track authority. As Clinton made the announcement the AFL-CIO, Ralph Nader and the CTC held an anti-Fast Track rally across the street. "We're committed to waging this campaign for as long as it takes with all the resources we have," AFL-CIO president John Sweeney told the crowd. The unions would spend at least $1 million on running television and radio commercials in 13 congressional districts across the country, and statewide in California, Sweeney told the crowd.[47]

While the AFL-CIO unveiled its plans to fight Fast Track, President Clinton and Vice President Gore took the unusual step of traveling across town to Capitol Hill to make their case to legislators. House Democrats gave them a chilly reception. Representative Gephardt said he could not support the legislation because it compromised "the basic goals of growth, opportunity, dignity of work, environmental quality, and democracy."[48] The White House had a tough sell on its hands.

Clinton and his aides were already going about the fight in entirely the wrong way. Seeing Fast Track as simply a procedural, inside-the-Beltway issue, the White House failed to remember that all politics is local: The most contentious political battles are decided not by the sentiment at the far end of Pennsylvania Avenue, but by the feelings in places like Peoria, Illinois. The White House did not recognize the intensity of emotions swirling around trade issues. Surrounded by other elites who embraced free trade, White House officials didn't see that a growing number of ordinary people were angry at the free trade status quo, and were prepared to do something about it. During the six-week Fast Track campaign, Clinton delivered just two Fast Track speeches outside of Washington.[49] As the President would later concede, he failed to speak to the American public, and it was his undoing.

The business community, however, knew that if it was going to get

Fast Track, it would have to affect the debate in the heartland. To counter the AFL-CIO media blitz, an ad-hoc coalition of corporations called "America Leads on Trade" began running newspaper ads in 43 cities nationwide targeting some 65 Representatives who were undecided. The U.S. Chamber of Commerce sent letters to every House Member asking them to support Fast Track. Corporate lobbyists also turned to their old astroturf tricks, using push polling to urge people to contact their Representatives and urge Fast Track passage. The letters were sometimes brazenly fake. A California Representative reported receiving pro-Fast Track letters with New York postmarks.[50]

While business groups attempted to manufacture support for Fast Track, the measure's opponents were working at the real grassroots. The five-year-old Citizens Trade Campaign was coming into its own, uniting disparate groups in a common cause. Environmentalists and blue-collar workers came together in at least six cities, including Dallas, Chicago, and New York, for joint anti-Fast Track rallies. Activists leafleted baseball games and handed out free peanuts with "free trade scorecards" attached that detailed NAFTA's failures.[51] Environmentalists began talking about workers' issues, and union members discussed how Fast Track—and the free trade agreements it would pave the way for—might impact the environment. In San Francisco, members of the Teamsters Union went to the farmers' market to distribute anti-Fast Track literature about how NAFTA undermined food safety in the United States.

Art Persyko, a rank-and-file Teamsters member who was involved in the San Francisco activism, says that working in coalition with other interest groups gave an extra dimension of energy to the anti-Fast Track campaign. Persyko recalls:

> The thing that I remember the best and like the best about this work has been working in coalitions and bringing people together. It inspired me to work harder. By melding organizations together we could really make a difference. It was fun and interesting and effective. You got the sense that we were starting to build community, and that's a powerful antidote to corporate globalization.[52]

Communities across the United States were responding to the CTC's warnings about Fast Track. Hundreds of thousands of citizen letters and phone calls opposing Fast Track were flooding the Capitol. The AFL-CIO set up an 800 number to help people call their Representatives. Taking advantage of new technologies, activists armed with cell phones went to job sites during workers' lunch breaks and asked them to call Washington. The steelworkers' union alone sent some 160,000 handwritten letters to Congress.[53] One Republican Representative from Wisconsin reported that Fast Track calls to his office were running 723 to 28 against, and that the only people for it were business lobbyists.[54]

Organized labor was waging a no-holds-barred campaign. The Teamsters paid for radio spots on stations frequently listened to by truckers while the garment workers union ran ads in Spanish-language newspapers. The AFL-CIO mailed more than 1 million anti-Fast Track leaflets nationwide. When Al Gore went to Iowa to stump in preparation for his 2000 presidential run, union workers picketed his speech.[55]

The labor movement's intense resistance to Fast Track and future trade agreements such as NAFTA was displayed in late September when the AFL-CIO held its annual convention in Pittsburg. During the three-day gathering, House Democratic leader Gephardt, Vice President Gore, and President Clinton each addressed the nation's 800 labor leaders. Gephardt won hearty applause with his demand that "if intellectual property and capital deserves protection in core Fast Track treaties, so do labor laws and labor rights and environmental laws."[56] Gore was careful not to mention Fast Track or other trade issues, and was treated respectfully. The union leaders' reception for Clinton revealed the dislike the President had incurred among labor officials because of his strong support for business priorities such as free trade deals. The President was greeted with what reporters called a "stony silence." Some trade unionists made a show of reading newspapers during his speech. At one point, a handful of people in the back of the room chanted "No Fast Track!"[57]

It was clear that Fast Track was in trouble. While Senate passage was assumed as a given, the bill's fate in the House—usually considered a more populist body—was uncertain. The Republican caucus, led by House Speaker Newt Gingrich (R-GA), mostly supported the free trade agenda. But 50 Republicans were expected to vote against Fast Track. That meant Gingrich needed the White House to line up about 70 Democrat supporters. Head counts showed Clinton had only half that number.

In late October, House Speaker Gingrich placed the Fast Track vote on the House schedule for the first week of November. Lobbying became even more intense. The White House sent a slew of Cabinet officials to Capitol Hill to pitch Fast Track. The President invited Members of Congress to the White House to make his case in person. Corporate lobbyists, and union members and environmental activists, swarmed over Congressional offices.

Opinion polls showed that a majority of the public was opposed to Fast Track. Two separate surveys put support for Fast Track at 37 percent, with 56 percent against.[58] A poll commissioned by the AFL-CIO showed that just one-quarter of the public thought NAFTA had been positive for the U.S. economy.[59] Yet despite this resistance to the free trade agenda, the conventional wisdom in Washington still predicted a White House win on Fast Track. Most pundits figured the Fast Track fight would echo the NAFTA fight: a nail-biter until the end, but ultimately another step forward in the decades-long embrace of free trade.

But in the last week of the campaign, Clinton was hardly helping to make that prediction come true. In a series of gaffes the President further estranged himself from House Democrats and, at the same time, illustrated the widening gulf between elite policy makers and the general public when it came to trade policy. First, the President said during a press conference that if the vote were taken in secret Fast Track "would pass overwhelmingly." Clinton was referring to the aggressive pressure by organized labor, and insinuating that Democrats were not voting their consciences, but only their campaign coffers. Opponents of the bill were outraged by the comment. Then, to make matters worse, a few days later the President again insulted opponents when he said that voting in favor of Fast Track was a "no brainer."[60]

But for most Members of Congress, voting *against* Fast Track was a no-brainer. The CTC and the AFL-CIO had based their strategy on making Fast Track a referendum on NAFTA, and it was working. Judged by the promises Clinton had made three years earlier, NAFTA had clearly been a failure. During the NAFTA debate, the President said the deal would lead to new exporting opportunities for U.S. business and create hundreds of thousands of U.S. jobs. Yet U.S. trade with Mexico had gone from a $1.7 billion yearly surplus to a $16 billion deficit.[61] According to some estimates, NAFTA had cost the United States approximately 400,000 manufacturing jobs.[62] Even the White House's most optimistic studies showed the agreement had created less than 100,000 jobs, far fewer than boasted earlier.[63]

NAFTA's much-heralded "side agreements" were also a disappointment. The environmental ministers of Canada, Mexico, and the United States had admitted that thus far the environmental side agreement had been a failure.[64] And of the seven cases filed under the labor side agreement, none had yet gone beyond initial consultations among the interested parties.[65] Privately, White House officials conceded that they had promised too much in trying to sell NAFTA. The White House even banned administration officials from using the term "NAFTA expansion" in trying to sell Fast Track.[66]

Fast Track's opponents were using the NAFTA's string of broken promises to devastating effect. In Florida, legislators were facing the rage of tomato and pepper farmers, who had been nearly wiped out since NAFTA went into effect. The state had lost 120 of its 200 winter tomato farms during that time.[67] Rep. Robert Menendez (D-NJ) complained that his district had lost 1,500 jobs due to factories relocating to Mexico. "These jobs have been driven out of business because of competition with cheap foreign labor," he told reporters.[68]

Fair trade forces also pointed out that NAFTA had been no winner for ordinary Mexicans, either. During the NAFTA debate, the deal's backers had warned that the Mexican economy would crash if the agreement didn't pass. The deal did pass, and still the Mexican economy tanked. To keep Mexico attractive for foreign investors—a key aim of NAFTA—government officials there had kept the peso artificially high. But in December of 1995 a financial crisis sent the economy into a tailspin. Millions of people lost their jobs, and average wages dropped some 20 percent. Bankruptcies skyrocketed, creating an entire political movement of angry debtors. Fast Track's opponents could easily claim that NAFTA had been a raw deal for U.S. citizens and Mexicans alike.

Fair trade activists were making headway arguing that their resistance to Fast Track wasn't necessarily about trade per se, but about the rules for making trade policy. That is, any deals negotiated by Fast Track would protect business interests, but not the interests of other groups. As one anti-Fast Track leaflet put it, the legislation would "strengthen business rights . . . while prohibiting . . . enforceable labor and environmental protections in future trade deals."[69]

In response to these criticisms, the White House and business lobbyists offered vague assertions that, in theory, more trade would lead to greater benefits for ordinary Americans. But many people found such arguments unconvincing. One Representative called the proponents' reasons for supporting the bill "esoteric."[70]

With the vote just days away, business and citizen groups were in a frenzy on Capitol Hill. Union members and CTC activists waited outside congressional offices to make their case to representatives. Lobbyists with the U.S. Chamber of Commerce set up a "war room" in a chamber of the House Ways and Means Committee. Bill Gates, the founder of Microsoft, ran a full-page ad in *The Washington Post* urging Fast Track passage.

Desperate to see the measure win, the White House returned to its NAFTA playbook and began offering Representatives all kinds of perks if they would support the measure. If the White House couldn't win the issue on its merits, perhaps it could succeed by buying votes. "It's blue light special time at the White House," one congressional aide told the press. "They're dealing hard."[71] The President promised special protections for tobacco and peanut farmers; agreed to fund a study to examine the impact of Canadian wheat exports; and offered Members much-coveted fundraising appearances. "I've been promised 16 bridges; now all I need is a river," joked one Democrat opposed to Fast Track.[72]

This time, however, Congress wasn't buying. Clinton already had too many outstanding IOUs. Gingrich and the White House decided to delay the vote—originally set for Friday, November 7—through the weekend to allow more time to twist arms. The President went on the Sunday morning talk shows to plead his case, but the votes were still not there. At 2:00 a.m. on Monday morning, Gingrich called the President to say that Fast Track did not have the votes to pass. The two agreed to postpone the measure indefinitely.

Fast Track's failure was a shocking reversal of the free trade agenda. For fair traders, it was an historic win, marking the first time since the 1940s that Congress had rebuffed a President on a trade-related issue.

The nation's leading newspapers and journalists, who had long reflected elite support for free trade policies, were stunned. A contributor to *The Washington Post* called the bill's failure a "victory for the flat-earth caucus."[73] *New York Times* columnist Thomas Friedman called the decision "harebrained," while that paper's editorial writers said Fast Track's demise represented a victory for "narrow political interests."[74]

The White House expressed surprise that Members of Congress would listen to their constituents rather than vote to salvage the President's reputation or support some abstract idea of trade's benefits. According to many political analysts, House Members had opposed Fast Track to cater to "parochial interests." What that point of view failed to realize was that when it came to trade policy, the interests of transnational corporations and ordinary citizens were sharply divergent. The gap between elite sentiment and popular feelings was widening. While 82 percent of elites—defined as elected officials, journalists, and policy experts—thought NAFTA had been good for the country, just 47 percent of the broader public agreed, according to one poll.[75] The business community and Clinton lost Fast Track because they made light of the growing public resistance to the free trade agenda.

"The Clinton folks underestimated how much resonance this had," says the CTC's Wallach. "They thought it was about trade and tariffs, whereas the people in the communities saw it was about food safety, and local zoning, and jobs."

The business lobby spent an estimated $5 million on its Fast Track campaign, more than twice what the AFL-CIO spent.[76] Yet big business and the White House failed to convince average citizens that more commercial deals such as NAFTA were in their interests. For most people, the evidence on the ground was clear. The free trade consensus had held for 50 years because trade issues had largely been left in the hands of policy elites. But as corporate globalization came to have a real impact on people's lives, ordinary citizens became involved in trade issues, and the result was the Fast Track defeat.

"I think this is not the last chapter in this story," Clinton said after the Fast Track postponement.[77] The President was right, but not in the way he thought. Congress would take up Fast Track again in 1998 and handily defeat the measure. The White House and the business community would keep misgauging the depth of popular suspicion of corporate-led globalization and, as it had in the Fast Track battle, the miscalculation would continue to cost them. Fair traders were set to win other struggles by taking to an international level the coalition building that was key to the Fast Track victory.

AN INVESTORS' BILL OF RIGHTS

In early 1997, as citizen groups were building opposition to Fast Track, Antonia Juhasz was working as a legislative assistant in the Washington offices of Congressman John Conyers (D-MI). Juhasz knew little about global trade and investment issues. Her area of expertise was Social Security policy and community redevelopment, and at the time she was working on using federal "block grants" to support women- and black-owned enterprises in America's inner cities. It had never occurred to her that international commercial agreements could undermine the issues she was working on. That is, until she met Mark Weisbrot, a policy analyst with the nonprofit Preamble Center. He warned her that a secretive investment agreement in the works could have the power to undermine all her efforts. According to Weisbrot, an international treaty was under negotiation that threatened the ability of citizens to use government funds to help build up local economies. The treaty, Weisbrot said, was called the Multilateral Agreement on Investments (MAI).

Juhasz had never heard of the MAI, and she wasn't alone. Even today, a majority of citizens probably still haven't heard of the MAI, despite an innovative grassroots campaign by fair trade groups. During 1997 and 1998, when the MAI became the key target of the Citizens Trade Campaign, the American media gave the agreement little attention,* even though the proposed investment deal was major news in

---

* A Nexis search for "Multilateral Agreement on Investment" reveals that *The New York Times* and *The Washington Post* together published just eight articles about the MAI in 1998, when the issue was most contentious. Most of the articles covered the agreement's demise, meaning that the papers did little to inform the public while there was a chance for citizens to influence the debate.

most other industrialized nations. The MAI's backers tried to craft a far-reaching commercial agreement without the public's knowledge and—had it not been for the efforts an international coalition of citizens groups—they would have succeeded.

Juhasz learned just how shadowy the MAI was when she called the offices of the U.S. Trade Representative (USTR) to follow up on Weisbrot's warnings. "I said, 'What can you tell me?'," Juhasz recalls.

> And they said, "There's nothing to tell. You're not on the relevant committee." The message was: "Don't worry your pretty little head about it." It felt really disempowering, because the USTR was treating me as a bother, and they were supposed to work for me, a Capitol Hill staffer. They didn't let me past the front door.[78]

Disturbed by the evasive treatment she had received from the Trade Representative's office, Juhasz did some more research on her own. "The more I looked into it, the more I saw this would invalidate everything I was doing—and no one knew about it," Juhasz says. The Capitol Hill staffer decided to quit her job with Conyers' office and go to work for the Preamble Center to help defeat the MAI.

Proposals for creating an international agreement focused solely on global investment were first floated in the World Trade Organization. But the poorer members of the WTO resisted, fearing that a global investment agreement would greatly enhance the power of transnational corporations over poor countries.[79] The wealthier countries decided to move forward anyway. They shifted negotiations to a less-well-known venue: the Organization for Economic Cooperation and Development (OECD), a think tank for the world's 28 richest nations. Holding the investment talks within the OECD gave the wealthier nations a chance to craft an agreement away from the glare of public attention.

The MAI negotiations started in May 1995 in the basement of the OECD's Paris headquarters, and continued on schedule for the next year and a half without public awareness that the talks were even occurring. But in January of 1997, one of the negotiators leaked the draft texts to activists with the Council of Canadians, a fair trade group that had fought both NAFTA and GATT. The Council quickly placed the proposed agreements on its Website, where all the world could see it.

Civil society groups were horrified by the planned investment treaty. The MAI's authors proposed a series of restrictions that would prohibit governments at any level from placing certain rules or standards on corporate behavior. The MAI called for "national treatment" of all corporations, which meant that governments would have to treat foreign and domestic companies the same. This would prevent the common practice of governments giving preferences to locally owned (or women-owned or minority-owned) businesses. It would forbid governments from placing ownership restrictions on foreign investments. The MAI would also prohibit so-called "performance requirements"—rules requiring foreign corporations to use local suppliers or hire a certain number of local workers. Limits on capital flows and rules requiring companies to reinvest a portion of their profits back into the local economy would also be banned.

Especially disturbing to fair trade activists, the MAI would expand the definition of expropriation (government seizure of a company's property) to include the financial impact of government regulations. If a law reduced a corporation's profits, the company could claim its property had been expropriated and demand compensation. Essentially, governments would be placed in the position of having to pay companies for the privilege of regulating them. Perhaps most worrisome of all, the MAI would create a dispute settlement system allowing transnational corporations to directly sue national governments to challenge regulations they objected to. A similar dispute mechanism already existed within Chapter 11 of NAFTA. The NGO community now feared it would be expanded to the entire globe.[80]

The leaking of the MAI draft text confirmed the accusations fair trade activists had been making for years: corporations were using international commercial agreements to promote deregulation and slip free of public accountability. The MAI would grant corporations a vast array of new rights while at the same time freeing them from responsibilities. Critics quickly dubbed the agreement an "investors bill of rights." An anti-MAI pamphlet warned:

> The MAI is designed to multiply the power of corporations over governments. If enacted in its current form, the MAI would radically limit our ability to promote social, economic, and environmental justice. In other words, it puts our democracy at risk.[81]

Through the first half of 1997 civil society groups prepared their campaign to stop the MAI. Nine environmental groups wrote a letter to U.S. Trade Representative Charlene Barshefsky complaining that "the treaty is being negotiated in haste, largely in secret, and with only token gestures at international dialogue with environmentalists and others in civil society."[82] The CTC launched a "campaign of inquiry" calling for opening the MAI talks to the public, and started distributing educational materials through its grassroots network to alert people about the little known commercial deal.

The MAI didn't garner real attention, however, until the Fast Track fight heated up. In Capitol Hill hearings over Fast Track, Members of Congress started asking hard questions about what international trade and investment deals the White House was already negotiating. Administration officials—who earlier in the year were denying the MAI even existed[83]—were forced to concede that investment talks were underway in Paris. Representatives wanted to know how the negotiations could be taking place without any congressional consultation or oversight, and they questioned the White House's rationale for its Fast Track request, pointing out that talks over an agreement every bit as complicated as GATT and the FTAA were occurring without Fast Track powers. Some Members of Congress started raising sharp objections to the MAI agenda. "Why would the U.S. willingly cede sovereign immunity and expose itself to liability for damages under vague language . . . ?," two dozen representatives asked the President in a letter.[84]

The pointed questions from Capitol Hill grabbed the interest of a handful of American reporters, who began to track the issue. In a front-page story, the openly right-of-center *Washington Times* called the agreement "an international bill of corporate rights."[85]

PEOPLE'S GLOBALIZATION

Interest at the grassroots was far ahead of the media. Websites dedicated to exposing and opposing the agreement mushroomed. Warnings about the MAI ricocheted around cyberspace, bouncing among some 1,000 sites set up worldwide to stop the agreement.[86] Activists were using the new communications technologies—often hailed as the backbone of globalization—to trip up corporate globalization itself. In doing so, citizens organizations and civil society groups were launching a sort of globalization from below, a people's globalization.

While opposition to the MAI was spreading over the Internet, Antonia Juhasz was busy using old-fashioned organizing strategies to drum up resistance to the investment pact. Juhasz began reaching out to local organizations and smaller policy groups one at a time to tell them how their agendas for social change could be undermined by the MAI. She showed how local living wage ordinances, bans on the sale of dangerous products, recycling laws, and public contract preferences for environmentally responsible or minority-owned firms could be ruled discriminatory to foreign investors, and therefore be rolled back by the MAI. The Clinton administration, along with corporate interests, was working at cross purposes to social advocates' efforts, she told one organization after another.

To help make the case that the MAI threat was real, Juhasz, CTC organizers, and other fair trade activists pointed to how NAFTA's investor protections were already leading to a rollback in public interest laws. NAFTA's Chapter 11 gave corporations the power to sue national governments directly to get compensation for any expropriation of their property. The definition of expropriation, however, was much broader than in U.S. law, and included any government rule, even health or environmental laws, that reduced profits. As reporting by William Greider would reveal, Chapter 11's sweeping definition of government expropriation was written by corporate lawyers involved in the NAFTA talks with the clear intention of attacking government restrictions on business. "The parties did not stumble into this," a source told Greider. "This was a carefully crafted decision."[87]

One of the first Chapter 11 cases showed the impact the so-called "investor-to-state" lawsuits could have on government regulations. In April of 1997 the Canadian government voted to ban a chemical additive to gasoline, MMT, that had been linked to nervous system disorders. Canadian environmentalists hailed the vote as a win for air quality and public health. But the victory was jeopardized when the Virginia-based manufacturer of MMT, Ethyl Corporation, filed a NAFTA Chapter 11 suit asking the Canadian government for $251 million in damages.[88] Although MMT was already banned by the U.S. Environmental Protection Agency, Ethyl claimed that the Canadian government's action was NAFTA-illegal and had lowered its profits. Fair trade activists were shocked by Ethyl's challenge.* Their predictions were coming true: A public interest law was under attack because it represented a barrier to profit making. The polluter would have to be paid not to pollute. Noting that the MAI contained investor-to-state lawsuits like Chapter 11, fair trade activists warned that the Ethyl case was just the tip of the iceberg. If the MAI became law, the assault on health, environmental, and labor regulations would accelerate, activists warned.

A growing number of people were getting the message. The Western Governors' Association released a report expressing concern over how the MAI could override local laws and impact the sovereignty of the states. The governors' report warned that the MAI could overturn many laws: an Arizona law restricting the sale of public lands to state residents, laws in Western states regarding standards for strip-mining, Oregon and Idaho regulations prohibiting the sale of unprocessed lumber to foreign companies, and a raft of laws designed to give preference to

---

* The NAFTA court eventually ruled in favor of Ethyl's claim and awarded the company $17 million. The Canadian government repealed its ban on MMT.

local business.[89] "It strikes right to the heart of our state government," an aide to Nebraska Governor Ben Nelson told the press. "We may be destroying states' rights or states' abilities to govern themselves just to promote international business."[90]

City officials were expressing similar concerns. CTC activists started working with local politicians to pass "MAI Free Zone" resolutions expressing a city's opposition to the proposed investment agreement. San Francisco was the first city to pass an anti-MAI resolution. Juliette Beck, then an organizer with the California arm of the CTC, said the effort was relatively easy. By identifying city laws that were in violation of MAI rules—among them the city's restriction on buying goods from Burma and an ordinance requiring companies doing business in the city to provide benefits to employees' gay and lesbian partners— Beck quickly won supporters on the city's Board of Supervisors. The city attorney's office was also an ally, and helped draft the language of the anti-MAI resolution. In the weeks before city officials voted on the resolution, Beck's California Fair Trade Campaign held several forums to spread the word about the MAI and build public support for the resolution. "Through the city government process we were able to educate a lot of different communities about the MAI," Beck recalls.[91] The city's supervisors passed the resolution unanimously.

Beck wrote up a journal of her experience passing the anti-MAI resolution and posted it on the Internet. Soon her e-mail in-box was full of messages from people across the country wanting advice on how they could pass similar measures in their community. Activists in Boulder, Seattle, Dallas, Los Angeles, and Olympia, Washington, were soon organizing their own campaigns to pass anti-MAI resolutions.

"It was amazing to see how the MAI negotiations ran against the grain of American values," Beck says. "People instantly got that this was un-American—the idea that this was being negotiated behind closed doors really scared people."

The spectre of the MAI tapped into people's deep-felt concerns about the increase in corporate power. Activists' arguments resonated with the growing number of citizens who felt they were losing control over their lives to forces beyond their influence. The MAI confirmed suspicions that unaccountable corporations—not elected governments—had the real power. "It is only big U.S. transnational corporations that are calling the shots, and strictly for their own benefit," a Seattle man wrote to his local newspaper at the time. "The original vision of the MAI is of a new world order governed by and for big business."[92]

"We are writing the constitution for a single global economy," Renato Ruggiero, the head of the WTO, had said of the MAI.[93] For many Americans, that was a chilling notion. The idea that a global constitution was being written that would eclipse the U.S. Constitution was made even more frightening by the fact that while business groups boasted of their involvement in the MAI negotiations, public interest groups were prevented from participating in the talks.[94] Ralph Nader called it a "slow motion *coup d'etat*."[95] When activists such as Beck and Juhasz told people about the MAI, the reaction was almost always the same: People were afraid that corporate power was short-circuiting democracy.

"People already had a sense that they were losing control of their day-to-day lives," Beck says. "And this treaty confirmed it, and heightened that fear. With the people I spoke to, the idea that international regulations could trump local laws was frightening."

By February of 1998, the MAI talks taking place in the basement of the OECD were running into trouble. Among journalists and activists alike the phrase "basement talks" had become shorthand for the shadowy MAI negotiations. The basement negotiating room was a metaphor for the entire investment deal: secretive, hidden from the view of the public. But citizen vigilance had dragged the MAI into the light of day, and the exposure put pressure on government trade officials to respond to the critics' concerns.

In Washington, Members of Congress were starting to echo those concerns as the grassroots complaints grew louder. Hearings on the MAI were scheduled in the House. Republicans started complaining that the MAI would overturn U.S. sanctions on countries such as Cuba and Libya. Representative David Bonior (D-MI), one of the leaders of the drive against Fast Track, delivered a fiery speech against the MAI during a Capitol Hill rally organized by the CTC. Activists delivered handcuffs to every congressional office accompanied by materials explaining how the MAI would "handcuff democracy."

The resistance was having an impact on the talks. In Paris, U.S. negotiator Charlene Barshefsky asked that environmental provisions be added to the investment pact. "This agreement is not good enough," Barshefsky told reporters, and said the MAI would require changes to U.S. laws that "we do not intend to change."[96] Negotiators began to express doubts that the talks would be completed by the April deadline.

The most influential pressure was coming from activists in Canada and France. As intense as opposition to the MAI had become among some sectors of Americans, it paled in comparison to the outrage in Canada and France, where the MAI was daily news. French and Canadian citizens shared worries that the MAI would strike down their countries' government subsidies to domestic media and arts companies. In both countries worries about the encroachment of American films, music, and television had struck a nationalistic nerve. Many people feared that corporate globalization was homogenizing their distinct cultures. The MAI would make the situation worse by preventing governments from supporting local TV and film industries. The prospect of commerce steamrolling cultural uniqueness ignited vehement opposition to the MAI among millions of Canadian and French citizens.

Increasingly, Canadian, French, and American activists—along with MAI opponents from other countries—were coordinating their efforts to stop the investment deal. More than 600 NGOs from 67 nations signed a statement calling for a suspension of the OECD talks and blasting the proposed deal for not "respecting the rights of countries . . . to democratically control investments into their economies."[97] MAI foes had met in France to plan how to scuttle the agreement, and were also working together via e-mail and the Internet. Activists shared information about each country's negotiating positions and swapped ideas about how to play the different governments against one another. Juhasz recalls:

> The international cooperation was amazing. A group of people who had never met each other were finding ways to work together. . . . The idea that there could be a meeting during the night in France and that the next morning we could have the meeting notes in DC made the governments see that we had a kind of power that hadn't been flexed before.

It was a power strong enough to defeat the MAI. As MAI negotiators prepared to meet again in April, anti-MAI protests took place in front of the U.S. Capitol and the French National Assembly. Seeing that their differences on the agreement were too wide to bridge, negotiators announced on April 28 that they were putting the negotiations on hold. After three years of talks, the MAI proposal was being shelved. Although negotiators tried to put a positive spin on the move by saying they would revisit the subject in six months, it was widely understood that the MAI in its current form was dead.

By driving a wedge between government officials and the corporate backers of the MAI, activists sunk the agreement. As soon as the MAI negotiators pledged to "address social concerns and particularly environmental and protection and labor issues," big business support evaporated.[98] For the transnational corporations backing the MAI, addressing such concerns was antithetical to the entire project. In trying to win the support of citizen groups, the governments lost the support of big business. As an official with the U.S. Chamber of Commerce said, the inclusion of social issues "made us lose our appetite."[99]

Grassroots resistance to the MAI also drained the Clinton

administration's enthusiasm. Still recovering from the bruising Fast Track battle, the White House had little stomach to wage another fight over globalization. Facing stiff NGO opposition and seeing only luke-warm support from business, the White House decided it wasn't worth going to the mat for the MAI. Without serious commitment from the U.S. government—which had initiated the MAI talks—the pact was bound to fail.

The MAI victory revealed how coalitions at the international level were essential for challenging corporate globalization. After all, the new commercial agreements were global in scope, so to stop them activists' efforts would have to be global as well.

The struggles against NAFTA, the GATT, and Fast Track led to an impressively broad-based fair trade coalition in the United States. The MAI fight cemented a similar coalition among citizens groups in doz-ens of countries. Now those distinct forces were set to come together to repeat their victories against Fast Track and the MAI, but on a much more dramatic scale. Activists around the world were organized and determined to take their fight against corporate globalization to another target, the WTO.

BEEF, BANANAS, & BURMA: THE ROAD TO SEATTLE

In January 1999 officials at the World Trade Organization announced that Seattle, Washington, had been chosen to host the next "ministerial level" trade talks, during which trade ministers from around the world would launch a new round of market-opening negotiations. The selec-tion of a U.S. city pleased President Clinton, who was eager to have a platform to jump-start his free trade agenda after the Fast Track defeat. Local officials applauded the decision, thinking that the WTO's so-called "Millennium Summit" would polish Seattle's image and fill hotels and shops. For free traders, Seattle seemed an ideal location for trumpeting the virtues of the WTO and free trade. The city was one of the country's largest ports, and local corporations such as Microsoft and Boeing were perfect examples of companies that benefited from globalization.

The Citizen's Trade Campaign was equally thrilled with the choice. Seattle, a city known for its liberalism, boasted the most unionized workforce of any city in the country. Environmental groups were strong throughout the Pacific Northwest, which in recent years had been the scene of pitched battles over logging, salmon fisheries, and dams. It was an ideal spot for recruiting people to protest the WTO's agenda.

Seattle reflected the worldviews of free traders and fair traders alike. For each side, the city offered a kind of *tabula rasa* over which to lay their visions of what globalization meant. Those competing visions were set to collide in spectacular fashion.

As soon as Seattle was announced as the host of the WTO's Millennial Summit, fair trade groups began preparing for protests to coincide with the meeting. "Everybody clear your calendars," read an e-mail Public Citizen's Global Trade Watch sent to its activist network on January 26. "We're going to Seattle at the end of November."[100] Public Citizen and its allies in the CTC saw the Seattle summit as a unique chance to highlight the failures of the free trade record. Since the meeting was occurring in the United States, the negotiations were bound to receive special media coverage. If fair trade organizers could put enough people in the streets to protest the WTO, they had a real opportunity of shifting the debate to the issues concerning them. And if they were lucky they might even be able to slow the WTO's agenda.

Returning to the ideas behind the successful campaign that made Fast Track a referendum on NAFTA, the CTC planned to base its WTO strategy on exposing the organization's track record. This time, however, the CTC's arguments wouldn't focus solely on jobs or food safety, but on a much larger concern: the WTO's threat to democracy itself.

In the first four years of its existence the WTO had made a series of decisions revealing a perspective that put global commerce before any other competing interest, whether it was promoting clean air, protecting endangered species, guaranteeing human rights, or trying to assist poor countries. The WTO's record was the organization's own worst enemy.

Researchers at Public Citizen had been compiling evidence of the WTO's record for years, and now the group shared its findings with the public. Lori Wallach and Michelle Sforza authored a book, *Whose Trade Organization?; Corporate Globalization and the Erosion of Democracy*, that exposed the WTO's history regarding environmental, social, and labor issues. The book was abridged and released as an 80-page pamphlet, *The WTO: Five Years of Reasons to Resist Corporate Globalization*. The CTC's old *Citizen's Guide to the GATT* was updated and re-released as *The Citizen's Guide to the WTO*.

The arguments centered on five WTO rulings involving: protections for endangered Sea Turtles; the U.S. Clean Air Act; a European Union (EU) ban on hormone-injected beef; an EU policy favoring bananas grown in former European colonies; and the state of Massachusetts' restrictions on contracting with companies doing business in Burma. In educating the general public about the WTO threat, many activists pared the five down to the three B's—bananas, beef, and Burma.

The WTO decision on sea turtles was a deja vu of the earlier GATT case involving dolphin-safe tuna. In 1989 Congress approved legislation intended to protect sea turtles, an endangered species, from the nets of shrimp fisherman. The law required all U.S. shrimp fishers to use what is called a turtle excluder device: a $400 grate that lets shrimp into the net but keeps turtles out. The law also prohibited shrimp imports from countries that didn't mandate turtle protection practices. In 1996, Thailand, Malaysia, India, and Pakistan challenged the U.S. law via the WTO's dispute panel. Two years later, the WTO ruled against the turtle protections as a barrier to trade and ordered U.S. officials to change the law.[101] The Sierra Club called the new rules "radically weakened."[102]

Another WTO decision involving U.S. environmental laws similarly outraged social activists. In January 1996, a WTO dispute panel ruled in favor of a Brazilian and Venezuelan challenge to portions of the U.S. Clean Air Act. In 1990, Congress amended the Act to call for a reduction in gasoline contaminants. Gasoline refineries were supposed to make their gas 15 percent cleaner than their 1990 gas. Foreign refineries would measure their progress from an industry average. Even though they were required to meet only average cleanliness levels, Brazil and Venezuela complained that the regulations unfairly discriminated against imported gas. The WTO agreed, and ordered the U.S. to change its law. The Environmental Protection Agency did so, while warning that the new rules would effectively be unenforceable and noting that the change "creates a potential for adverse environmental impact."[103]

Of course, what goes around comes around, and just as the United States had been the target of WTO decisions so too had U.S. corporations urged the American government to challenge other nations' laws as barriers to trade.

In 1988, the European Union banned the sale of beef (foreign or domestic) that had been treated with artificial hormones. U.S. beef and biotechnology companies saw the ban cutting into their profits, and in 1996 succeeded in urging U.S. trade officials to file a WTO complaint against the hormone ban. WTO arbitrators agreed with the U.S. position and ordered the EU to remove the ban. To the relief of environmentalists and public health advocates, the EU refused, despite the threat of trade sanctions. Still, the WTO's reasoning upset activists. The WTO said the EU hormone ban was impermissible because it was enacted in advance of scientific certainty about the effects of hormone-treated food. The Europeans responded that they were using the "precautionary principle," a pillar of public health policy that says substances should be proven safe *before* being put on the market. The WTO verdict troubled the NGO community because it revealed a WTO bias against national preferences. Social activists argued that people have a right to not purchase foods they don't want. The WTO evidently thought differently, and viewed such preferences as an unacceptable barrier to trade.[104]

The EU also ran afoul of the WTO because of its desire to assist former European colonies. Under a treaty called the Lomé Convention, the EU had established preferential tariffs and quotas for certain products coming from former colonies. The Lomé agreement also provided direct assistance to family farmers, since banana cultivation in the Caribbean, the main beneficiary of the deal, lay mostly with small landholders, as opposed to the giant plantations in Central and South America. The arrangement was intended as compensation for centuries of imperialism. But Chiquita Banana, a U.S.-based company, objected to the system, and in 1996 the corporation convinced U.S. officials to submit a WTO challenge, even though very few bananas are grown in the United States. A year later, a WTO panel ruled that the Europeans' preference system was in fact WTO illegal. The EU refused to change its law, and the Clinton administration, with WTO permission, imposed $190 million of annual trade sanctions on the EU.[105] Once again, citizen groups were shaken by the WTO's thinking. A group of wealthy countries had been trying to assist poor farmers, yet that was impermissible in the eyes of the WTO. For many activists, that reasoning represented a kind of tyranny of the bottom line.

Activists' final WTO horror story dealt with a controversy the WTO had never formally ruled on, but in which the organization still played a significant role. In 1996 the state of Massachusetts and several U.S. cities passed laws saying they would penalize bids from corporations with operations in Burma, a country ruled by a repressive military junta. In 1997, the EU and Japan asked for a WTO "consultation" (generally the first step before filing a formal complaint) on whether the Massachusetts selective purchasing law was a barrier to trade. The EU argued that the selective purchasing law violated WTO rules barring the use of "political" criteria in awarding government contracts. The EU challenge was soon pre-empted by a legal challenge to the law by corporate groups. Still, the very fact that the WTO had a prohibition against making purchasing decisions based on political criteria was deeply disturbing. Didn't consumers—whether individuals or state governments—have the freedom to decide how they would spend their money? The mere threat of the WTO challenge chilled the prospect of laws similar to the Burma purchasing restrictions. For example, when Maryland legislators considering a law aimed at human rights abuses in Nigeria, U.S. State Department officials showed up at the Maryland statehouse to warn that the law could lead to a WTO dispute. The proposal was defeated.[106]

These cases, among others, showed that the WTO represented a threat to the environment, human rights, public health and safety, and workers. The WTO's power to overturn public interest laws revealed the organization's danger to democracy. Control over the kinds and means of industrial production had been taken from democratic bodies. Unelected trade bureaucrats had the ability to use trade sanctions to compel a country to change laws enacted by elected officials. Yes, the EU had twice rebuffed WTO mandates, but the United States had not. Activists warned that small nations could not resist a WTO decision, opening the door for many more rollbacks of government regulations.

In making their case against the WTO, Public Citizen and other groups also pointed to the secrecy shadowing the WTO's dispute resolution process. The WTO hearings, held in Geneva, Switzerland, did not permit journalists or NGO representatives to witness the arguments. Only national governments enjoyed access to briefs and other tribunal documents. Unlike court systems in many counties, the WTO arbitrators did not accept briefs from interested third parties. There was no mechanism for independent appeals, a bedrock standard of the rule of law. The secrecy surrounding the WTO tribunals, activists said, clearly violated the democratic principle of transparent decision-making.

Citizen activists also objected to the makeup of WTO arbitration panels. WTO rules allowed each country in a dispute to choose one judge, while the third judge would be agreed upon jointly. The rules also required judges to have prior experience on GATT panels or service as a trade bureaucrat with a member country. This requirement kept out judges with backgrounds in environmental or labor law and narrowed the range of opinion on the WTO bench, assuring that disputes would be heard by judges already committed to the WTO's worldview. Activists also complained that the judge selection process contained no conflict of interest rules, allowing the involvement of individuals with connections to corporations with a stake in the case.

A Public Citizen pamphlet noted that the closed-door WTO tribunals represented

> . . . an insidious shift in decision-making away from democratic, accountable fora—where citizens have a chance to fight for the public interest—to distant, secretive and unaccountable international bodies, whose rules and operations are determined by corporate interests.[107]

Activists noted that while the U.S. government had given some 500 corporate representatives access to WTO negotiating texts, public interest groups were not given the same access. The unequal treatment raised questions about who, exactly, was writing the rules for the new global economy, and who those rules would benefit. The WTO's vast powers fed worries about who was in control: Was it elected governments, or was it a far-off trade body that acted as a shill for corporate interests? Wallach sums it up this way:

"People were worried about who is making the decisions," notes Lori Wallach. She adds:

People ask themselves, "Am I going to be able to decide?" It's all about who decides, who controls our lives. You don't have to be an environmental activist or have a Ph.D. in trade to worry about food safety and the quality of your meat. . . . We saw Seattle as a chance where, if we did things right, we could take the opposition to the next level.

The pieces were in place to make Seattle a showdown over corporate globalization. The CTC had matured from a small coalition in the early 1990s to a real political force, with grassroots activists across the country. Major organizations were mobilizing for Seattle. The victories over Fast Track and the MAI brought new people into the fair trade movement and gave activists a sense that the public was on their side. Organizers were hearing from more and more people worried about the shape of the global economy.

"After the MAI we had this whole coalition looking for things to do, and we saw that investment was going to be included in the WTO talks and we all just shifted in that direction," says Antonia Juhasz, who by 1999 had moved to WTO organizing with the American Lands Alliance. "It meant that we were organizing easily a year-and-a-half before Seattle. We had a whole network already built up."

In February, Public Citizen opened an office in Seattle. Throughout the summer, groups around the country were educating their constituents about the WTO and urging people to make plans for traveling to Seattle. The message was simple: "End Corporate Rule. November 30, Seattle," one widely circulated anti-WTO flier read.

In May, the CTC released a statement signed by more than 600 NGOs from 65 countries outlining civil society's views on the upcoming WTO summit. Saying that the WTO functioned principally "for the benefit of transnational corporations" and had "contributed to the concentration of wealth in the hands of a few," the groups said there should be no increase in the WTO's powers. The civil society groups said that instead of expanding its purview into new areas, the WTO should undertake "a comprehensive and in-depth review and assessment" of the impacts of its policies. "The failure ... of the MAI demonstrates broad public opposition to the deregulation of the global economy," the statement said. A review of the WTO would provide a chance to "develop an alternative, humane and sustainable international system of trade."[108]

The statement served as one of the central demands of the protesters in Seattle. "No new round—turn around," became the slogan.

By the fall of 1999, anti-WTO organizing was in full swing. The human rights organization Global Exchange and a political theater group called Art and Revolution sponsored a two-week roadshow from California to Canada featuring speakers and performers. The show traveled up the West Coast encouraging people in small communities and big cities to prepare for what had already been dubbed "The Battle in Seattle." A growing number of organizations signed on to a statement calling for nonviolent civil disobedience to shut down the WTO meeting. The goal was to involve thousands of people in a large, Gandhian-style protest to communicate intense resistance to WTO policies. The Ruckus Society, a group specializing in training activists in nonviolent direct action, and the Rainforest Action Network, an environmental group, invited more than 100 organizers to an "action camp" in the woods south of Seattle to prepare for civil disobedience against the WTO.[109]

The CTC and the AFL-CIO started preparations for holding a major march and rally the first day of the trade summit, November 30. A new generation of union leaders had come to see the WTO as every bit a threat to workers as NAFTA. The AFL-CIO objected to the WTO's resistance to addressing the issue of labor rights, and worried that the WTO, by making it easier for companies to move production facilities around the world, was fostering a race to the bottom. The AFL-CIO launched a major WTO education effort. Labor councils and local unions made arrangements to bus thousands of workers to Seattle.

Environmentalists—from major national organizations like the Sierra Club to local conservation groups—were encouraging people to go to Seattle. At first glance, the Pacific Northwest would seem an unlikely place to seal the budding labor-green alliance against corporate globalization. Disputes over logging and protecting the habitats of endangered species like the spotted owl had sharply divided communities in the region, becoming something of a national metaphor for the tensions between environmental protection and protecting good-paying jobs. Yet the West Coast was also the site of some truly innovative collaborations between workers and environmentalists. For example, on California's north coast locked-out aluminum workers and forest activists had joined forces to form the Alliance for Sustainable Jobs and the Environment. The workers wanted their jobs back and the activists wanted to save trees, and they shared a common enemy in the Maxxam Corporation. A worker and an environmentalist from the Alliance traveled together throughout the Northwest giving speeches and bringing together their constituencies to learn about the WTO.

The WTO was undermining the interests of so many different constituencies that it was easy to unite disparate groups. "These agreements do so much harm that they bring together many different kinds of people," notes Teamster activist Art Persyko. "People were concerned about an international government that didn't seem to work in the interests of ordinary people. They saw this as undermining our democratic rights as citizens."

"The metaphor for the WTO was an octopus, reaching its tentacles into all the things we cared about," recalls Juliette Beck, who was organizing WTO opposition for Global Exchange.

> I would go to talks and begin by saying that the WTO is the greatest threat to democracy ever—it is at once rule-maker, judge, and jury. There are no checks and balances. You would get these blank stares. Could this really be happening, people wondered. But then I would go back to that community a few months later and people would have these very technical questions about the WTO. People had clearly gone out and done a lot of research on the web on their own. And then it was very clear to them that the WTO was a government of, by, and for the global corporations.

By November, it was apparent to organizers that the protests in Seattle were going to be big. The AFL-CIO rented Seattle's Municipal Stadium for its rally on the 30th, while Public Citizen contracted a church in downtown for a week to serve as a combination teach-in forum and activist gathering spot. The WTO meetings were scheduled to last four days, and the CTC had divided the week into themes. There would be a day for environmental issues, a day for farmers to talk about the WTO's impact on agriculture and food safety, a human rights day, a day for trade unions. Websites were set up that listed ways to get to Seattle and offered homestays for out-of-town visitors. Organizers promised "the protest of the century."[110]

People opposed to the WTO started pouring into Seattle the weekend after Thanksgiving. The International Forum on Globalization, a think tank made up of scholars from around the world, hosted a three-day, sold-out teach-in at Seattle's Benaroya Symphony Hall, just blocks from where the WTO talks would begin in a few days. Some 3,000 people heard speakers from five continents explain how WTO policies were exacerbating environmental destruction, lowering living standards, and sabotaging democracy. Martin Khor, director of the Malaysia-based Third World Network, told the teach-in audience:

> An African cabinet minister was told by WTO officials that he would

have to change his country's constitution to meet WTO rules. "But don't worry," the officials told the minister. "We have already written the changes, and we have them right here for you."[111]

All across Seattle anti-WTO activities were occurring. The local labor council and human rights groups conducted a "people's tribunal" that indicted Union Carbide and other corporations for crimes against humanity.[112] Media activists set up an "Independent Media Center" to give freelance writers, radio reporters, and videographers a location to file stories and place video footage on the Internet.

Hundreds of people protested against sweatshop abuses in front of a GAP store in the city's trendy Capitol Hill neighborhood, while activists with Global Exchange dropped an anti-sweatshop banner over the front of an Old Navy downtown. In a particularly dramatic move, activists with the Ruckus Society and the Rainforest Action Network scaled a construction crane above Interstate 5 and dropped a huge banner with two giant street signs: an arrow pointing one way with the word "Democracy," and one pointing the other direction with the letters "WTO."

The flood of people into Seattle began to surprise even organizers. "We were impressed as anyone by what was happening" says Jia Ching Chen, an activist who had spent the fall planning for the nonviolent civil disobedience action. "Even though we had been working on it for months, we were surprised by the number of people who showed up."[113]

Hundreds of people were gathering at a warehouse about 10 blocks from downtown where an ad-hoc group called the Direct Action Network had set up what it called a "Convergence Center." Part soup kitchen and part political war room, the warehouse was the hub for people wanting to engage in the civil disobedience. Several times a day, trainings were held to give people the basics in nonviolent direct action. During the evenings a "spokescouncil" brought together "affinity groups"—autonomous collections of people ranging from 10 to 30 people—to discuss strategy and tactics. Dozens of affinity group spokespeople representing thousands of people attended the nightly meetings leading up to the summit. The meetings, often lasting hours, focused on details for staging a massive sit-in to physically shut down the WTO meeting.

Monday, November 29—the day before the trade talks were scheduled to start—witnessed the first flurry of protests. A demonstration against genetically engineered foods and cultural homogenization took place in front of a McDonald's. The protest was led by José Bové, a leader of the French Farmers' Confederation who had become famous for dismantling a French McDonald's with his tractor. In a glimpse of things to come, several protesters broke a McDonald's window before being upbraided by the rest of the crowd, including Bove.[114]

In Seattle Harbor, representatives from the Sierra Club and the United Steelworkers threw a "Seattle Tea Party." Crying "No globalization without representation," activists threw symbolic representations of imported Chinese steel, shrimp, and hormone-treated beef into the harbor as examples of goods tainted by WTO decisions.[115]

Downtown, 2,000 people marched to express their outrage at the WTO's environmental record. "Save Our Forests, Clearcut the WTO," read the banner at the front of the march. A woman held a placard that said, "The WTO Is A Hazardous Waste." Hundreds of marchers were dressed in blue and green sea turtle costumes to symbolize the WTO's shrimping decision. The human sea turtles carried pennants featuring a photo of a turtle and the caption, "I am not a trade barrier."

"The boat's off course, and everyone knows it," a Sierra Club member said while marching. "If we can't decide what's going into our food anymore, then something's very wrong."[116]

Activities continued into the night. As Seattle city officials and WTO representatives gathered at the Superdome for a pre-summit dinner, thousands of people holding hands circled the stadium. The protest had been called by the faith-based group Jubilee2000, and was organized to demand immediate debt cancellation for the world's poor countries. Across town, some 5,000 people attended "The People's Gala," an anti-WTO warmup rally featuring hip hop artists, 1960s protest leader Tom Hayden, and U.S. Senator Paul Wellstone.[117]

For all of its energy, Monday was just the opening act. Though protests were scheduled for the entire week, organizers had pinned most of their efforts on Tuesday, the opening day of the summit. The date, November 30, had gained its own shorthand; activists dubbed it N30.

The civil disobedience plans were no secret. For weeks protest organizers had been meeting with Seattle police to share with them the outline of their plans and to make sure the lines of communication were open. And on November 29, activists held a press conference in the hotel where many WTO delegates were staying to announce their intention to shut down the meetings. Yet somehow city officials and WTO representatives didn't get the message, or they didn't believe the protesters' claims. However unlikely it may have seemed, the protesters were poised to make history.

THE BATTLE OF SEATTLE

November 30 began with sheets of rain sweeping in from Puget Sound. Two hours before dawn thousands of people began converging at a waterfront park near Seattle's historic Pike Place Market. On the other side of downtown, thousands more were massing near a community college campus. In the cold drizzle activists assembled giant puppets—grim corporate reapers, colorful butterflies—and formed into their affinity groups. Some people danced to shake off the chill. A bare-shouldered Scotsman in a kilt fortified the crowd by jumping up on a dumpster and shouting "You think this is bad weather? This is nothing!" Just as the first hints of dawn appeared, the ponchoed crowds set off to encircle the convention center where the WTO talks were to begin that morning.

Masses of demonstrators surged through Seattle's downtown. The crowds came upon intersections that had already been blocked by activists who woke in the very early morning to "lock down" key points. Forming circles of about 20 people, activists put their arms into strong plastic tubes, inside of which two people clasped U-shaped bicycle locks; to break the lockdowns, police would have to sunder some two dozen people. While some marchers reinforced the lockdown groups, ranks of protesters continued toward the convention center. Lines of police tried to block the way, but the protesters vastly outnumbered them, and in a series of flanking maneuvers forced the police to surrender one city block after another.

Law enforcement officials had been caught off guard. Inside a Starbucks just a few hundred yards from the convention center, Washington State Patrol Chief Annette Sandberg looked up from her coffee to see demonstrators streaming past the window, cops nowhere in sight. A call came across the police radio from a member of the County Sheriff's force: "Sheriff, we're trapped. . . . We have no backup."[118] The 400 cops on the streets faced protesters coming at them from all directions. Police lines fell back to the last intersections before the convention center. Thousands of demonstrators now stood between the convention center and the hotels where most of the WTO delegates were staying.

WTO officials had planned to formally open their Millennial Summit with a ceremony at the Paramount Theater, one block northwest of the convention center. But by 8:00 a.m. the theater was cut off. Police officials had set up two lines of barriers in front of the theater: a rope line a half block away and then a semicircle of buses forming a barricade in front of the theater's marquee. The rope line fell without police resistance, and protesters climbed on top of the busses, waving flags and chanting. A handful of WTO officials, including WTO Director General Michael Moore, had managed to get inside ahead of the protesters, but the vast majority of dignitaries now had no way of entering.

Some 15,000 protesters effectively controlled the streets of downtown Seattle. Lines of people locked elbows, forming a giant human chain around the convention center. In some places the lines were four people deep. Realizing that they had so quickly succeeded in shutting down the city's core, a jubilation swept through the protesters. Many people started dancing. A Teamsters union semi-truck equipped with a giant sound system began playing Bob Marley tunes.

WTO delegates were trapped outside the convention hall as protesters stood their ground, refusing to let anyone pass their lines. Unable to get near the convention center, trade officials wandered the streets befuddled. "Interesting, very interesting," a Israeli delegate muttered as she took in the scenes of people dancing and shouting slogans.[119]

"I don't believe we should have the corporations running the world," an 82-year-old activist from Concord, Massachusetts, said as she stood locked arm in arm with other protesters. "We work so hard to get environmental laws, labor laws, human rights laws. I just don't believe corporations should rise above government rules."[120]

Some delegates seemed to sympathize with the protesters. "It's part of the democratic process," a South African delegate said. "We do this in our country all the time."

In some spots, however, interactions between demonstrators and delegates turned tense and even erupted into shoving matches as trade officials tried to push their way through the protesters. "You people are nuts," the trade minister from Estonia shouted after being rebuffed by protesters.[121]

While the direct action protesters held their ground downtown, the AFL-CIO started its rally at the Municipal Stadium near the Seattle Space Needle. "End Corporate Rule," "Labor Rights, Not Trade Wrongs," and "Make Trade Work For Working Families," read signs in the sea of 30,000 union members.

The trade controversy had come a long way from the old debate pitting proctectionists against internationalists. Many of the unionists in the crowd—such as Boeing engineers and dockworkers*—were from industries that relied on international trade. They weren't against trade per se, but rather the rules governing trade, which they saw as stacked in big business's favor.

"The rules of this new global economy have been rigged against workers, and we're not going to play them anymore," the president of the garment workers union said to thunderous applause.[122] Workers were protesting in Seattle, Teamsters president James Hoffa, Jr. told the crowd, to fight corporate greed. "We are going to change the WTO or we are

---

* In a powerful sign of solidarity, dockworkers from San Diego to Seattle staged a work stoppage from 10:00 a.m. to 1:00 p.m. on November 30 to show their support for the WTO protesters.

going to get rid of the WTO," the Teamsters leader said.[123]

The rally's international feel also pointed to a new kind of thinking within organized labor. Challenging the free trade agenda wasn't just about protecting American jobs, it was about guaranteeing labor rights everywhere. Trade unionists from more than 100 countries were at the rally, and labor leaders from Malaysia, Barbados, Argentina, and South Africa addressed the crowd. The struggle against the WTO was global and protecting the environment and human rights was a universal desire. "It is a demonstration of all working class people all over the world," a labor leader from Barbados thundered to the union rally. "Rich country, poor country, white country, black country, all countries!"[124]

A wave of discontent that had been building for years was crashing onto Seattle. Even in the midst of the peaceful and prosperous 1990s there lurked a deep disquiet. As a poll published before the Seattle meetings showed, support for globalization split sharply along class lines. Among families earning $75,000 or more a year, 63 percent of people saw globalization as positive; among families earning less than $50,000 a year, support for globalization fell to 37 percent.[125] Suspicions about the global economy's benefits were not limited to the political fringe. Millions of Americans feared the increase in corporate power, and now those emotions were emerging in a spectacular fashion. "I'm not super-radical or anything," a protester holding a cardboard representation of genetically modified corn said. "I'm for democracy, human rights and the environment. The world has to be about more than money."[126]

The Seattle police, meanwhile, were fed up with the protesters jamming the streets. The demonstrators had utterly paralyzed the WTO's meetings. Top officials, including Secretary of State Madeleine Albright and United Nations Secretary-General Kofi Annan, were trapped in their hotels. Something had to be done.

At approximately 10:30 a.m. Seattle police unleashed a volley of tear gas, pepper spray, and rubber bullets on the protesters in an attempt to clear a corridor between delegates' hotels and the convention hall. As trade officials looked on from the windows of their hotels, police bludgeoned the protesters. A woman on a megaphone shouted to the police, "we are peaceful," and in the next instant she was hit with a stream of chemical spray and fell back on the pavement writhing in pain. The police fired rubber bullets at point blank range, threw concussion grenades, swung batons. Wounded activists fell back from the front lines— heads bleeding, faces swollen by the toxic chemicals—and were treated by protester-medics who had come prepared to treat casualties. "They sprayed me right in the face," an activist said as a medic treated his eyes with solution. "We were just sitting there chanting to the delegates, and they sprayed us with tear gas."[127]

Protest organizers had expected police backlash, but they were shocked by the intensity of the onslaught. "I had been protesting my entire life," says Antonia Juhasz, "and I had never experienced anything like that. It was a real rude awakening."

Organizers had anticipated that, facing massive civil disobedience, police would engage in arrests. But the police were too badly outnumbered by the activists, and they decided to rely on force instead. It didn't work. Whenever a group of protesters retreated, a new set took their place. Even with their superior firepower, the police could not budge the thousands of demonstrators.

The activists were also aided by the unique structure of their affinity group model. While the law enforcement officials' top-down, hierarchical system forced cops on the front lines to keep radioing back to command officers for instructions, the protesters were able to react immediately to changes in the street scene. Each affinity group was independent within the larger mass of protesters, and so if a group of people decided they wanted to retreat or advance, they just did it. In the tear gas fog of the street clashes, the protesters' loose decision-making structure gave them a clear tactical advantage.[128]

Activists were outsmarting law enforcement officials inside the convention center as well. Three activists with Global Exchange—Medea Benjamin, Juliette Beck, and author Kevin Danaher—used their formal NGO credentials to get into the Paramount Theater. The several hundred trade representatives inside the theater were glum, anxiously watching TV coverage of the street battles just outside. The three activists decided to address the delegates. The trio walked calmly onto the stage and approached the podium. "Since we're a bit slow in getting started today," Global Exchange founder Medea Benjamin told the startled delegates, "I thought we should have a discussion that is long overdue about why the WTO is not addressing labor rights or human rights or the environment." A squad of police quickly hustled the three off stage, but the episode left the delegates shaken. No place, it seemed, was safe from the hordes outside.

At 1:00 p.m. WTO officials announced what had been obvious for hours—the opening meetings would be cancelled. The news quickly swept through the activists' ranks. The crowd was ecstatic. The protesters had accomplished their goal of shutting down the WTO. Yet that didn't mean the activists were going to abandon their blockades. Talk began to spread of holding the streets through the night. It seemed possible. All that was needed was reinforcements from the labor rally.

Even as WTO officials announced that the trade talks would be cancelled for the day, the 30,000-strong union rally was marching out of Municipal Stadium. Organized labor was eager to put on a show of force to pressure U.S. negotiators and WTO officials to address labor rights within the WTO framework. But union leaders were worried about associating too closely with the direct action protesters engaging in civil disobedience. The unions wanted to be radical, but not necessarily militant. And so as the labor march snaked downtown—in places within blocks of the ongoing melee—labor stewards were careful to direct their members away from the confrontation. Not all the union marchers, however, followed the stewards' directions. A few thousand marchers split off from the main parade and joined the direct action protesters.

The presence of the several thousand trade unionists immediately changed the dynamic of the standoff between the cops and the protesters. Since dawn the police had contended with young college students, environmental activists, and human rights advocates. Now the police officers faced their physical match—brawny steelworkers, dockworkers, and burly teamsters making their way to the front of the protest lines. It seemed the conflict was set to become even messier.

And it did, but in a way few people anticipated. All day a group of about 100 protesters—dressed entirely in black and accompanied by drummers banging a martial rhythm—had been moving through the crowds. They made for an unusually dour presence among the exuberant protesters. The self-described anarchists called themselves the "Black Bloc," and they had a different idea of direct action than the people staging the massive sit-in. The Black Bloc wanted to make a statement that they thought would be more powerful than nonviolent civil disobedience. After biding their time throughout the day, the arrival of the labor reinforcements gave them their chance.

Protected from the police by thick ranks of protesters, the Black Bloc members set about to destroy any symbol of corporate capitalism they could find. Reaching into their backpacks for pipes and hammers, the anarchist contingent began smashing the windows of FAO Schwartz, Banana Republic, Planet Hollywood, and Old Navy. Several Black Bloc members picked up a *USA Today* dispenser and hurled it through a Starbucks storefront. A half dozen climbed on top of the Nike Town roof and methodically dismantled the large chrome Nike letters there.

Taken aback by the broken glass, many of the protesters in the crowd chanted, "Shame, shame, shame." A handful of people—ironically, some of the very people who made Nike sweatshops a household name—tried to protect the Nike Town windows, arguing with the anarchists that wanton destruction would discredit the protest's aims in the eyes of most Americans. Unconvinced, the Black Bloc moved on to attack the

Warner Brothers Store and Nordstroms. A few overturned garbage cans
and lit them on fire. As the light began to fade from the sky, the scene
looked very much like anarchy indeed.[129]

Meanwhile, the police were preparing a counterattack. Since mid-
morning law enforcement officials and Secret Service officers had been
urging Seattle Mayor Paul Schell to declare a state of emergency and
impose a curfew in downtown. The mayor resisted. Calling a state of
emergency would effectively shut down the labor march, and the mayor,
a 1960s Vietnam War protester, did not want to be seen as quashing
dissent. By the afternoon, however, the labor march was winding down
and the situation downtown was heating up. A furious Secretary of State
Albright called the state's Governor and told him to do something. The
Secret Service and the FBI, anxious about President Clinton's scheduled arrival in Seattle the next day, demanded the area be cleared of
protesters. At 3:24 p.m. Mayor Schell declared a state of emergency
and asked the Governor to bring in the National Guard.[130]

The police officers downtown had almost run out of tear gas by noon.
To restock, the Seattle police had to send officers to nearby cities to
pick up more gas canisters. Then the police used plain clothes officers
carrying duffle bags to sneak them through the protester lines. By 4:00
p.m. the authorities had enough ammunition to clear downtown.[131]

Authorities launched a barrage of tear gas. It was a fusillade unlike
anything from earlier in the day, canister after canister of gas accompanied by concussion grenades to disorient the protesters. Clouds of tear
gas enveloped the crowd. The union marchers and direct action protesters retreated. Black Bloc members, now bolstered by local youths who
had come downtown to loot, formed a kind of rear guard, taunting the
advancing police and occasionally hurling spent tear gas canisters at the
lines of cops. Slowly the Black Bloc retreated into the Capitol Hill neighborhood where, after a lengthy standoff with police, the remnants of the
day's protest finally dispersed.

The day ended in a way few would have predicted, with National
Guard troops patroling a curfew zone in the city's battered downtown
among wreckage later estimated at $3 million in damage.

Though shaken by the destruction and police abuse, activists were
overjoyed. The alliance of trade unions, environmentalists, animal rights
activists, human rights groups, and others had achieved their central
goals. The WTO had been prevented, at least for a day, from meeting.
More important, the protests had punctured the veil of secrecy surrounding the organization. In a single day the WTO had become a household
name, and not a very pretty one.

FAILURE IS NOT AN OPTION?

During the next three days, protests continued to rattle downtown Seattle. The vast majority of demonstrators left the city after November 30, but thousands of activists had planned to stay throughout the week, and they were determined to keep the heat on the WTO.

On early Wednesday morning a few thousand activists, hopeful of repeating their success, entered the "no-protest" curfew zone inside Seattle's downtown and again tried to block the streets. This time, however, the police knew what to expect, and the demonstrators were at a fraction of their earlier size. The protesters were kept blocks away from the convention center. By mid-morning, police arrested some 600 people engaged in a nonviolent sit-in. In the afternoon, police used a barrage of tear gas to disperse a few thousand people who had gathered near the Pike Place Market.

By Thursday the clashes between activists and police had cooled, though the mood in the streets remained tense. Farmers organizations and environmentalists held a festive rally on the waterfront to express their opposition to the WTO's support for genetically modified crops. Small farmers from France, the United States, India, and Mexico told a crowd of 3,000 people that WTO policies were favoring the interests of giant agribusiness corporations over the needs of family farmers.

Like the labor march two days earlier, the farmers' rally showed that the WTO demonstrations were as much an international protest as an American one. "We've marched with farmers from Japan, France, everywhere," said an almond farmer from California. "Many of the marchers didn't even know English. They were singing in Japanese. It's the most solidarity I've ever seen."[132]

On Thursday afternoon, thousands of people participated in a protest against the way in which the protesters were being treated. To symbolize how the no-protest curfew zone was limiting citizens' free speech rights, activists staged a silent march. Lines and lines of protesters with their mouths taped shut streamed past the equally silent lines of helmeted, shield-bearing cops.

Yet even as the protesters were being kept out of earshot of the WTO delegates, their message was getting through. The activists' passion had rattled the trade ministers and unsettled the talks. The disorder in the streets was mirrored by a disarray inside the meeting rooms.

On Wednesday—as Seattle storekeepers recovered from the damage to downtown—President Clinton delivered a speech to WTO officials, saying that some of the protesters' complaints should be addressed. "It's imperative," the President told the trade ministers over lunch, "that the

WTO become more open and accessible. If the WTO expects to have public support grow for our endeavors, the public must see and hear, and in a very real sense, actually join in the deliberations."[133]

But Clinton's call for greater transparency within the WTO was overshadowed by comments he had made on his way to the summit. Talking with a reporter from the *Seattle Post-Intelligencer* while at the airport, the President said the WTO should establish a working group to

> ... develop these core labor standards, and then they ought to be part of every trade agreement, and ultimately I would favor a system in which sanctions would come for violating any provision of a trade agreement.[134]

Clinton was echoing some of the protesters' demands that the WTO give workers and the environment the same kind of protections it afforded investors and intellectual property. The comment quickly inflamed delegates from the developing world, who charged that binding rules on labor rights would be used to discriminate against goods from their nations. White House aides tried to spin Clinton's remarks, offering that the President hadn't really intended to say what he said. But the damage had been done. Developing countries said they would fight any U.S. agenda that included labor provisions in the WTO.*

As Clinton spoke to the trade ministers, reporters across Seattle scrambled to make sense of the protests. The nation hadn't seen anything like the Seattle conflict since the height of the Vietnam War, and newspapers and television networks were anxious to explain the activists' passion to a startled public. The corporate accountability movement, which had simmered just beneath the surface of politics throughout the 1990s, had in the space of less than a week boiled up to the surface of the popular consciousness.

Many pundits expressed shock that resistance to the WTO was so deep and that the passions of the protesters had gone so far. Influential *New York Times* columnist Thomas Friedman derided the fair trade ac-

---

* Many commentators pointed to poor governments' opposition to labor rights as evidence that the protesters were out of touch with the needs of the world's impoverished majority. In return, fair trade activists pointed to the presence of international trade unionists at the Seattle protests. Ordinary workers in the world's poor countries desperately wanted enforceable international labor protections. It was the business owners from their countries who opposed such protections. Corporate executives from developing countries feared losing their "comparative advantage" of paying low wages and suppressing trade union rights. And it was the business interests, not the interests of trade unions, that were represented by their countries' trade delegations. The split between workers from poor countries and trade officials from poor countries mirrored the division between elites and working people in the United States on trade policy.

tivists as "a Noah's ark of flat-earth advocates."[135] Friedman, along with several other commentators, said the protesters' criticisms and demands were inconsistent: While the activists decried the power of a secretive global government, they wanted new rules that could only be enacted by such a government. Friedman was right, but not in the way he thought. The activists weren't anti-globalist, they were anti-corporate. Among protesters there wasn't a question of whether the new global economy should have rules. The heat in the streets was over who should be writing the rules: corporations, or citizens. News commentators had difficulty understanding the protesters because they failed to recognize that the conflict was over governance, not globalization.

The protests were exposing the inherent tensions of corporate globalization. As the global economy expanded, ordinary people were increasingly at the mercy of forces beyond their control. This prompted a desire for more social insurance, more regulations, to cushion against the vicissitudes of the global economy. Yet the system envisioned by WTO officials prohibited new rules and demanded deregulation. The delegates were trapped in a kind of Catch-22, pinned between the expectations of their citizens and the interests of their corporations.

Those internal contradictions of corporate globalization roiled the Seattle talks. Clinton's remarks about labor rights had ignited the suspicions of developing countries, and now other conflagrations were starting to spread. The summit had become a kind of high-stakes catfight, with disagreements breaking out in all quarters. The U.S. government—prodded by American biotech and agribusiness corporations—was demanding that the EU lower its farm subsidies and end its restrictions on genetically modified food. The Europeans refused to budge. EU negotiators were also resisting American attempts to introduce some of the MAI rules into the WTO. Developing countries, meanwhile, were causing their own stir by demanding that the richer nations implement the tariff reductions called for in the Uruguay Round, which many had been remiss in doing. Feeling that in the past they had given more than they received, many poor countries said they wouldn't agree to any new WTO rules until the old ones had been implemented.

The negotiating impasse was partly the work of the international NGO coalition that had come out of the MAI fight. Since January, citizen activists from around the world had been holding monthly conference calls to strategize ways to scuttle the Seattle summit. The "Our World Is Not For Sale Coalition"—which included activists from Asia, Europe, Africa, and the Americas—figured that if they could use public pressure to force their individual governments to hold on to certain positions, they could monkeywrench the talks.

The international citizen coalition's strategy rested on the idea that if the WTO were to truly act like a democracy, the organization would not be able to function. As one free trader explained it, the WTO system was set up precisely to restrain domestic groups from influencing international trade talks.[136] Insulating the negotiations from the unruliness of democracy was seen as a virtue by many WTO delegates. Even as tens of thousands of people protested against the organization's structure, some WTO officials privately defended the secrecy, saying that without it country negotiators would not feel free to make politically risky concessions.[137] The secrecy was essential if the negotiators were to be able to sacrifice the interests of their citizens to the imperatives of free trade. The fair trade forces calculated that if the negotiators were exposed to public scrutiny, the talks would fail.

Two issues—labor rights and concerns about genetically modified food—showed the strategy in action. By staging a massive show of strength in Seattle, the U.S. labor movement forced Clinton to propose a workers' rights agenda within the WTO. Clinton's preferred successor, Vice President Al Gore, needed the AFL-CIO's grassroots energy to win the presidential election less than a year away, and Clinton's proposal was a way of showing his administration's support for workers. And yet by appeasing his domestic supporters, Clinton alienated many WTO delegates.

In a similar fashion, environmentalists and farmers in Europe had been putting pressure on EU negogiators not to concede anything to the Americans when it came to genetically modified foods. Yet if European negotiators stuck to the demands of their citizens, they would not be able to reach a compromise with the American negotiating team.

While U.S. and EU negotiators bickered, delegates from the developing nations were launching their own protest about the undemocratic nature of the WTO talks. In theory, the WTO was supposed to operate on consensus, with all member countries participating equally in the negotiations. In reality, however, negotiations in the past had been dominated by the wealthy countries, which wrote the agreements almost exclusively among themselves and then sought approval from the developing nations, who were asked to sign onto a fait accompli. Officials from the world's rich countries who assumed they could manage a similar process in Seattle were about to be proven wrong.

In the months leading up to the Seattle summit, officials from 10 of the world's wealthiest countries had secretly written a draft agreement for the November talks. But some delegates from poorer countries found out about the closed meetings and managed to get a leaked copy of the draft. When, on the second day of the Seattle summit, a paper was distributed that was supposed to reflect the negotiations that had taken place there so far, a few people realized that the two drafts were identical. Trade officials from the wealthy countries claimed to have included concessions sought by the developing world; yet it was clear they had done nothing of the kind. Dozens of delegates were outraged.[138] "This is a sham," one delegate from the developing world told a reporter. "We are just like the environmentalists. We are frozen out of the process."[139] "They have been treating us like animals," an Egyptian trade official said, "keeping us out in the cold and telling us nothing."[140]

By Thursday night, it was clear the trade talks were in jeopardy. The major powers had not come to agreement on any significant issues, and several smaller nations were threatening to leave the summit unless the closed-door proceedings were opened to all nations. Still, despite these troubles, few expected the summit would fail completely. During a Washington press conference held right before Seattle, U.S. Trade Representative Charlene Barshefsky had announced that "failure is not an option."[141] And even as success seemed increasingly elusive, Barshefsky told the other delegates in Seattle that they would get an agreement "by whatever means."[142]

Trade negotiators, led by Barshefsky, worked through Thursday night and into Friday morning without sleep. In Washington, President Clinton called leaders around the world to urge them to put pressure on their negotiators to force a compromise.[143]

On Friday morning, as bleary eyed WTO delegates struggled to reach some sort of agreement, the protests continued. About 2,000 people marched through downtown, past surreal scenes of boarded-up store windows and Santa Clauses flanked by National Guard troops. A half dozen activists with Global Exchange, the Rainforest Action Network, and Friends of the Earth once again used their NGO credentials to get inside the talks, where they unfurled a banner reading, "No Globalization Without Representation," before being dragged away by security.

Delegates from the developing world remained angry at what they saw as a lack of representation. Several tried to get inside the so-called "Green Room," where talks were taking place among the biggest countries, but they were rebuffed. It was the last straw. In the evening, eight Latin American countries released a statement saying they would not sign any deal because they had been excluded from the talks. With countries pulling out of the talks, an agreement looked impossible.

At 10:30 p.m. Barshefsky told the delegates that the meetings were adjourned. "It would be best to take a timeout," she said simply.[144] WTO officials started heading to the airport without even bothering to release a final communique. The summit had been a complete failure.

"THIS IS WHAT DEMOCRACY LOOKS LIKE"

Exceeding even their own expectations, fair trade activists had prevented the WTO from launching a new round of trade talks and expanding its power. The national and international coalitions painstakingly assembled during the course of earlier political fights had overturned the best laid plans of the world's most influential corporations. Labor and environmental groups played the world's governments off each other rather than allowing themselves to be played against each other. Anti-corporate sentiment had revealed itself to be a powerful force. The grassroots globalization movement showed it was capable of changing the course of world history.

News of the talks' collapse raced among the few thousand activists still in Seattle. In front of the county jail—where hundreds of people had gathered to express solidarity with those still in custody from arrests two days earlier—the announcement was greeted with wild shouts and cheers. Activists hugged and danced. A chant went up from the crowd, accompanied by a steady drum beat. Over and over, the people chanted: "This is what democracy looks like! This is what democracy sounds like! This is what democracy feels like!"

CONCLUSION
Building a Movement for Global Democracy

PROTESTS AGAINST CORPORATE RULE did not end in Seattle. Just four months after the demonstrations against the WTO, tens of thousands of people gathered in Washington, DC, to protest the policies of the WTO's cousins: the International Monetary Fund (IMF) and the World Bank, institutions that promote corporate interests and free-market fundamentalism at the expense of the world's poor majority. Similar demonstrations against the IMF and World Bank took place in Washington in September 2002.

Corporate accountability groups have also kept the heat on individual companies. Since the Seattle protests, campaigners have successfully compelled Home Depot and Loew's to stop selling products made with old-growth timber, and they have convinced Starbucks to offer "Fair Trade-certified" coffee, which guarantees farmers a living wage. Public health advocates are pressuring Coca-Cola to provide health insurance to its African workers. Activists are demanding that M&M/Mars use Fair Trade-certified chocolate. And a wide range of groups are urging grocery chains to disclose whether their products contain genetically modified crops.

Mass protests outside meetings of the WTO, IMF, and World Bank drew heightened public attention to such corporate accountability initiatives. They also, of course, intensified debate about the global economy. By demonstrating widespread public resistance to the status quo, the protests kick-started a rethinking about corporate globalization. The large-scale demonstrations, combined with the wide range of corporate accountability struggles, forced even conservative observers into a reassessment of corporate behavior. As *BusinessWeek* noted: "There's no point in denying that multinationals have contributed to labor, environmental, and human-rights abuses."[1]

Such admissions are no small victory. By channeling the public's mistrust of big business into action, the corporate accountability movement has helped establish popular agreement that too much corporate power is a real danger. That fact that corporate accountability groups were able to do this even at the height of an economic boom speaks volumes about the depth of opposition to corporate power.

As we all know, the boom turned to bust. A few months after the anti-WTO protests, the NASDAQ began a nose-dive, and the Dow Jones Industrial Average and the S&P500 soon followed. The irrational exuberance of the 1990s evaporated as U.S. stock markets lost some $7.5 trillion in value between the spring of 2000 and the spring of 2003. Economic growth has been sluggish; an estimated 3 million people have lost their jobs.

In 2002, the tragedy of recession turned into the farce of scandal. The collapse of energy giant Enron was the largest bankruptcy in U.S. history and signaled trouble on the horizon. A cascade of corporate scandals followed in which one major corporation after another announced that it had engaged in improper accounting. Corporate giants in the newly deregulated communications industry—Adelphia, Global Crossing, Qwest, and WorldCom—went down the tubes after admitting that they had misled the public about their profits—or lack of them. The demise of WorldCom, one of the world's biggest long distance companies, eclipsed the Enron failure as the largest bankruptcy in U.S. history. Arthur Andersen, among the largest and most reputable accounting firms, was wiped out after it was shown that the firm's accountants helped cook the books at Enron. In the wake of these infamies, even those who may have once viewed big business with adulation now regarded it with suspicion. A *CBS News* poll in July 2002 found just six percent of Americans saying they had "a lot of confidence in business."

History shows that crises provide opportunities for change. The increased dissatisfaction with corporate behavior gives corporate campaigners an opening to push for sweeping reforms. More people than ever are open to questions about whether it is in society's best interest to leave corporations free from accountability to the public.

Yet even as the corporate accountability movement is poised to achieve new gains, the specters of terrorism and war overshadow activists' ambitions. Since the September 11 terrorist attacks, war and security issues have dominated the headlines. International conflict has replaced economic globalization as the premier political drama.

The corporate accountability movement, then, finds itself at a crossroads between vast opportunity and creeping insignificance. The challenge facing anti-corporate activists is how to keep questions about corporate power in the public mind.

RESPONSIBILITY vs. ACCOUNTABILITY

War may dominate the headlines, but that does not mean domestic issues have dropped from public consciousness. Opinion surveys taken in the spring of 2003 showed that most Americans were more concerned with the state of the economy than with the war in Iraq. People's memories are long when it comes to ways in which they have been wronged—for example, being deceived by corporate executives. In any case, one doesn't need a long memory to witness corporate wrongdoing. The drip-drop of corporate scandals continues: In early 2003, the Providian Financial group, a banking firm, admitted it had overstated earnings by nearly 20 percent between 1999 and 2003, while the owner of the Giant grocery store chain said it had overstated earnings by $500 million during 2001 and 2002.[2] There is a great amount of grist to feed anti-corporate sentiment.

But will public disgust with corporate behavior lead to systemic change? Much of the answer hinges on the distinction between corporate *responsibility* and corporate *accountability*.

During the summer of 2002—as the wave of corporate scandals became a tsunami—politicians of all stripes, including MBA President Bush, were heard talking about corporate responsibility. "There's no capitalism without conscience," the President told a Wall Street audience in July of that year.[3] Responsibility is fine, but it's not the same as true accountability. Responsibility is *voluntary*: it calls for individuals or institutions to behave in an acceptable manner. Accountability is *mandatory*: it requires a certain standard of behavior and includes penalties if those standards are not met. When activists demand corporate accountability, they are saying that companies should be bound by law, that corporations should answer to the higher authority of citizen democracy.

Responsibility relies on morals, the conscience Bush spoke of. But conscience is often insufficient to guard against abuses. This is why accountability is based on the rule of law: the principle that everyone must play by the same rules.

Of course, many of the America's top executives did not play by the rules. The wealth and privilege showered on business leaders evidently convinced many of them that they were so powerful they did not have to obey the rules. As the corporate crime wave proves, self-policing will not work with those who see themselves above the law. Tom Paine captured the necessity for the rule of law when he wrote: "A body of men holding themselves accountable to nobody ought not to be trusted by anybody."[4]

No wonder trust in Corporate America is at an all-time low.[5] Millions of Americans feel betrayed, knowing that while they followed the rules, the corporate crooks didn't. "The whole system is rigged in favor of an elite two or three percent of the population," a self-described middle-class woman said at the height of the corporate scandals.[6]

The corporate establishment is on the defensive. After a year of non-stop scandals, big business's image is in tatters. After decades of downsizing, Corporate America cannot plausibly claim that it benefits workers. And after the collapse of Enron and WorldCom, the free market fundamentalists will have a difficult time trumpeting the alleged virtues of deregulation. The corporate ascendancy has stalled.

During the 1990s, citizens succeeded in scoring some impressive victories over big business. Now campaigners have a chance to take those wins a step further and go on the offensive. The time for corporate responsibility and voluntary initiatives is over. This is the time to demand lasting accountability.

Corporate campaigners now have an opportunity to push for a whole new set of rules that will radically* change the relationship between citizens and corporations.

BEYOND END-OF-PIPELINE POLITICS

The real outrageousness of 2002's summer of scandal is not how many laws were broken by corporate executives, but how few laws they needed to break to do what they did. The maneuvers that led to several companies' downfall are not only legal, but widely practiced. Offshore tax havens, accounting firm conflicts-of-interest, and boards stacked with the friends and relatives of executives are just part of business as usual. Enron and WorldCom didn't have to break the rules because they had already written the rules themselves through their influence in Washington. Since the corporations helped set up the system that was intended to guard against abuses, it can hardly be surprising that the system failed.

Nor should it be surprising that the government response was lackluster. President Bush mouthed a few pieties, but even Wall Street was left unimpressed by the President's commitment to real reform, and the stock markets, hungry for stability, tanked in the days following Bush's speeches on corporate responsibility. On Capitol Hill, lawmakers quickly cobbled together legislation to close some of the most egregious loopholes that had permitted corporate abuses. The Sarbanes-Oxley bill put in place some long overdue changes—among them requiring independent oversight of auditors, stiffer penalties for those convicted of fraud, and new protections for company whistle-blowers. But this was not, as some claimed, "landmark legislation." The overall weakness of the law

---

* Radical does not mean extreme. When we say radical change, we mean change that gets to the root of the problem, since radical comes from the Latin *radic*, for root.

was apparent in the fact that the powerful Business Roundtable backed its passage, and that one of its sponsors, Michael Oxley (R-OH) has a long history of supporting corporate interests. Meaningful reform rarely comes from the people who the reforms are meant to target.

The most assertive response to the corporate scandals came from outside Washington. State attorneys general, led by New York Attorney General Elliot Spitzer, marshaled their resources to punish corporate fraud. Spitzer forced Merrill Lynch to pay $100 million in fines after it was shown that the firm's analysts were recommending stocks that they thought were worthless. Then, in December 2002, Spitzer secured a settlement with nine other Wall Street firms, making them pay $900 million in fines and agree to separate their underwriting and research divisions to reduce conflicts of interest.

Yet these successes were less than what they appeared. The New York Attorney General's deal didn't include an indictment of a single person or institution, and it halted a broader investigation into the financial sector's operations. Syndicated columnist Arianna Huffington derided the agreement as a "sweetheart deal" and "kid-glove treatment."[7] The settlement let the corporate crooks off the hook.

The problem with these efforts—from the President's halfhearted bully pulpit to the congressional legislation and even the Spitzer settlements—is that they spring from the assumption that the corporate scandals were caused by a few bad apples. In fact, the entire apple barrel is rotted clear through. The revelations of corporate corruption are just high-profile examples of a wholesale breakdown in the system of checks and balances between the public interest and big business power. When it comes to corporate crimes, the scandals of 2002 are just the tip of the iceberg.

The timid congressional reforms and the weak attorney general settlement addressed the *consequences* of corporate corruption without tackling its *causes*. They came nowhere near the roots of the corporate rule crisis. The official response was a clear example of "end-of-pipeline politics." Reformers scrambled to clean up the effluent coming out of the factory rather than trying to get inside the factory itself and address the problem at its source.

End-of-pipeline strategies are doomed to failure. There is simply too much effluent—not just common fraud, but the week-to-week layoffs, environmental destruction, and rights abuses—coming out of the big business establishment. Trying to clean up all the corporate horseshit is a Herculean task on a par with clearing the Aegean Stables.

This dilemma reveals the centuries-old question that confronts all social change movements: reform or revolution? Should corporate accountability campaigners seek to enact immediate, but limited, reforms?

Or should they set their sights on a transformation of the entire system? Are they mutually exclusive?

In a globalized economy wracked by growing social inequities and the threat of ecological collapse, the question of reform or revolution has no easy answer. The sweatshop seamstress needs relief now, and a reform agenda can provide it. Yet tinkering around the edges won't solve the environmental crisis spurred by corporate globalization.

The way to split this Gordian knot is by pushing reforms that, if enacted, would be truly transformative, reforms that dance on the edge of revolution. Corporate accountability activists must direct their energies to campaigns with system-changing goals. The corporate accountability movement's victories to date have been half-wins, precarious victories vulnerable to reversal. Most corporate campaigns are piecemeal efforts that focus on a specific abuse and target, at most, a handful of companies. They are end-of-pipeline struggles. It is now time to move beyond end-of-pipeline politics and embrace strategies that can lead to a deep transformation of global corporate capitalism.

The goal, after all, is not just to improve the behavior of corporations. We do not want somewhat less environmental destruction or somewhat less social injustice. In order to save the environment and equalize social opportunity, it is necessary to change the structures of power and the rules of the game. As Dr. Martin Luther King, Jr. said: "True compassion is not merely tossing a coin to a beggar. True compassion comes to see that an edifice which produces a beggar needs restructuring."

The corporate accountability movement's task is to guide such a restructuring of the status quo. Success depends on ensuring democratic control over corporations.

EMPOWERING DEMOCRACY

In seeking to bring big business under public control, anti-corporate forces face a daunting Catch-22: To hold corporations accountable, new laws are needed to mandate different corporate behavior; yet, because of the realities of corporate rule, enacting such laws will be incredibly difficult. But those difficulties don't mean that the corporate accountability movement should give up on government action. Doing so would be a no-struggle position, an unconscionable surrender. Democratic government, after all, is supposed to be "we the people," and that principle should never be compromised, especially in our minds. If Steve Biko, the martyred South African Black Consciousness leader, was correct when he said "the most powerful weapon in the hands of the oppressor is the mind of the oppressed," then it is also true that the most powerful weapon in the hands of the *oppressed* is the mind of the oppressed. The idea is to reclaim democracy, to empower citizens to themselves return power to the democratic system.

Many of the reforms proposed in the wake of the summer of scandal had to do with corporate governance—how corporations are internally organized. Again, the assumption was that the chicanery had been an aberration, and that if only shareholders and board members had exercised more supervision of executives there would have been no crisis. Many people said the scandals resulted from a collapse in accountability within corporate headquarters, not because of a larger failure by society at large to hold corporations accountable. This misses the point. The problem is not corporate governance, though there is much room for internal democratization inside an essentially authoritarian heirarchy. The problem is that we have a corporate government.

SEPARATION OF CORPORATIONS AND THE STATE

The first step toward reclaiming our democracy is to enact a separation between corporations and the state.* The founders of the U.S. republic understood that when a single segment of the population dominates society, democracy is at risk. This principle applies to the economic realm just as it does to the religious sphere. Fundamentalism is always a threat to freedom, whether it's a fundamentalism of faith or a fundamentalism of commerce. As long as one class of people—whether monsignors or millionaires—holds a monopoly on power, democracy is compromised.

One of the most obvious ways to separate corporations and the state is to cut the leash between Corporate America and Capitol Hill. Most of our lawmakers have ceased to act as watch dogs for the public interest and now serve as lap dogs for corporate interests. Corporate rule will remain as long as this disgraceful arrangement persists.

Unfortunately, the Supreme Court has upheld corporate political donations as a "right," arguing that constitutional free speech protections cover this renting of our politicians. And well-intentioned efforts such as the McCain-Feingold bill to reduce the flow of campaign cash have

---

* To call for a separation of corporations and the state is not to deny the government a role in the economy. To the contrary, citizens have every right to use government as a mechanism to ensure that corporations work in the best interests of society. The point is to say that corporations should not be controlling the state, as is now the case. This is not a new idea. As far back as 1910 President Theodore Roosevelt stated: "We must drive the special interests out of politics. That is one of our tasks today . . . The citizens of the United States must effectively control the mighty commercial forces which they have themselves called into being. There can be no effective control of corporations while their political activity remains. To put an end to it will be neither a short nor an easy task, but it can be done."

been only moderately successful: Money, like water, always manages to find a crack to flow through. If halting corporate campaign contributions is not an option, then freeing political candidates from the very need to raise money is the solution. Full public financing of campaigns is a key step to empowering democracy and restoring citizen rule.

Already, citizens in several states have put in place ambitious public financing systems. With the assistance of campaigners from the Washington, DC-based clean elections group, Public Campaign, residents in Arizona, Maine, Massachusetts, and Vermont have set up—either via ballot initiatives or through their legislatures—systems that come closest to full public financing of elections. The first elections that occurred with public financing rules demonstrated how divorcing politics from profits could reinvigorate the electoral process. By giving candidates independence from corporate contributions, the public financing systems have enabled more grassroots activists to run for office, while also giving a boost to smaller parties on both the left (the Green Party) and the right (the Libertarian Party).

The drive for public financing of elections should be taken to other states, starting with the 11 states that already give candidates partial financing. In expanding the effort for clean elections, campaign finance reform activists should consider reworking their appeals to citizens. Currently, much of the reform rhetoric centers on the pernicious behavior of ill-defined "special interests." There needs to be more of a focus on who specifically is buying our democracy. People should be asked directly: Do you think corporations should run the government? The overwhelming majority will answer, "no."

PUBLIC CONTROL OVER THE PUBLIC AIRWAVES

While activists struggle for public financing of elections, they should also be demanding greater public control over the airwaves. One of the major reasons elections have become so expensive is that candidates are dependent on television and radio to get their message out. To run a competitive race for U.S. Senate in many states costs tens of millions of dollars, in large part because candidates are compelled to buy huge amounts of TV and radio ads. What many people forget is that the airwaves dominated by large corporations are actually owned by the public. The entertainment and news companies have to lease their space on the broadcast frequencies from the federal government. So when political candidates spend millions of dollars to communicate with the public, they are paying to use property that they already own a part of.

Corporate accountability activists must put new effort into demanding a shift in control over the public airwaves from corporations to the rightful owners: we the people. For years groups such as Fairness and Accuracy in Reporting (FAIR) and Media Alliance have sought to democratize the media. Corporate accountability groups should lend energy and resources to those existing initiatives. But we also need a new organization, a formalized network that can link the many small organizations opposed to corporate control of the media. Just as the Fifty Years Is Enough Network connects hundreds of groups critical of the IMF and the World Bank, a network focused on securing public control of the public airwaves could join the hundreds of alternative news organizations, radio stations, video producers, and political groups that understand if we don't open up the media to reflect the diversity of the United States—the most diverse country in world history—we will always be fighting uphill battles for the public mind.

The demands of such a network could be simple. Political candidates should be given substantial amounts of free air time during campaigns, and throughout the year community groups, non-profits, and other non-governmental organizations should be given airtime as well. If the infotainment corporations refuse to comply with these public service requirements, they will lose their broadcast licenses. The demand for free airtime should be part of an antitrust campaign to break up the media empires.

The appeal to the public should be straightforward: For democracy to work, debate is essential. Political debate in the United States has atrophied because the public airwaves are controlled by commercial institutions that make their money by selling the public mind to corporate advertisers. Because the viewers are the commodity being sold, the media companies have no interest in educating people. They want the commodity to be stupid, scared, and passive—the perfect consumer. The answer is to break the corporate grip on the public airwaves and open the doors of media access. If we want an active citizenry, we need thinking, self-confident citizens.

Freeing political candidates from dependence on corporate contributions and broadening public access to the means of communication would be a tonic for democracy. Those reforms, if enacted, would breath new life into the political system, and go a long way toward establishing citizen rule. This would pave the way for other badly needed reforms: a repeal of corporate welfare, a halt to the revolving door between business and government, and the establishment of stricter civil and criminal liabilities for corporate executives.

The citizens' movement challenging the power of big business must transform itself from an anti-corporate struggle into a pro-democracy struggle. This is not just semantics. Most people are more enthusiastic about campaigns that are positive and forward thinking rather than negative and reactive. Equally important, the movement's definition of itself will guide its strategy and tactics. If we hope to achieve democratic goals, then it must be clear that the struggle against corporate power is a fight for real democracy.

DISMANTLING CORPORATE RULE

Establishing mechanisms of true democracy would create a counterweight to unelected corporations. Yet even a massive overhaul of the political system would not get to the root of corporate power. For that to happen, activists must begin challenging the legitimacy of the corporation itself. They must ask: Where does corporate power come from, and how can it be brought under public control?

To date, corporate accountability activists have been very successful at disrupting corporate rule. The task now must be to *dismantle* corporate rule. If the goal is to redraw the balance of power between society and big business, the corporate accountability movement needs to focus on removing the sources of corporate authority.

A consensus is emerging within corporate accountability organizations that one of the best ways to get at the roots of corporate power is to target the basis of corporations' legal standing: the corporate charter. As explained in Chapter 1, the first corporations were understood to be creations of the state. The corporation was an artificial creature, owing its very existence to the public, and allowed to operate only if it fulfilled some public service.

Yet over the last 150 years corporate lawyers and free market fundamentalists have sought to advance the idea that corporations are natural creations—organic beings that result from individuals freely agreeing to enter into a shared relationship. The idea that the corporation has rights apart from what is granted by the state has led to a series of judicial rulings giving corporations many of the same protections as flesh-and-blood persons. Courts have ruled that corporations enjoy freedom of speech rights as well as due process protections and freedom from unreasonable search and seizure. But there is virtually no popular support for the notion that corporations are the same as people. The idea violates common sense: Ask anyone on the street if they think a corporation is a person, and most people will say, "no."

The courts seem divided on the issue, with many judges still committed to the principle that corporations exist only with the consent of the people. "Corporations are artificial entities created by law," Supreme Court Justices Byron White, William Brennan, and Thurgood Marshall wrote in a 1978 dissenting opinion over whether corporations should be given free speech rights. "The State need not permit its own creation to consume it."[8]

Activists can remind citizens of the original intent of corporations by waging campaigns focused on chartering laws. Chartering laws should be changed to reform corporate governance structures, federal charters should be established, and activists should exercise existing state rules that allow for revoking corporate charters.

A first step would be to rewrite the charter laws to require broader participation on corporate boards. Workers, consumers, shareholders, company suppliers, and local community leaders should all have a voice on company boards. Such a system of stakeholder capitalism—as opposed to stockholder capitalism—already exists in Germany (no economic underachiever), where a supervisory board made up of many different constituencies is the final corporate authority. Requiring diverse points of view on corporate boards would improve corporate behavior because it would force companies to consider a wider range of interests when making decisions.

But the impact of such a reform would be blunted unless it were adopted across the United States, and this is difficult because each state has its own chartering rules. If a state were to enact progressive changes in its corporate chartering system, it would run the risk of driving some businesses out of its jurisdiction. This threat of a race-to-the-bottom points to the need for a federal chartering system.

At the turn of the last century, as states were competing with each other to water down their charter requirements, progressive reformers pushed the idea of federal chartering as a way to establish a floor for business standards. Presidents Roosevelt, Taft and Wilson all supported the idea of federal incorporation. Even *The Wall Street Journal* backed the plan, as did the National Association of Manufacturers, which said national chartering would be "a national blessing." The momentum for federal chartering was lost after the Federal Trade Commission was established in 1914. But the idea has remained attractive to corporate accountability reformers. During the Depression, the proposal was again discussed, and in the 1976 book, *Taming the Giant Corporation*, Ralph Nader made federal chartering a central part of a reform agenda.[9]

Federal chartering is as needed now as it was then. In an age of megacorporations, state chartering makes about as much sense as state passports or state postal services. Aside from establishing a single national standard for business behavior, federal incorporation would also give activists a chance to put in place some long overdue reforms. For example, federal charters could create new rules, and tighten existing ones, to ensure that companies' top management and directors be held liable—both in civil and criminal courts—for corporate wrongdoing. Executives and shareholders of corporations currently enjoy virtual immunity when it comes to harm committed against workers, employees, or the environment, and this limited liability is a central source of corporate power. Company officials would certainly be more careful about their businesses' behavior if they knew they could be held personally liable for crimes committed by their corporations.

Given the corporate grip on the Capitol, putting a federal chartering system in place won't happen immediately. In the meantime, corporate accountability activists should take advantage of existing laws that allow for corporate charters to be revoked.

The early American idea that corporations were artificial entities was manifested through laws that strictly limited company life spans. Corporations were not originally intended to be immortal. Corporate charters in the 19th century routinely put a time limit on company operations, anywhere from 3 to 20 years. And when a corporation caused harm or exceeded its mandate, its charter could be revoked through a legislative process called *quo warranto* ("by what authority"). In stating that corporations were not entitled to eternal existence, charter revocation rules underscored the idea that owning a company was a privilege—granted by the people—and not a right.

Not until the end of the 19th century did corporate charters permit corporations to exist in perpetuity. Yet even today, every state except Alaska has some sort of provision for revoking company charters. Corporate accountability activists are already setting their sites on reviving the principle that if companies routinely violate the public interest, they should not be permitted to do business. Corporate crime must be followed by real punishment, including corporate death sentences.

Some anti-corporate activists have already tried to repeal company licenses. Activists in New York have sought to revoke the charter of Union Carbide (now owned by Delaware-based Dow Chemical), while groups in California tried to repeal Unocal Oil's charter. Activists in California are currently seeking to establish—via the state's referendum system—a "three-strikes-and-you're out" law to hold corporations accountable for illegal behavior. Any company that commits three "major violations"—defined as grossly negligent behavior that results in deaths, or fine or damages above $1 million—should lose the privilege to operate in the state.[10] The idea has commonsense appeal: Corporate recidivism should be no more tolerated that individual recidivism.

While strengthening public control of the corporate charter is essential, it cannot serve as a substitute for continuing to target specific abuses. The corporate campaign—for all of its noted limitations—remains an important tactic. Campaigns targeted at individual companies hold a kind of David vs. Goliath drama that grabs the public imagination. Exclusively legalistic strategies risk losing the attention of ordinary citizens. The idea should be to combine the two approaches: Every corporate accountability campaign should include some effort to repeal the charter of the targeted company. At the very least, attempting to revoke corporate charters will raise the stakes of individual campaigns and help put the companies on the defensive.

And when a charter revocation effort first becomes successful, it will be the shot heard around the world.

REDEFINING PROGRESS

A charter revocation or two would give corporations new incentives to do less harm, but it would not ensure perfect behavior. This is for the simple reason that corporate responsibility is an oxymoron. Corporations, after all, are set up to evade responsibility. As Ambrose Bierce put it in *The Devil's Dictionary*: a corporation is "an ingenious device for obtaining individual profit without individual responsibility."[11]

The very structure of the corporation leads to misbehavior. Corporations cannot be socially responsible because their only true legal duty is to maximize profits for shareholders. The essential corporate dictum is: Privatize profits, socialize costs.

Under current law, it is actually illegal for corporate executives to act in the public interest. This is because of so-called fiduciary responsibility rules. If a CEO were to decide to sacrifice some profits to keep a factory in the United States and save U.S. jobs, shareholders would be entitled to sue that CEO for failing to fulfill the duty to maximize profits. Until these fiduciary responsibility laws are changed, real corporate accountability will be impossible. We must redesign the corporation's internal logic and refocus its obligation to society at large, not just shareholders.

Author and entrepreneur Paul Hawken has stressed the need for a "triple bottom line." Corporations' legal obligations would be expanded to include the environment, workers, and community. Success and progress would be measured not just by profits, but also by how a company treats the earth, its employees, and its neighbors.

Robert Hinkley, a former corporate attorney, has proposed an elegantly simple way to put this idea into practice. The law in Maine, Hinkley's home state, says: "The directors and officers of a corporation shall exercise their powers . . . with a view to the interest of the corporations and their shareholders." Hinkley adds a modest amendment: " . . . but not at the expense of the environment, human rights, the public safety, the communities in which the corporation operates, or the dignity of the employees."

The addition is only 25 words, yet it has revolutionary potential. It could, for example, outlaw the internal combustion engine, force an increase in wage levels, and eliminate unnecessary layoffs. By redefining the corporation's reason for being, the Hinkley amendment would help create a more ecologically sustainable and socially just economy.

Every state has some law similar to the Maine statute, making the amendment universally applicable. Hinkley suggests phasing in the law over 10 to 15 years. No starry-eyed idealist—he worked for 20 years as a securities law expert—Hinkley believes the idea would face less resistance than might be expected.

"I once sat next to a Republican Delaware legislator at a dinner in New York," Hinkley told a reporter, "and he said to me—'Bob, that's a great idea. You get it passed in the other 49 states and I'll get it done in Delaware.'"[12]

The corporate accountability movement should accept the challenge.

SIZE MATTERS

It is essential that these attacks on corporate power be aimed at the largest companies. The corporate accountability movement is not against business; it's opposed to the arrogant power of big business. Corporate accountability efforts have been, and should remain, focused on the minority of companies that are harming the public interest with near impunity.

Take, for example, the proposed federal chartering system. Federal incorporation would apply to only the largest corporations, those whose reach crosses state lines. It would be silly to ask Joe's Hamburger Stand to go to Washington, DC, to get a license to operate. The idea would be to create a dual chartering system in which most companies would continue get their charters through state offices, while the giant corporations would have to get licenses from both state and federal officials. A modest step would be to require federal chartering for only those companies—the few hundred largest—that already are required to certify their quarterly earnings. From there, federal incorporation could be expanded to include any corporation with yearly revenues of more than $250 million, which would mean a few thousand businesses.

Although Hinkley's amendment would apply to all companies, in practice it would only affect a handful of corporations for the simple reason that the vast majority of locally owned businesses already behave fairly responsibly. Because they are rooted in place, most business owners' behavior is tempered by the expectations of their neighbors.

The corporate abuses are due in large part to the fact of absentee ownership. The directors of the largest corporations have no connection to the people or environments their decisions impact: They do not have to witness the depression that sweeps a town after a round of layoffs or smell the toxic vapors coming from a refinery's towers. Their detachment is what permits them to behave irresponsibly. Absentee ownership fosters absence of conscience.

"The local guy in downtown Ellsworth, Maine has to walk through town everyday," says Hinkley. "If he messes with the public interest, the local people will not do business with his company and he will be out of business. It is the large public corporations that are creating the problem."[13]

Just 2,500 U.S. companies have a net worth of $500 million, while 99 percent of U.S. corporations are capitalized at less than $10 million.[14] The corporate accountability movement's challenge is to enlist the support of that 99 percent in order to fundamentally transform the behavior of the other 1 percent. This can happen by appealing to small business owners' faith in the free enterprise system. After all, giant corporations harm local entrepreneurs just as often as they harm their workers and the environment, as the bankrupt owners of countless independent bookstores, family-owned video stores, and Main Street hardware shops can attest. We must choose between two opposing definitions of "free enterprise": the freedom of corporations to go anywhere and do anything to people and planet, or the freedom of everyone to be enterprising.

In forcing that choice, anti-corporate campaigners can gain the assistance of small businesses in overthrowing big business.

POPULISM FOR THE NEW CENTURY

The necessity of recruiting small business owners into anti-corporate struggles points to the larger need of bringing more "conservatives"—those who believe in conserving community and nature—into the movement.

In 2000, Ralph Nader was obviously the anti-corporate candidate. His Green Party run centered on the crisis of corporate rule, and his candidacy brought issues of corporate power into the larger political debate. Even the ever-cautious Al Gore felt moved to occasionally employ populist rhetoric as he criticized HMOs, Big Pharma, Big Tobacco, and the "powerful forces arrayed" against ordinary citizens. It is worth noting that the combined Nader-Gore vote in the 2000 presidential election was the largest center/left vote total since Lyndon Johnson crushed Barry Goldwater in 1964. This helps prove the popular resonance of corporate accountability politics. And what about those centrist Democrats who blame Gore's flirtation with populist themes for Bush's ultimate victory? Democratic pollster Stanley Greenberg points out that Gore's polling numbers rose dramatically *after* he began attacking big business. And of course Gore received a half million more votes than the Texas Governor.

In 1996, however, the anti-corporate insurgence came from the right, not the left. Styling himself a "pitchfork populist," conservative commentator Pat Buchanan was unforgiving in his assaults on big business, especially when it came to worker layoffs. Buchanan said he wanted to wrench the Republican Party away from Wall Street and give it back to the people on Main Street. He did not succeed, but he briefly riled the political conventional wisdom.

As described in the last chapter, these left and right strands of anti-corporate sentiment have come together in limited ways to combat corporate globalization. It's essential to deepen this tactical alliance and find other ways that the two camps can work together. By uniting these forces, the groundwork can be laid for a broad-based, anti-corporate populism for the 21st century.

To say the least, constructing a new populist movement will not be easy. It is one thing to work with unlikely allies to defeat a common foe; it is something entirely different to maintain that alliance to build a common good. There is no doubt that Nader's voters and Buchanan's supporters have vastly different worldviews and ideas of what would constitute a perfect society. Yet that does not mean there is no room for future collaboration.

Political alliances do not depend on the partisans agreeing on everything. Rather, they rest on finding some sort of common ground. A good place to start strengthening ties between left and right anti-corporate forces is on the ground of America's rural landscape.

As the 2000 election proved, there is a vast cultural divide between urban and rural America. But that divide closes when it comes to concerns over corporate power. Rural communities know all too well the brutal effects of corporate rule. A decade after the farm crisis first came to the public's attention, rural bankruptcies and farm foreclosures continue to devastate small towns across the country. Millions of farmers have been ruined as agribusiness giants such as Archer Daniels Midland and Cargill depress prices ever further. In response to this calamitous situation, rural communities have fought back against the might of big business. Nine states have passed referenda prohibiting non-family-owned corporations from engaging in farming; at least eight Pennsylvania townships have passed laws to keep out factory farms.[15] Anti-corporate sentiment is alive and well in the heartland.

Shared anti-corporate politics promise to close the vast gap between the cities and the countryside. In doing so, a truly left-right corporate accountability movement has the potential to fundamentally alter the political map. The lines of political debate would be redrawn. No longer would politics hinge on cultural tensions between the left and right. Instead, politics would become a matter of up and down: the corporate elites versus ordinary people.

FORMING THE FINGERS INTO A FIST

The corporate accountability movement's diversity is its greatest strength. Biologists tell us that a field with an assortment of plants is healthier than a monocrop: So it is with social movements. Yet while maintaining bouquet consciousness, it is also important to develop organizational coordination. Call it unity of diversity. Anti-corporate activists must find new ways of working together so that the sum of their efforts will be greater than the individual parts. Think of a hand: Each finger alone is breakable, but unified in a fist they are far stronger.

The foundations for bringing corporate accountability activists into greater collaboration are already in place. For the last three years, people from around the United States have come together for the "Empowering Democracy" conference, a chance for activists to share skills, swap strategies, and hatch future plans. The annual gathering has already distinguished itself as an incubator for new alliances among activists.

The big business meltdown during 2002's summer of scandal also forged new partnerships among anti-corporate organizations. Feeling a great sense of urgency to respond to the crisis with far-reaching reform proposals, groups wrote an 11-point "Unity Statement on Corporate Accountability." Demanding a "fundamental transformation of the relationship between corporations and society," the statement lays out a set of long-overdue reforms, including many of those mentioned above, such as democratizing the charter system and separating corporations and the state. The statement also calls for re-regulating utility markets, stronger oversight of accounting firms, forcing corporations to pay their fair share of taxes, and tighter liability rules for corporate directors. To date more than 200 citizen groups have endorsed the statement.[*]

It is past the time to bring these ad-hoc efforts into a more permanent structure. An agenda as large and as forward-looking as the one sketched here cannot be tackled by individual organizations. To coordinate the disparate elements of this far-flung movement, activists should begin

---

[*] The Unity Statement is available online at: www.citizenworks.org.

work to establish a Corporate Accountability Network (CAN).

CAN would not be an institution seeking to dominate the movement. It would be a *network*: a hub for sharing news about ongoing campaigns, a public source for information, a clearinghouse for tactics that work, and a venue for offering proposals for further collaborative action. CAN would not promote one specific tactic above any other; it would seek to create the space for diverse tactical approaches to interact and develop a truly democratic strategy for ending corporate rule.

CAN's central responsibility would be to unite the disparate threads of the corporate accountability movement around systemic reforms tackling corporate power. The idea is to create the biggest tent possible: One in which revolutionaries and reformers, local groups and national ones feel comfortable.

CAN would also serve as a catalyst for mass mobilizing. Corporate elites are intent on demobilizing people, on encouraging complacency, apathy, and cynicism. CAN would help identify pressing needs and urgent actions so that, when necessary, individual groups could focus all of their efforts on a certain problem. It's the strategy of the organized swarm—combining separate energies into a single force, a perfect storm capable of overturning the status quo.

ACTING GLOBALLY

Creating an anti-corporate populist movement in the United States will be a major achievement. But if activists solely focus on corporate rule in the United States, their victories will by Pyrrhic. The stories in this book teach that, because corporate power is transnational, responses to corporate abuses must be equally transnational.

Corporations have no allegiance to any nation or country, and a large part of their power comes from not being rooted in place. When faced with being barred from doing business in Burma, Unocal Oil threatened to relocate to Malaysia. When Boeing moved its headquarters from Seattle to Chicago, company directors admitted they made the move in order to feel less attachment to Seattle and so be more comfortable acting solely in the interests of shareholders; not surprisingly layoffs in Seattle have followed. As Thomas Jefferson once observed: "Merchants have no country. The mere spot they stand on does not constitute so strong an attachment as that from which they draw their gain."[16] If citizens were to end corporate rule in the United States, many companies would simply move their headquarters to "friendlier" countries.

The global economy is lawless because corporations, operating across borders, have simply gone beyond the law. While public oversight of corporations—when it exists—remains limited to the nation-state, big business has become truly international.

The situation is reminiscent of the challenges faced by American anti-corporate activists at the turn of the last century. Corporations had become national in scope, yet business regulations reached no farther than state lines. It took two generations for the law to catch up to reality and to establish meaningful national regulations for corporate behavior. Citizens today confront a similar task: how to write the rules for a global economy. The world is at a constitutional moment. The decisions made today will determine the shape of international laws for generations to come. The question is whether corporate interests will dominate international relations, or if citizens around the planet will unite to hold corporations accountable for their actions.

Fortunately, efforts are well underway to ensure that this constitutional moment is not squandered. Corporate accountability movements in Europe, Asia, Africa, and Latin America are working together to make sure the global economy is set up in such a way to benefit the world's majority. Activists are challenging the "free trade" status quo, while suggesting alternatives to the current path. Groups in the United States are demanding real transparency into the workings of transnational corporations. And organizations are pushing for binding international rules on corporate behavior.

Citizens in the Western Hemisphere opposed to the planned Free Trade Area of the Americas (FTAA) have produced an "Alternatives for the Americas" that offers a blueprint for socially responsible and environmentally sustainable international commerce.[17] Citizens are not consenting to corporations writing the constitution of the global economy; they are writing their own rules themselves. The rallying cry of this global justice movement has been radical yet simple: The needs of people and planet should take priority over profits.

While anti-corporate forces defy the global rule makers, they are also proposing systemic solutions to address the abuses of specific transnational corporations. Organizations in the United States are pressuring the U.S. Congress to pass legislation that would force transnational companies to disclose basic information about their overseas operations. When corporations operate in the United States, they are required to make public the details of their pollution discharges, the kinds of chemicals they use, and the number and cause of workplace injuries. But when the same companies operate outside U.S. borders, they are not required to supply the same information to the communities in which they operate. A coalition of groups—including Amnesty International, Friends of the Earth USA, the AFL-CIO, Earth Rights International, and Global Exchange—is working to close this gap. The International Right to Know coalition wants to ensure that communities everywhere are provided the basic information they need to monitor corporate practices. The initiative is admittedly modest: The proposed law would not require changes in corporate behavior, only disclosure. Yet, as the stories in this book have shown, transparency is the first crucial step toward real accountability.[18]

While demanding transparency, citizen groups are at the same time taking the next step toward global corporate accountability. Friends of the Earth International has developed a legally binding international framework for corporate behavior. The proposed international treaty—endorsed by hundreds of organizations around the world—would place mandatory rules on corporate behavior. The corporate accountability convention, unveiled at the UN Earth Summit in Johannesburg in 2002, would require companies to consult with communities before undertaking major activities, conduct environmental impact assessments of all their projects, and issue regular reports about their operations. The convention would also tighten the legal liability rules for companies and their directors. Corporate executives would be held personally responsible if their companies violate the laws of the countries where they do business. The treaty includes a variety of penalties—suspension of stock exchange listings, withholding of public subsidies, and even removal of limited liability status—if a company breaks the rules of the treaty. The convention is a crucial step in creating an international rule of law governing corporate behavior.[19]

Who would enforce such a treaty? The United Nations is an obvious first choice. Unfortunately, the UN's recent record on holding corporations accountable is not impressive. The institution disappointed many anti-corporate activists when it launched its "Global Compact," a limited and nonbinding code of conduct for transnational corporations. Many activists complained that the system—little more than a vague pledge on a piece of paper—would do nothing to improve corporate behavior while allowing the signatory companies to wrap themselves in UN legitimacy. Even some UN agencies have pointed out the limitations of the approach: "Multinational corporations are too important and too dominant a part of the global economy for voluntary codes to be enough," the UN Development Program has declared.[20]

Just as activists should not give up on Congress, neither should we take a no-struggle approach to the UN, despite its failings. The institution remains a potential vehicle for establishing global democracy and an international rule of law. Campaigners should set their sites on democratizing the United Nations. Insofar as the UN becomes truly democratic, it can be a vehicle for demanding corporate accountability.

A first step would be to revive the UN Center on Transnational Corporations (UNCTC). From 1977 to 1992, the center acted as a forum for discussing the problems of corporate behavior. It also came close to establishing a sweeping— though voluntary—code of conduct for corporations. The center and the code of conduct eventually became the victims of the U.S. government's opposition to the program.

In the short term, a new Center on Transnational Corporations could serve as a venue for investigating the impacts of corporate behavior and encouraging discussion and debate about the effects of corporate rule. Eventually, the Center could help draft, oversee the ratification of, and implement the proposed international treaty on corporate accountability. The Center could also establish a corporate chartering system for transnational businesses, since international corporate charters are needed just as much as national charters. By re-establishing corporate issues under UN jurisdiction, the UN could become a progressive counterweight to the power of the WTO.

Given the U.S. government's historic resistance to addressing corporate issues via the UN, momentum for a binding corporate accountability convention must come from international activist networks. It will be the responsibility of U.S. organizations to stay in close contact with their partners around the world to find ways to assist in this endeavor. In an age of corporate globalization, international citizen cooperation is essential for bringing corporations under democratic control.

A GLOBALIZATION OF CONSCIENCE

Fortunately, international cooperation among corporate accountability groups is growing. During the last decade, a form of grassroots globalization has developed to combat corporate globalization. Trade unions have formed relationships among workers in different countries. Environmentalists in Europe and North America have linked with Indigenous groups in the global south to stop oil extraction and rainforest destruction. Human rights groups have forged connections with threatened communities in all corners of the globe. Fair trade organizations have linked producers in the world's poor countries to consumers in the wealthier nations. And activists from all these movements have united to challenge the WTO and IMF.

In the immediate aftermath of the terrorist attacks on September 11, 2001, it appeared that the new realities of war and conflict would set back the budding grassroots globalization. Wars, after all, tend to muzzle dissent and distract from other priorities. The Spanish-American war killed the Populist Movement; World War I sidetracked the Progressive Era reforms; the Vietnam War drowned the Great Society. As the rubble smoldered at ground zero, it seemed that the corporate accountability movement could be a casualty of the terrorists' attacks.

But if wars undermine social justice movements, they also breed resistance—the kind of resistance displayed by the new global peace movement. The belligerence of the Bush White House has ignited an international backlash that promises to bring new energy and new supporters to the global justice movement.

The most dramatic and inspiring example of grassroots globalization occurred in February 2003, when more than 10 million people around the world came together to protest the Bush administration's war on Iraq. As the sun rose on February 15, the anti-war marches began. Peace marchers took to the streets of Seoul, Tokyo, and Melbourne to oppose an invasion of Iraq. More than one million people carrying anti-war banners paraded past Rome's Coliseum. Peace demonstrations occurred across Spain, and London witnessed the largest protest in British history. Up to 400,000 people clogged Manhattan's East Side as Nobel Peace Prize winner Archbishop Desmond Tutu led crowds in a chant of "Peace! Peace! Peace!" In snowy Minneapolis nearly 10,000 people streamed through the city's downtown, while in Phoenix thousands marched in t-shirts. The coordinated demonstrations marked the single biggest day of global protests in world history.

The worldwide protests were made possible by globalization. These were wired demonstrations, organized and planned through the World Wide Web. But make no mistake—this was not your CEO's globalization. The peace demonstrations represented, not a globalization of commerce, but a globalization of *conscience*.

The challenge facing the corporate accountability movement is how to join with this vibrant global movement for peace. How can we bring together the global peace and global justice movements? How can grassroots globalization reach its full potential?

The answer lies in building a movement dedicated not simply to preserving the peace, but to *creating* justice. Citizen groups must expand their efforts to address the root causes of violence, not just its consequences. Tackling corporate rule must be a central part of this agenda, for true security requires abolishing the environmental, political, and economic injustices that feed the fear and resentment propelling war.

The global justice movement's long-standing concerns fit naturally with the global peace movement's agenda. Each peace rally is, in a sense, a cry for safety. But safety, to paraphrase Dr. Martin Luther King, is not just the absence of war—it is the presence of justice. Without limiting our dependence on petroleum, we will not be safe. Without helping citizens around the world achieve real democracy, we will not be safe.

Without ensuring that all people everywhere have a roof over their heads and enough food to eat, we will not be safe. Lasting security rests on putting the corporate accountability movement's ideals of democracy and fairness at the center of our national and international priorities.

It should be obvious enough: damming rivers, demolishing forests, and setting up sweatshops does not earn friends. Dictating economic policy to dozens of nations from within the walls of the IMF does not win allies. In many parts of the world, U.S. companies and U.S.-dominated economic institutions serve as de facto ambassadors for the United States. U.S. corporations are synonymous with America. If those companies act abusively, it helps breed the anti-Americanism that terrorist recruiters thrive on. Holding transnational corporations accountable is essential for encouraging the goodwill that is key to real security.

While putting corporate misbehavior in the context of global security, anti-corporate activists should confront transnational businesses on the ambivalent nature of their own patriotism. Since September 11, there has been much discussion about who is patriotic and who is not. That question should be put to the transnational corporations that dominate the U.S. economy. After all, companies that lay off thousands of workers so they can move production to low-wage havens overseas or who relocate their legal headquarters to Bermuda to avoid paying taxes are certainly not acting patriotically. During the roaring '90s, many corporations proudly called themselves international businesses. General Electric CEO Jack Welch portrayed GE as a "borderless company," while an executive of Colgate-Palmolive explained: "The United States does not have an automatic call on our resources. There is no mindset that puts this country first."[21] Campaigners should force companies to explain why, if they feel that way, they think they are entitled to U.S. government bailouts, massive subsidies, and tax breaks. Corporate accountability activists should make clear that corporate interests are often inimical to the national interest.

In the wake of the February 2003 global peace rallies, *The New York Times* wrote: "There may still be two superpowers on the planet: the United States and world public opinion."[22] Mobilizing that public opinion is key not just for stopping war, but also for ending corporate rule and halting the ecological destruction and social injustice that plague the planet. Keeping the power of public opinion on the move will be crucial for building the better world people are hungry for.

THE RACE TO THE TOP

Challenging corporate power is not enough. While working to dismantle corporate rule, activists must also create subsitutes to the status quo.

Unless citizens are given other options to business as usual, they will not wholeheartedly join the anti-corporate struggle. It is unrealistic to ask people to abolish corporations as we know them without providing some kind of alternative. We cannot expect people to jump from a sinking ship unless we give them a life raft.

Perhaps the corporate accountability movement's greatest test is showing people that there is a better way of organizing society. The corporate elites have constructed a system driven by money and profits. In response, we must offer a vision of a world based on life and liberty. The corporations are leading a race to the bottom. It is our duty to start a race to the top. Anti-corporate activists must put new efforts into constructing the better world we know is possible.

The first step is to vow noncooperation with the corporate system. All power—even tyrannical power—depends on some measure of popular aquiescence. Public participation in the corporate economy is fundamentally what gives corporations their power. If we refuse to consent, big business will lose much of its might. That's because the corporations need us more than we need them. If you want a hamburger, you can get it from Joe's Hamburger Stand down on the corner. But without your dollars, McDonald's is done for.

Noncooperation, however, only goes so far, especially if there are not easy and readily available alternatives to the status quo. Most people would happily pay more for shoes and clothes not made in sweatshops.[23] But their natural question is: "If I don't buy Nike or Gap, then what should I buy?"

A green/fair economy is already sprouting at the grassroots to meet this demand for better ways of living. Organic farming is growing far more rapidly than chemical farming, with sales expected to top $11 billion in 2003. Sales of Fair Trade-certified products broke the $100 million mark for the first time in 2000, while "no-sweat" garment manufacturers such as Ben Cohen's Sweat-X in Los Angeles are reporting dramatic sales gains. The Co-op America Business Network has more than 2,000 green/fair trade companies as members, while socially responsible investment funds now control $639 billion in assets.[24]

Anti-corporate activists should help deepen the roots of this alternative economy. This does not have to be difficult. It means supporting neighborhood retailers and mom-and-pop stores to keep resources in the local economy. It includes buying organic foods that are locally grown and searching out sweat-free, organic clothing. It requires a consciousness about the power of our own dollars.

Individual efforts can be greatly magnified by making them public policy and using the power of the government's purse to bolster the green/fair economy. At the national level, this would mean lobbying for a halt to the massive subsidies for the fossil fuel industry and shifting that money into renewable energies such as wind and solar. At the local level, citizens should pressure their states, cities, and counties to pass legislation that would, among other things, mandate governments to favor local businesses and give priority to companies that have a commitment to environmentally sustainable and socially responsible business practices. Such laws not only will improve communities' quality of life, but they can also serve as a political tripwire against the WTO.

WTO rules forbid discriminating against goods because of the product's origin or the production methods used in its manufacturing. By deliberately violating those rules and favoring green/fair enterprises, citizens can create jurisdictional challenges that will hamstring the WTO's authority. If we are at a constitutional moment globally, then we should seek to provoke constitutional crises that will force society to decide who it wants making the rules—local communities, or transnational corporations. The goal is to ensure as much local control as possible, to guarantee communities the right to determine their own future. The idea is that—by anchoring the green/fair economy at the local level—community can serve as an antidote to corporatization.

Building a green/fair economy is an ecological necessity: The planet can no longer afford an economy based solely on short-term gain, an economy that sees no value in a 2,000-year-old redwood tree until it is cut down and made into marketable commodities. Creating a green/fair economy is also a moral necessity: We can no longer tolerate the impoverishment of the many to bankroll the privilege of a few. And, for anti-corporate activists, the green/fair economy is a political and strategic necessity. Trying to reform the laws in the face of corporate rule has proven nearly impossible. It is time to consider that, in addition to trying to retool the economy by taking over politics, we should take over the economy so we can retool politics.

People will not rebel against the status quo unless they see a way out. This is why a green/fair economy is so desperately needed. Building something, being part of movement that is forward-looking, will inspire people with a hope that no rear guard struggle against corporate abuses ever can. People will dare to resist only if they know another world is possible.

"Another world is possible"—that's the motto of the World Social Forum, an annual international gathering of social activists designed as a response to the corporate-centered World Economic Forum in Davos, Switzerland. For the last three years, tens of thousands of activists from around the world have gathered in Porto Alegre, Brazil, to discuss ways of resisting corporate globalization and building the green/fair economy. African trade unionists, Indigenous peasants, European human rights activists, and Asian environmentalists have come together to lay the foundations for an economy that prioritizes life values above money values.

At the 2003 conference, award-winning Indian writer Arundhati Roy captured the hope and promise that so many people around the world feel. She made clear that not only is resistance to the corporate system not futile, it is winning:

> The corporate revolution will collapse if we refuse to buy what they are selling: their ideas, version of history, war, weapons, and their notion of inevitability. They need us more than we need them. Another world is not only possible, she is on her way. On a quiet day, I can hear her breathing.

Can you?

RESOURCES

In Global Exchange's corporate accountability work we have found the following organizations to be reliable. Our apologies to any organizations we left out.

180 Movement for Democracy and Education
P.O. Box 251701
Little Rock, AR 72225
Tel: 501-244-2439
www.corporations.org/democracy

50 Years Is Enough Network
3628 12th St NE
Washington, DC 20017
Tel: 202-IMF-BANK (202-463-2265)
50years@50years.org
www.50years.org

ACORN National
88 3rd Avenue
Brooklyn, NY 11217
Tel: 718-246-7900
www.acorn.org

Alliance for Democracy
681 Main Street
Waltham, MA 02451
Tel: 781-894-1179
www.thealliancefordemocracy.org

Amazon Watch
255 Third Street, Suite 206
Oakland, CA 94607
Tel: 510-419-0617
www.amazonwatch.org

AFL-CIO
815 16th Street, N.W.
Washington, DC 20006
Tel: 202-637-5000
www.aflcio.org

California Global Corporate Accountability Project
Nautilus Institute
125 University Ave.
Berkeley, CA 94710-1616
Tel: 510-295-6100
www.nautilus.org/cap

Campaign ExxonMobil
611 South Congress, Suite 200
Austin, TX 78704
Tel: 1-877-SAVE-TIGE(r)
www.campaignexxonmobil.org

Center for Economic Justice (CEJ)
733 15th St., NW, Suite 928
Washington, DC 20005
Tel: 202-393-6665
www.econjustice.net

Center for Responsive Politics
1101 14th Street, NW, Suite 1030
Washington, DC 20005
Tel: 202-857-0044
www.opensecrets.org

Citizen Works
P.O. Box 18478
Washington, DC 20036
Tel: 202-265-6164
www.citizenworks.org

Co-Op America
1612 K Street NW, Suite 600
Washington, DC 20006
Tel: 800-58-GREEN/202-872-5307
www.coopamerica.org

Consumer Action (CA)
717 Market Street #310
San Francisco, CA 94103
Tel: 415-777-9456
www.consumer-action.org

Corporate Accountability Project
1434 Elbridge Street
Philadelphia, PA 19149
Tel: 215-743-4884
www.corporations.org

Corporate Europe Observatory
Paulus Potterstraat 20
1071 DA Amsterdam
Netherlands
Tel/fax: +31-20-6127023
www.xs4all.nl/~ceo/

CorpWatch
P.O. Box 29344
San Francisco, CA 94129
Tel: 415-561-6568
www.corpwatch.org

EarthRights International (ERI)
1612 K St. NW, Suite 401
Washington, DC 20006
Tel: 202-466-5188
www.earthrights.org

Fair Trade Federation
1612 K Street NW, Suite 600
Washington, DC 20006
Tel: 202-872-5329
www.fairtradefederation.com

Focus on the Global South
C/o CUSRI, Chulalongkorn University
Bangkok 10330 Thailand
Tel: +66-2-2187363-65
www.focusweb.org

Food First/Institute for Food and Development Policy
398 60th Street
Oakland, CA 94618
Tel: 510-654-4400
www.foodfirst.org

Friends of the Earth-US
1025 Vermont Ave., NW, Suite 300
Washington, DC 20005
Tel: 877-843-8687
www.foe.org

Global Exchange (GX)
2017 Mission Street, Suite 303
San Francisco, CA 94110
Tel: 415-255-7296
www.globalexchange.org

INFACT
46 Plympton Street
Boston, MA 02118
Tel: 617-695-2525
www.infact.org

Institute for Agriculture and Trade Policy
2105 First Avenue South
Minneapolis, MN 55404
Tel: 612-870-0453
www.iatp.org

Institute for Policy Studies (IPS)
733 15th St., NW, Suite 1020
Washington, DC 20005
Tel: 202-234-9382
www.ips-dc.org

Interfaith Center for Corporate Responsibility
475 Riverside Drive, Room 550
New York, NY 10115
Tel: 212-870-2295
www.iccr.org/

International Development Exchange (IDEX)
827 Valencia Street, Suite 101
San Francisco, CA 94110-1736
Tel: 415-824-8384
www.idex.org

International Forum on Globalization (IFG)
1009 General Kennedy Avenue, #2
San Francisco, CA 94129
Tel: 415-561-7650
www.ifg.org

International Center for Research on Women
1717 Massachusetts Avenue, NW
Suite 302
Washington, DC 20036
Tel: 202-797-0007
www.icrw.org/

International Confederation of Free Trade Unions (ICFTU)
5 Boulevard du Roi Albert II, Bte 1
1210 Brussels
Belgium
Tel: +32 (0)2 224 0211
www.icftu.org/

International Labor Rights Fund
733 15th St., NW #920
Washington, DC 20005
Tel: 202-347-4100
www.laborrights.org/

Investor Responsibility Research Center (IRRC)
1350 Connecticut Ave., NW, Suite 700
Washington, DC 20036-1702
Tel: 202-833-0700
www.irrc.org/

International Right to Know Campaign
Friends of the Earth—United States
1025 Vermont Ave., NW
Washington, DC 20005
Tel: 202-783-7400 x121
www.irtk.org/

Jubilee USA Network
222 East Capitol St. NE
Washington DC
Tel: 202-546-4468
www.jubileeusa.org/

McSpotlight
BM McSpotlight
London; WC1N 3XX, UK
www.mcspotlight.org

Monsanto vs. Schmeiser
www.percyschmeiser.com/

Multinational Monitor
P.O. Box 19405
Washington, DC 20036
Tel: 202-387-8030
www.essential.org/monitor/monitor.html

Program on Corporations, Law & Democracy (POCLAD)
P. O. Box 246
S. Yarmouth, MA 02664-0246
Tel: 508-398-1145
www.poclad.org/

Project Underground
1916-A M.L.King, Jr. Way
Berkeley, CA 94704
Tel: 510-705-8981
www.moles.org

Public Campaign
1320 19th St., NW, Suite M-1
Washington, DC 20036
Tel: 202-293-0222
www.publicampaign.org

Public Citizen's Global Trade Watch/Citizens Trade Campaign
1600 20th St. NW
Washington, DC 20009
Tel: 202-588-1000
http://www.citizen.org/trade/

Public Information Network
P.O. Box 95316
Seattle WA 98145-2316
Tel: 206-723-4276
http://www.endgame.org/

Rainforest Action Network
Rainforest Action Network
221 Pine St., Suite 500
San Francisco, CA 94104
Tel: 415-398-4404
www.ran.org

Redefining Progress
1904 Franklin Street, 6th Floor
Oakland, CA 94612
Tel: 510-444-3041, ext. 303
www.rprogress.org/

Shareholder Action Network
1612 K St., NW, Suite 650
Washington, DC 20006
Tel: 202-872-5313
www.shareholderaction.org

Stakeholder Alliance
733 15th St., NW, Suite 1020
Washington, DC 20005
Tel: 202-234-9382
www.stakeholderalliance.org

Stop the FTAA
www.stopftaa.org/

**Students Transforming and
Resisting Corporations (STARC)**
2732 SE Belmont
Portland, Oregon 97214
Tel: 503-235-0760
www.corpreform.org/

Take Back The Media
1072 Casitas Pass Road #125
Carpinteria, CA 93013
info@takebackthemedia.com
www.takebackthemedia.com

Third World Network (TWN)
121-S, Jalan Utama, 10450
Penang, Malaysia.
Tel: 60-4- 2266728/2266159
www.twnside.org.sg/

Tobin Tax Initiative
CEED/IIRP, PO Box 4167
Arcata, CA 95518-4167
Tel: 707-822-8347
www.ceedweb.org/iirp/

TransFair USA
1611 Telegraph Ave., Suite 900
Oakland, CA 94612
Tel: 510-663-5260
www.transfairusa.org/

United for a Fair Economy
37 Temple Place, 2nd Floor
Boston, MA 02111
Tel: 617-423-2148
www.ufenet.org/

**United Students Against
Sweatshops**
888 16th Street NW, Suite 303
Washington, DC 20006
Tel: 202-NO SWEAT
www.usasnet.org

Who Owns What in the Media
www.cjr.org/owners/

**Women's Environment and
Development Organization**
355 Lexington Avenue, 3rd Floor
New York, NY 10017-6603
Tel: 212-973-0325
www.wedo.org

**Women's International League for
Peace and Freedom**
1213 Race Street
Philadelphia, PA 19107
Tel: 215-563-7110
www.wilpf.org

Working Assets
101 Market Street, Suite 700
San Francisco, CA 94105
Tel: 877-255-9253
www.workingassets.com

END NOTES

Introduction
THE INSURRECTION AGAINST CORPORATE POWER

1. David Henry, "Mergers: Why Most Big Deals Don't Pay Off," *BusinessWeek*, October 14, 2002.
2. Richard Grossman and Ward Morehouse, "Minorities, the Poor & Ending Corporate Rule," *The Boycott Quarterly*, Spring 1996.
3. Thomas Hartmann, *Unequal Protection* (New York: Rodale Press, 2002), p. 37.
4. Sarah Anderson and John Cavanagh, *The Rise of Corporate Global Power* (Washington, DC: Institute for Policy Studies, 2000).
5. David Korten, *When Corporations Rule the World* (San Francisco and Bloomfield, CT: Berrett-Koehler and Kumarian Press, 2000), p. 126.
6. Political bribery statistics can be found online at www.opensecrets.org, the Website for The Center for Responsive Politics, and www.commoncause.org, Common Cause's Website.
7. Quote in Ronnie Dugger, "Crimes Against Democracy: Citizens' Address to the Members of Congress," October 26, 1999.
8. Program on International Policy Attitudes, "Americans on Globalization: A Study of U.S. Public Attitudes," March 28, 2000.
9. Donald Barlett and James Steele, "What Corporate Welfare Costs," *Time*, November 9 and 16, 1998. Also see Ralph Nader, *Cutting Corporate Welfare* (New York: Seven Stories Press, 2000).
10. Barlett and Steele ...
11. Leonard Weiner, "The Tax Man Goeth." *U.S. News & World Report*, August 19, 2002.
12. Statistics are available online from Citizens for Tax Justice, www.ctj.org.
13. See www.opensecrets.org and www.commoncause.org.
14. John Cassidy, "The Greed Cycle," *The New Yorker*, September 23, 2002.
15. "Corporate Irresponsibility: There Ought to Be Some Laws; A Study of the Political and Policy Implications of Public Attitudes Toward Corporate America," EDK Associates, New York, July 29, 1996.
16. Clay Chandler, "US Corporations: Good Citizens or Bad?" *Washington Post National Weekly Edition*, May 20-26, 1996.
17. EDK Associates, "Corporate Irresponsibility."
18. Richard Stevenson, "Do People and Profits Go Hand in Hand?" *The New York Times*, May 9, 1996.
19. EDK Associates, "Corporate Irresponsibility."
20. Cassidy, "The Greed Cycle ..."
21. Aaron Bernstein, "Too Much Corporate Power?" *BusinessWeek*, September 11, 2000.
22. Jeffrey L. Seglin, "In Bad Times, It's Easier to Blame," *The New York Times*, May 19, 2002.

23. "In NGOs We Trust." *PR News*, December 18, 2000.

24. Bernstein, "Too Much Corporate Power ..."

25. *Threshold*, The Movement Magazine of the Student Environmental Action Coalition, January 1996.

26. "Fighting Corporate Power," *Guild Notes*, Fall 1998, p. 5.

27. From the Website of the Austin, TX, Chapter of the Alliance for Democracy: www.main.org/alliance.

28. "Corporations Put Environmentalists Under Fire Worldwide," Amnesty International press release, February 20, 2003. For more details, see Amnesty's full report, *Environmentalists Under Fire*.

29. From the Sierra Club Website: www.sierraclub.org/trade/resources/globalrep.asp.

30. Jarol Manhein, *The Death of a Thousand Cuts: Corporate Campaigns and the Attack on the Corporation* (Mahwah, NJ: Lawrence Erlbaum Publishers, 2001), Appendices A and B. Manheim's estimates are certainly understated because he does not count local campaigns; for example, the efforts against big box retailers. A great many corporate accountability initiatives never make the national headlines and so escape notice.

31. Daphne Wysham, "Women Take on Oil Companies in Nigeria," *Economic Justice News*, October 2002.

32. Bernstein, "Too Much Corporate Power ..."

33. Howard Zinn, *A People's History of the United States* (New York: Harper Collins, 1995), p. 282.

Chapter 1
CORPORATE POWER vs. PEOPLE POWER
A History of U.S. Corporate Accountability Struggles

1. Thom Hartmann, *Unequal Protection* (New York: Rodale Press, 2002), pp. 47-48.

2. Ibid, pp. 51-52.

3. Ibid, p. 57.

4. Ibid, p. 58.

5. Ralph Nader, Mark Green and Joel Seligman, *Taming the Giant Corporation* (New York: W.W. Norton & Company, 1976), p. 34.

6. Kevin Phillips, *Wealth and Democracy* (New York: Broadway Books, 2002), p. 304.

7. Nader, Green and Seligman, *Taming ....* Also see Jack Beatty, *Colossus: How the Corporation Changed America* (New York: Broadway Books, 2001), p. 60.

8. Thomas Dublin, "The Boston Manufacturing Company." pp. 67-74 of Beatty, *Colossus ...*

9. Arthur M. Schlesinger, Jr., *The Age of Jackson* (Boston: Little Brown and Co., 1945), p. 335.

10. Ibid.

11. Howard Zinn, *A People's History of the United States* (New York: Harper Collins, 1995), pp. 216-225.

12. Phillips, pp. 15-31.

13. Schlesinger, p. 81.

14. Ibid., p 76.

15. Ibid., p. 105.

16. Ibid., p. 102.

17. Ibid., pp. 123-24.

18. Ibid., p. 110.

19. Richard Grossman, and Frank T. Adams, "Taking Care of Business," p. 64 of Dean

Ritz, ed., *Defying Corporations, Defining Democracy* (New York: Apex Press, 2001).
20. Phillips, p. 304.
21. Zinn, p. 217.
22. Grossman, in Ritz, p. 65.
23. Zinn, p. 217.
24. Schlesinger, p. 337.
25. Alfred D. Chandler, Jr., "The Railroads: The First Modern Business Enterprises, 1850s-1860s," in Beatty, pp. 103-105.
26. Ibid., pp. 99-102.
27. Zinn, pp. 247-48.
28. Phillips, p. 305.
29. Beatty, p. 151.
30. Zinn, pp. 233 and 248.
31. Nader, Green, Seligman, *Taming* ..., p. 21.
32. Peter Kellman, "You've Heard of Santa Clara, Now Meet Dartmouth," in Ritz, pp. 89-91; and Beatty, pp. 83-84.
33. Grossman, in Ritz, p. 68; and Zinn, p. 254.
34. Charles Derber, *Corporation Nation* (New York: St. Martin's Press, 1998), pp. 129-130; and Beatty, pp. 83-84.
35. Derber, pp. 131-134.
36. Michael Kazin, *The Populist Persuasion* (New York: Basic Books, 1995), p. 63.
37. Robert McMath, *American Populism: A Social History, 1877-1898* (New York: Hill and Wang, 1992), p. 75.
38. Zinn, pp. 240-46; and Beatty, p. 126.
39. Zinn, pp. 267-270.
40. Ibid., p 272.
41. McMath, pp. 55 and 77.
42. Derber, p. 191.
43. McMath, p. 72.
44. Derber, p. 183.
45. McMath, p. 115.
46. Zinn, p. 252.
47. McMath, p. 191; and Kazin, p. 10.
48. McMath, pp. 161-62 and p. 168.
49. Edmund Morris, *Theodore Rex* (New York: Random House, 2001), p. 418.
50. Phillips, p. 307.
51. Zinn, p. 251 and p. 294.
52. Ibid., p. 311.
53. Kazin, p. 62.
54. Ibid., p. 68.
55. Morris, p. 495.
56. Ibid., p. 360.
57. Ibid., p. 139.
58. Beatty, p. 138.
59. Deber, p. 152.
60. Phillips, p. 307.
61. David M. Kennedy, *Freedom from Fear: The American People in Depression and War, 1929-1945* (Oxford: Oxford, 1999), p. 25.
62. Marchand, Ronald, "AT&T: The Vision of a Loved Monopoly," in Beatty, pp. 177-205.

63. Beatty, p. 258; and Kennedy, p. 24 and p. 41.

64. Kennedy, pp. 85-88.

65. Ibid., p. 141.

66. Ibid., p. 168.

67. Ibid., p. 182.

68. John Steinbeck, *The Grapes of Wrath* (New York: Penguin, 1976 rev. ed.), p. 43.

69. Kennedy, p. 217.

70. Kazin, p. 114; and Kennedy, p. 196.

71. Kennedy, pp. 88 and 223.

72. Ibid., pp. 280-282.

73. Kazin, pp. 135-150.

74. Kazin, p. 139.

75. Kennedy, p. 314.

76. Derber, pp. 30-36.

77. Ibid., p. 356.

78. http://coursesa.matrix.msu.edu/~hst306/documents/huron.html

79. Ralph Nader, Keynote Address at the Consumer Assembly, November 2, 1967, in *The Ralph Nader Reader* (New York: Seven Stories Press, 2000), p. 259.

80. Beatty, p. 471; and Phillips, p. 335.

81. "The World's View of Multinationals," *The Economist*, January 29, 2000.

82. This statistic, which compares corporate sales with country GDP, has become among corporate accountability activists' favorites, and is scattered among contemporary anti-corporate literature. The original source is Sarah Anderson and John Cavanagh's studies for the Institute for Policy Studies.

83. David Korten, *When Corporations Rule the World* (San Francisco and Bloomfield, CT: Berrett-Koehler and Kumarian Press, 2001), p. 210.

84. "The World's View of Multinationals," *The Economist*, January 29, 2000.

Chapter 2
"WOULD YOU WANT *YOUR* SISTER
TO WORK THERE?"
The Conflict Over Sweatshops

1. Transcript from ABC's *Prime Time Live*, May 22, 1996.

2. All quotes are from author interviews.

3. Edna Bonacich and Richard Applebaum, *Behind the Label: Inequality in the Los Angeles Apparel Industry* (Berkeley: University of California Press, 2000), p. 8.

4. Bill Bufford, "Sweat is Good," *The New Yorker*, April 26 and May 3, 1999.

5. National Labor Committee report on El Salvador's Exmodica Factory, Spring 2001. Available at http://www.nlcnet.org/elsalvador/0401/exmodica.htm

6. Tim Connor, *Still Waiting for Nike to Do It* (San Francisco: Global Exchange, 2001), pp. 64-65.

7. Charles Kernaghan, *Behind the Label: Made in China* (New York: National Labor Committee, 1998); and Phillip P. Pan, "Worked Till They Drop; Few Protections for Chinas' New Laborers," *The Washington Post*, May 13, 2002.

8. Collegiate Apparel Research Initiative, *La Lucha Sigue: Stories from the People of the Kukdong Factory* (Mexico: Collegiate Apparel Research Initiative, 2001).

9. Witness for Peace, *From the Maquila to the Mall* (Washington, DC: Witness for Peace, 1997).

10. Collegiate Apparel Research Initiative, *La Lucha Sigue* ...

11. Human Rights Watch, *Sex Discrimination in Mexico's Maquiladora Sector* (New York: Human Rights Watch, 1996).

12. National Labor Committee report on El Salvador ...

13. Rajiv Chandrasekaran, "Indonesian Workers in Nike Plants List Abuses," *The Washington Post*, February 23, 2001.

14. Hong Kong Christian Industrial Committee, *Labour Practices in Chinese Contract Factories Making Disney Products* (Hong Kong: Hong Kong Christian Industrial Committee, 2001); and Phillip P. Pan, "Poisoned Back Into Poverty; As China Embraces Capitalism, Hazards to Workers Rise," *The Washington Post*, August 4, 2002.

15. For a more in-depth analysis of this dynamic, see Naomi Klein, *No Logo: Taking Aim at the Brand Bullies* (New York: Harper Collins, 2000), pp. 195-200.

16. National Labor Committee report on El Salvador ...

17. Author interviews with workers, July 1999.

18. Hong Kong Christian Industrial Committee, *Labour Practices* ...

19. National Labor Committee report on El Salvador ...

20. Author interview.

21. Connor, *Still Waiting* ...

22. Hong Kong Christian Industrial Committee, *Labour Practices* ...

23. Witness for Peace, *From the Maquila to the Mall* ...

24. Bonacich and Applebaum, *Behind the Label* ..., p. 3.

25. George White, "Workers Held in Near-Slavery, Officials Say," *The Los Angeles Times*, August 3, 1995.

26. Calvin Woodward, "Sweatshops a Tough Target in a Scattered Garment Industry," Associated Press, August 4, 1995.

27. Bettijane Levine, "Sweatshop Charges Put a Wrinkle in Consumerism. Many Shoppers and Industry Insiders Say They Would Now Consider Factors Such as Treatment of Workers in Making a Purchase of Business Decision," *The Los Angeles Times*, August 24, 1995.

28. Alan Finder, "Conversations: Robert B. Reich, How an American Industry Gets Away With Slave Labor," *The New York Times*, August 20, 1995.

29. Testimony of Robert Hall, Vice President, Government Affairs Counsel National Retail Federation, before the California Senate Industry Relations Committee, August 25, 1995.

30. Author inteview.

31. "Giffords Give Cash to Sweatshoppers," The Associated Press, May 25, 1996.

32. Barry Bearak, "Stitching Together a Crusade. Charles Kernaghan Tries to Put One of America's Best-Known Corporate Giants on the Spot as He Battles for Haiti's Garment Workers. Contractors Claim They Provide the Tattered Island's 'Only Ray of Hope,'" *The Los Angeles Times*, July 25, 1996.

33. Bob Herbert, "Nike's Pyramid Scheme," *The New York Times*, June 19, 1996.

34. "It's Err Jordan for Nike—Lobby," *The Daily News,* June 7, 1996.

35. Ira Berkow, "Jordan's Bunker View on Nike's Slave Labor," *The New York Times*, July 12, 1996.

36. Bearak, "Stitching Together a Crusade ..."

37. Earnings report from National Labor Committee press release, January 30, 1996, citing *Financial Times*.

38. Herbert, "Nike's Pyramid Scheme."

39. William Goldschlag, "Kathie Lee Ready to Listen. Worker Begs to Tell Gifford of Abuse," *The New York Daily News*, May 30, 1996.

40. As quoted in Klein, p. 350.

41. Stuart Silverstein and George White, "US Singles Out Big Retailers on Clothing Sales. JC Penney Says It Is 'Perplexed' by Charges that It Sold Goods Made by Alleged Sweatshops. Macy's Parent Has No Comment," *Los Angeles Times*. May 21, 1996.

42. Reuters, "Sweatshops 'Growing Problem' in U.S., Reich Says," May 25, 1996.

43. As quoted in Randy Shaw, *Reclaiming America: Nike, Clean Air, and the New National Activism* (Berkeley: University of California Press, 1999), p. 24.

44. John Allen, "The Human Cost of Doing Business," *The Tidings*, Southern California's Catholic Weekly, January 7, 1997.

45. Joanna Ramey, "Reich Sees Summit as 'Turning Point' in Sweatshop Wars," *Women's Wear Daily*, July 17, 1996.

46. Bob Herbert, "The Wrong Indonesian," *The New York Times*, November 1, 1996.

47. Shaw, p. 108. For more on the trade politics at the time, see Canellos, Peter S., "Free Trade Faces Renewed Assault. Public Fear of Agreements Growing Amid Accusations of Child Labor Abuses," *The Boston Globe*, July 14, 1996.

48. John F. Harris and Peter McKay, "Companies Agree to Meet on 'Sweatshops,'" *The Washington Post*, August 3, 1996.

49. Paula L. Green, "Clinton Names Officials to Consumer Apparel Panel," *Journal of Commerce*, August 5, 1996.

50. Harris, McKay, "Companies Agree ..."

51. Author interview.

52. As quoted in Shaw, p. 44.

53. Joanna Ramey, "Church Groups Line Up with Reich on Sweatshops," *Women's Wear Daily*, October 23, 1996.

54. Lucille Renwick, "Teens' Efforts Give Soccer Balls the Boot. Students Persuade LAUSD to Stop Buying Gear from Countries That Use Child Labor," *The Los Angeles Times*, December 23 1996.

55. Shaw, p. 73.

56. Charles Kernaghan, NLC memo to Disney Campaign Supporters, January 17, 1997.

57. Peter H. King, "Where Does This Stuff Come From?" *The Los Angeles Times*, December 8, 1996.

58. William J. Holstein, "Santa's Sweatshop," *U.S. News & World Report*, December 16, 1996.

59. Bonacich and Applebaum, p. 298.

60. Shaw, p. 13.

61. Shaw, p. 14.

62. Ibid.

63. As quoted in Klein, p. 197.

64. Shaw, p. 22. Also, author interview with Jeff Ballinger.

65. Jeff Ballinger e-mail, December 7, 1999.

66. For more on Nike's production flight, see the study by N. Landrum, New Mexico State University, 2000.

67. Shaw, p. 16.

68. Author interview.

69. Author interview.

70. As quoted in Gary Gereffi, Ronie Garcia-Johnson, and Erika Sasser, "The NGO-Industrial Complex," *Foreign Policy*, July-August 2001.

71. Timothy Egan, "The Swoon of the Swoosh," *The New York Times Magazine*, September 13, 1998.

72. Klein, p. 51.

73. Klein, p. 17.

74. Egan, "Swoon of the Swoosh ...

75. For the complete Nguyen story, see Shaw, pp. 47-51.

76. Bob Herbert, "Nike's Boot Camp," *The New York Times*, March 28, 1997.

77. Jeff Manning, "Nike Plants Balk at $2.36 a Day," *The Oregonian*, April 3, 1997; and Tim Shorrock, "Nike Workers Stage Strike in Indonesia; Thousands Take to the Streets in a Dispute over the Minimum Wage," *Journal of Commerce*, April 24, 1997.

78. Manning, "Nike Plants Balk ...."

79. Shorrock, "Nike Workers Stage Strike ..."

80. Insight courtesy of Shaw, see p. 53.

81. Albom and Salter as quoted in Shaw, pp. 53-54.

82. On Andrew Young episode, see Shaw, pp. 65-69; Dana Caneday, "Nike's Asian Factories Pass Young's Muster," *The New York Times*, June 25, 1997; and Ellen Neuborne, "Young Gives Nike Fair Review after Plant Tours," *USA Today*, June 25, 1997.

83. *BusinessWeek* and *New Republic* as quoted in Shaw, pp. 67-68.

84. For the complete Bronx story, see Klein, pp. 372-374.

85. David Gonzalez, "Youthful Foes Go Toe to Toe With Nike," *The New York Times*, September 27, 1997.

86. As quoted in Klein, p. 374.

87. Shaw, p. 76, citing *USA Today*.

88. As quoted in Klein, p. 113.

89. October 28, 1997 letter from women's organizations.

90. On the campus revolt, see Shaw, pp. 82-84.

91. As quoted in Klein, p. 371.

92. Steven Greenhouse, "Nike Shoe Plant in Vietnam Is Called Unsafe for Workers," *The New York Times*, November 8, 1997.

93. Steven Greenhouse, "Voluntary Rules on Apparel Labor Proving Elusive," *The New York Times*, February 1, 1997.

94. Glenn Burkins, "Clinton Plan to Eliminate Sweatshops in Apparel Industry Called Too Weak," *The Wall Street Journal*, April 15, 1997.

95. Editorial, "A Modest Start on Sweatshops," *The New York Times*, April 16, 1997.

96. Greenhouse, "Voluntary Rules ..."

97. Steven Greenhouse, "Groups Reach Agreement for Curtailing Sweatshops," *The New York Times*, November 5, 1998.

98. Ibid.

99. Ibid.

100. Verena Dobnik. "Spurred by Kathie Lee Scandal, White House Offers Sweatshop Pact." The Associated Press, November 6, 1998.

101. Medea Benjamin, "Toil and Trouble: Student Activism in the Fight against Sweatshops," in Geoffrey D. White, et al., eds., *Campus, Inc.: Corporate Power in the Ivory Tower* (New York: Promethus Books, 2000).

102. Ibid.

103. UNITE, "Was Your School's Cap Made in This Sweatshop?" Summer 1998.

104. Author interview.

105. As quoted in Benjamin, "Toil and Trouble ..."

106. Benjamin, "Toil and Trouble ..."

107. Author interview with Tom Wheatley.

108. Steven Greenhouse, "Activism Surges at Campuses Nationwide, and Labor Is at

Issue," *The New York Times*, March 29, 1999.

109. Ibid; and Nancy Cleeland. "Students Give Sweatshop Fight the College Try." *The Los Angeles Times*, April 22, 1999.

110. Greenhouse, "Activism Surges ..."

111. Author interview.

112. Steven Greenhouse, "Student Critics Push Attacks on an Association Meant to Prevent Sweatshops," *The New York Times*, April 25, 1999.

113. Benjamin, "Toil and Trouble ..."

114. Author interview.

115. Details of WRC structure taken from WRC website: http://www.workersrights.org/faq.html

116. Steven Greenhouse, "Nike Identifies Plants Abroad Making Goods for Universities," *The New York Times*, October 8, 1999.

117. Author Interview.

118. Author Interview.

119. Mary Beth Marklein, "Making them sweat. Students step up pressure to hold colleges accountable for apparel," *USA Today*, April 13, 2000.

120. On campus protests, see: "Labor, religious, environmental groups join anti-sweatshop campaign," *Associated Press*, April 19, 2000; David Kinney, "Penn Staters camp out to protest sweatshops," *Associated Press*, April 7, 2000; Susan Ochs, "Molly McGrath won't take no for an answer," *In These Times*, April 3, 2000.

121. Marcella Fleming, "Compromise prompts 5 to end fast. Purdue students go without food 10 days, incensed that school apparel is made in bad working conditions," *The Indianapolis Star*, April 8, 2000.

122. "Nike refuses to comply with WRC, cancels Brown U. contract," *Brown Daily Herald*, April 3, 2000.

123. Jim Irwin, "Nike Kills U. of Michigan Talks," *The Associated Press*, April 27, 2000.

124. Statement from Nike Founder and CEO Philip H. Knight Regarding the University of Oregon, April 24, 2000.

125. Tim Connor, *Still Waiting for Nike to Do It* (San Francisco: Global Exchange, 2001), pp. 80-90.

126. After a 2000 BBC investigation revealed child laborers working at a Cambodian plant making clothing for Nike and Gap, both retailers terminated their contracts with the factory. For more details see Wayne Arnold, "Translating Union Into Khmer." *The New York Times*, July 12, 2001.

127. Editorial, "How to Battle Sweatshops," *The Washington Post*, February 2, 2001.

128. Tim Vickery, "Who's watching the shop floor," *Christian Science Monitor*, April 30, 2001.

129. Transcript from ABC's *Prime Time Live*, May 22, 1996.

130. Author interview with Nikki Bas.

131. *Washington Post*, "How to Battle ..."

132. Vickery, "Who's watching ..."

133. As quoted in Connor, *Still Waiting for Nike ...*, p. 6.

134. Connor, *Still Waiting for Nike ...*, pp 91-95.

135. Many retailers have joined an alternative monitoring group created by the American Apparel Manufacturer's Association. That system, best described as an auditing regime, was created without any NGO or union involvement. For more information, see Paula L. Green, "Industry to Oversee Textile Factories," *Journal of Commerce*, November 6, 1998.

136. Author interview.
137. Wayne Arnold, "Translating Union into Khmer," *The New York Times*, July 12, 2001.

Chapter 3
FLIPPER vs. THE WTO
The Fight for Dolphin-Safe Tuna

1. Author interview. All Mark Palmer quotes came from author interview.
2. Todd Steiner, David Phillips, and Mark Palmer, *The Tragedy Continues: Killing of Dolphins by the Tuna Industry* (San Francisco: Earth Island Institute, 1988.), p. 17.
3. Ibid., p. 27.
4. Kenneth Brower, "The Destruction of Dolphins," *The Atlantic Monthly*, July 1989.
5. Ibid.
6. Ibid.
7. Robert Gabriel, "Making Waves: Risking His Life to Record the Killing of Dolphins, Sam LaBudde Changed from Unfocused Drifter to Darling of the Environmental Movement," *The Los Angeles Times*, October 19, 1989.
8. Steiner et al., "Tragedy Continues ..." pp. 30-33.
9. Ibid.
10. Brower, "The Destruction ..."
11. For a detailed account of LaBudde's adventures, see Brower, and Gabriel.
12. Greg Johnson, "Tuna Canners Send Buyers a Message with 'Dolphin-Safe' Labels," *The Los Angeles Times*, November 20, 1990.
13. Louis Sahagun, "Protests Urge Tuna Boycott Over Killings of Dolphins," *The Los Angeles Times*, April 12, 1988.
14. Greg Johnson, "'Dolphin-Safe' Claims Remain Cause for Debate," *The Los Angeles Times*, December 11, 1990.
15. Author interview. All Sara Meghrouni quotes came from author interviews.
16. The assertion that the NMFS lacked the funds to pay for observers came from Mark Palmer.
17. Michael Parrish, "Film Turns Tide for Dolphins at StarKist: A Rock n' Roll Executive Carried the Public's Message," *The Los Angeles Times*, April 14, 1990.
18. For details on the struggles within Heinz, as well as further details on Jerry Moss's involvement, see: Patrick K. Connor, "Saving the Dolphin," *This World*, June 17, 1990.
19. David Ranni, "Heinz Acquisition Plans Exclude Big Names," *The Pittsburg Press*, September 7, 1989.
20. "An Open Letter from the U.S. Fishermen of the Eastern Tropical Pacific Ocean." No single author listed. There is no date on the letter, but it was clearly written sometime in 1988 or 1989.
21. Anthony Ramirez, "'Epic Debate Led to Heinz Tuna Plan," *The New York Times*, April 16, 1990.
22. David Phillips, "Breakthrough for the Dolphins: How We Did It," *Earth Island Journal*, Summer 1990.
23. Dan Morain, "U.S. Told to Ban Tuna Imports: Judge Orders Embargo until Foreign Fleets Prove They Are Reducing Number of Dolphins They Kill. Mexico Would Be Among Nations Most Affected," *The Los Angeles Times*, August 29, 1990.
24. General Agreement on Tariffs and Trade (GATT) Secretariat. "United States—Restrictions on the Imports of Tuna: Report of the Panel," August 16, 1991. Last available online at: www.ciesin.org.

25. Ibid.

26. Ibid.

27. Michael Parrish, "Pact May Stop Dolphin Deaths in Tuna Fishing," *The Los Angeles Times*, June 17, 1992.

28. Bob Davis, "U.S., Mexico, Venezuela Set Accord on Tuna," *The Wall Street Journal*, March 20, 1992.

29. Juanita Darling and Michael Parrish, "Mexico Backs Away from Pact on Tuna Trade. Some See the Latest Action as an Effort to Gain a NAFTA Bargaining Chip," *The Los Angeles Times*, November 4, 1992.

30. Timothy Noah and Bob Davis, "Tuna Boycott Is Ruled Illegal By GATT Panel—Blow to U.S. Policy to Save Dolphins May Escalate Attacks on Trade Pace," *The Wall Street Journal*, May 23, 1994.

31. Alexander Cockburn, "Al Gore, Green Groups & Narco-Traffickers," *The Nation*, August 12/19, 1996.

32. David Phillips, "Open Letter to Members of the Environmental Community Re: Greenpeace and the Tuna/Dolphin Issue," December 10, 1996.

33. Testimony of Lori Wallach Before the House Resources Fisheries, Wildlife and Oceans Subcommittee, February 29, 1996. Provided by Public Citizen.

34. Eugene Linen, "Chicken of the Sea? A Dolphin-Safe Tuna Flap Makes the U.S. Squirm," *Time*, March 4, 1996.

35. Barbara Dudley, "It's Time to Set the Record Straight about Tuna and Dolphins." Advertisement in *The Nation*, October 28, 1996. And Mark Palmer interview.

36. As of this writing, the issue had not been settled. On January 1, 2003, the government seemed to approve the new, looser definition of dolphin-safe tuna. But a week later the Bush administration announced a 90-day delay to make time for discussions with Earth Island Institute. For more, see Christopher Marquis, "Rule Weakening Definition of 'Dolphin Safe' Is Delayed," *The New York Times*, January 10, 2003.

Chapter 4
UP IN SMOKE
Tobacco Profits vs. Public Health

1. Stanton A. Glantz, John Slade, Lisa A. Bera, Peter Hanauer, Deborah E. Barnes, *The Cigarette Papers* (Berkeley: University of California Press, 1996), p. 6.

2. Tara Parker-Pope, *Cigarettes: Anatomy of an Industry from Seed to Smoke* (New York: New Press, 2001), pp. 2-7.

3. Parker-Pope, pp. 67-68.

4. Insights courtesy of Richard Kluger, *From Ashes to Ashes: America's Hundred-Year Cigarette War, the Public Health, and the Unabashed Triumph of Philip Morris* (New York: Vintage, 1996), from the Foreword.

5. Carrick Mollenkamp, Adam Levy, Joseph Menn, Jeffrey Rothfeder, *The People vs. Big Tobacco: How the States Took on the Cigarette Giants* (Princeton: Bloomberg Press, 1998), p. 15.

6. Parker-Pope, pp. 21-22.

7. Mollenkamp, et. al. p. 64.

8. For company profiles, see Parker-Pope pp. 30-37.

9. For the health effects, see Parker-Pope pp. 110-111.

10. Kluger, p. 737.

11. Glantz, et al., Preface.

12. For the history of opposition, see Parker-Pope, pp. 146-147.

13. Parker-Pope, pp. 81-86

14. Ibid., pp. 112-113.

15. Kluger, pp. 255-260.

16. Parker-Pope, p. 118.

17. Ibid., p. 93.

18. For Koop's role, see Kluger, pp. 536-540.

19. Parker-Pope, p. 122.

20. Kluger, p. 672.

21. For Deep Cough history, see Kessler, pp. 79-94.

22. On the beginnings of FDA offensive against tobacco, see David Kessler, *A Question of Intent: A Great American Battle with a Deadly Industry*, pp. 3-66.

23. Mollenkamp, et al., pp. 50-51.

24. For legal history and arguments, see Parker-Pope, pp. 149-150.

25. Ibid., p. 150.

26. Mollenkamp, pp. 73-74.

27. Peter J. Boyer, "Big Guns," *The New Yorker*, May 17, 1999.

28. Mollenkamp, p. 30.

29. Williams history, Mollenkamp, pp. 37-47.

30. Ibid., p. 40.

31. Ibid., p. 111.

32. Kessler, p. 188.

33. Mollenkamp, p. 51.

34. Kevin Sack, "For the Nation's Politicians, Big Tobacco No Longer Bites," *The New York Times*, April 22, 1997.

35. FDA struggle, see Kessler.

36. Mollenkamp, p. 115.

37. Kessler, p. 353.

38. Mollenkamp, p. 56.

39. Mollenkamp, pp. 116-118.

40. Ibid., pp. 187-191.

41. Robert Weissman, "The Great Tobacco Bailout," *Multinational Monitor*, July-August 1997.

42. John M. Broder, "Tobacco Critics Begin Attacking Proposal, Calling It Soft on the Cigarette Industry," *The New York Times*, June 24, 1997.

43. Ibid.

44. For more on the 1978 and 1980 California initiatives, see Stanton Glantz and Edith D. Balbach, *Tobacco War: Inside the California Battles*, pp. 1-32.

45. For details on Proposition 99, see ibid., pp. 75.

46. Authors interview.

47. John Mintz and Saundra Torry, "In Their Own Words. Internal Tobacco Company Documents Reveal the Long Campaign to Recruit Young Smokers," *Washington Post National Weekly Edition*, January 19, 1998.

48. Ceci Connolly and John Mintz, "How Big Tobacco Got Smoked," *Washington Post National Weekly Edition*, April 6, 1998.

49. Ibid.

50. Howard Kurtz, "The Switch-Hitter on Smoking," *Washington Post National Weekly Edition*, June 29, 1998.

51. Bob Hohler, "How the Tobacco Deal Went Up in Smoke," *The Boston Globe*, June 19, 1998.

52. INFACT, The 1997 People's Annual Report.

53. Hohler.

54. Jonathan Weisman, "Industry Painted Tobacco Bill as Tax, Power Grab. Conservatives, Ads Slowed and Finally Stopped Legislation," *The Baltimore Sun*, June 19, 1998.

55. "Smiles in a Smoky Room," (Editorial) *The Los Angeles Times*, June 19, 1998.

56. "FDA Has No Authority to Regulate Nicotine or Cigarettes, 4th Cir. Rules," *Tobacco Industry Litigation Reporter*, August 28, 1994.

57. Action on Smoking and Health (ASH) Website, www.ash.org.uk/papers.

58. Hubert H. Humphrey III, "Still a Threat," *The New York Times*, November 24, 1998.

59. Ross Hammond, *Addicted to Profit: Big Tobacco's Expanding Global Reach* (Washington, DC: Essential Action, 1998), p. 13.

60. Parker-Pope, p. 30.

61. Hammond, p. 14.

62. Ibid.

63. Connolly and Mintz.

64. Hammond, p. 21.

65. Ibid.

66. Anne Platt McGinn, "The Nicotine Cartel," *World Watch*, July-August, 1997.

67. Nisid Hajari, "Where There's Smoke," *Time Asia*, September 9, 1997.

68. Robert Weissman, "Taking on Tobacco Imperialism: Interviews with Tobacco Control Advocates from Around the World," *Multinational Monitor*, July-August 1997.

69. Hammond, p. 21.

70. Platt McGinn.

71. Peter Eng, "Multinational Tobacco Companies Look to Asia's Young Market," The Associated Press, February 12, 1996.

72. David Dahl, "Tobacco Industry Targets Third World," Scripps Howard News Service, April 20, 1996.

73. Robert Weissman, "Marlboro Man Goes East," *Multinational Monitor*, January-February, 1992.

74. Weissman, "Taking on Tobacco Imperialism."

75. Hammond, p. 18 and pp. 36-37.

76. Jane Perlez, "Fenced in at Home, Marlboro Man Looks Abroad," *The New York Times*, June 24, 1997.

77. Hammond, p. 36.

78. Ibid.

79. Ibid.

80. Parker-Pope, p. 50.

81. Ibid.

82. William Carlsen, "Tobacco Firms Find New Markets Abroad," *San Francisco Chronicle*, June 4, 1997.

83. Platt McGinn.

84. Leslie Chang, "Chinese Lawyers Lay Plan to Take on Big Tobacco," *Wall Street Journal*, May 16, 2001.

85. Hammond, pp. 19, 20, and 38.

86. Elizabeth Olson, "Big Tobacco Said to Fight Swiss Smoking Laws," *The New York Times*, January 15, 2001.

87. Hammond, p. 22.

88. Langley, Alison. "W.H.O. Adopts Tobacco Pact But Many Countries Object," *The New York Times*, March 1, 2003.

89. Linda Greenhouse, "High Court Holds FDA Can't Impose Rules on Tobacco," *The New York Times*, March 22, 2000.

90. Eric Lichtblau, "U.S. Lawsuit Seeks Tobacco Profits," *The New York Times*, March 18, 2003.

91. Quoted in ibid.

92. Rick Bragg and Sarah Kershaw, "Juror Says a 'Sense of Mission' Led to Huge Tobacco Damages," *The New York Times*, July 16, 2000.

Chapter 5
Citizen Diplomacy vs. Corporate Profits
Defending Human Rights in Burma

1. Author interview.

2. Open Society Institute, *Burma: Country in Crisis* (New York: Open Society Institute, 1998), p. 1.

3. Ibid., p. 1.

4. Peter Ackerman and Jack Duvall, *A Force More Powerful* (New York: St. Martin's Press, 2000), p. 472.

5. Edward Klein, "The Lady Triumphs," *Vanity Fair*, October 1995, p. 126.

6. Open Society Institute, p. 1.

7. U.S. State Department, *Human Rights Report on Burma*, February 2001, p. 10.

8. Blaine Harden, "The New Burmese Leisure Class: Army Capitalists," *The New York Times*, November 21, 2000.

9. Blaine Harden, "Grim Regime," *The New York Times*, November 14, 2001.

10. Human Rights Watch, *World Report 2000* (New York: Human Rights Watch, 2001).

11. U.S. State Department, p. 2.

12. Ibid., p. 18.

13. Harden, "Grim Regime."

14. U.S. State Department, p. 28.

15. Open Society Institute, p. 15.

16. Linda Kwon, ed., *The Free Burma Coalition Manual*, 1997.

17. Harden, "The New Burmese Leisure Class".

18. Open Society Institute, p. 7.

19. Ibid., p. 7.

20. Harden, "Grim Regime."

21. Author interview with Zarni.

22. Kwon, pp. 12-13.

23. Kwon, p. 19.

24. Authors interview with Zarni.

25. Kwon, p. 48.

26. Author interview with Zarni.

27. Ibid.

28. Zarni and Michael W. Apple, "Conquering Goliath: The Free Burma Coalition Takes Down PepsiCo," from *Campus, Inc.: Corporate Power in the Ivory Tower*, Geoffry D. White, ed. (New York: Prometheus Books, 2000), p. 280.

29. Authors interview.

30. Desmond Tutu, "Burma as South Africa," *Far Eastern Economic Review*, September 16, 1993.

31. Kwon, p. 39.

32. Ibid., p. 41.

33. Author interview with Simon Billenness.

34. Ibid.

35. Michael Kranish, "Proposed Sanctions on Burma a Hot Issue for Weld, Kerry," *The Boston Globe*, June 14, 1996.

36. Free Burma Coalition Website, www.freeburmacoalition.org; and *The Washington Post*, June 23, 1999.

37. Meg Vaillancourt, "Mass. Becomes First State to Boycott Burma Business," *The Boston Globe*, June 26, 1996.

38. Sen. Mitch McConnell, Speech Before the Paul Nitze School of International Studies, Johns Hopkins University, May 14, 1996. See Kwon, p. 135.

39. Sarah Jackson-Han, "Controversial Burma Sanctions Bill Galvanizes U.S. Oil Firms," *Agence France Presse*, July 9, 1996.

40. Earthrights International Report,"Total Denial," July, 1996.

41. George Soros, Testimony on May 22, 1996 Before Senate Committee on Banking, Housing and Urban Affairs. See Kwon, p. 138.

42. Salpukas, Agis. "US Oil Companies Risk Unstable Politics on the Hill," New York Times News Service, May 23, 1997.

43. Frank Phillips, "Apple Cites Mass. Law in Burma Decision," *The Boston Globe*, October 4, 1996.

44. FBC Website, www..freeburmacoalition.org.

45. Author interview with Billenness.

46 Michael S. Lelyveld, "Massachusetts Moves to Amend Myanmar Sanctions; State Aims to Squash EU, Japanese Objections," *Journal of Commerce*, April 28, 1998.

47. Simon Billenness, *Investing for a Better World* (monthly publication of Franklin Research's Insight), April 1998.

48. Fred Hiatt, "Massachusetts Takes on Burma," *The Washington Post National Weekly Edition*, February 8, 1999.

49. USA Engage Website, www.usaengage.org.

50. Author interview with Robert Stumberg.

51. Michael S. Lelyveld, "Industry Group Takes Massachusetts to Court of Myanmar Sanctions; Complain Charges State with Violating the Constitution," *Journal of Commerce*, May 1, 1998.

52. Evelyn Iritani, "Coalition Challenges Myanmar Trade Ban; Suit Has Direct Implications for Similar Laws in California Cities," *The Los Angeles Times*, May 1, 1998.

53. Michael S. Lelyveld, "Judge Hears Argument Against Myanmar Sanctions," *Journal of Commerce*, September 24, 1998.

54. Michael S. Lelyveld, "Massachusetts Sanctions Struck Down," *Journal of Commerce*, November 6, 1998.

55. Robert Stumberg, "Preemption & Human Rights: Local Options after *Crosby v NFTC*." *International Law Journal of Georgetown University Law Center*, Fall 2000.

56. John Donnelly, "High Court Tackles Mass. Burma Law; Justices Question Whether States Can Discourage Trade with Nation," *The Boston Globe*, March 23, 2000.

57. Linda Greenhouse, "Justices Weigh Issue of States' Making Foreign Policy," *The New York Times*, March 23, 2000.

58. Linda Greenhouse, "State Law on Myanmar Boycott is Voided," *The New York Times*, June 20, 2000.

59. "Total Denial Continues," EarthRights International, 2000.

60. Evelyn Iritani, "Myanmar Project Fueling International Controversy; US Is Part of Consortium Building Gas Pipeline. Critics, however, Question Partnership with Brutal

Regime," *The Los Angeles Times*, November 24, 1996.

61. Evelyn Iritani, "Judge Rejects Suit Accusing Unocal of Conspiring with Myanmar," *The Los Angeles Times*, September 7, 2000.

62. Sheri Prasso, "A Company without a Country? Unocal Says It Won't Leave Burma, but It May De-Americanize," *Business Week,* May 5, 1997.

Chapter 6
TRADING DEMOCRACY
Rule-Making in the Global Economy

1. Author interview.

2. Susan Ariel Aaronson, *Taking Trade to the Streets: The Lost History of Public Efforts to Shape Globalization* (Ann Arbor: University of Michigan Press, 2001), p. 41.

3. Aaronson, p. 49.

4. Aaronson, p. 50.

5. Aaronson, p. 111.

6. As quoted by Aaronson, pp. 113-114.

7. Aaronson, p. 115.

8. As quoted by Aaronson, p. 108.

9. As quoted by Aaronson, p. 119.

10. As quoted by Aaronson, p. 125.

11. For a in-depth account of how Clinton came to his decision, see John B. MacArthur, *The Selling of 'Free Trade'* (New York: Hill and Wang, 2000), pp. 159-164.

12. As quoted by MacArthur, p. 185.

13. MacArthur, pp. 167-173.

14. MacArthur, p. 216.

15. MacArthur, p. 199.

16. As quoted by MacArthur, p. 199.

17. As quoted by David C. Korten, *When Corporations Rule the World* (West Hartford, CT: Kumarian Press, 2001), p. 125.

18. William Greider, "The Right and U.S. Trade Law: Invalidating the 20th Century." *The Nation*, http://www.thenation.com/doc.mhtml?i=20011015&s=greider

19. As quoted by MacArthur, p. 91.

20. For more details on the USA*NAFTA campaign, see MacArthur, pp. 216-223.

21. Author interview with Lori Wallach.

22. MacArthur, p. 222.

23. As quoted by MacArthur, p. 248.

24. MacArthur, pp. 263-264.

25. As quoted by MacArthur, p. 274.

26. As quoted by Aaronson, p. 89.

27. As quoted by Aaronson, p. 151.

28. As quoted by Aaronson, p. 108.

29. Peter Behr, "Dole Joins President on GATT; Senate GOP Leader Gets 'Escape Hatch' on Trade Arbitration," *The Washington Post*, November 24, 1994.

30. Thomas L. Friedman, "Dole Explains Trade Treaty Stand," *The New York Times*, September 14, 1994.

31. Peter Behr, "GATT's Got Their Tongues; Trade Treaty's Friends and Foes Take Their Fight to TV with a Blitz of Advocacy Ads," *The Washington Post*, August 12, 1994.

32. Robert Weissman, "GATT: The Final Act," *Multinational Monitor*, October 1994.

33. Behr, "GATT's Got Their Tongues ..."

34. Peter Behr, "Congress to Cast Vote on Historic Trade Pact; GATT's Issues Transcend Political Parties," *The Washington Post*, November 28, 1994.

35. Peter Behr, "GATT Is Legislative Landmark, but Trade Remains a Divisive Issue," *The Washington Post*, December 2, 1994.

36. Weissman, "GATT: The Final Act,"

37. Thomas L. Friedman, "President Vows Victory on Trade," *The New York Times*, September 28, 1994.

38. Michael Janofsky, "Trade Pact Casts Shadow for Garment Workers," *The New York Times*, December 12, 1994.

39. Keith Bradsher, "Big Push on Trade: Making the Deals; Plenty of Favors Made for Industry Backing," *The New York Times*, September 30, 1994.

40. Weissman, "GATT: The Final Act ..."

41. Allen R. Myerson, "In Trade-Pact War, Clashes Outside the Capital Are Heavy," *The New York Times*, November 24, 1994.

42. David E. Sanger, "Administration Says Deal with Dole on Trade Is Near," *The New York Times*, November 23, 1994.

43. Helen Dewar, "Senate Approves GATT on Big Bipartisan Vote," *The Washington Post*, December 2, 1994.

44. Bob Herbert, "Business Beats Brooklyn," *The New York Times*, November 30, 1994.

45. Peter Behr, "Voter Shift Threatens Old Trade Coalition," *The Washington Post*, October 7, 1994.

46. Kevin Phillips, "Clinton's Loss on Fast Track, Combined with the Stock Market Drop and Sharpening Divisions in Society, All Point to Trouble Ahead," *The Los Angeles Times*, November 16, 1997.

47. Frank Swoboda, "Labor Plans Ads, Lobbying on Trade Pact; 'Fast Track' Request Called Unacceptable," *The Washington Post*, September 17, 1997.

48. David Espo, "Clinton Launches Lobbying Effort for Fast-Track Legislation," The Associated Press, September 16, 1997.

49. John F. Harris and Peter Baker, "Clinton Neglected to Sell 'Fast Track' to U.S. Public," *The Washington Post*, November 12, 1997.

50. Paul Wiseman, "Final 'Fast Track' Lobbying Intensifies," *USA Today*, November 7, 1997.

51. John M. Broder, "Party, Spurned, Repays Clinton with Rebellion," *The New York Times*, November 11, 1997.

52. Author interview.

53. Jill Abramson and Steven Greenhouse, "Labor Victory on Trade Reveals Power," *The New York Times*, November 11, 1997.

54. Wiseman, "Final 'Fast Track' Lobbying..."

55. Mike Glover, "Gore Shrugs Off Questions about Money Raising and Trade Fight," The Associated Press, October 27, 1997.

56. Terence Hunt, "Clinton Not Expecting to Win Union Converts on Trade Legislation," The Associated Press, September 23, 1997.

57. Peter Baker, "Don't Punish Democrats Over Trade, Clinton Urges; Unionists React Cooly to 'Fast Track' Speech," *The Washington Post*, September 25, 1997.

58. Art Pine, "Polls Show Many in U.S. Ready to Adandon Protectionism. But Bill Still Faces Tough Battle,"*The Los Angeles Times*, October 14, 1997.

59. Paul Wiseman, "Administration Pushes Hard as Fast-Track Comes to Fore," *USA Today*, October 7, 1997.

60. Rob Wells, "House Vote on Trade Bill Delayed," The Associated Press, November 8, 1997.

61. "Three Years of NAFTA Facts," Public Citizen Fact Sheet, January 1, 1997.

62. Robert E. Scott, "Focusing on Workers in the Fast-Track Talk," *Los Angeles Times*, November 2, 1997.

63. Alison Mitchell, "Clinton Faces Off With Congress on Trade," *The Washington Post*, September 17, 1997.

64. Alexander Cockburn, "Clinton on a Fast Track to No Place," *Los Angeles Times*, November 13, 1997.

65. Richard Stevenson, "Union Misgivings on NAFTA are Clinton's Latest Worry," *The New York Times*, November 4, 1997.

66. William Safire, "Tracking the Fast Track," *The New York Times*, October 26, 1997.

67. Helen Dewar, "Florida Torn over 'Fast Track' Trade-Offs; Agriculture and Political Pressure Keep State Straddling the Fence on Global Commerce," *The Washington Post*, November 29, 1997.

68. Rob Wells, "Vote on Trade Bill Delayed," The Associated Press, November 7, 1997.

69. California Fair Trade Campaign leaflet, Fall 1997.

70. Alison Mitchell, "President Issues Last-Minute Plea on Trade Measure," *The New York Times*, November 7, 1997.

71. Jim Drinkard, "White House Dealing to Win Trade Votes," The Associated Press, November 7, 1997.

72. John E. Yang and Terry M. Neal, "'Fast Track' Hits 'Brick Wall,'" *The Washington Post*, November 9, 1997.

73. James K. Glassman, "A Victory for the Flat-Earth Caucus," *The Washington Post*, November 11, 1997.

74. Thomas L. Friedman, "The New American Politics," *The New York Times*, November 13, 1997; and Editorial "'Fast Track' Is Derailed," *The New York Times*, November 11, 1997.

75. John F. Harris and Peter Baker, "Clinton Neglected to Sell 'Fast Track' to U.S. Public," *The Washington Post*, November 12, 1997.

76. David Espo, "Trade Issue Entangled with Abortion," The Associated Press, November 7, 1997.

77. John F. Harris, "Clinton Offers Assurances on Free Trade," *The Washington Post*, November 15, 1997.

78. Author interview.

79. R.C. Longworth, "New Rules for Global Economy," *Chicago Tribune*, December 4, 1997.

80. For a detailed analysis of the MAI, see Maude Barlow and Tony Clarke, *The Multilateral Agreement on Investment and the Threat to American Freedom* (Toronto: Stoddard Publishing, 1998).

81. Ad Hoc Working Group on the MAI, *The MAI—Democracy for Sale* (New York: Apex Press, 1998).

82. Center for International Environmental Law, Community Nutrition Institute, Defenders of Wildlife, Friends of the Earth, Greenpeace, Institute for Agriculture and Trade Policy, National Wildlife Federation, Sierra Club, World Wildlife Fund. Letter to Charlene Barshefsky, February 13, 1997.

83. Tim Breen, "Lawmakers, Advocacy Groups Bludgeon Investment Treaty," *Environment and Energy Daily*, March 9, 1998.

84. Ron Klink and Cliff Stearns (Members of Congress), Letter to President Clinton,

November 5, 1997.

85. Lorraine Woellert, "Trade Storm Brews Over Corporate Rights," *The Washington Times*, December 15, 1997.

86. David Rowan, "Corporations vs States: Meet the New World Government," *The Guardian*, February 13, 1998.

87. Greider, "The Right and U.S. Trade Law ..."

88. Ruth Abramson, "Paying the Polluters?" *Maclean's*, September 1, 1997.

89. Quoted in Public Citizen Briefing Paper, "The Alarming Multilateral Agreement on Investment," April 1997.

90. Woellert, "Trade Storm Brews."

91. Author interview.

92. Dick Burkhart. "Time to Stop MAI Altogether," Letters to the Editor, *The Seattle Times*, May 14, 1998.

93. The Ruggiero comment, cited repeatedly in anti-MAI literature, was uttered at the WTO's 1996 Ministerial Summit in Singapore.

94. Michelle Sforza, Scott Nova, Mark Weisbrot, "A Concise Guide to the Multilateral Agreement on Investment," Preamble Briefing Paper, May 20, 1997.

95. Fred Hiatt, "Foreign Affairs in Annapolis," *The Washington Post*, March 30, 1998.

96. John Maggs, "US Balks at Proposed Investment Pact," *Journal of Commerce*, February 17, 1998.

97. Joint NGO statement, "International Organizations Oppose the Multilateral Agreement on Investment." Available online at http://www.citizen.org/trade/issues/mai/Opposition/articles.cfm?ID=1676.

98. R.C. Longworth, "Treaty to Govern International Investment Granted a Reprieve; Talks Are Extended, But Problems Remain," *Chicago Tribune*, February 18, 1998.

99. Maggs, "US Balks ..."

100. Greg Miller, "Email in January Launched Cyberspace Planning for the Actions, Including Aid in Finding Seattle Locations," *The Los Angeles Times*, December 2, 1999.

101. For complete details on the sea turtle case, see Peter Fugazzotto and Todd Steiner, *Slain by Trade: The Attack of the World Trade Organization on Sea Turtles and the U.S. Endangered Species Act* (San Francisco: Sea Turtle Restoration Project, 1998).

102. Jonathan Peterson, "Activists Bring Turtles' Cause to WTO Fishbowl."

103. Lori Wallach and Michelle Sforza, *The WTO: Five Years of Reasons to Resist Corporate Globalization* (New York: Seven Stories Press, 1999), pp 28-30.

104. Ibid., pp. 42-43.

105. Ibid., pp. 57-58.

106. Ibid., pp. 62-63.

107. Ibid., p. 14.

108. Statement from Members of International Civil Society Opposing a New Round of Comprehensive Trade Negotiations, May 25, 1999.

109. James Cox, "Protesters Plan to Disrupt WTO Talks," *USA Today*, September 15, 1999.

110. Ibid.

111. Big Noise Films, "Showdown in Seattle: Five Days that Shook the WTO." Distributed on VHS by Deep Dish Television.

112. "The New Trade War," *The Economist*, December 4, 1999.

113. Author interview.

114. Laurence Cruz, "Protesters Launch 'Battle in Seattle' against WTO," Associated Press, November 29, 1999.

115. Steven Greenhouse, "A Carnival of Derision to Greet the Princes of Global Trade," *The New York Times*, November 28, 1999.

116. Sam Howe Verhovek, "Trade Talks Start in Seattle Despite a Few Disruptions," *The New York Times*, November 29, 1999.

117. Steve Pearlstein, "Trade Theory Collides with Angry Reality," *The Washington Post*, December 3, 1999.

118. For a blow-by-blow account of the Seattle street conflicts, see Paul de Armond, "Black Flag Over Seattle," *Albion Monitor*, March 2000.

119. Jonathan Peterson, Jonathan Iritani and Kim Murphy, "Protest Delays Start of World Trade Summit," *The Los Angeles Times*, December 1, 1999.

120. Kim Murphy, "In the Streets of Seattle, Echoes of Turbulent '60s," *The Los Angeles Times*, December 1, 1999.

121. Peterson, Iritani, and Murphy, "Protest Delays ..."

122. Sam Howe Verhovek and Steven Greenhouse, "National Guard Is Called to Quell Trade-Talk Protests," *The New York Times*, December 1, 1999.

123. George Tibbits, "WTO Session Disrupted, Ministers Insist They Will Carry On," The Associated Press, December 1, 1999.

124. Big Noise Films, "Showdown in Seattle: Five Days that Shook the WTO."

125. Andrew Kohut, "Globalization and the Wage Gap," *The New York Times*, December 3, 1999.

126. Timothy Egan, "Free Trade Takes on Free Speech." *The New York Times*, December 5, 1999.

127. Luis Cabrera, "Protesters, Police Clash on Seattle's Streets," The Associated Press, December 1, 1999.

128. For more on the protesters' strategic and tactical advantages, see de Armond, "Black Flag ..."

139. Paul de Armond; and Timothy Egan, "Black Masks Lead to Pointed Fingers in Seattle," *The New York Times*, December 2, 1999.

130. Ibid.

131. Ibid.

132. Jonathan Peterson, "Activists Bring Turtles' Cause to WTO Fishbowl," *The Los Angeles Times*, December 3, 1999.

133. David Sanger, "President Chides World Trade Body in Stormy Seattle," *The New York Times*, December 2, 1999.

134. David Sanger, "Talks and Turmoil: After Clinton's Push, Questions about Motive," *The New York Times*, December 3, 1999.

135. Thomas Friedman, "Senseless in Seattle," *The New York Times*, December 1, 1999.

136. Karel van Wolferen, "Will the New World Trade Organization Work?" *The Washington Post*, June 26, 1994.

137. Greenhouse, "Trade Ministers Sidestep a Tricky Issue ..."

138. Evelyn Iritani, "Poor Nations Defy, Derail WTO 'Club,'" *Los Angeles Times*, December 5, 1999.

139. Jonathan Peterson, and Evelyn Iritani, "Agreement on Key Issues Eludes Trade Ministers," *The Los Angeles Times*, December 3, 1999.

140. John Burgess, "Green Room's Closed Doors Couldn't Hide Disagreements," *The Washington Post*, December 5, 1999.

141. Peterson and Iritani, "Agreement on Key Issues ..."

142. Ibid.

143. Evelyn Iritani and Jonathan Peterson, "Raucous WTO Meeting Ends Without

Accord," *The Los Angeles Times*, December 4, 1999.

144. Steve Pearlstein, "WTO Negotiators' Reach Far Exceeded Grasp of Complexities," *The Washington Post*, December 5, 1999.

Conclusion
BUILDING A MOVEMENT FOR GLOBAL DEMOCRACY

1. Aaron Bernstein, "Global Capitalism: Can It Be Made to Work Better?" *BusinessWeek*, November 6, 2000.

2. Alex Berenson, "Bank Overstated Its Earnings 18% For 1999-2000," *The New York Times*, March 4, 2003; and Crough, Gregory and Kapner, Suzanne. "Grocery Chain Owner Overstate Earnings," *The New York Times*, February 25, 2003.

3. David Sanger, "Bush, on Wall St., Offers Tough Stance," *The New York Times*, July 10, 2002.

4. Thomas Paine, "The Rights of Man," p. 229 in *The Thomas Paine Reader* (New York: Penguin Books, 1987).

5. For detailed polling numbers on the public's opinion of corporations, see Time/CNN poll published July 2002. The poll was conducted by Harris polling July 10-11, 2002. Last available on-line at: www.time.com/time/2002/corporate/poll. And a Newsweek poll, "Troubling Signs for Bush," July 29, 2002.

6. Matthew Miller, "It's Not Just Harken—It's the Whole Rigged System." *The San Francisco Chronicle*, July 14, 2002.

7. Arianna Huffington, "Spitzer Gets Beat by the Gangs of New York," Syndicated Column, January 15, 2003.

8. As quoted in Charles Derber, *Corporation Nation* (New York: St. Martin's Press, 1998), p. 166.

9. The quote from the National Association of Manufacturers appears in Ralph Nader, Mark Green, and Joel Seligman, *Taming the Giant Corporation* (New York: W.W. Norton, 1976), p. 68.

10. For more details on the three strikes proposal, visit www.corporate3strikes.org.

11. As quoted by Kate Jennings, "The Hypocrisy of Wall Street Culture," *The New York Times*, July 14, 2002. Ambrose Bierce, *The Devil's Dictionary* (New York: Dover Publications, 1993), p. 19.

12. Russell Mokhiber and Robert Weissman, "A Corporate Lawyer Speaks Out." Syndicated column, March 22, 2002.

13. Ibid.

14. Thom Hartmann, *Unequal Protection* (New York: Rodale Press, 2002), p. 37.

15. For more information on the restrictions against corporate farms, visit the Website of the Community Environmental Legal Defense Fund, www.celdf.org.

16. As quoted by Nader, et. al. "Taming the Giant ...," p. 241.

17. The complete Alternatives for the Americas document is available online at: www.economicjustice.org/alternatives/

18. To learn more about the International Right to Know campaign, visit www.irtk.org.

19. The draft corporate accountability convention is available online at: www.foei.org/publications/corporates/accountpr.html.

20. As quoted in ibid.

21. William Greider, "Pro Patria, Pro Mundus. It's Time to Ask "Borderless Corporations: Which Side Are You On?" *The Nation*, October 26, 2001.

22. Patrick E. Tyler, "Analysis: A New Power in the Streets," *The New York Times*, February 17, 2003.

23. According to a 2000 survey, 76 percent of American consumers say they would spend $5 more on a $20 garment if it was certified as not made in a sweatshop. See Steve Kull, "Americans on Globalization," Program on International Policy Attitudes, Marhc 28, 2000, p. 31.

24. On organic sales figures, see the Organic Consumers Association, online at www.oca.org; for Fair Trade numbers, visit the Website of the Fair Trade Federation, www.fairtradefederation.org; for statistics on socially responsible investing, see the Website of Co-op America, www.coopamerica.org.

INDEX